A Little Snow Fairy

Sugar

2

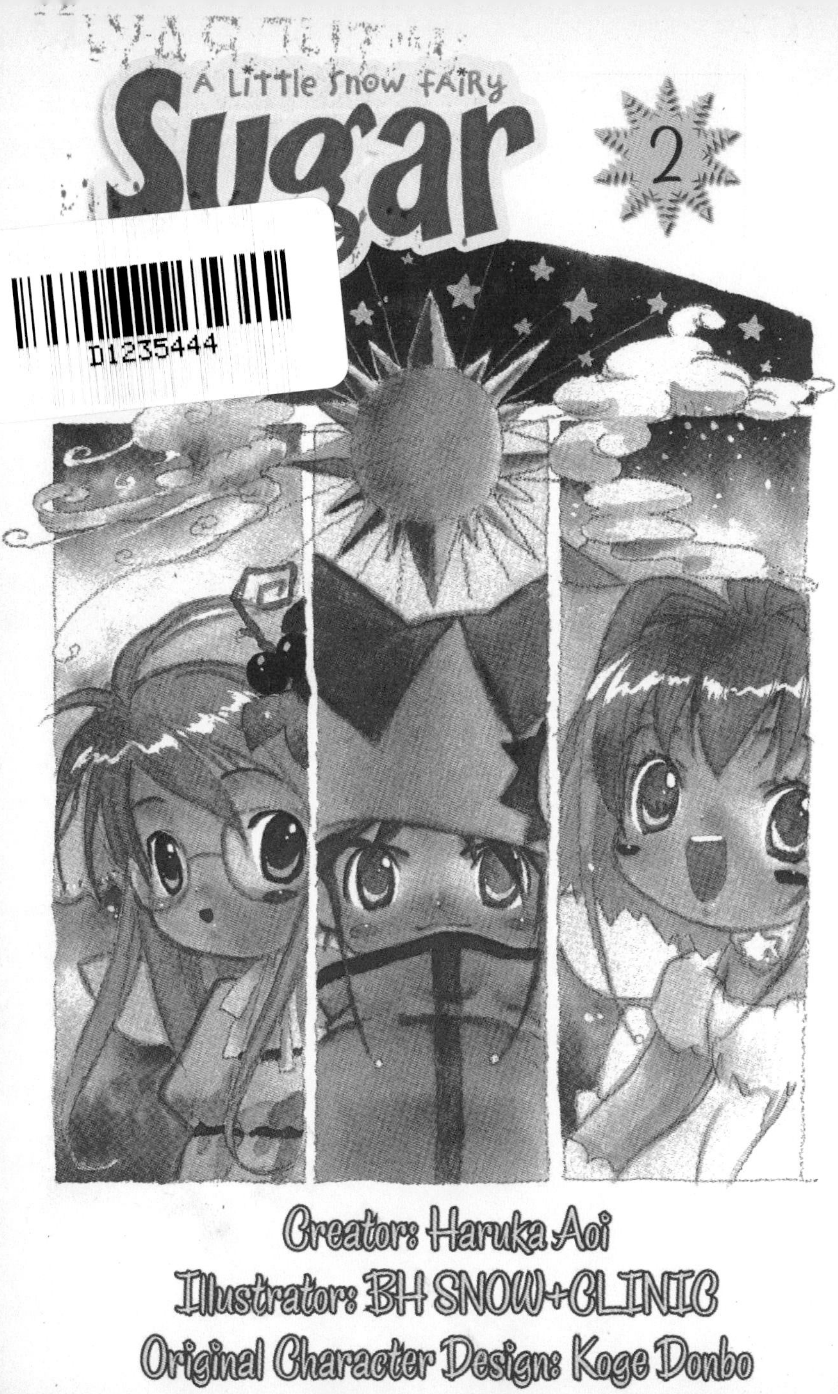

Creator: Haruka Aoi
Illustrator: BH SNOW+CLINIC
Original Character Design: Koge Donbo

CHAPTER 5 The Bear Pianist......................3

CHAPTER 6 The Pianist He Admires......31

CHAPTER 7 What I Want to Be...............63

CHAPTER 8 I've Decided!.......................95

CHAPTER 9 For Twinkles.......................119

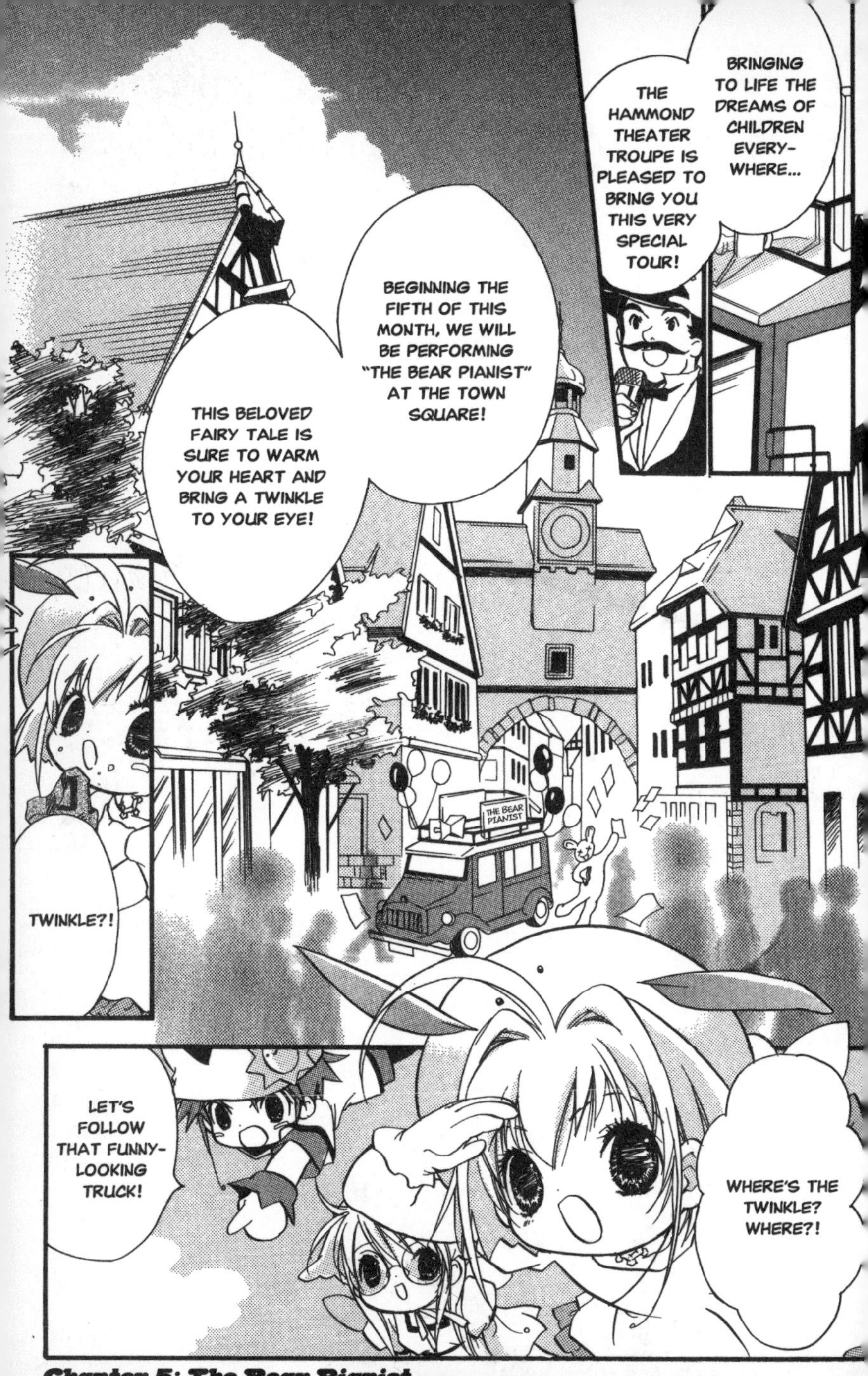
BRINGING TO LIFE THE DREAMS OF CHILDREN EVERY-WHERE...
THE HAMMOND THEATER TROUPE IS PLEASED TO BRING YOU THIS VERY SPECIAL TOUR!
BEGINNING THE FIFTH OF THIS MONTH, WE WILL BE PERFORMING "THE BEAR PIANIST" AT THE TOWN SQUARE!
THIS BELOVED FAIRY TALE IS SURE TO WARM YOUR HEART AND BRING A TWINKLE TO YOUR EYE!
THE BEAR PIANIST
TWINKLE?!
WHERE'S THE TWINKLE? WHERE?!
LET'S FOLLOW THAT FUNNY-LOOKING TRUCK!

Chapter 5: The Bear Pianist

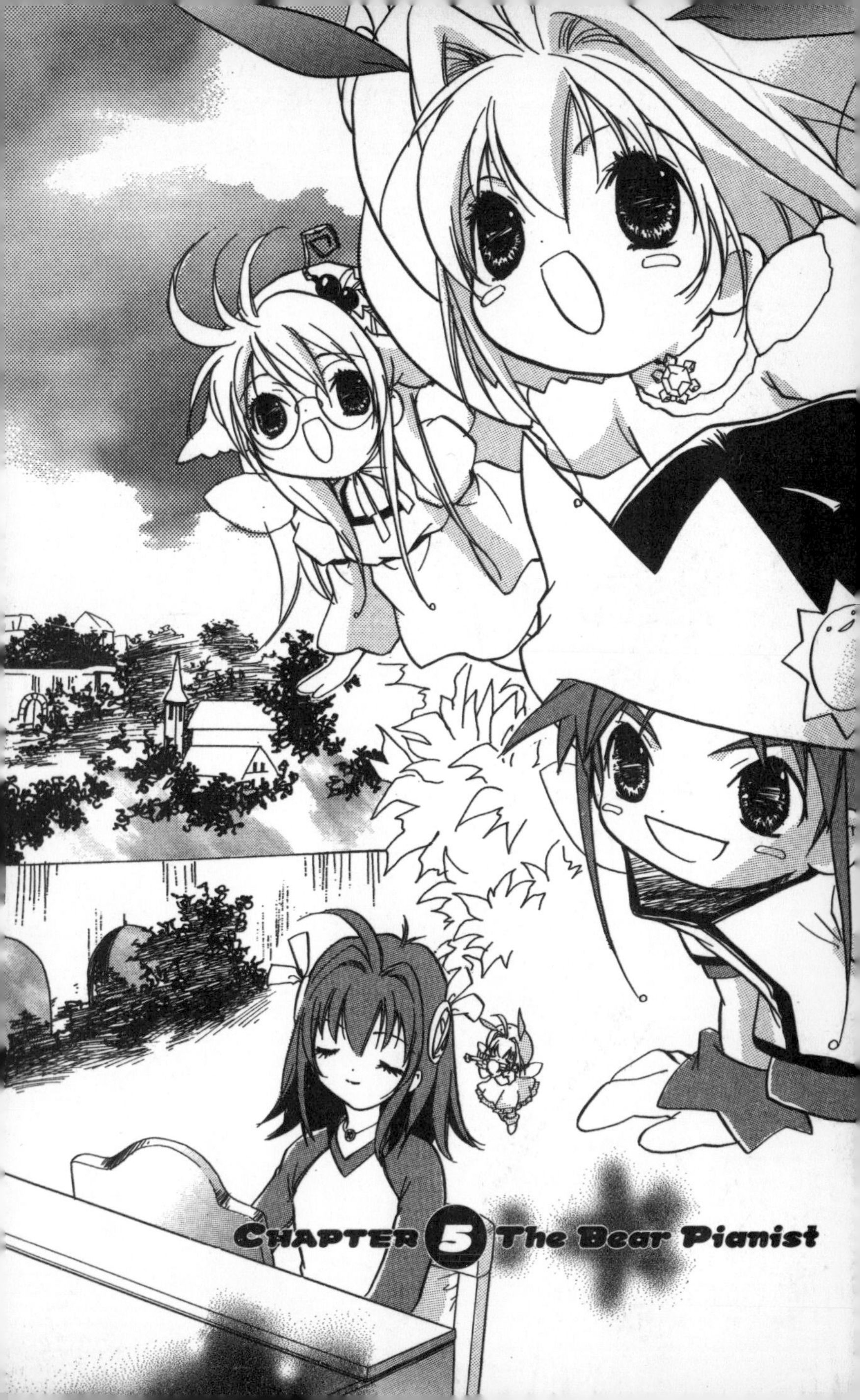
CHAPTER 5 The Bear Pianist

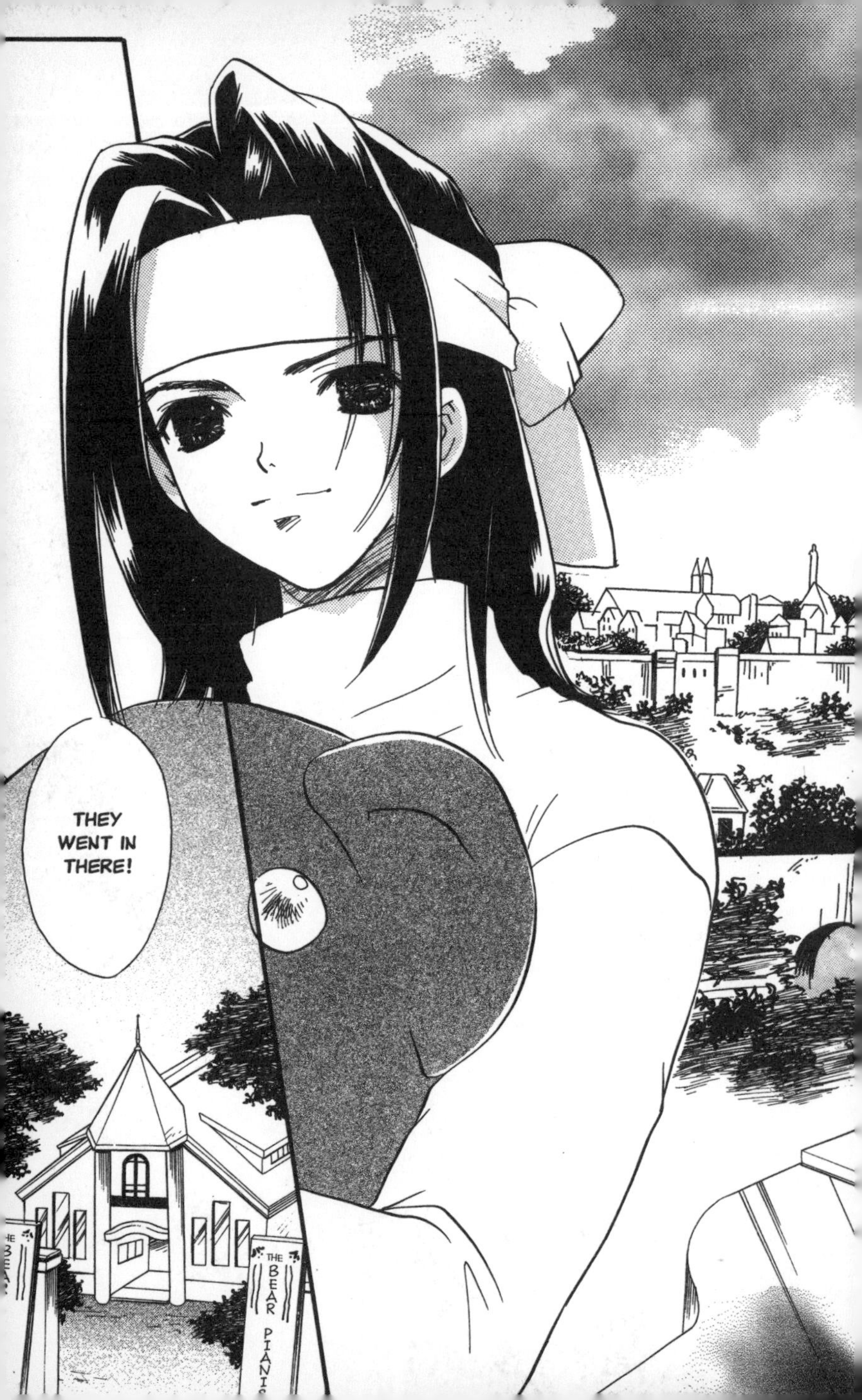
THEY WENT IN THERE!
THE BEAR

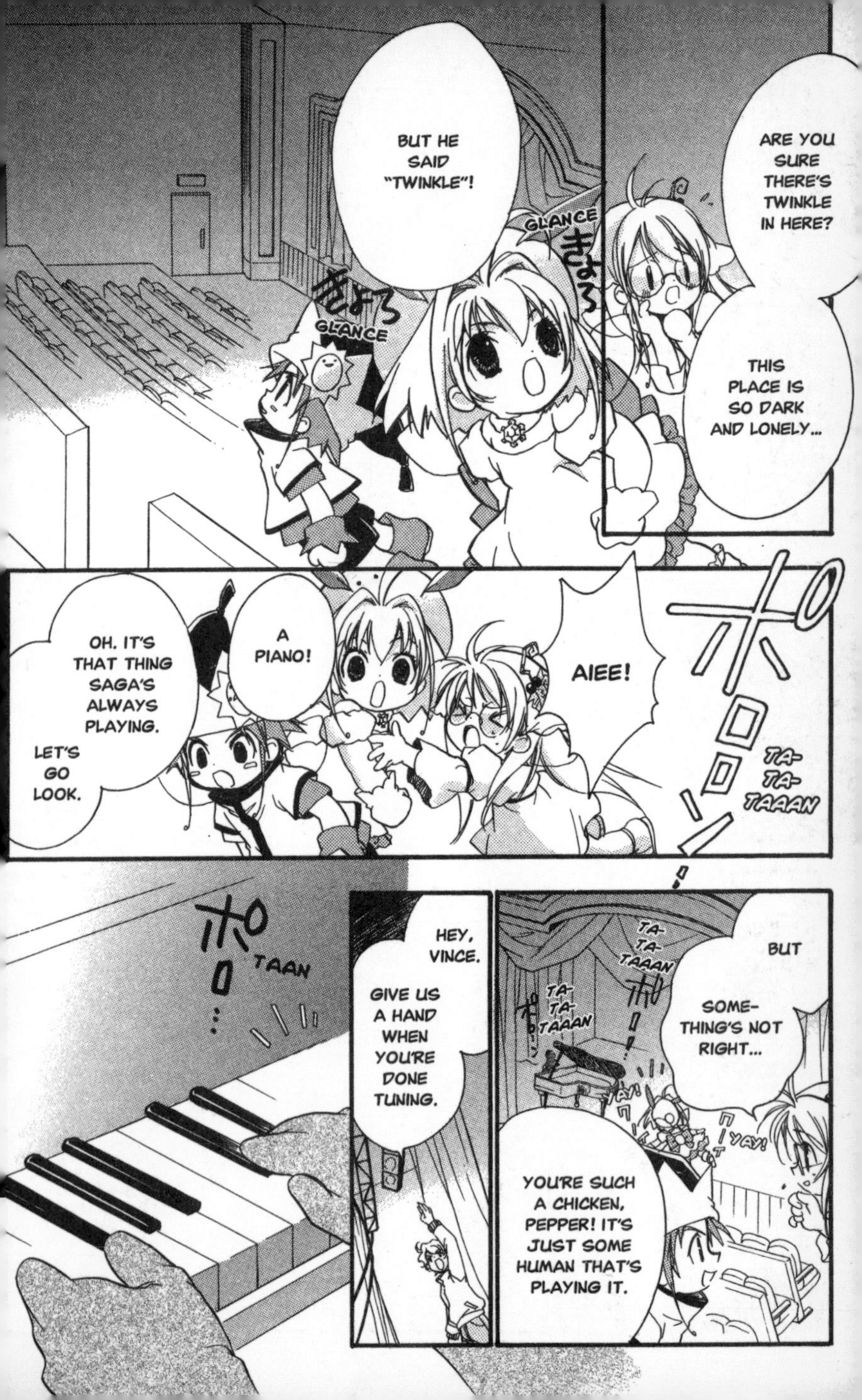
ARE YOU SURE THERE'S TWINKLE IN HERE?
THIS PLACE IS SO DARK AND LONELY...
GLANCE
きょろ
BUT HE SAID "TWINKLE"!
きょろ
GLANCE
TA-TA-TAAAN
AIEE!
A PIANO!
OH. IT'S THAT THING SAGA'S ALWAYS PLAYING.
LET'S GO LOOK.
BUT
SOME-THING'S NOT RIGHT...
TA-TA-TAAAN
TA-TA-TAAAN
YAY!
YAY!
YOU'RE SUCH A CHICKEN, PEPPER! IT'S JUST SOME HUMAN THAT'S PLAYING IT.
HEY, VINCE.
GIVE US A HAND WHEN YOU'RE DONE TUNING.
TAAN

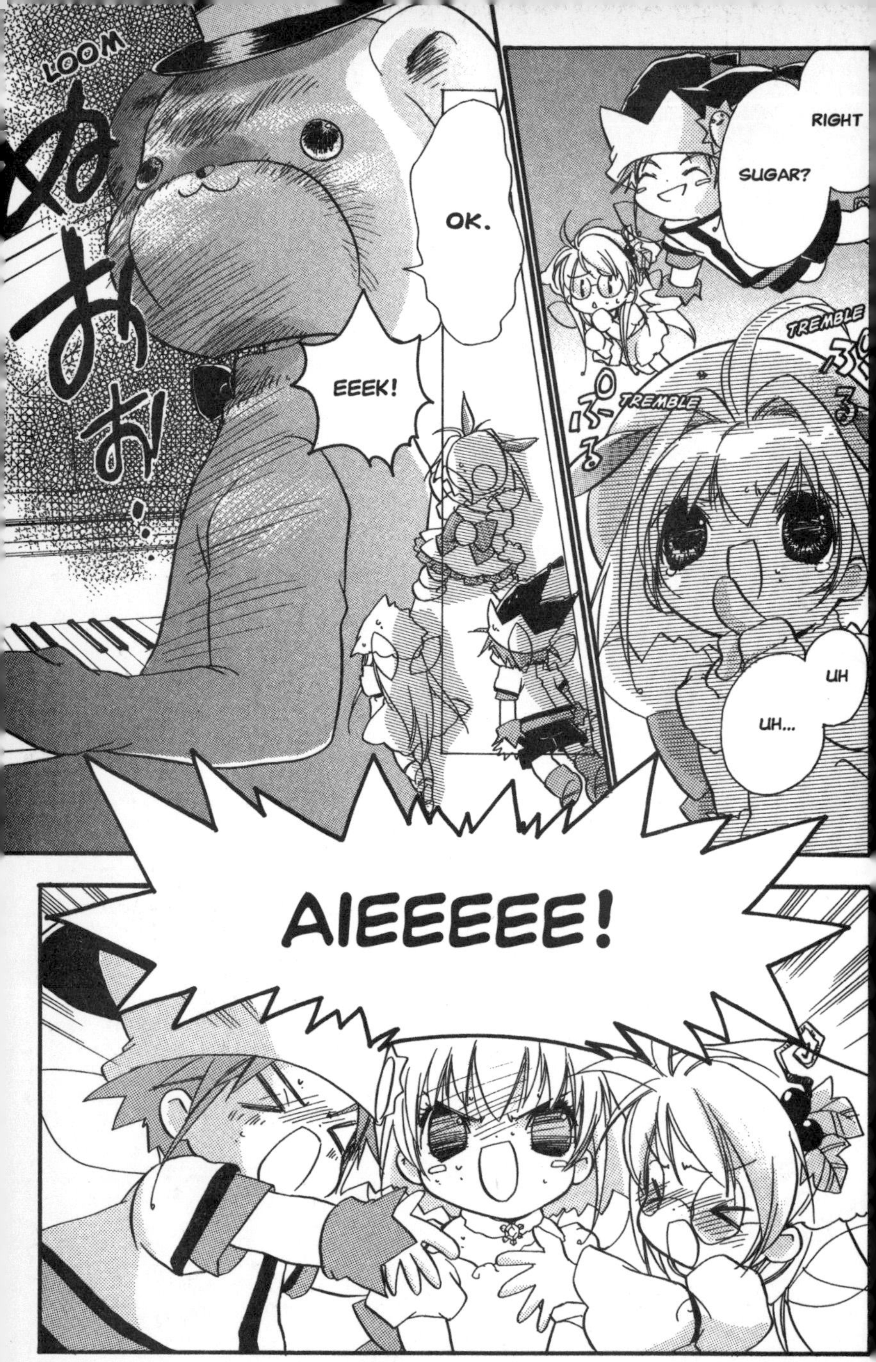
RIGHT SUGAR?
TREMBLE
TREMBLE
UH UH...
OK.
EEEK!
LOOM
ぬおお!
AIEEEEEE!

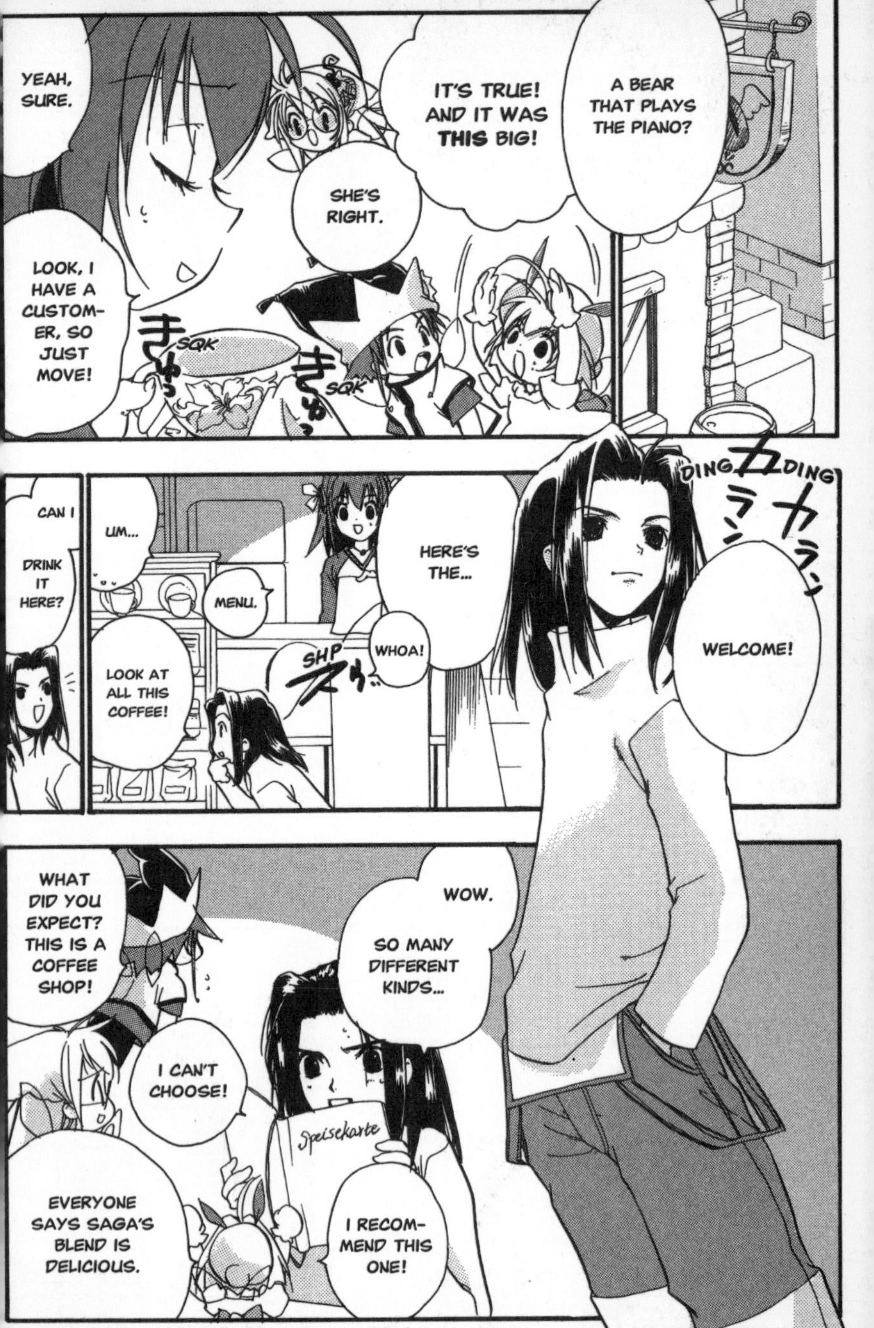
A BEAR THAT PLAYS THE PIANO?
IT'S TRUE! AND IT WAS THIS BIG!
SHE'S RIGHT.
YEAH, SURE.
LOOK, I HAVE A CUSTOM-ER, SO JUST MOVE!
SQK
SQK
DING DING
カラン カラン
WELCOME!
HERE'S THE...
WHOA!
SHP
MENU.
UM...
LOOK AT ALL THIS COFFEE!
CAN I DRINK IT HERE?
WOW.
SO MANY DIFFERENT KINDS...
WHAT DID YOU EXPECT? THIS IS A COFFEE SHOP!
I CAN'T CHOOSE!
Speisekarte
I RECOM-MEND THIS ONE!
EVERYONE SAYS SAGA'S BLEND IS DELICIOUS.

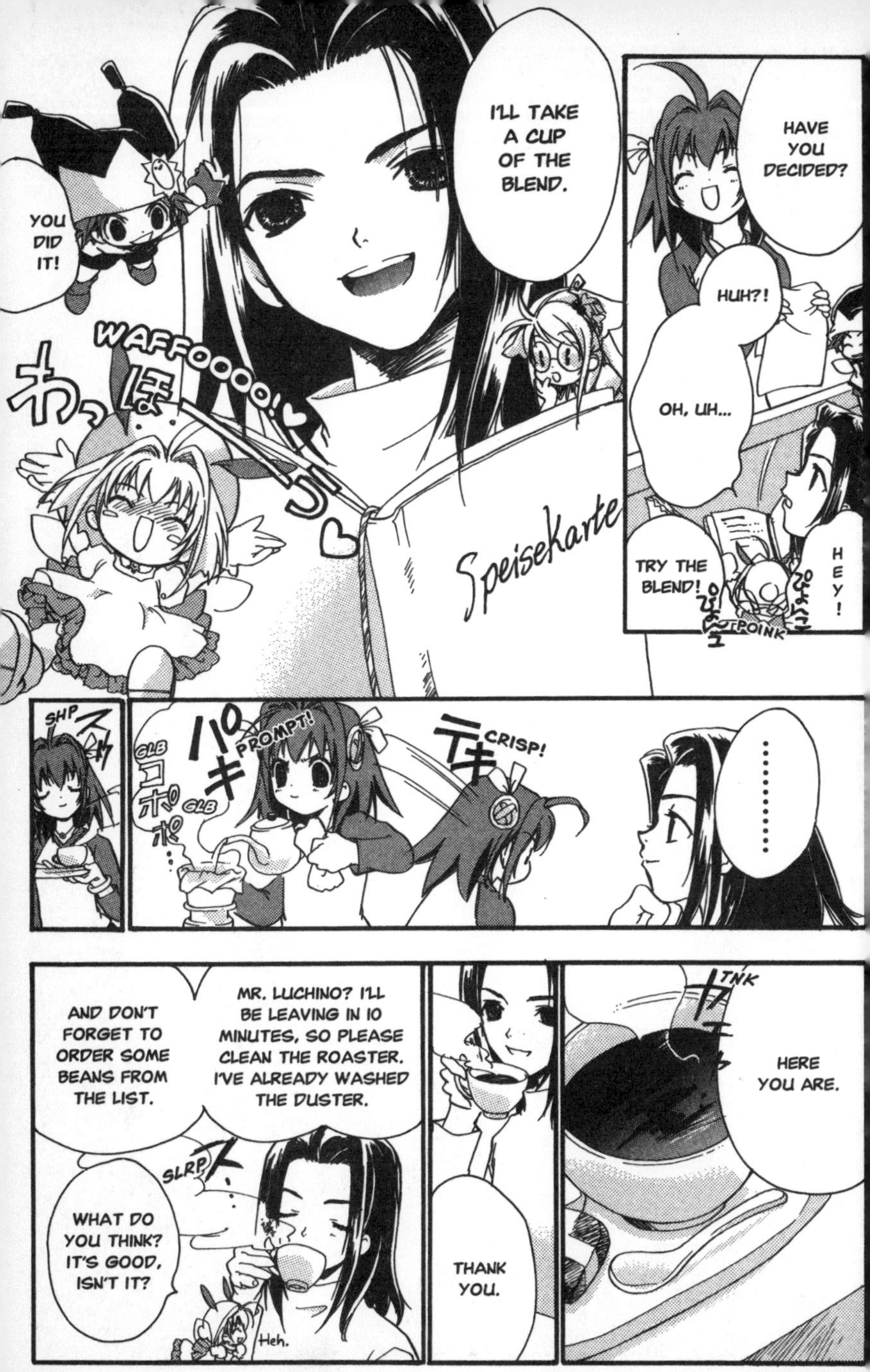
HAVE YOU DECIDED?
HUH?!
OH, UH...
HEY!
TRY THE BLEND!
POINK
I'LL TAKE A CUP OF THE BLEND.
YOU DID IT!
WAFFOOOOO!
Speisekarte
......
CRISP!
PROMPT!
GLB
GLB
SHP
HERE YOU ARE.
TNK
THANK YOU.
MR. LUCHINO? I'LL BE LEAVING IN 10 MINUTES, SO PLEASE CLEAN THE ROASTER. I'VE ALREADY WASHED THE DUSTER.
AND DON'T FORGET TO ORDER SOME BEANS FROM THE LIST.
SLRP
WHAT DO YOU THINK? IT'S GOOD, ISN'T IT?
Heh.

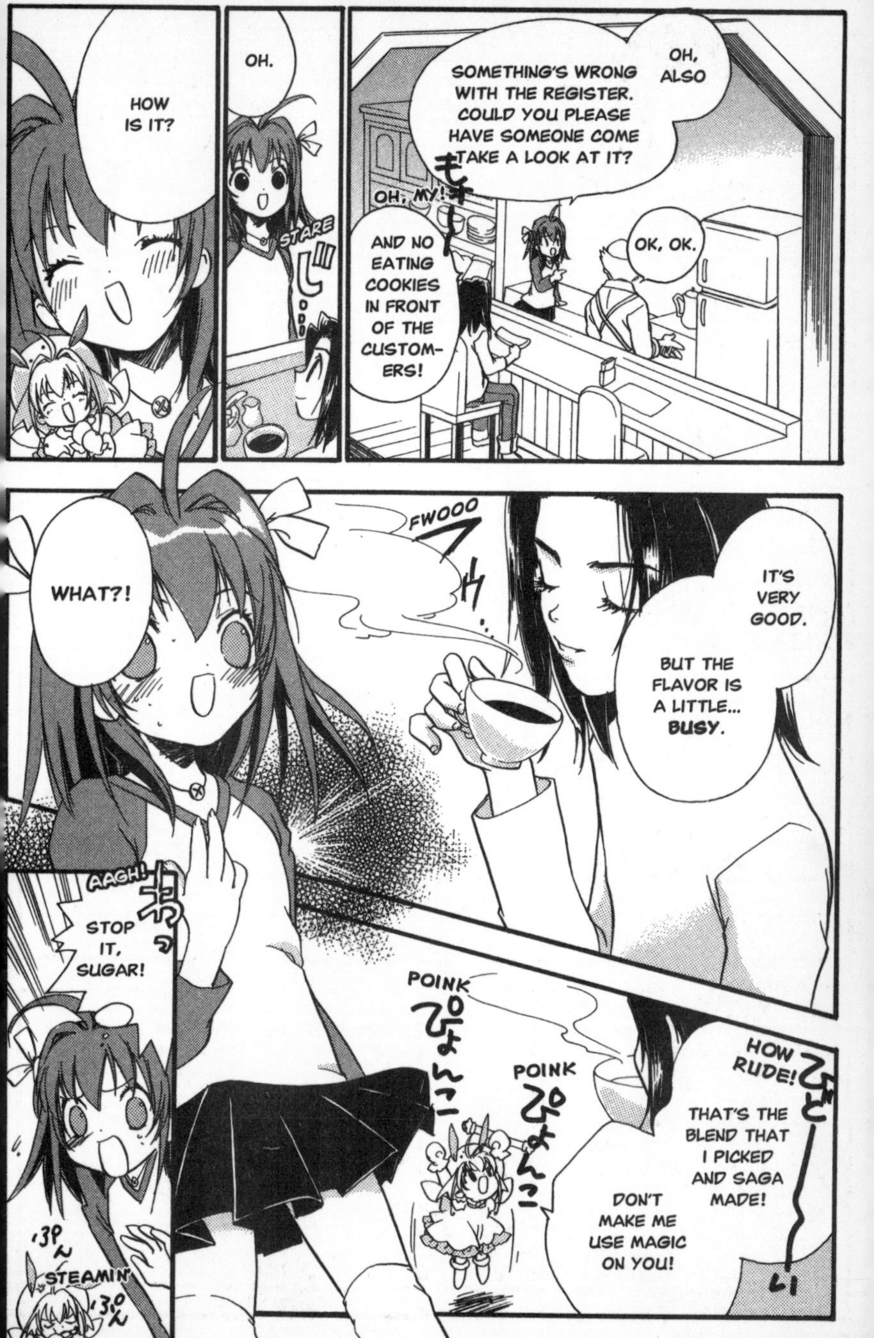
OH, ALSO
SOMETHING'S WRONG WITH THE REGISTER. COULD YOU PLEASE HAVE SOMEONE COME TAKE A LOOK AT IT?
OK, OK.
OH, MY!
AND NO EATING COOKIES IN FRONT OF THE CUSTOMERS!
OH.
STARE
HOW IS IT?
IT'S VERY GOOD.
BUT THE FLAVOR IS A LITTLE... **BUSY**.
FWOOO
WHAT?!
HOW RUDE!
THAT'S THE BLEND THAT I PICKED AND SAGA MADE!
DON'T MAKE ME USE MAGIC ON YOU!
POINK
POINK
AAGH!
STOP IT, SUGAR!
STEAMIN'

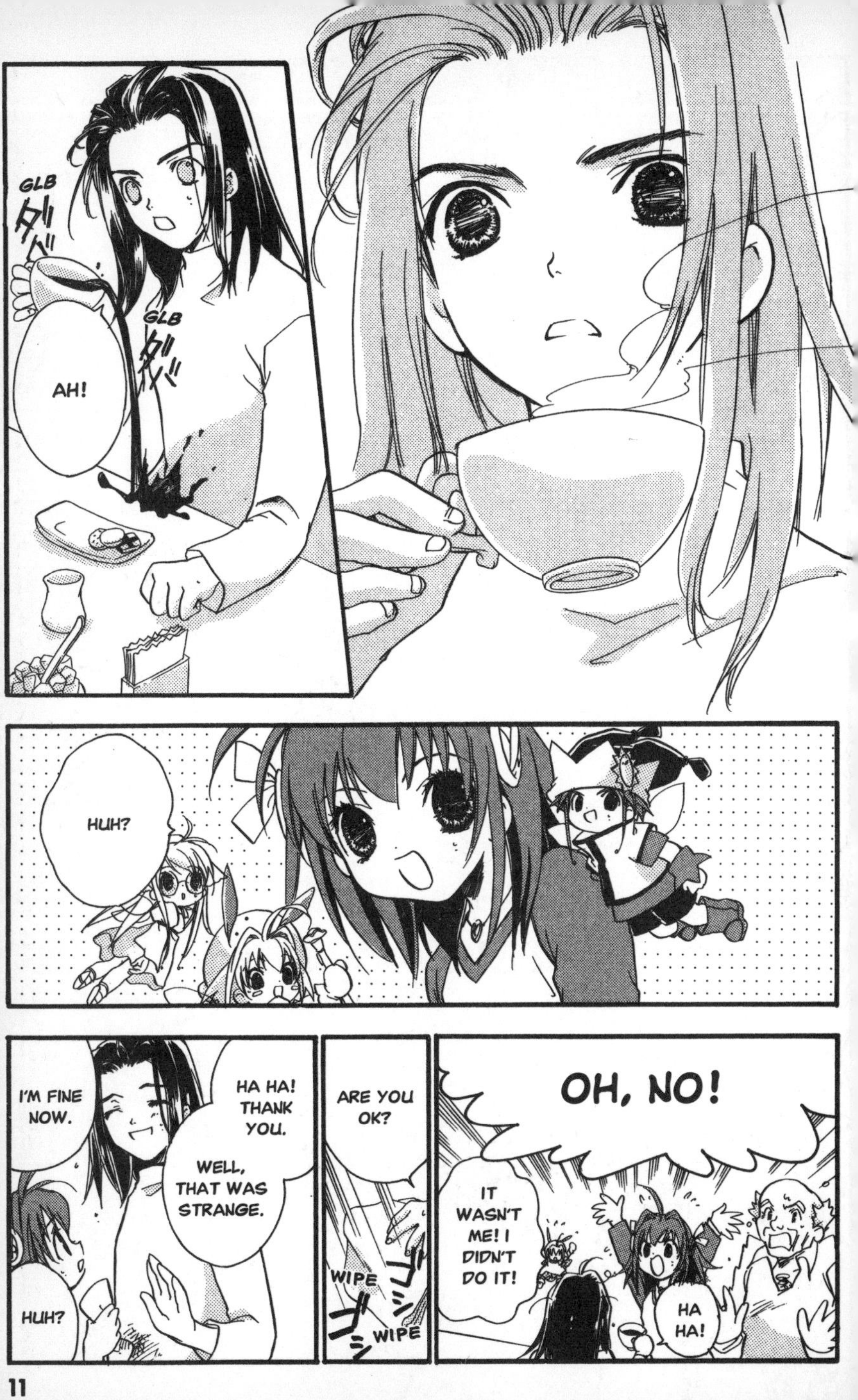
GLB
GLB
AH!
HUH?
OH, NO!
IT WASN'T ME! I DIDN'T DO IT!
HA HA!
ARE YOU OK?
WIPE
WIPE
HA HA! THANK YOU.
WELL, THAT WAS STRANGE.
I'M FINE NOW.
HUH?

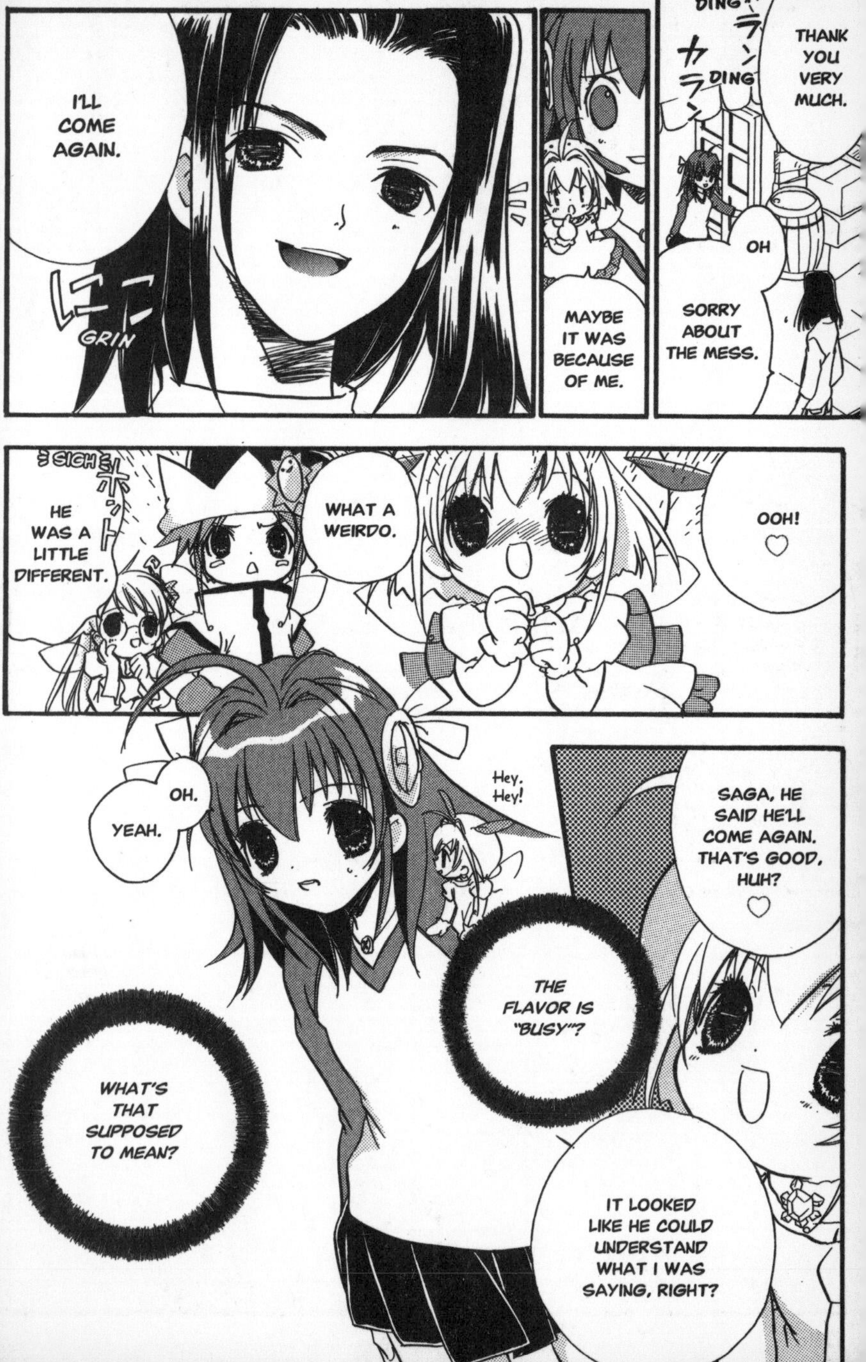
DING
カラン
DING
カラン
THANK YOU VERY MUCH.
OH
SORRY ABOUT THE MESS.
MAYBE IT WAS BECAUSE OF ME.
I'LL COME AGAIN.
GRIN
OOH! ♡
WHAT A WEIRDO.
SIGH
HE WAS A LITTLE DIFFERENT.
SAGA, HE SAID HE'LL COME AGAIN. THAT'S GOOD, HUH? ♡
Hey. Hey!
OH.
YEAH.
THE FLAVOR IS "BUSY"?
WHAT'S THAT SUPPOSED TO MEAN?
IT LOOKED LIKE HE COULD UNDERSTAND WHAT I WAS SAYING, RIGHT?

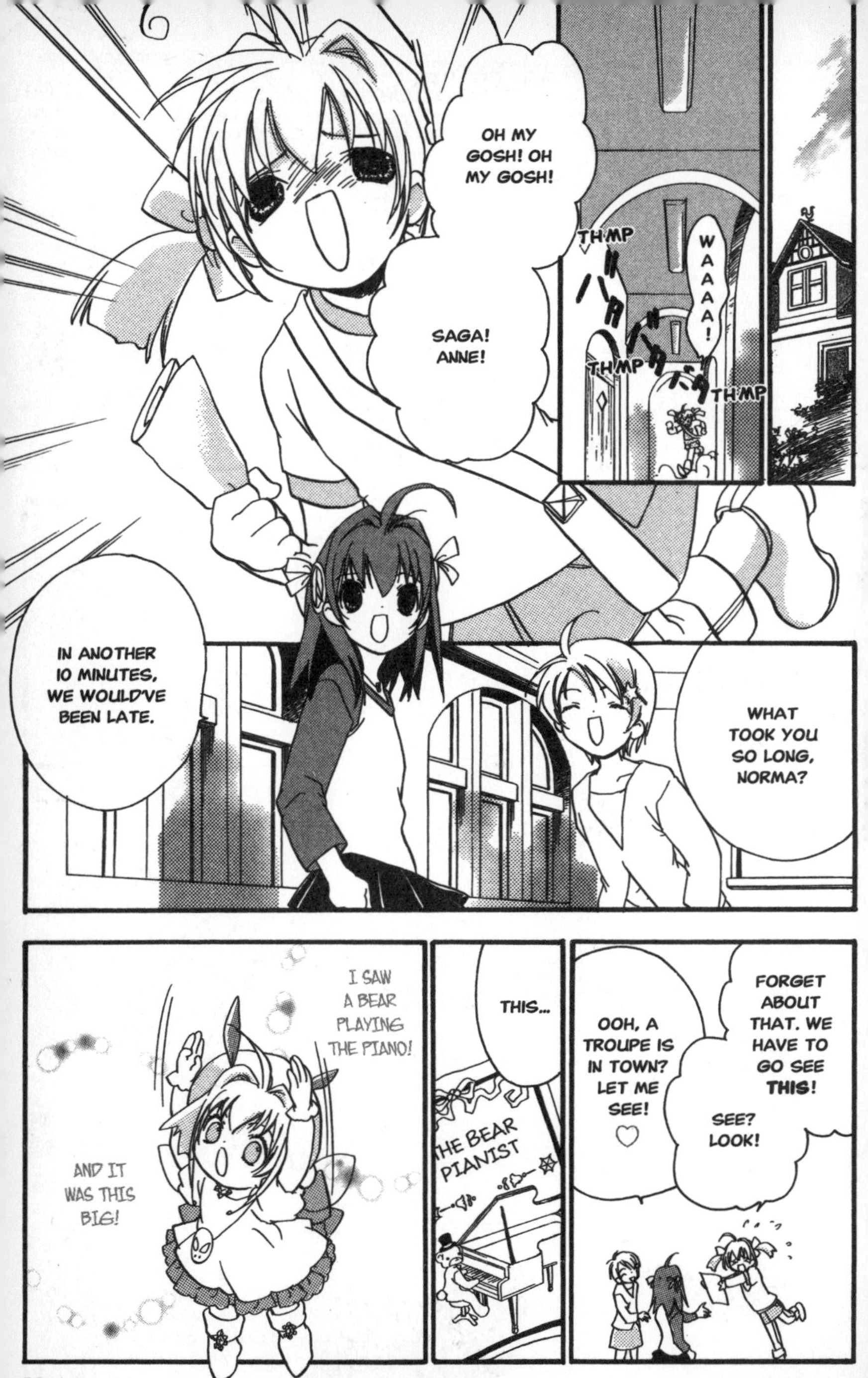
THMP
WAAAA!
THMP
THMP
OH MY GOSH! OH MY GOSH!
SAGA! ANNE!
WHAT TOOK YOU SO LONG, NORMA?
IN ANOTHER 10 MINUTES, WE WOULD'VE BEEN LATE.
FORGET ABOUT THAT. WE HAVE TO GO SEE THIS!
SEE? LOOK!
OOH, A TROUPE IS IN TOWN? LET ME SEE! ♡
THIS...
THE BEAR PIANIST
I SAW A BEAR PLAYING THE PIANO!
AND IT WAS THIS BIG!

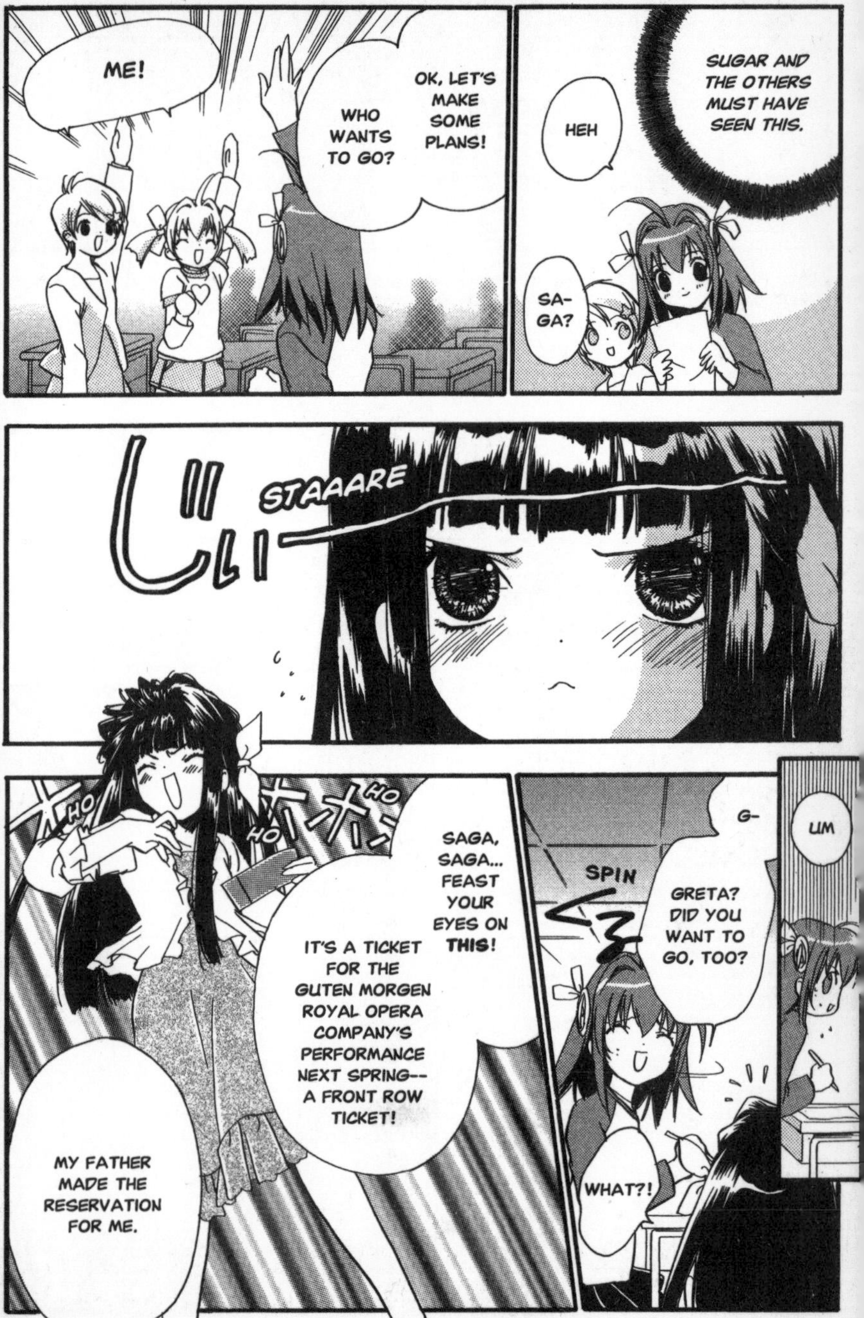
SUGAR AND THE OTHERS MUST HAVE SEEN THIS.
HEH
SA-GA?
OK, LET'S MAKE SOME PLANS!
WHO WANTS TO GO?
ME!
STAAARE
UM
G-
GRETA? DID YOU WANT TO GO, TOO?
SPIN
WHAT?!
HO HO HO
SAGA, SAGA... FEAST YOUR EYES ON THIS!
IT'S A TICKET FOR THE GUTEN MORGEN ROYAL OPERA COMPANY'S PERFORMANCE NEXT SPRING-- A FRONT ROW TICKET!
MY FATHER MADE THE RESERVATION FOR ME.

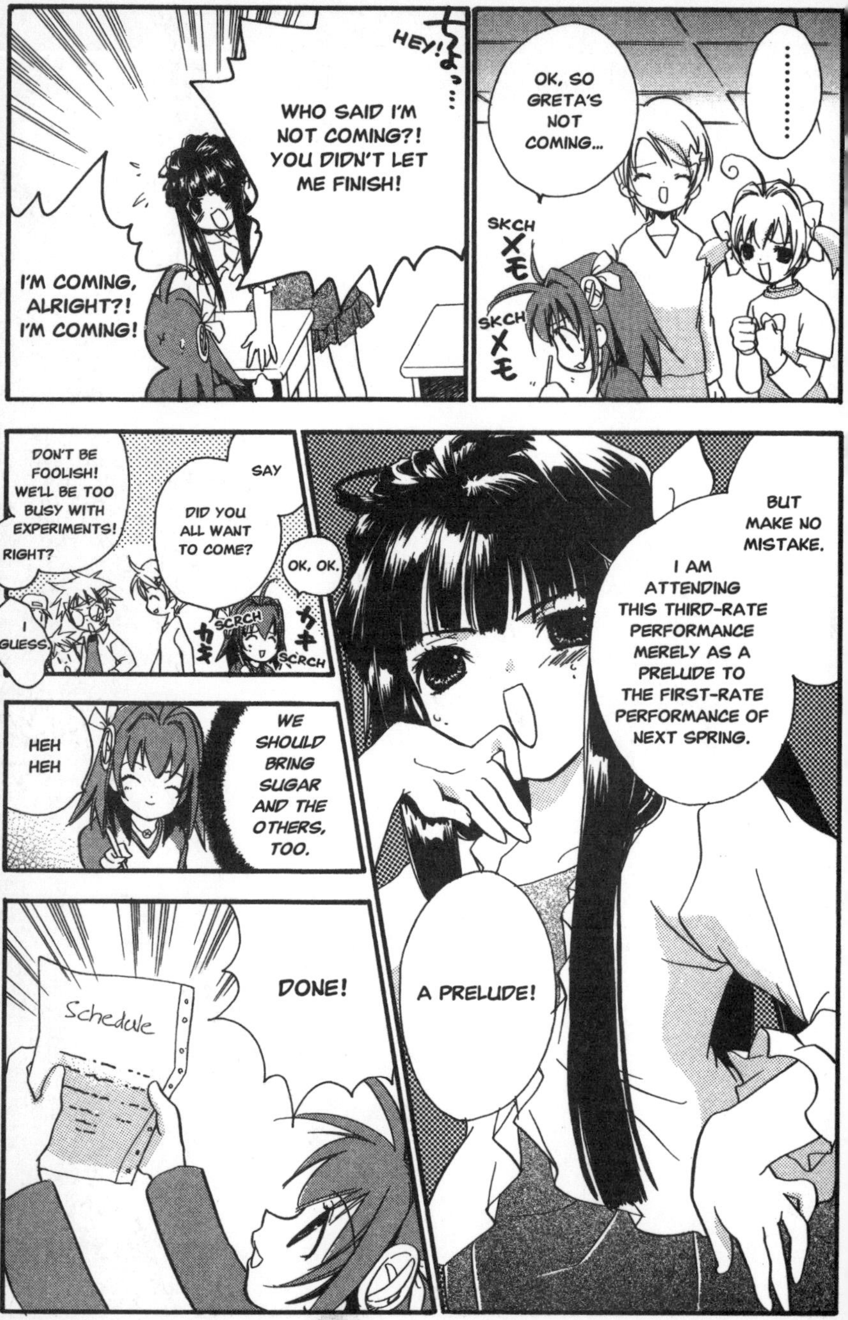
......
OK, SO GRETA'S NOT COMING...
SKCH
メモ
SKCH
メモ
HEY! ちょっ...
WHO SAID I'M NOT COMING?! YOU DIDN'T LET ME FINISH!
I'M COMING, ALRIGHT?! I'M COMING!
BUT MAKE NO MISTAKE.
I AM ATTENDING THIS THIRD-RATE PERFORMANCE MERELY AS A PRELUDE TO THE FIRST-RATE PERFORMANCE OF NEXT SPRING.
SAY
DID YOU ALL WANT TO COME?
OK, OK.
SCRCH
カキ
カキ
SCRCH
DON'T BE FOOLISH! WE'LL BE TOO BUSY WITH EXPERIMENTS!
RIGHT?
I GUESS.
WE SHOULD BRING SUGAR AND THE OTHERS, TOO.
HEH HEH
A PRELUDE!
DONE!
Schedule

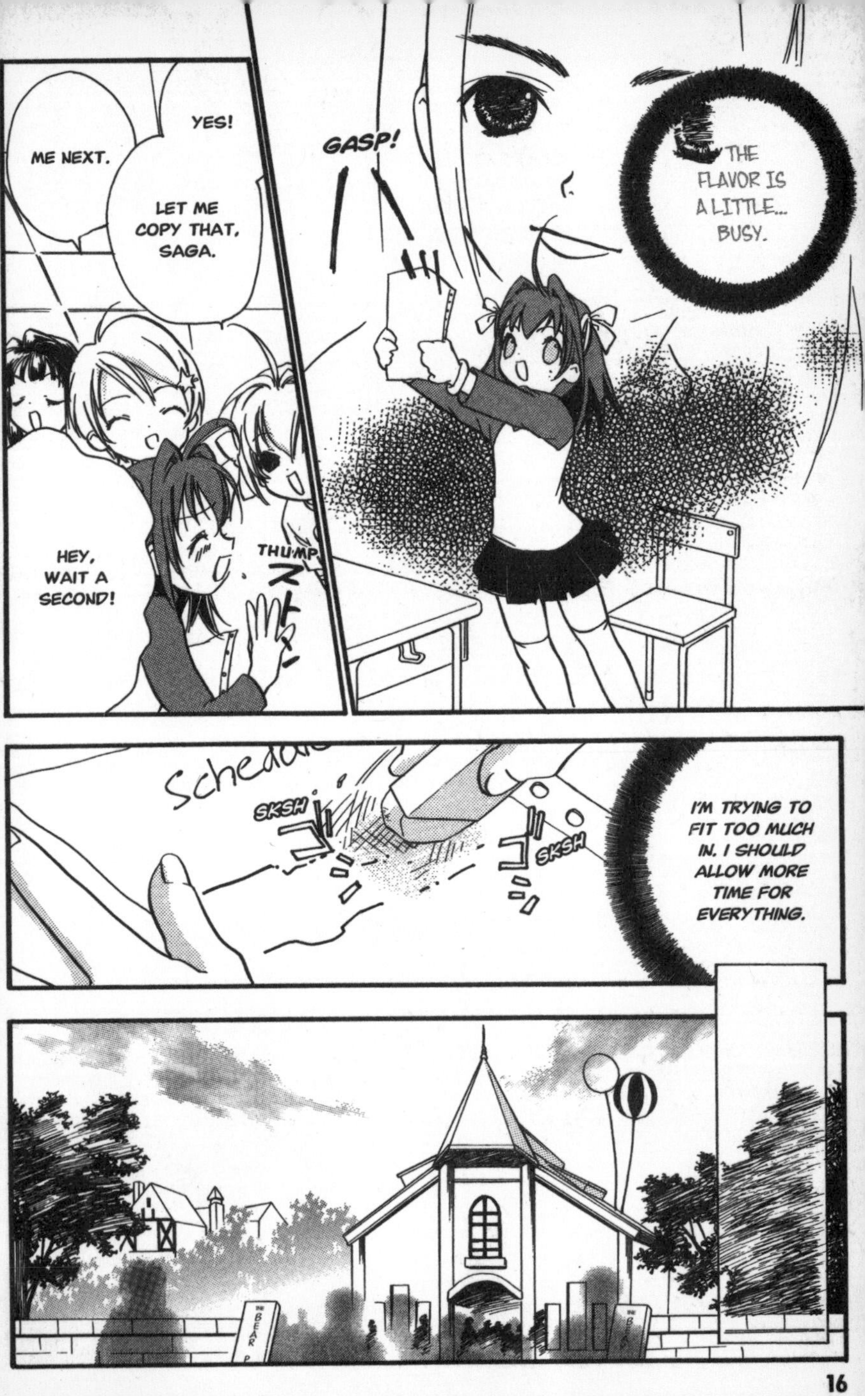
THE FLAVOR IS A LITTLE... BUSY.
GASP!
YES!
LET ME COPY THAT, SAGA.
ME NEXT.
THUMP
HEY, WAIT A SECOND!
I'M TRYING TO FIT TOO MUCH IN. I SHOULD ALLOW MORE TIME FOR EVERYTHING.
SKSH
SKSH

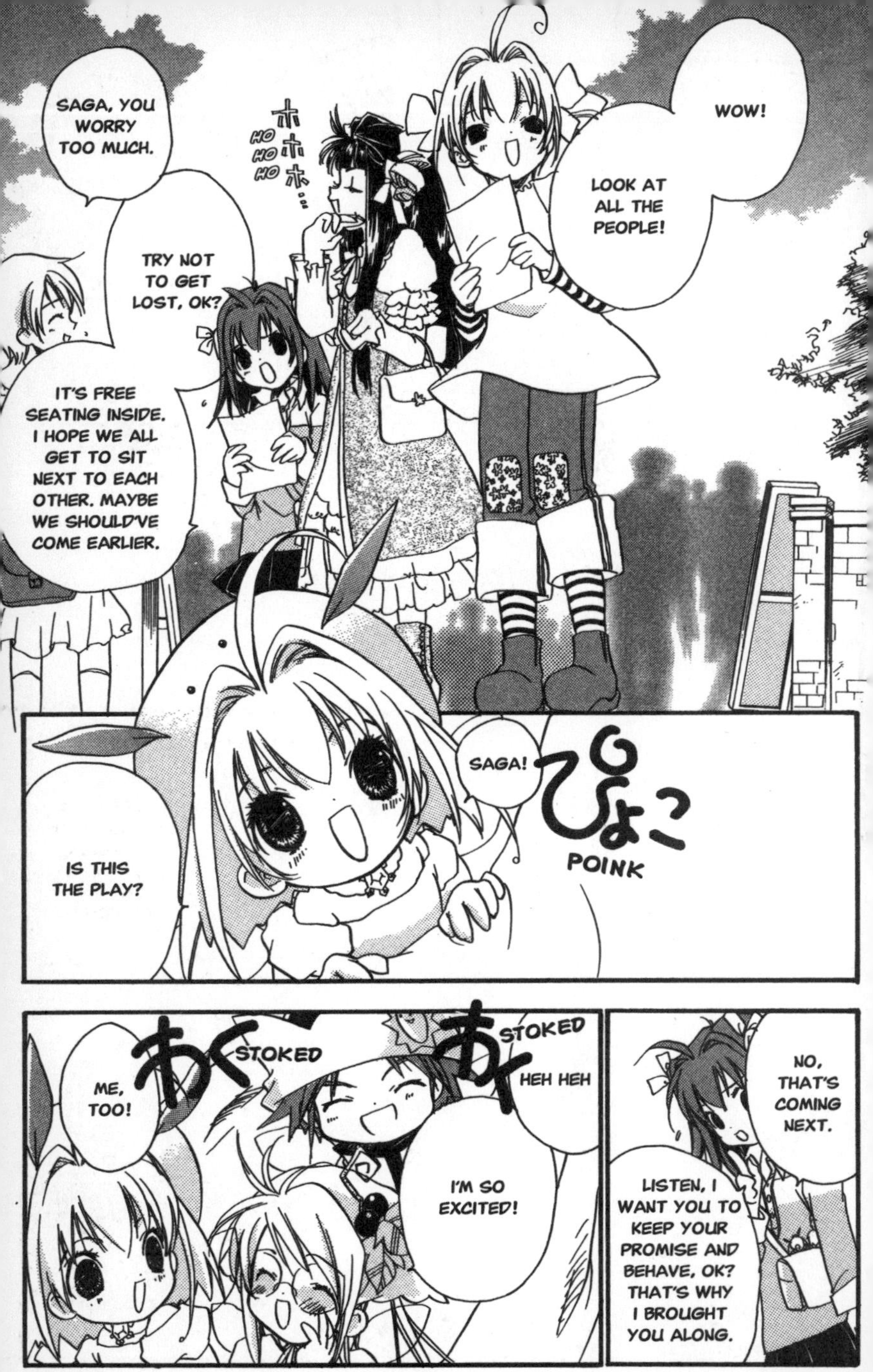

WOW!
LOOK AT ALL THE PEOPLE!
ホホホ…
HO HO HO
SAGA, YOU WORRY TOO MUCH.
TRY NOT TO GET LOST, OK?
IT'S FREE SEATING INSIDE. I HOPE WE ALL GET TO SIT NEXT TO EACH OTHER. MAYBE WE SHOULD'VE COME EARLIER.
ぴょこ
POINK
SAGA!
IS THIS THE PLAY?
NO, THAT'S COMING NEXT.
LISTEN, I WANT YOU TO KEEP YOUR PROMISE AND BEHAVE, OK? THAT'S WHY I BROUGHT YOU ALONG.
わく
STOKED
わく
STOKED
HEH HEH
I'M SO EXCITED!
ME, TOO!

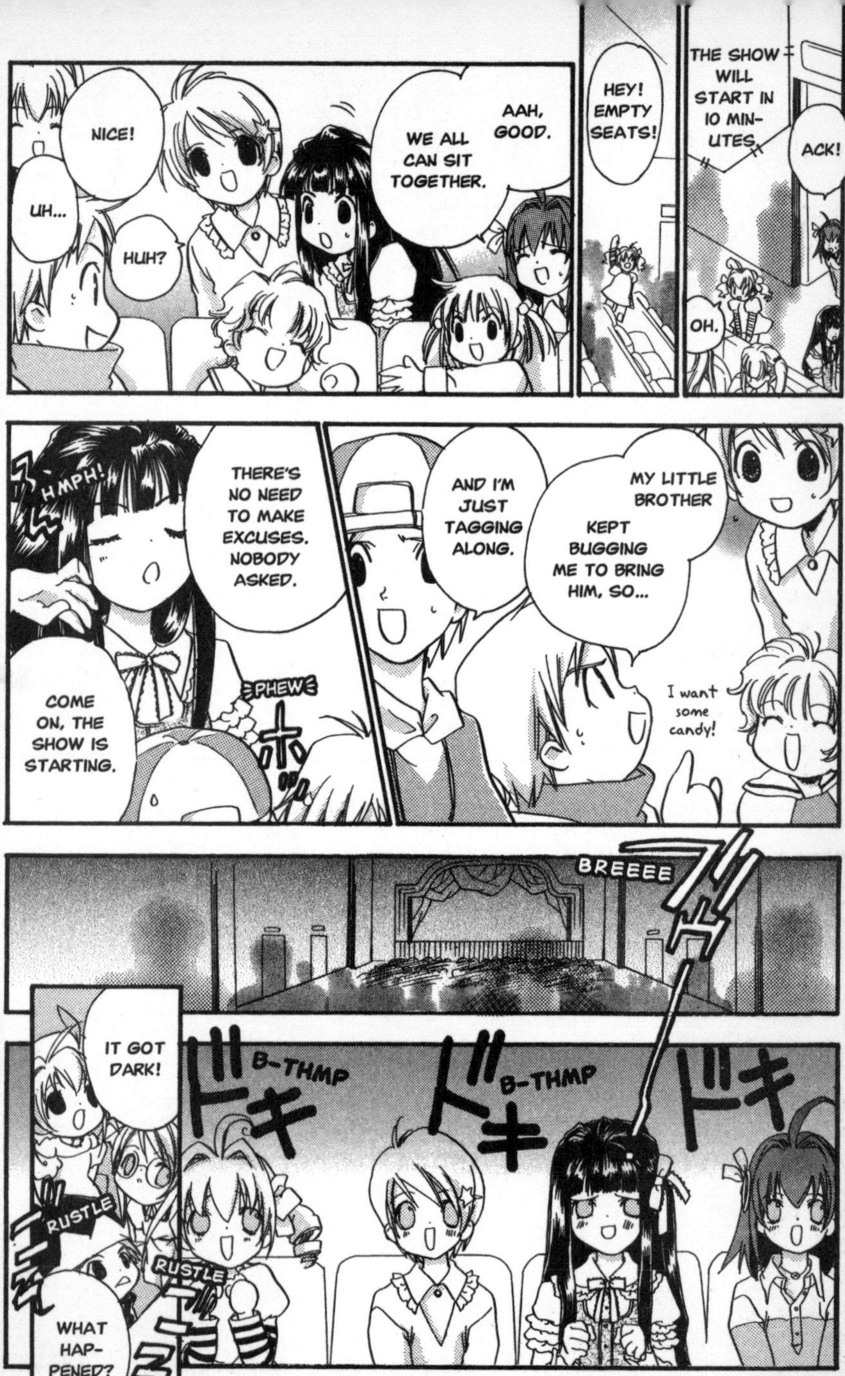
THE SHOW WILL START IN 10 MIN-UTES.
ACK!
OH.
HEY! EMPTY SEATS!
AAH, GOOD.
WE ALL CAN SIT TOGETHER.
NICE!
UH...
HUH?
MY LITTLE BROTHER
KEPT BUGGING ME TO BRING HIM, SO...
I want some candy!
AND I'M JUST TAGGING ALONG.
HMPH!
THERE'S NO NEED TO MAKE EXCUSES. NOBODY ASKED.
PHEW
COME ON, THE SHOW IS STARTING.
BREEEE
ドキ
B-THMP
IT GOT DARK!
ドキ
B-THMP
ドキ
RUSTLE
RUSTLE
WHAT HAP-PENED?

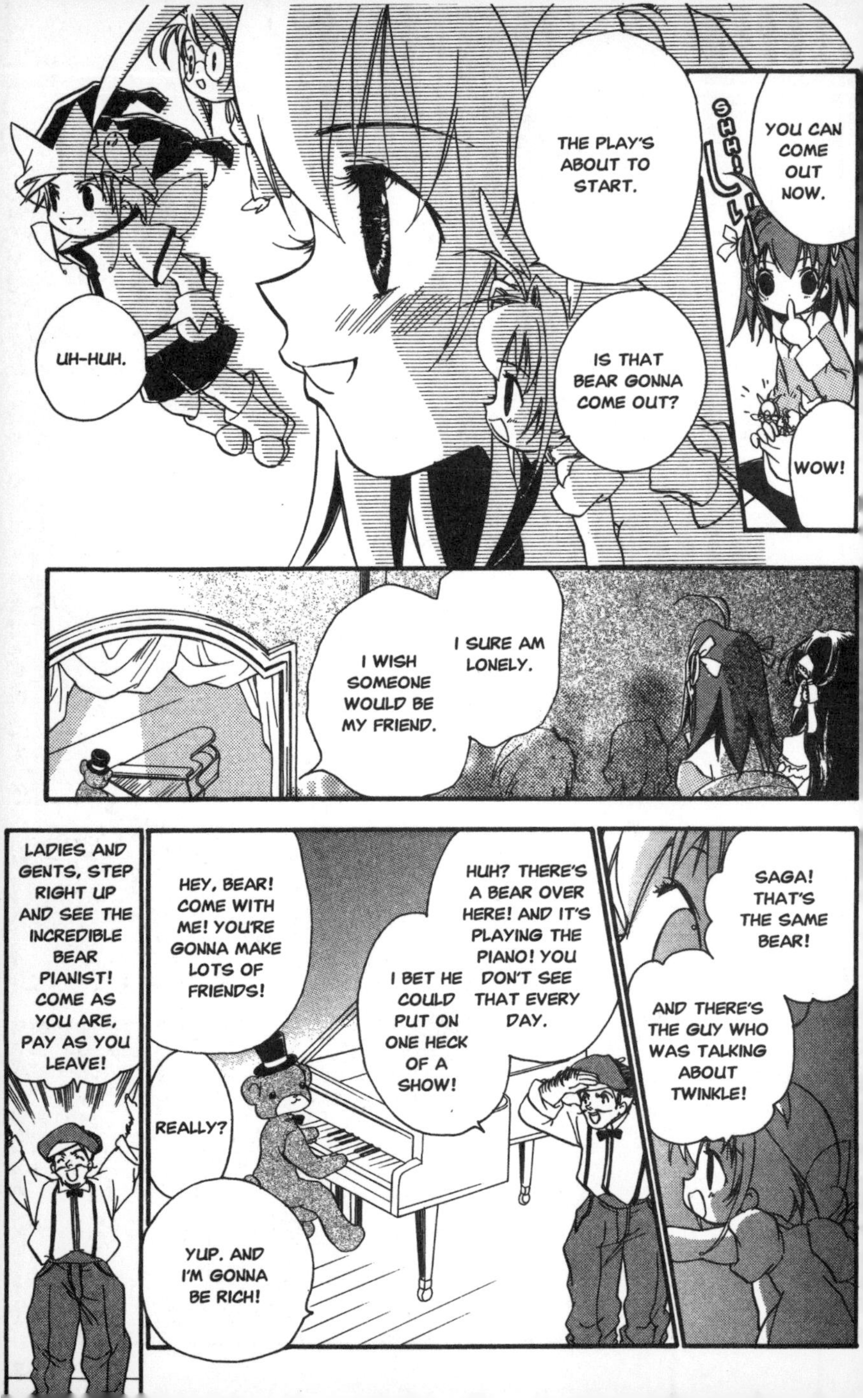
YOU CAN COME OUT NOW.
SHH!
WOW!
THE PLAY'S ABOUT TO START.
IS THAT BEAR GONNA COME OUT?
UH-HUH.
I SURE AM LONELY.
I WISH SOMEONE WOULD BE MY FRIEND.
SAGA! THAT'S THE SAME BEAR!
AND THERE'S THE GUY WHO WAS TALKING ABOUT TWINKLE!
HUH? THERE'S A BEAR OVER HERE! AND IT'S PLAYING THE PIANO! YOU DON'T SEE THAT EVERY DAY.
I BET HE COULD PUT ON ONE HECK OF A SHOW!
HEY, BEAR! COME WITH ME! YOU'RE GONNA MAKE LOTS OF FRIENDS!
REALLY?
YUP. AND I'M GONNA BE RICH!
LADIES AND GENTS, STEP RIGHT UP AND SEE THE INCREDIBLE BEAR PIANIST! COME AS YOU ARE, PAY AS YOU LEAVE!

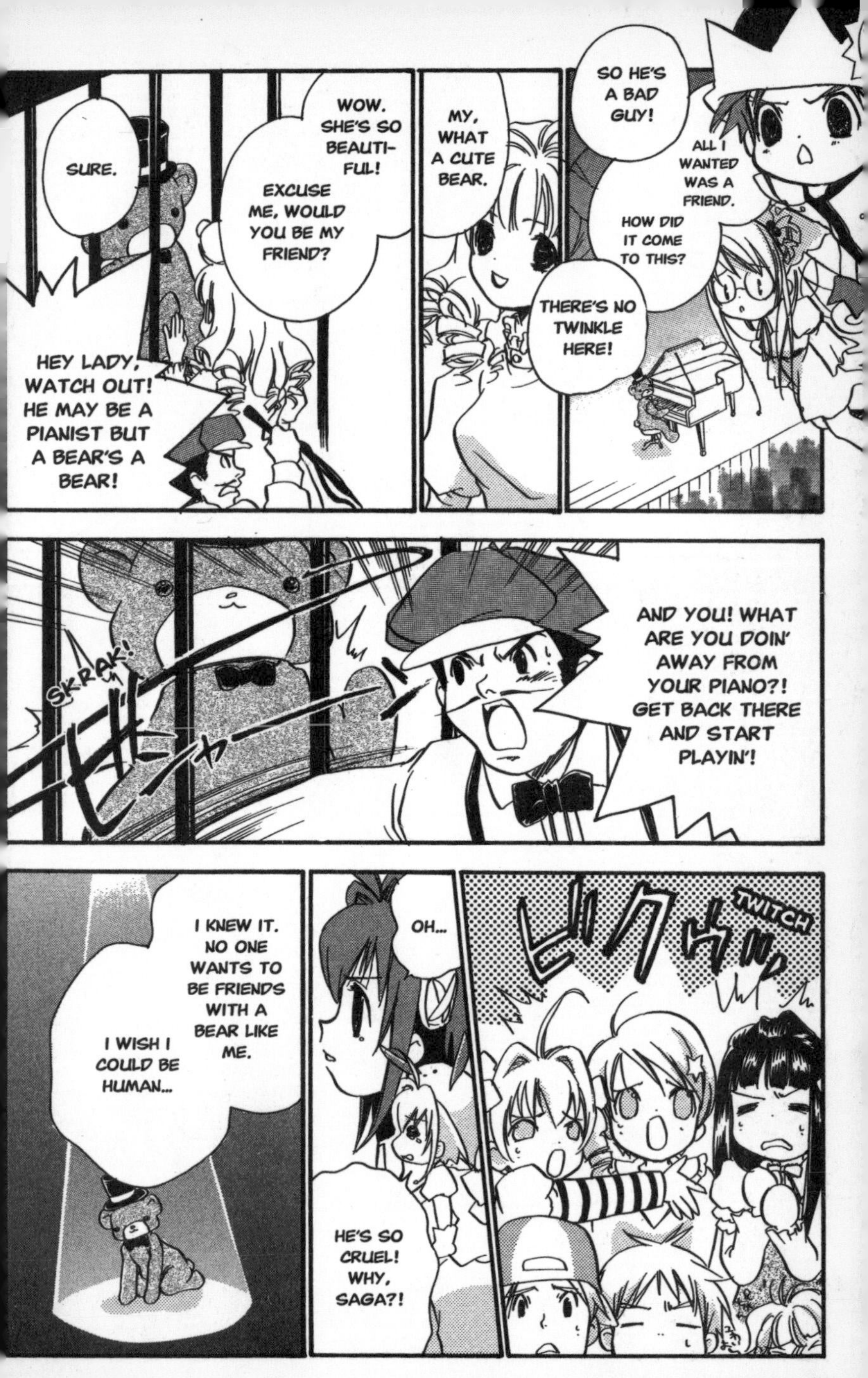
SO HE'S A BAD GUY!
ALL I WANTED WAS A FRIEND.
HOW DID IT COME TO THIS?
THERE'S NO TWINKLE HERE!
MY, WHAT A CUTE BEAR.
WOW. SHE'S SO BEAUTI-FUL!
EXCUSE ME, WOULD YOU BE MY FRIEND?
SURE.
HEY LADY, WATCH OUT! HE MAY BE A PIANIST BUT A BEAR'S A BEAR!
AND YOU! WHAT ARE YOU DOIN' AWAY FROM YOUR PIANO?! GET BACK THERE AND START PLAYIN'!
SKRAK!
TWITCH
OH...
HE'S SO CRUEL! WHY, SAGA?!
I KNEW IT. NO ONE WANTS TO BE FRIENDS WITH A BEAR LIKE ME.
I WISH I COULD BE HUMAN...

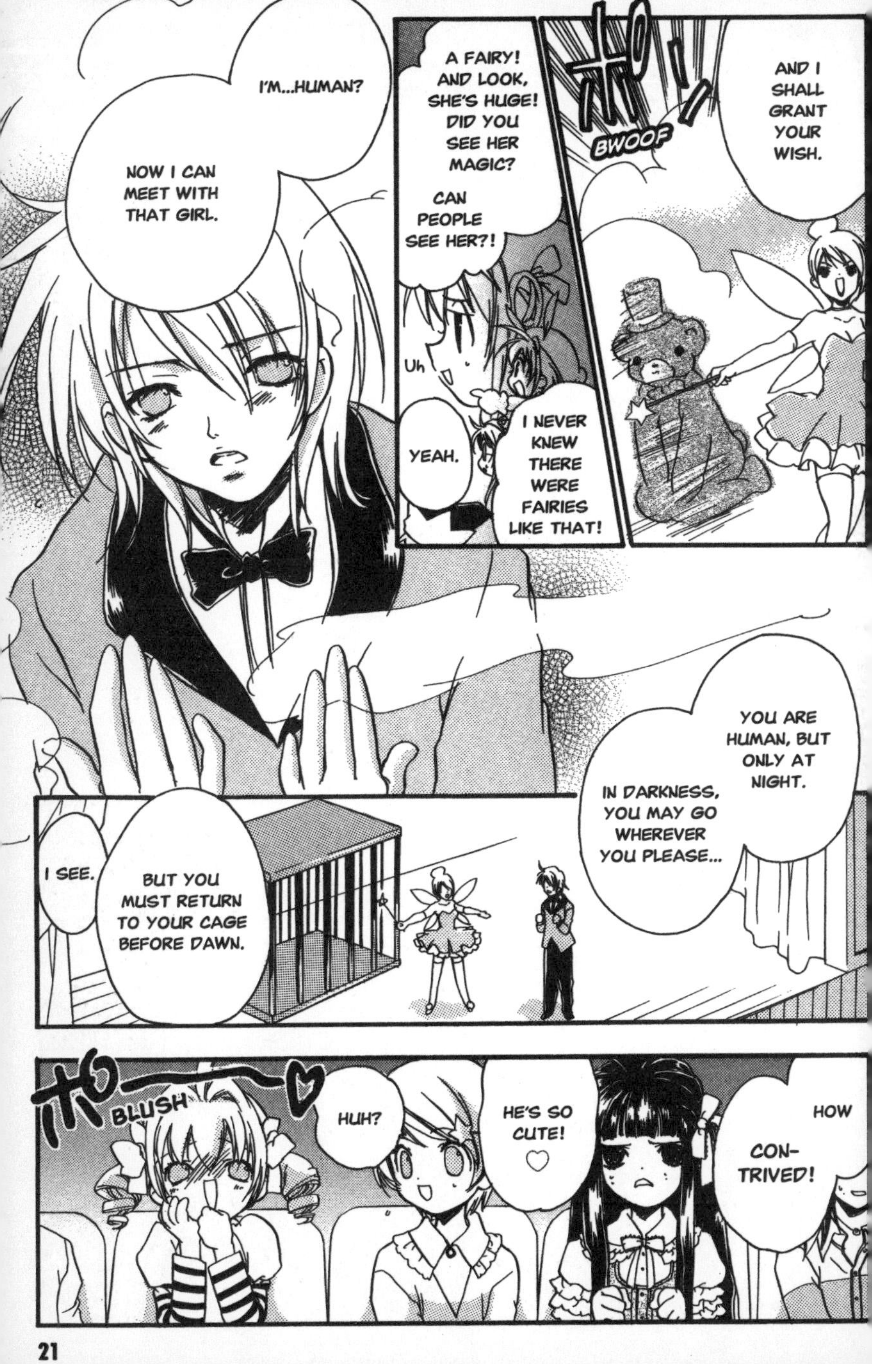
BWOOF
AND I SHALL GRANT YOUR WISH.
A FAIRY! AND LOOK, SHE'S HUGE! DID YOU SEE HER MAGIC?
CAN PEOPLE SEE HER?!
I NEVER KNEW THERE WERE FAIRIES LIKE THAT!
Uh
YEAH.
I'M...HUMAN?
NOW I CAN MEET WITH THAT GIRL.
YOU ARE HUMAN, BUT ONLY AT NIGHT.
IN DARKNESS, YOU MAY GO WHEREVER YOU PLEASE...
BUT YOU MUST RETURN TO YOUR CAGE BEFORE DAWN.
I SEE.
HOW CON-TRIVED!
HE'S SO CUTE!
HUH?
BLUSH

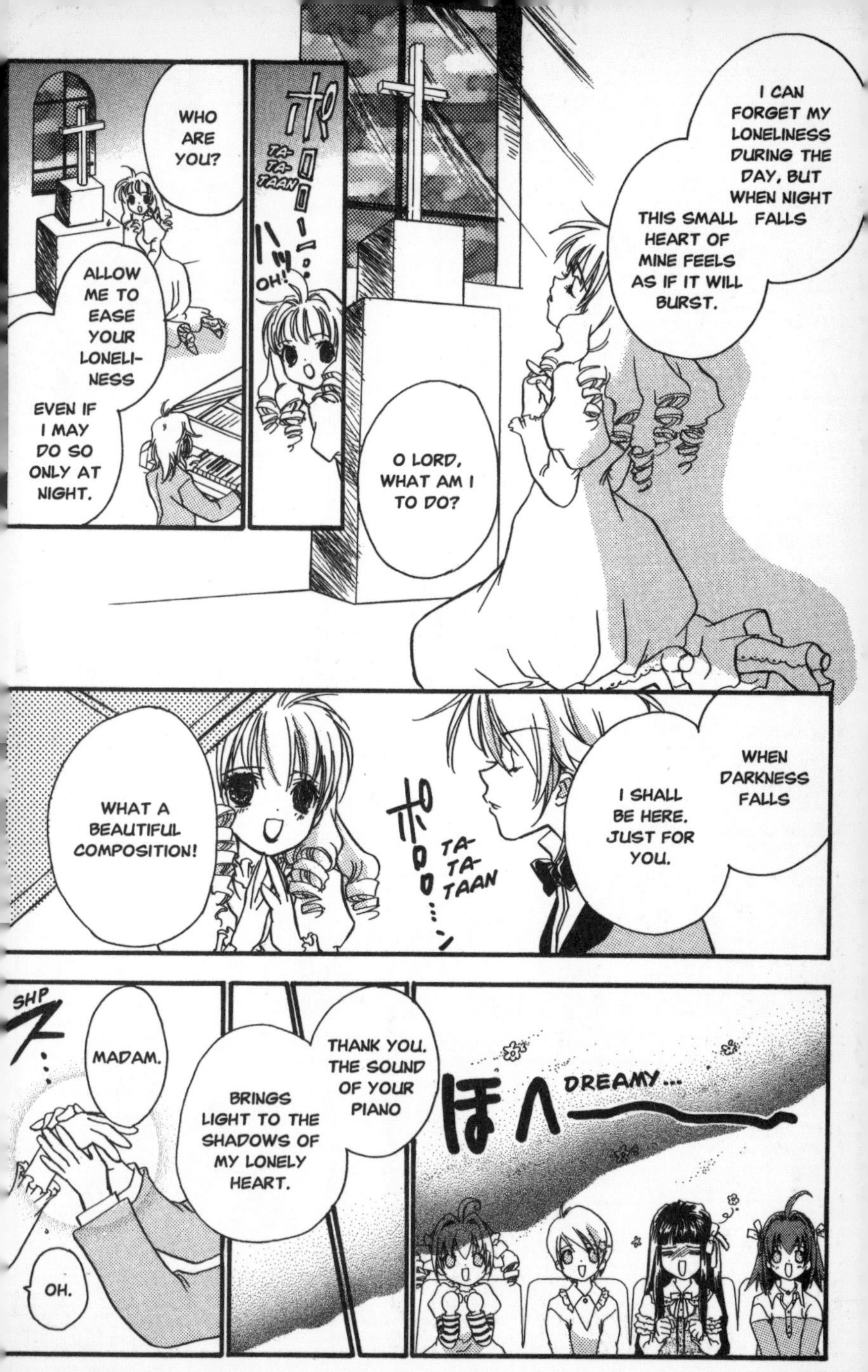
I CAN FORGET MY LONELINESS DURING THE DAY, BUT WHEN NIGHT FALLS
THIS SMALL HEART OF MINE FEELS AS IF IT WILL BURST.
O LORD, WHAT AM I TO DO?
ポロロー
TA-TA-TAAN
ハッ
OH!
WHO ARE YOU?
ALLOW ME TO EASE YOUR LONELINESS
EVEN IF I MAY DO SO ONLY AT NIGHT.
WHEN DARKNESS FALLS
I SHALL BE HERE. JUST FOR YOU.
ポロロ…ン
TA-TA-TAAN
WHAT A BEAUTIFUL COMPOSITION!
ほへ〜
DREAMY...
THANK YOU. THE SOUND OF YOUR PIANO
BRINGS LIGHT TO THE SHADOWS OF MY LONELY HEART.
MADAM.
SHP
OH.

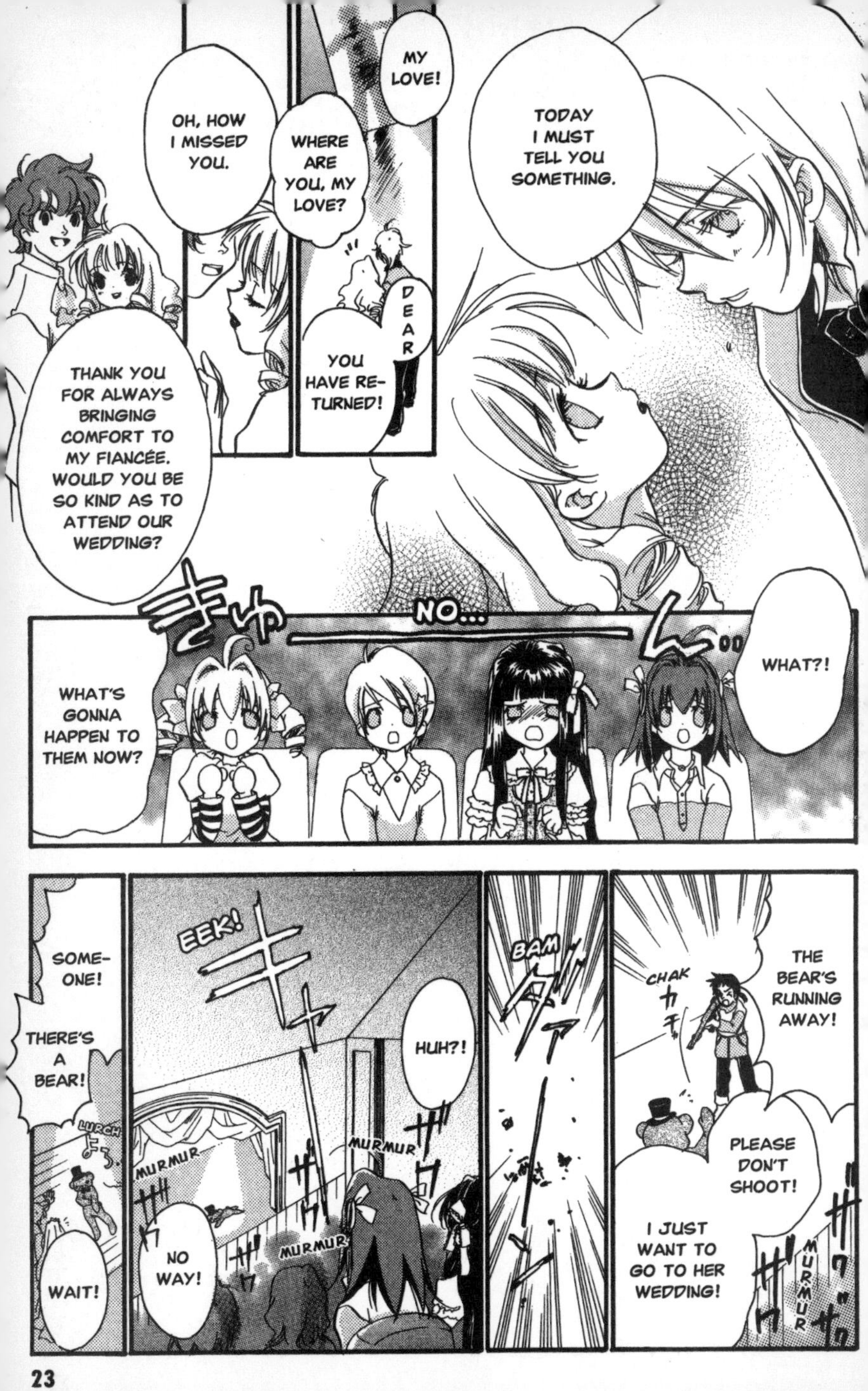

OH, HOW I MISSED YOU.
THANK YOU FOR ALWAYS BRINGING COMFORT TO MY FIANCÉE. WOULD YOU BE SO KIND AS TO ATTEND OUR WEDDING?
WHERE ARE YOU, MY LOVE?
MY LOVE!
DEAR
YOU HAVE RE-TURNED!
TODAY I MUST TELL YOU SOMETHING.
きゅ
NO...
ん
WHAT'S GONNA HAPPEN TO THEM NOW?
WHAT?!
SOME-ONE!
THERE'S A BEAR!
LURCH
WAIT!
EEK!
HUH?!
MURMUR
MURMUR
MURMUR
NO WAY!
BAM
CHAK
THE BEAR'S RUNNING AWAY!
PLEASE DON'T SHOOT!
I JUST WANT TO GO TO HER WEDDING!
MURMUR

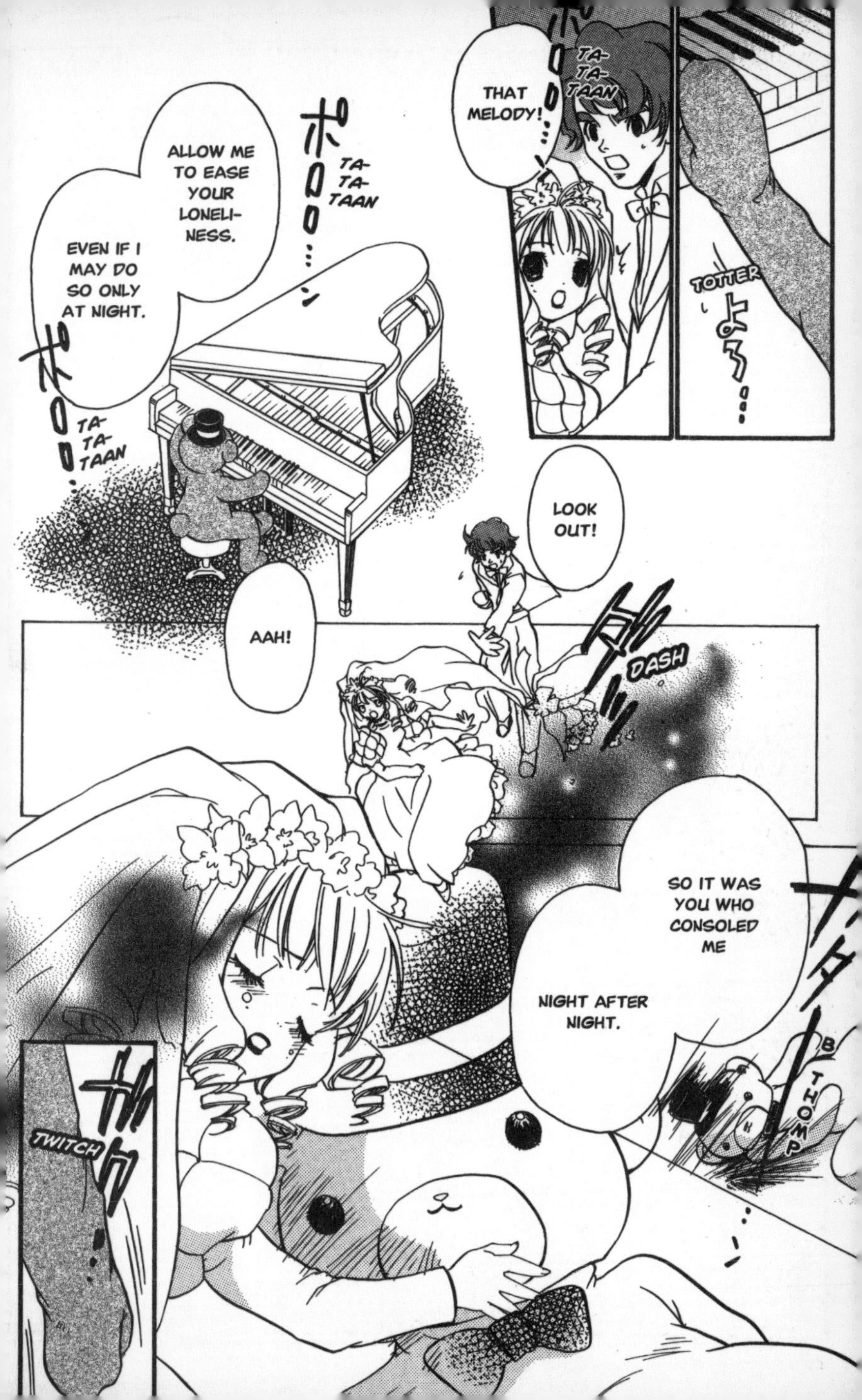
TOTTER
TA-TA-TAAN
THAT MELODY!
TA-TA-TAAN
ALLOW ME TO EASE YOUR LONELI-NESS.
EVEN IF I MAY DO SO ONLY AT NIGHT.
TA-TA-TAAN
LOOK OUT!
DASH
AAH!
B THOMP
SO IT WAS YOU WHO CONSOLED ME
NIGHT AFTER NIGHT.
TWITCH

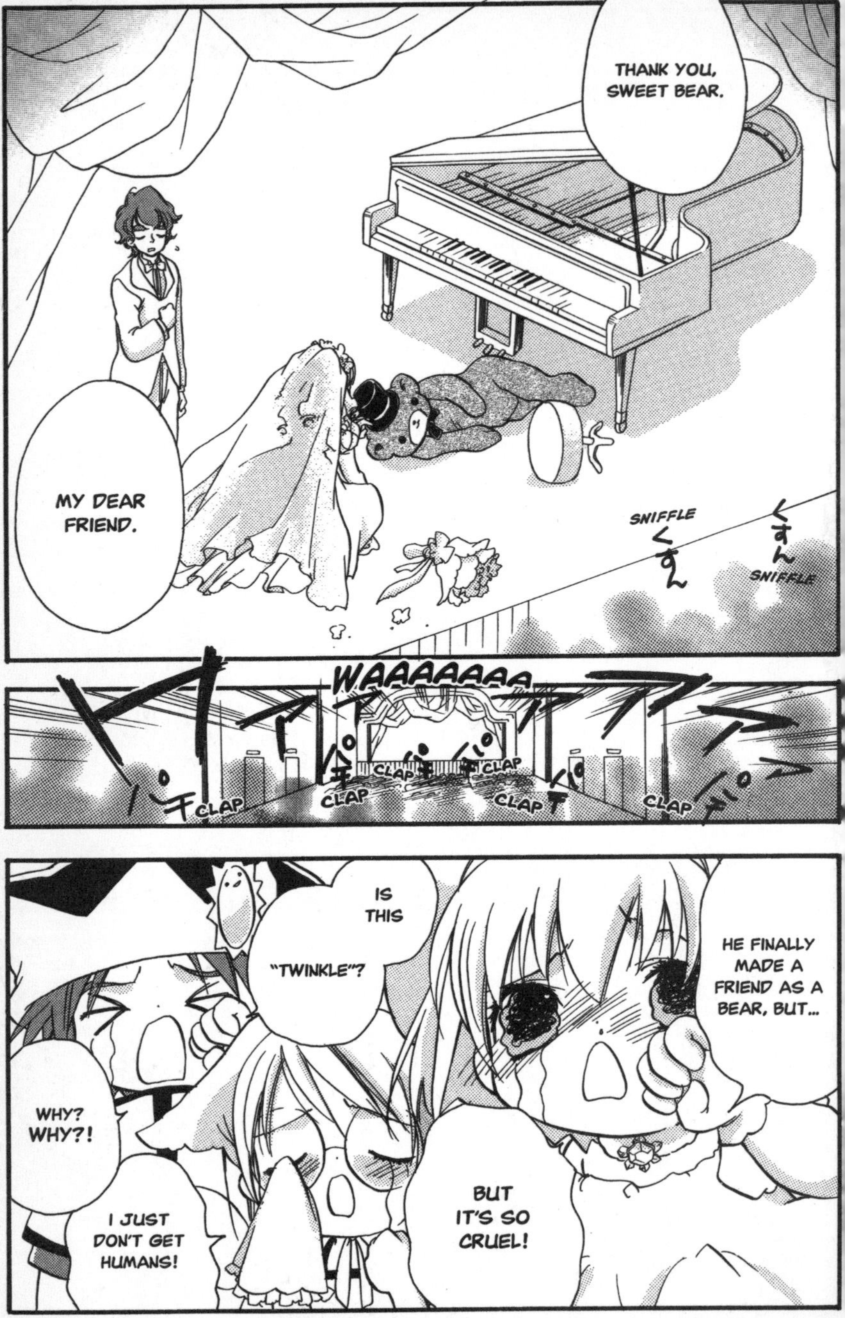
THANK YOU, SWEET BEAR.
MY DEAR FRIEND.
くすん
SNIFFLE
SNIFFLE
くすん
WAAAAAAA
CLAP
CLAP
CLAP
CLAP
CLAP
CLAP
HE FINALLY MADE A FRIEND AS A BEAR, BUT...
BUT IT'S SO CRUEL!
IS THIS "TWINKLE"?
WHY? WHY?!
I JUST DON'T GET HUMANS!

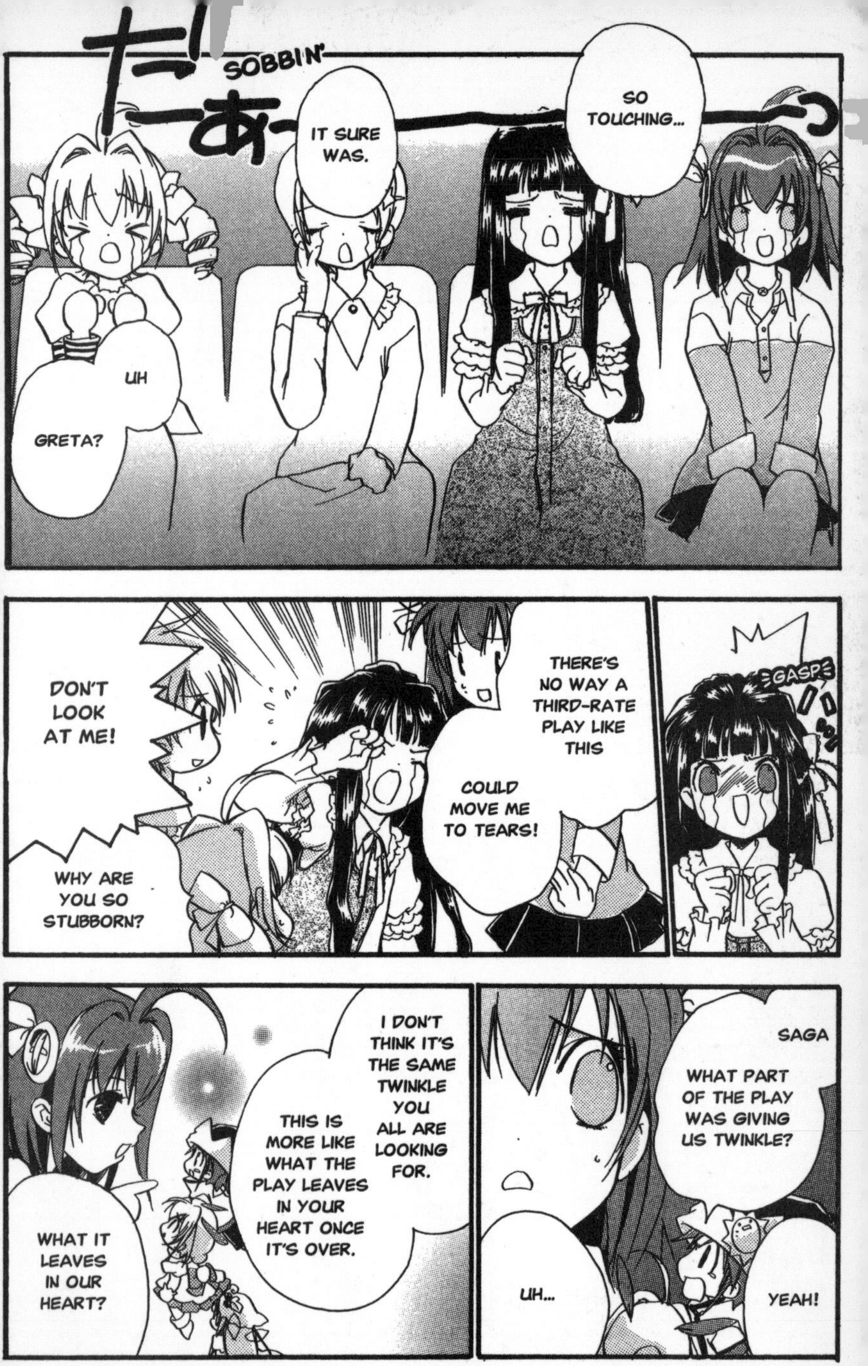
SOBBIN'
SO TOUCHING...
IT SURE WAS.
UH
GRETA?
GASP
THERE'S NO WAY A THIRD-RATE PLAY LIKE THIS
COULD MOVE ME TO TEARS!
DON'T LOOK AT ME!
WHY ARE YOU SO STUBBORN?
SAGA
WHAT PART OF THE PLAY WAS GIVING US TWINKLE?
YEAH!
UH...
I DON'T THINK IT'S THE SAME TWINKLE YOU ALL ARE LOOKING FOR.
THIS IS MORE LIKE WHAT THE PLAY LEAVES IN YOUR HEART ONCE IT'S OVER.
WHAT IT LEAVES IN OUR HEART?

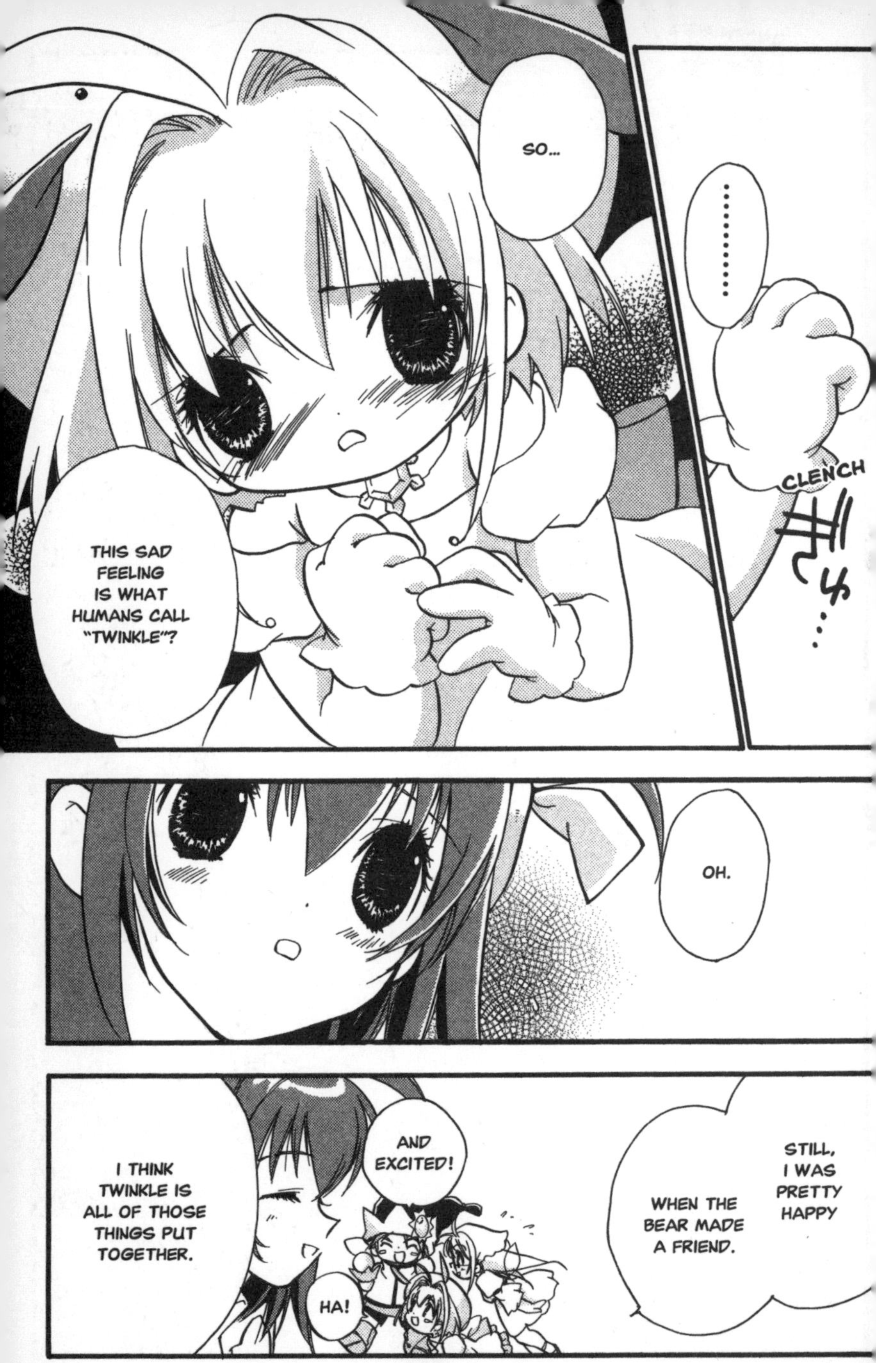
......
CLENCH
SO...
THIS SAD FEELING IS WHAT HUMANS CALL "TWINKLE"?
OH.
STILL, I WAS PRETTY HAPPY WHEN THE BEAR MADE A FRIEND.
AND EXCITED!
HA!
I THINK TWINKLE IS ALL OF THOSE THINGS PUT TOGETHER.

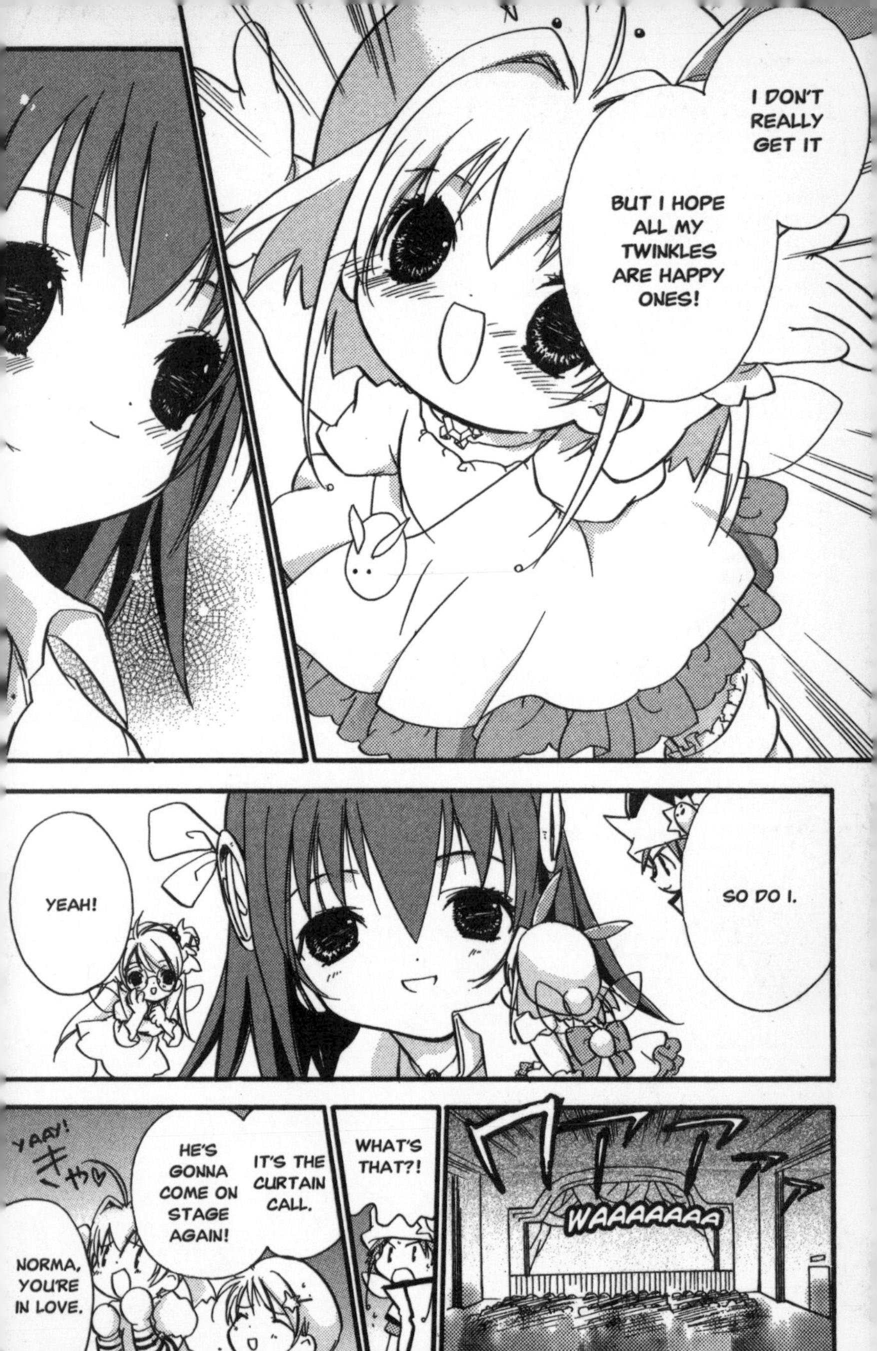
I DON'T REALLY GET IT
BUT I HOPE ALL MY TWINKLES ARE HAPPY ONES!
SO DO I.
YEAH!
WAAAAAAA
WHAT'S THAT?!
IT'S THE CURTAIN CALL.
HE'S GONNA COME ON STAGE AGAIN!
YAAY!
NORMA, YOU'RE IN LOVE.

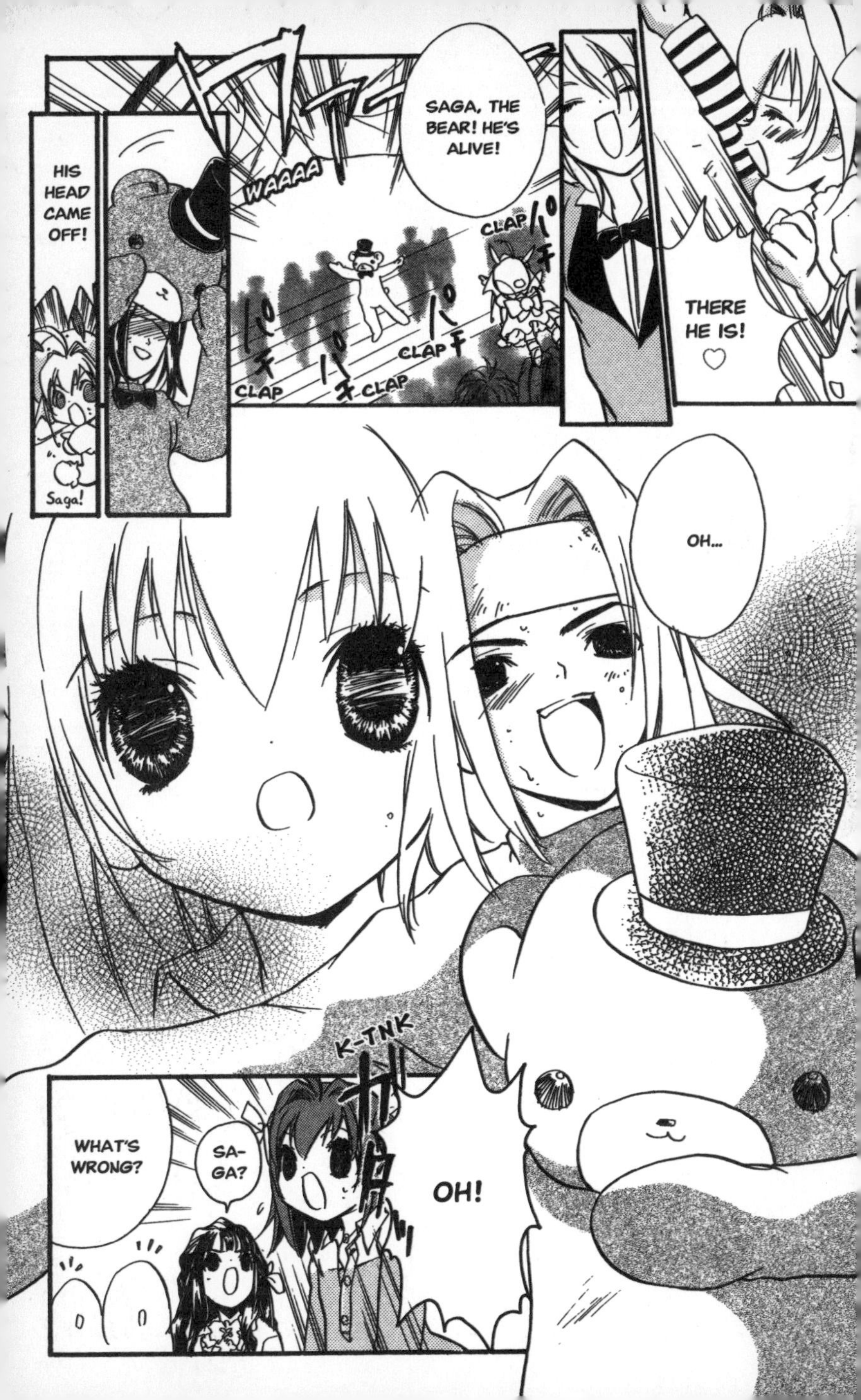
THERE HE IS!
SAGA, THE BEAR! HE'S ALIVE!
WAAAA
CLAP
CLAP
CLAP
CLAP
HIS HEAD CAME OFF!
Saga!
OH...
K-TNK
OH!
SA-GA?
WHAT'S WRONG?

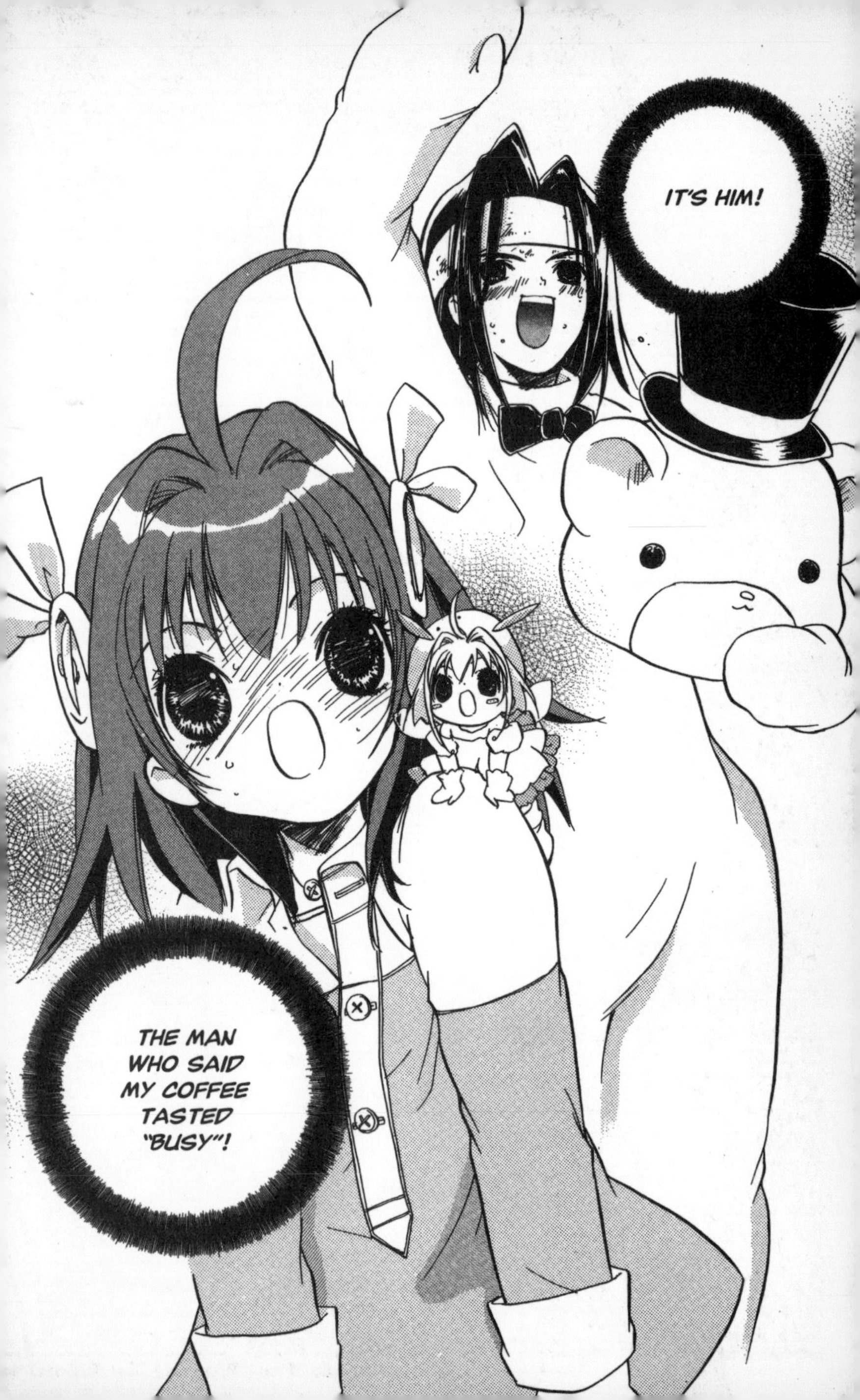
IT'S HIM!
THE MAN WHO SAID MY COFFEE TASTED "BUSY"!

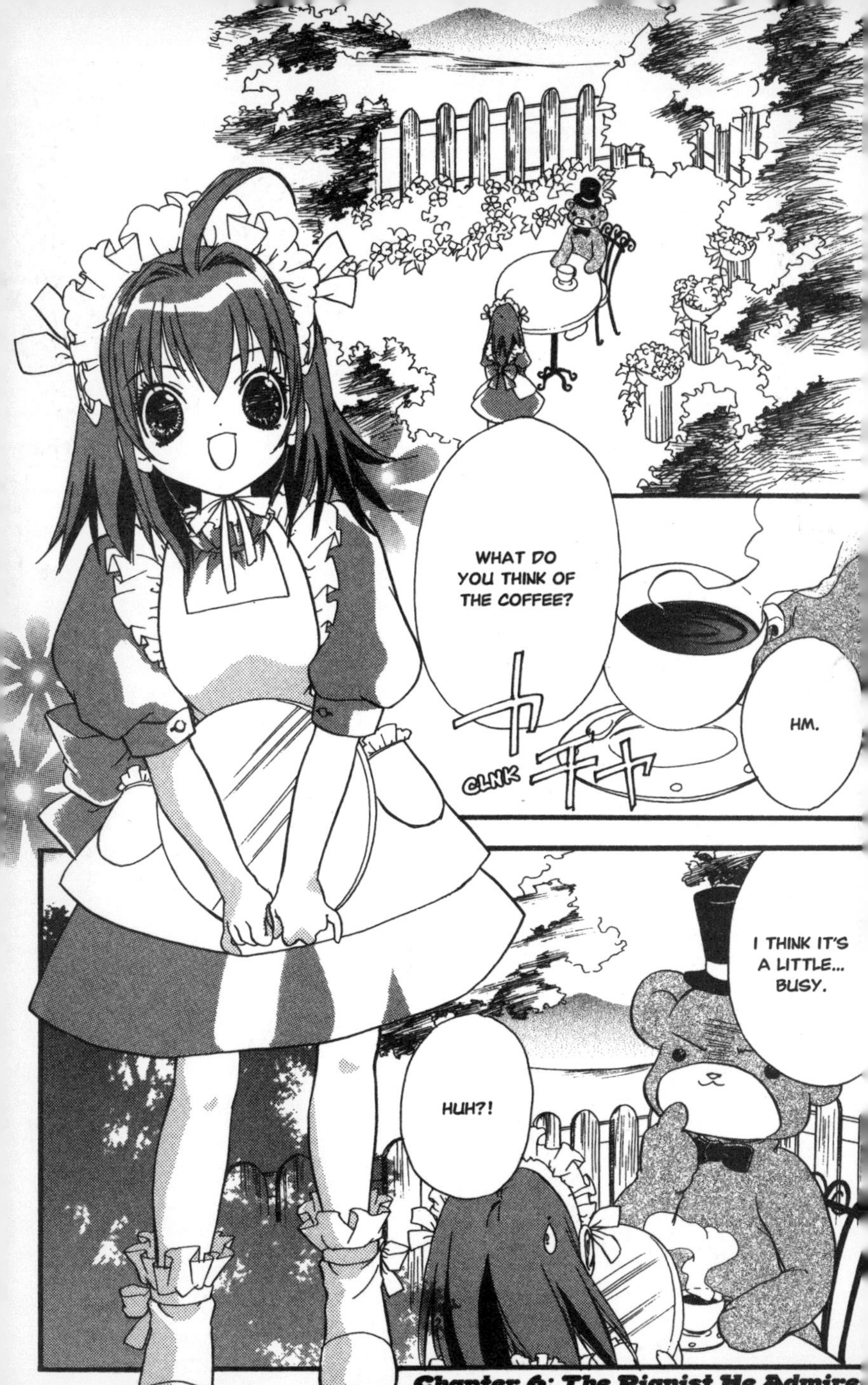
WHAT DO YOU THINK OF THE COFFEE?
CLNK
HM.
I THINK IT'S A LITTLE... BUSY.
HUH?!

Chapter 6: The Pianist He Admire

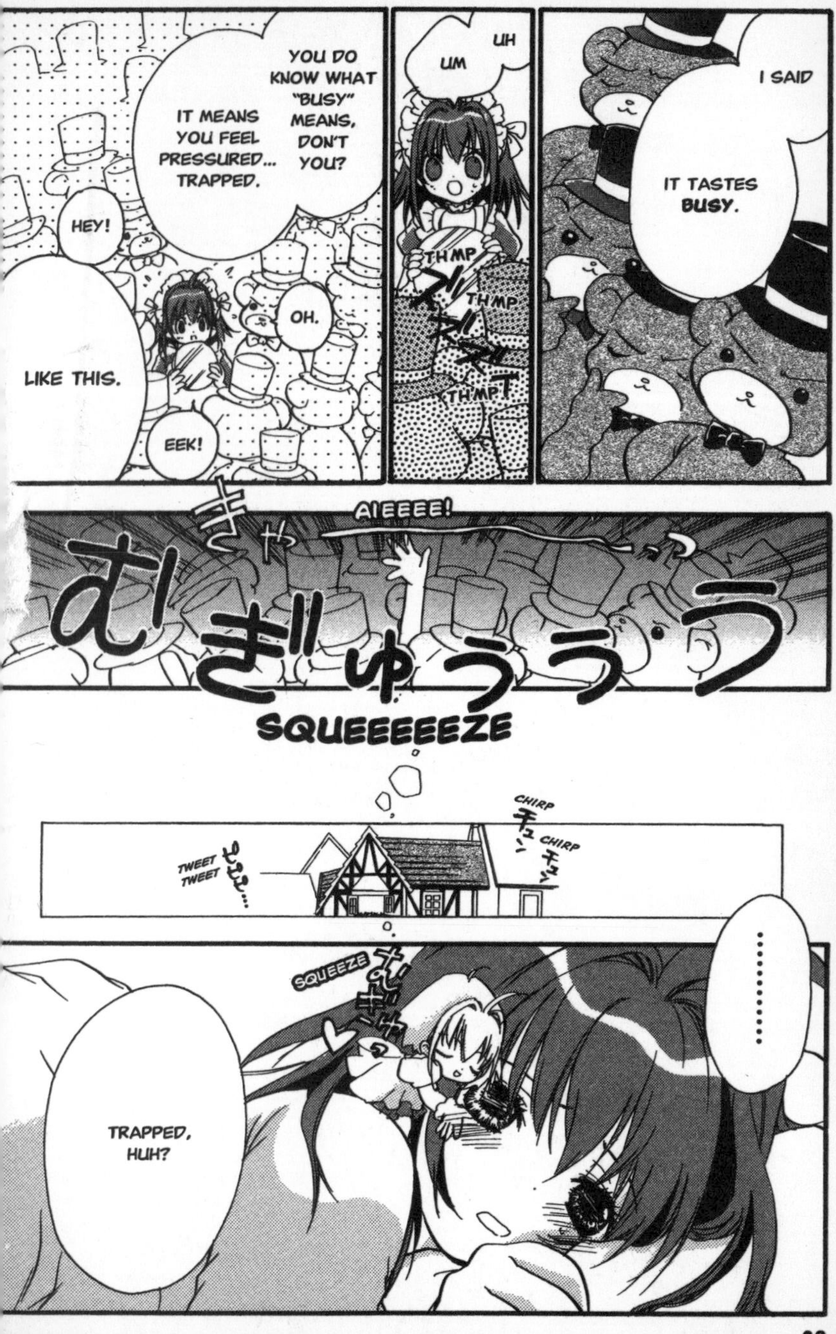
I SAID
IT TASTES BUSY.
UH
UM
THMP
THMP
THMP
YOU DO KNOW WHAT "BUSY" MEANS, DON'T YOU?
IT MEANS YOU FEEL PRESSURED... TRAPPED.
HEY!
OH.
LIKE THIS.
EEK!
AIEEEE!
SQUEEEEEEZE
CHIRP
CHIRP
TWEET TWEET
SQUEEZE
....
TRAPPED, HUH?

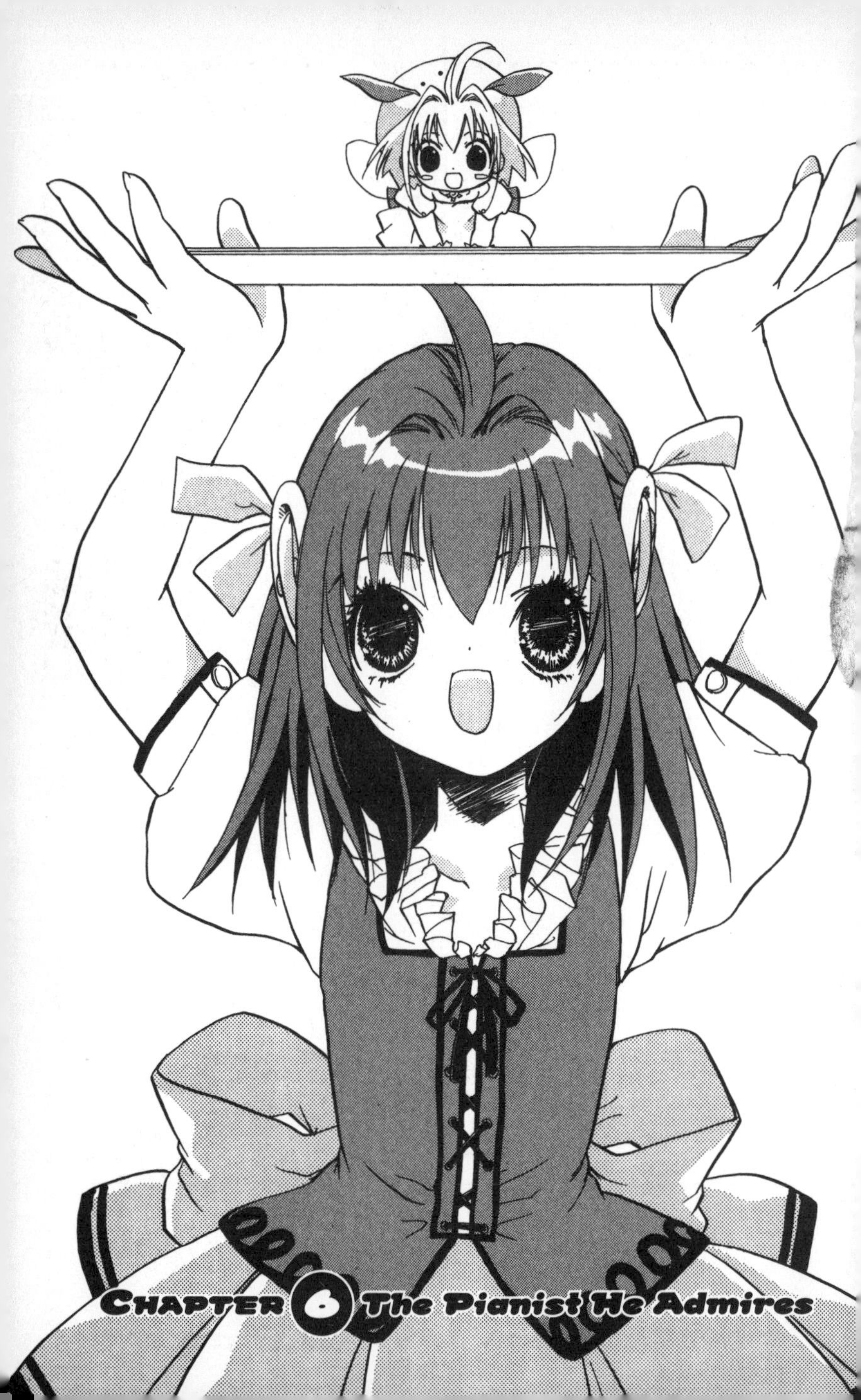
CHAPTER 6 The Pianist He Admires

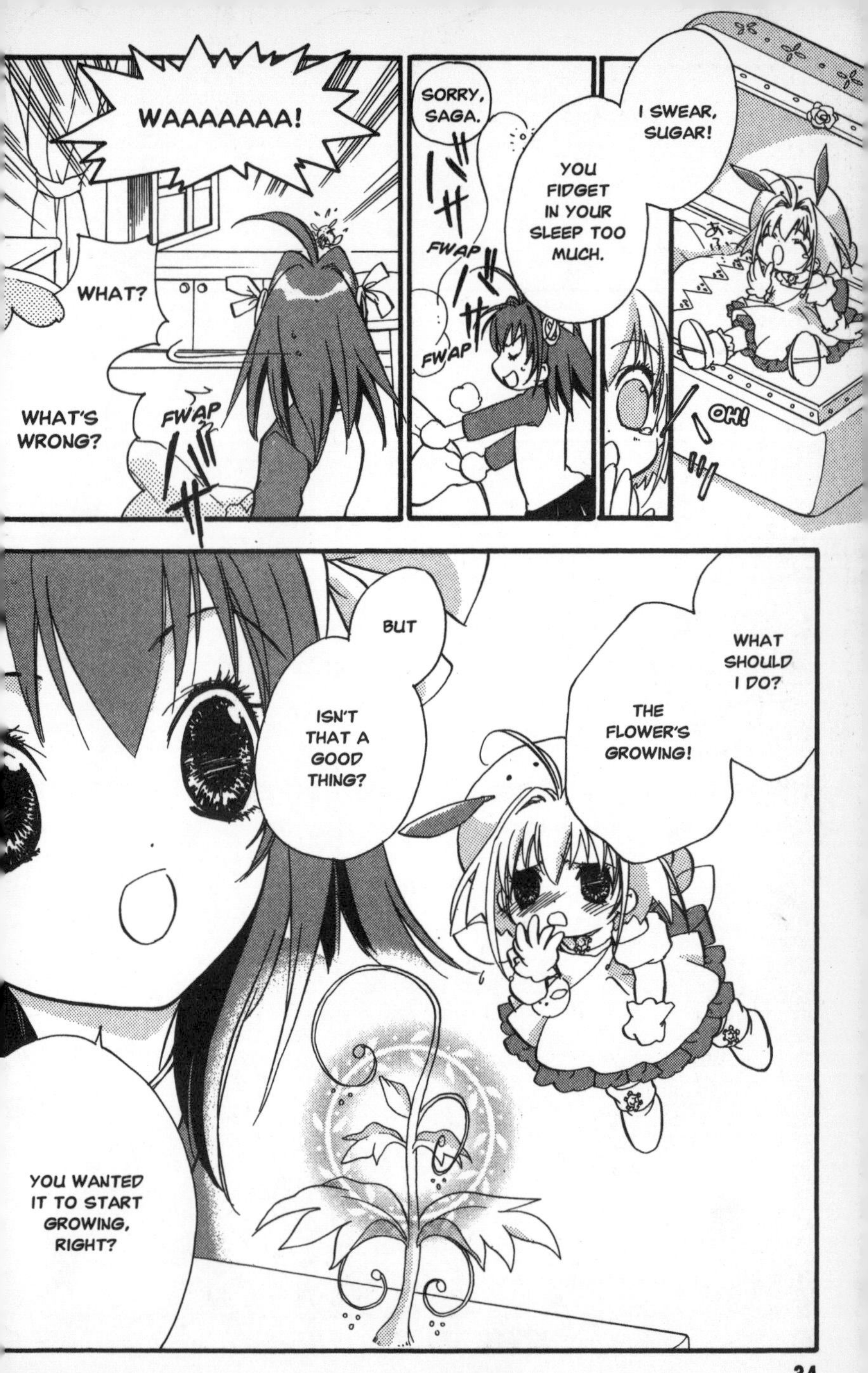
I SWEAR, SUGAR!
YOU FIDGET IN YOUR SLEEP TOO MUCH.
OH!
SORRY, SAGA.
FWAP
FWAP
WAAAAAAA!
WHAT?
WHAT'S WRONG?
FWAP
WHAT SHOULD I DO?
THE FLOWER'S GROWING!
BUT
ISN'T THAT A GOOD THING?
YOU WANTED IT TO START GROWING, RIGHT?

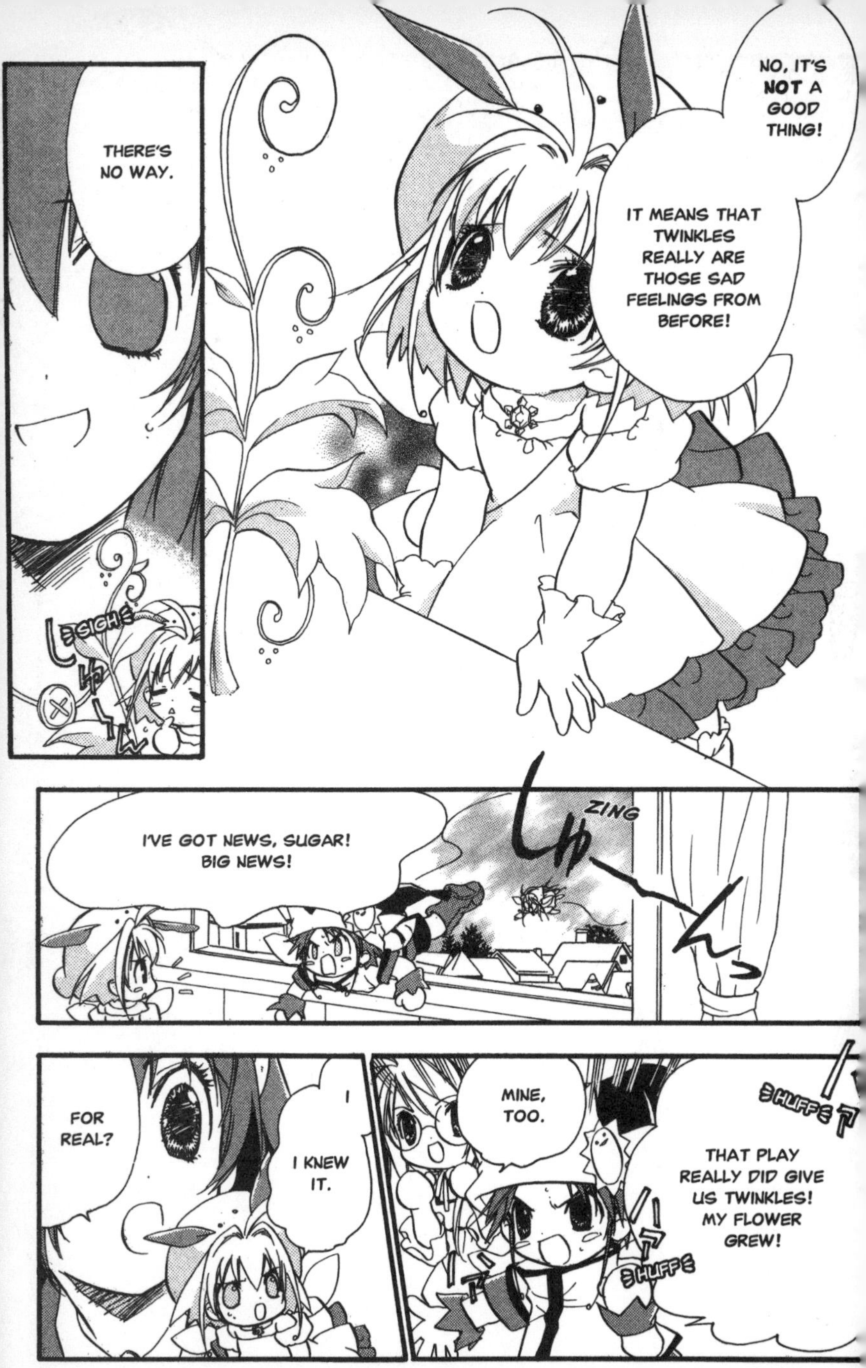

NO, IT'S **NOT** A GOOD THING!
IT MEANS THAT TWINKLES REALLY ARE THOSE SAD FEELINGS FROM BEFORE!
THERE'S NO WAY.
SIGH
I'VE GOT NEWS, SUGAR! BIG NEWS!
ZING
HUFF
THAT PLAY REALLY DID GIVE US TWINKLES! MY FLOWER GREW!
HUFF
MINE, TOO.
I
I KNEW IT.
FOR REAL?

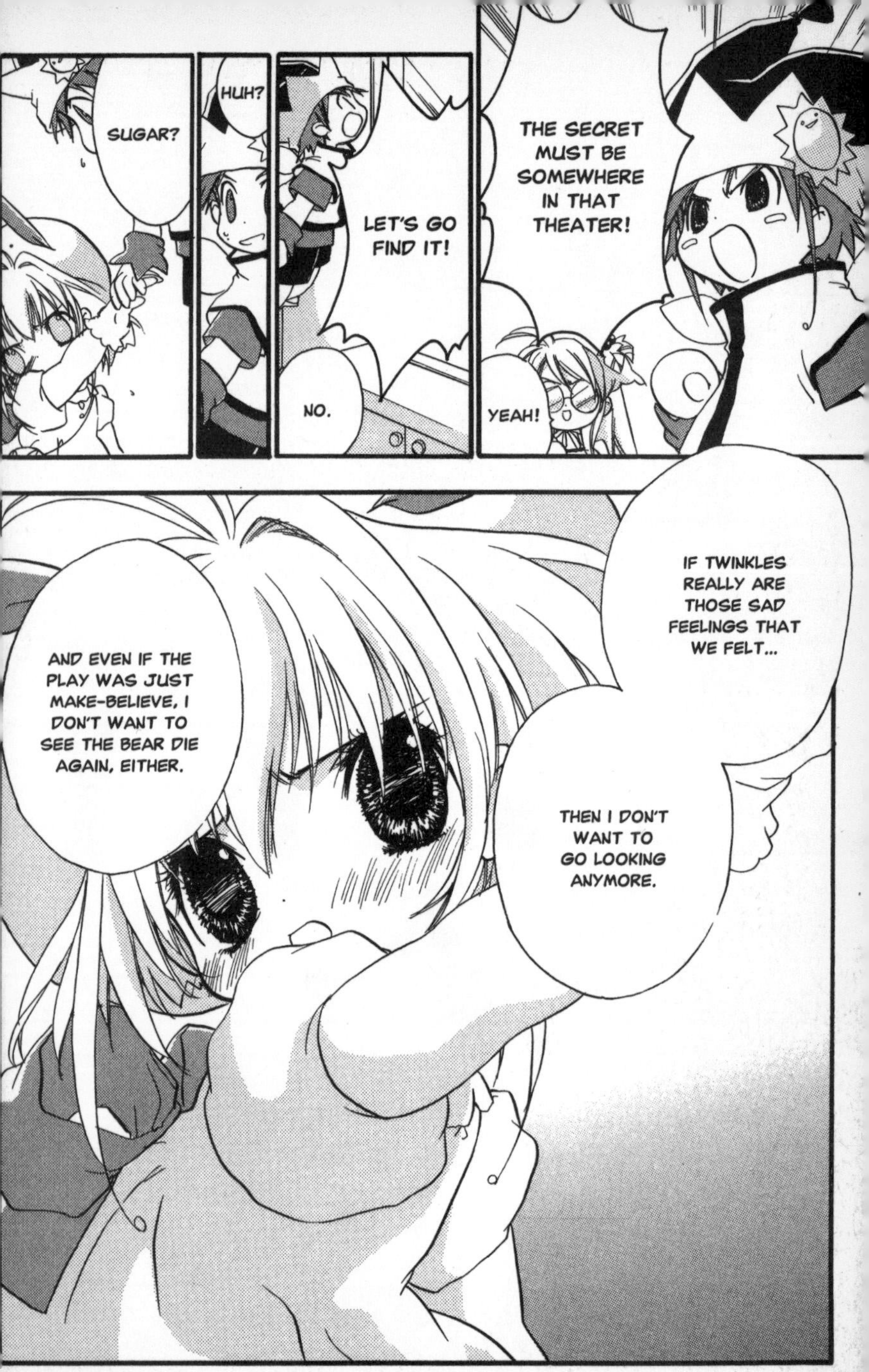
THE SECRET MUST BE SOMEWHERE IN THAT THEATER!
YEAH!
LET'S GO FIND IT!
NO.
HUH?
SUGAR?
IF TWINKLES REALLY ARE THOSE SAD FEELINGS THAT WE FELT...
THEN I DON'T WANT TO GO LOOKING ANYMORE.
AND EVEN IF THE PLAY WAS JUST MAKE-BELIEVE, I DON'T WANT TO SEE THE BEAR DIE AGAIN, EITHER.

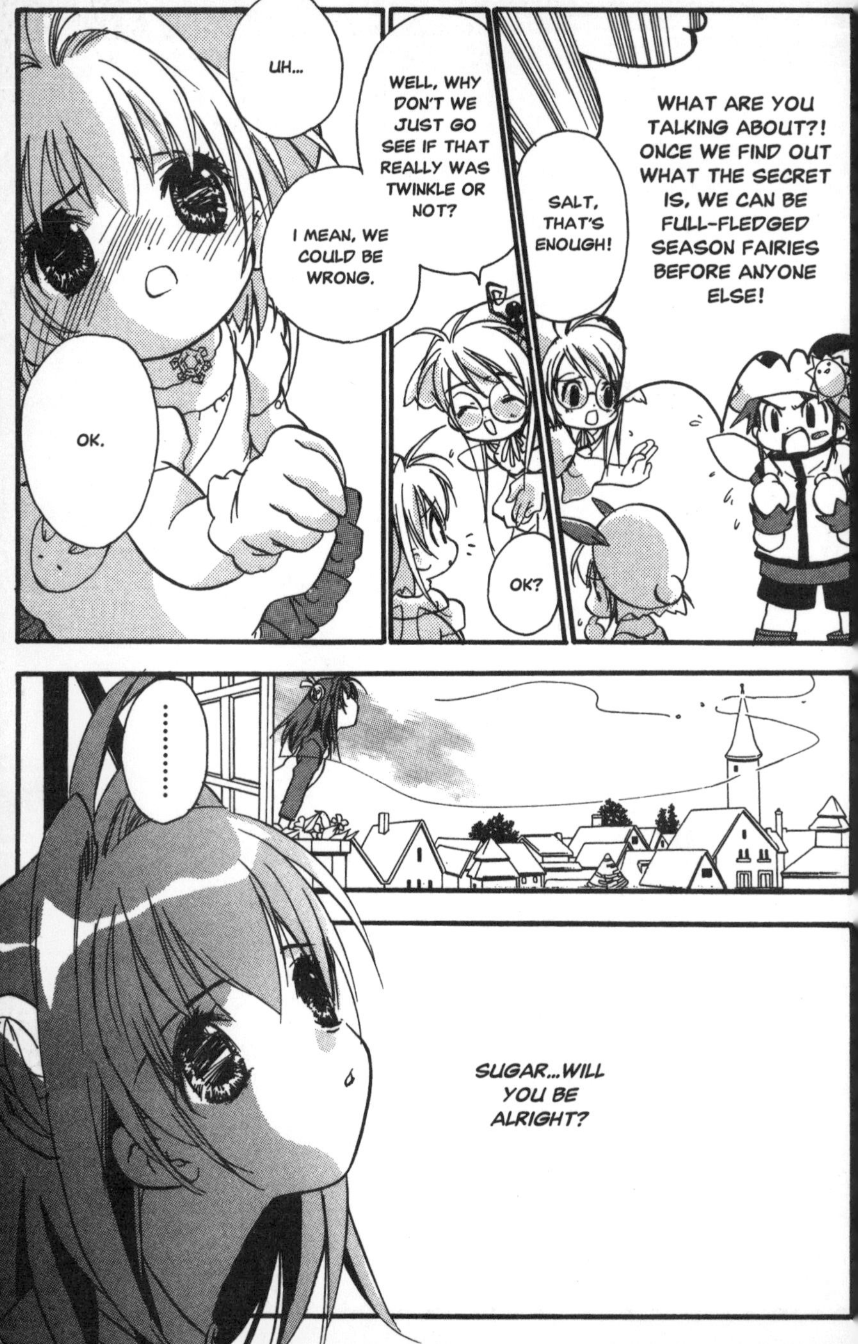

WHAT ARE YOU TALKING ABOUT?! ONCE WE FIND OUT WHAT THE SECRET IS, WE CAN BE FULL-FLEDGED SEASON FAIRIES BEFORE ANYONE ELSE!
SALT, THAT'S ENOUGH!
WELL, WHY DON'T WE JUST GO SEE IF THAT REALLY WAS TWINKLE OR NOT?
I MEAN, WE COULD BE WRONG.
OK?
UH...
OK.
....
SUGAR...WILL YOU BE ALRIGHT?

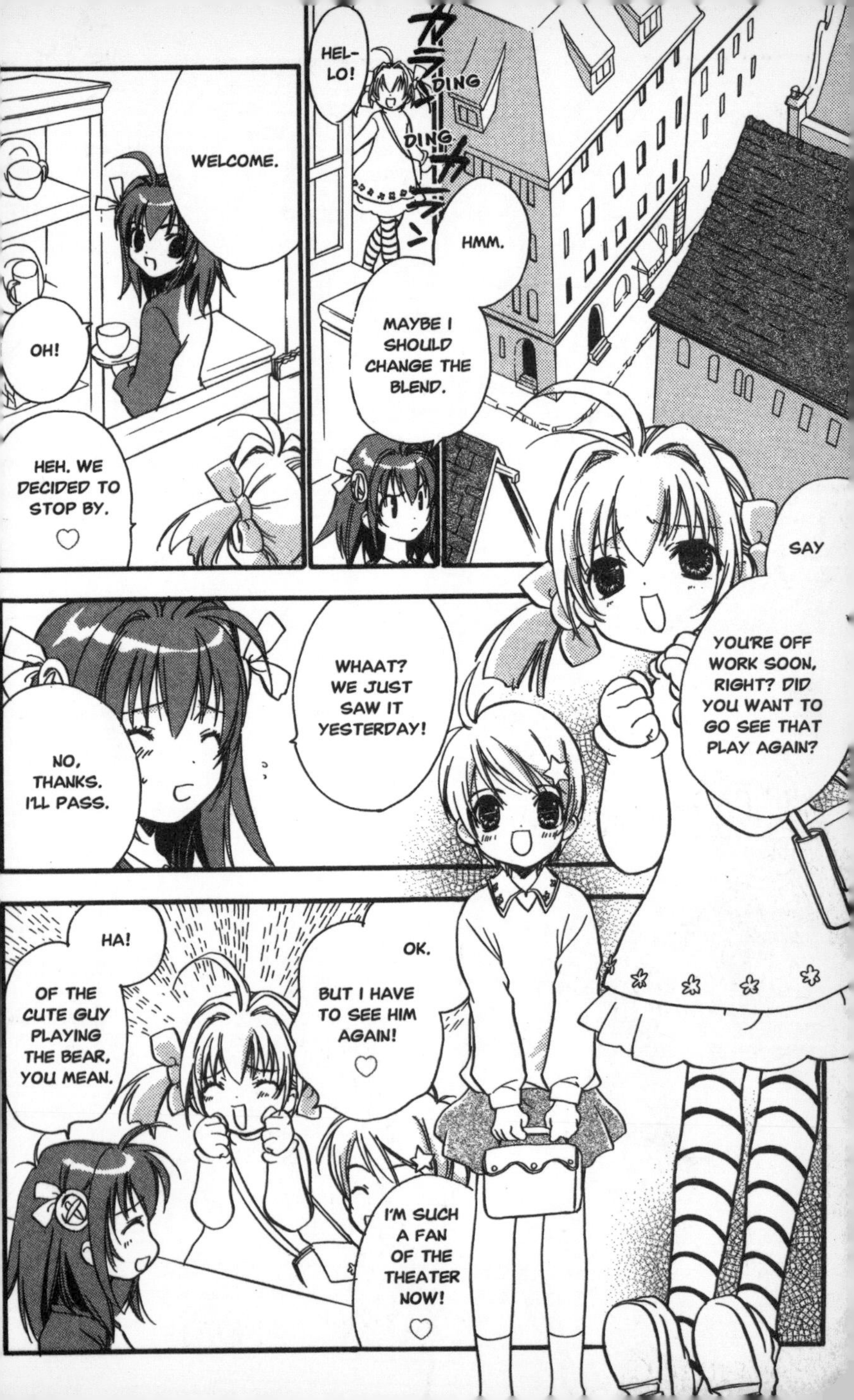
HEL-LO!
DING
DING
HMM.
MAYBE I SHOULD CHANGE THE BLEND.
WELCOME.
OH!
HEH. WE DECIDED TO STOP BY. ♡
SAY
YOU'RE OFF WORK SOON, RIGHT? DID YOU WANT TO GO SEE THAT PLAY AGAIN?
WHAAT? WE JUST SAW IT YESTERDAY!
NO, THANKS. I'LL PASS.
OK.
BUT I HAVE TO SEE HIM AGAIN! ♡
I'M SUCH A FAN OF THE THEATER NOW! ♡
HA!
OF THE CUTE GUY PLAYING THE BEAR, YOU MEAN.

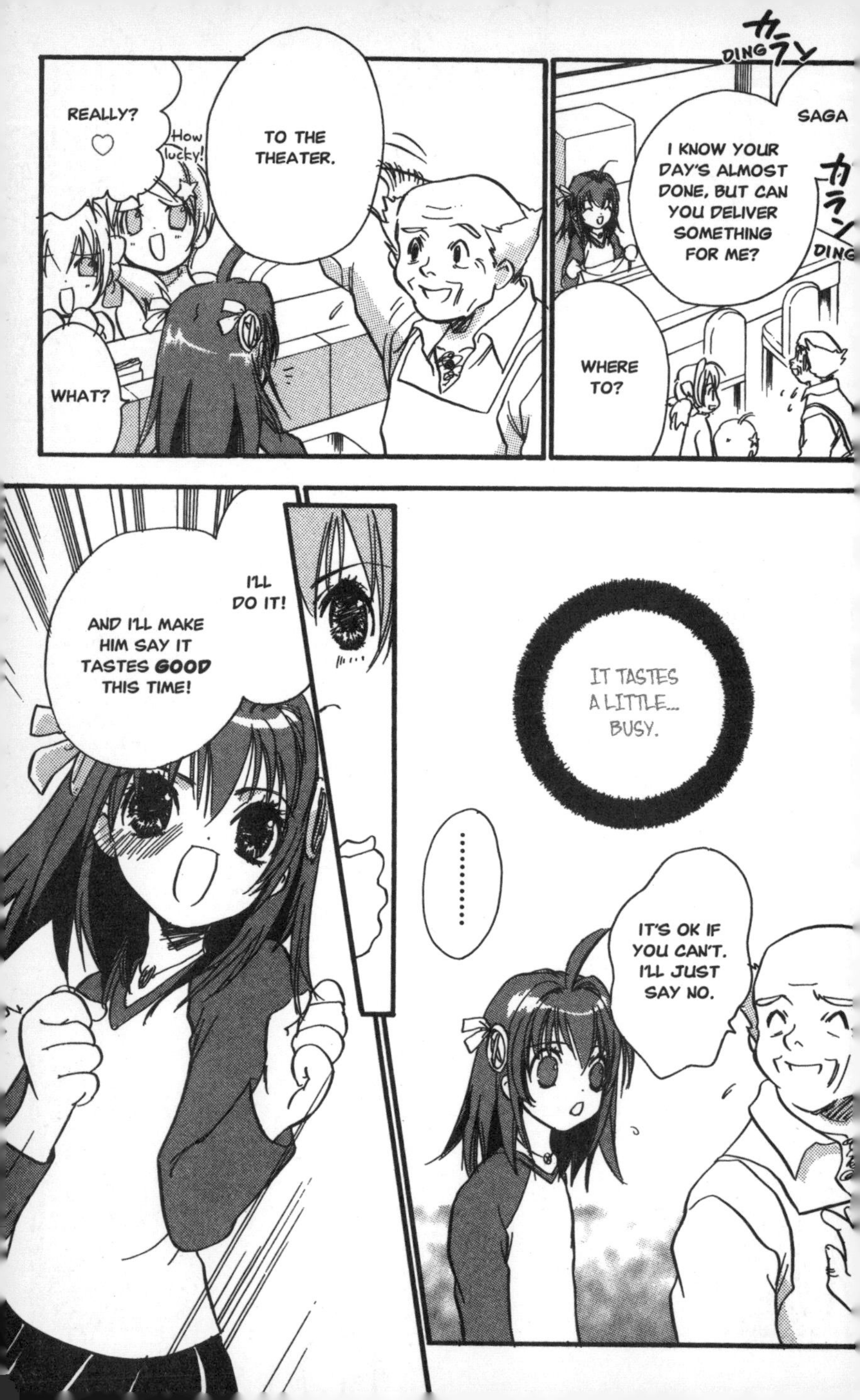
カラン
DING
SAGA
I KNOW YOUR DAY'S ALMOST DONE, BUT CAN YOU DELIVER SOMETHING FOR ME?
カラン
DING
WHERE TO?
TO THE THEATER.
REALLY? ♡
How lucky!
WHAT?
IT TASTES A LITTLE... BUSY.
....
IT'S OK IF YOU CAN'T. I'LL JUST SAY NO.
I'LL DO IT!
AND I'LL MAKE HIM SAY IT TASTES **GOOD** THIS TIME!

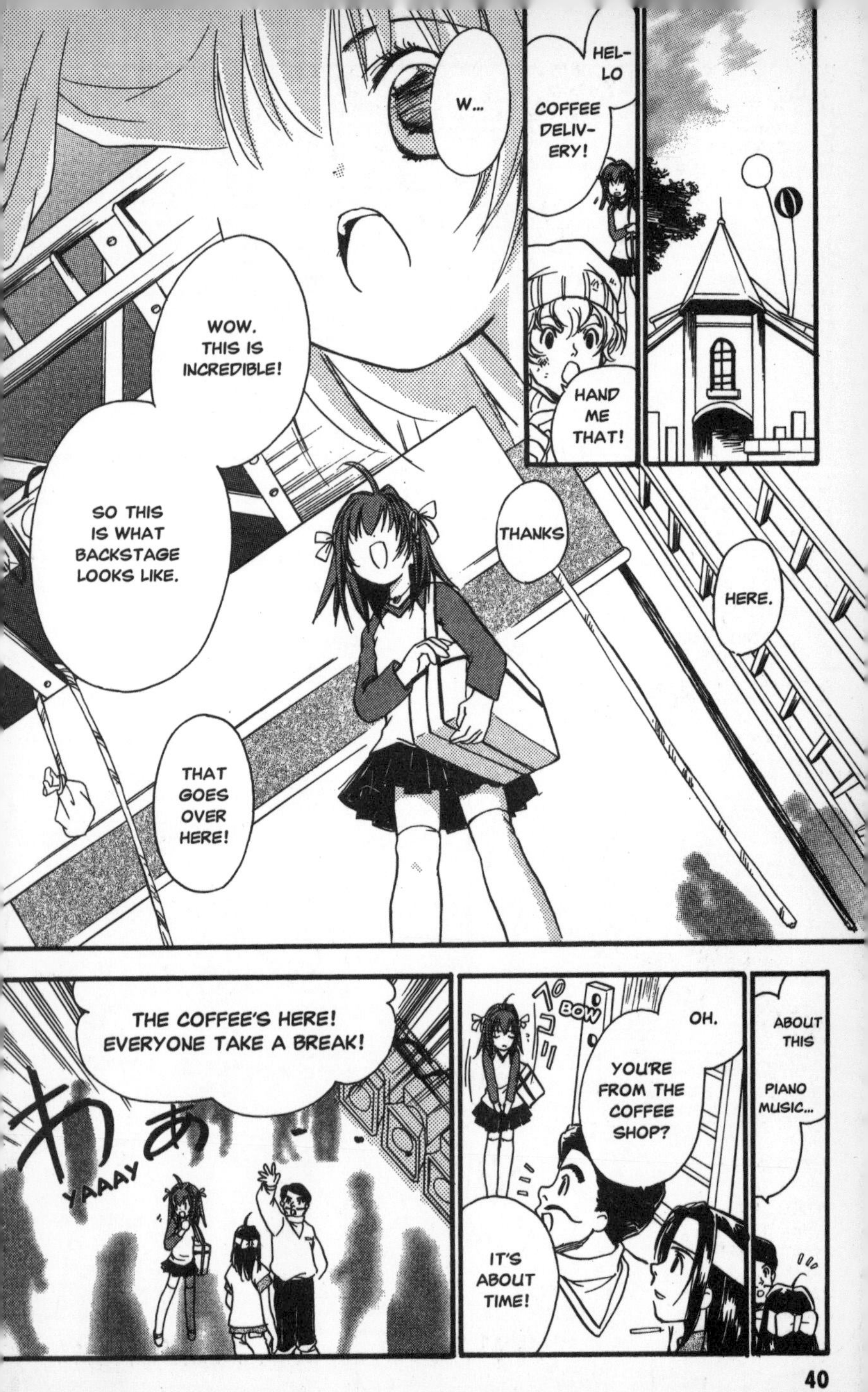
HEL-LO
COFFEE DELIV-ERY!
HAND ME THAT!
W...
WOW. THIS IS INCREDIBLE!
SO THIS IS WHAT BACKSTAGE LOOKS LIKE.
HERE.
THANKS
THAT GOES OVER HERE!
ABOUT THIS
PIANO MUSIC...
OH.
YOU'RE FROM THE COFFEE SHOP?
BOW
IT'S ABOUT TIME!
THE COFFEE'S HERE! EVERYONE TAKE A BREAK!
YAAAY

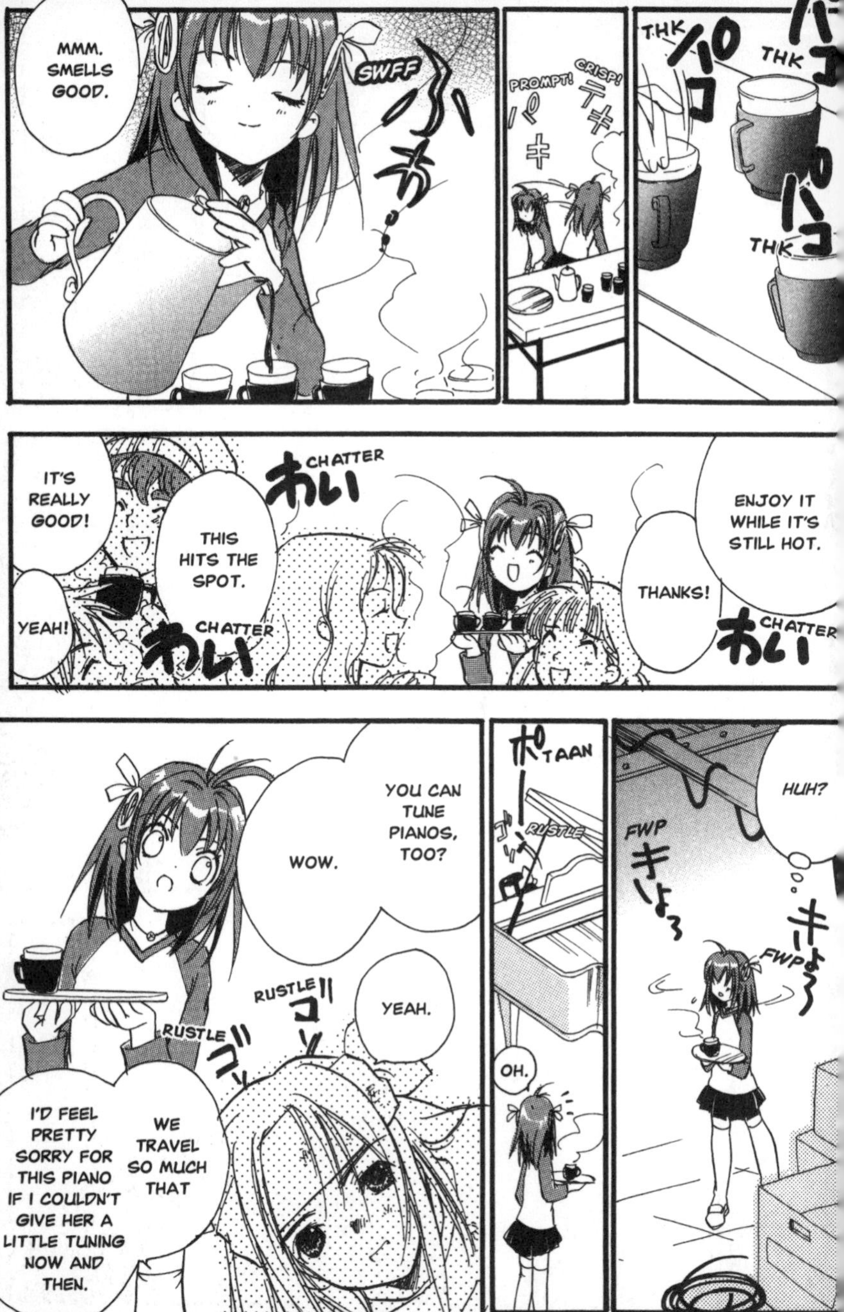
THK
THK
THK
CRISP!
PROMPT!
SWFF
MMM. SMELLS GOOD.
ENJOY IT WHILE IT'S STILL HOT.
THANKS!
CHATTER
CHATTER
THIS HITS THE SPOT.
IT'S REALLY GOOD!
YEAH!
CHATTER
HUH?
FWP
FWP
TAAN
RUSTLE
OH.
YOU CAN TUNE PIANOS, TOO?
WOW.
YEAH.
RUSTLE
RUSTLE
WE TRAVEL SO MUCH THAT
I'D FEEL PRETTY SORRY FOR THIS PIANO IF I COULDN'T GIVE HER A LITTLE TUNING NOW AND THEN.

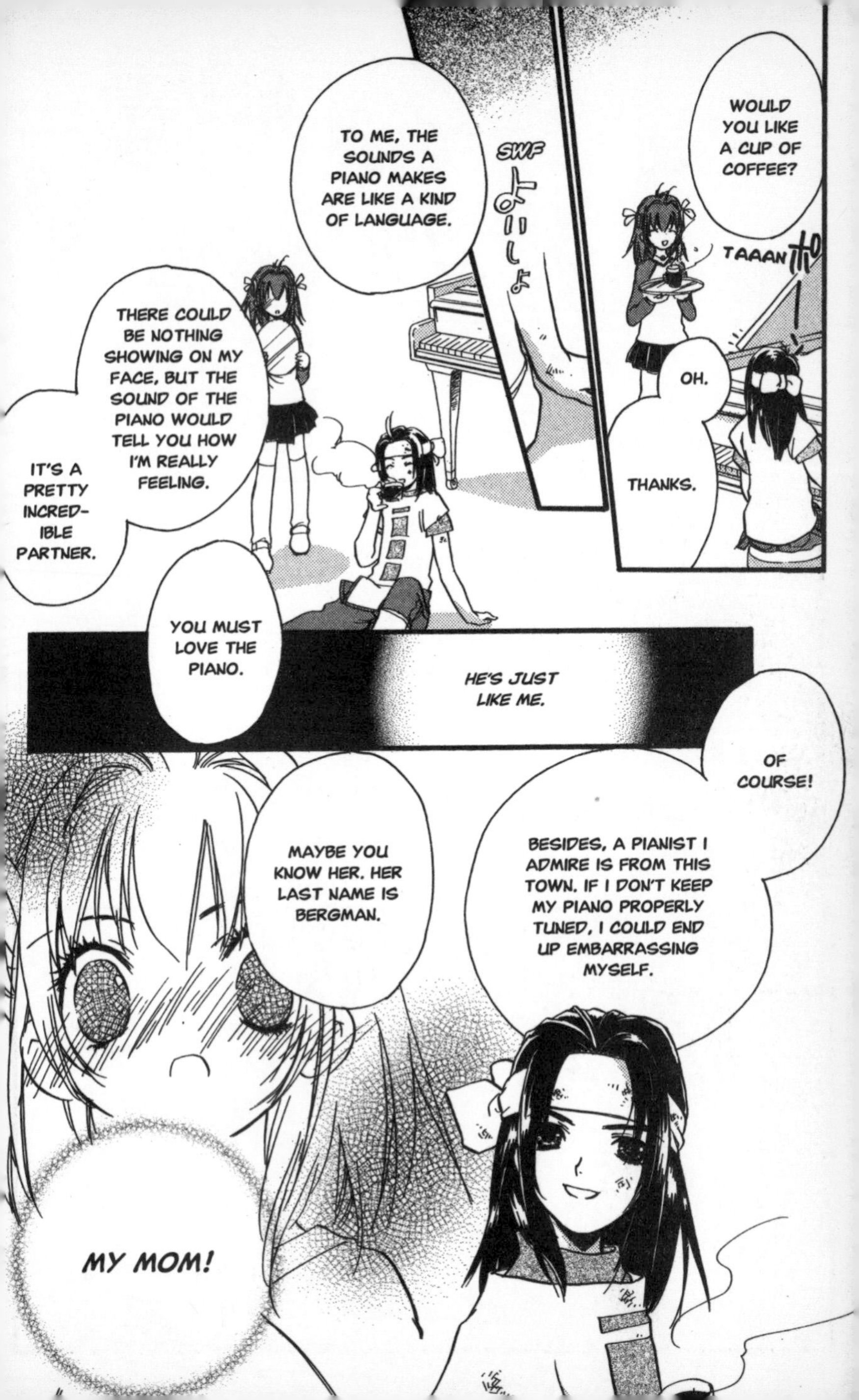
WOULD YOU LIKE A CUP OF COFFEE?
TAAAN
OH.
THANKS.
SWF
TO ME, THE SOUNDS A PIANO MAKES ARE LIKE A KIND OF LANGUAGE.
THERE COULD BE NOTHING SHOWING ON MY FACE, BUT THE SOUND OF THE PIANO WOULD TELL YOU HOW I'M REALLY FEELING.
IT'S A PRETTY INCRED-IBLE PARTNER.
YOU MUST LOVE THE PIANO.
HE'S JUST LIKE ME.
OF COURSE!
BESIDES, A PIANIST I ADMIRE IS FROM THIS TOWN. IF I DON'T KEEP MY PIANO PROPERLY TUNED, I COULD END UP EMBARRASSING MYSELF.
MAYBE YOU KNOW HER. HER LAST NAME IS BERGMAN.
MY MOM!

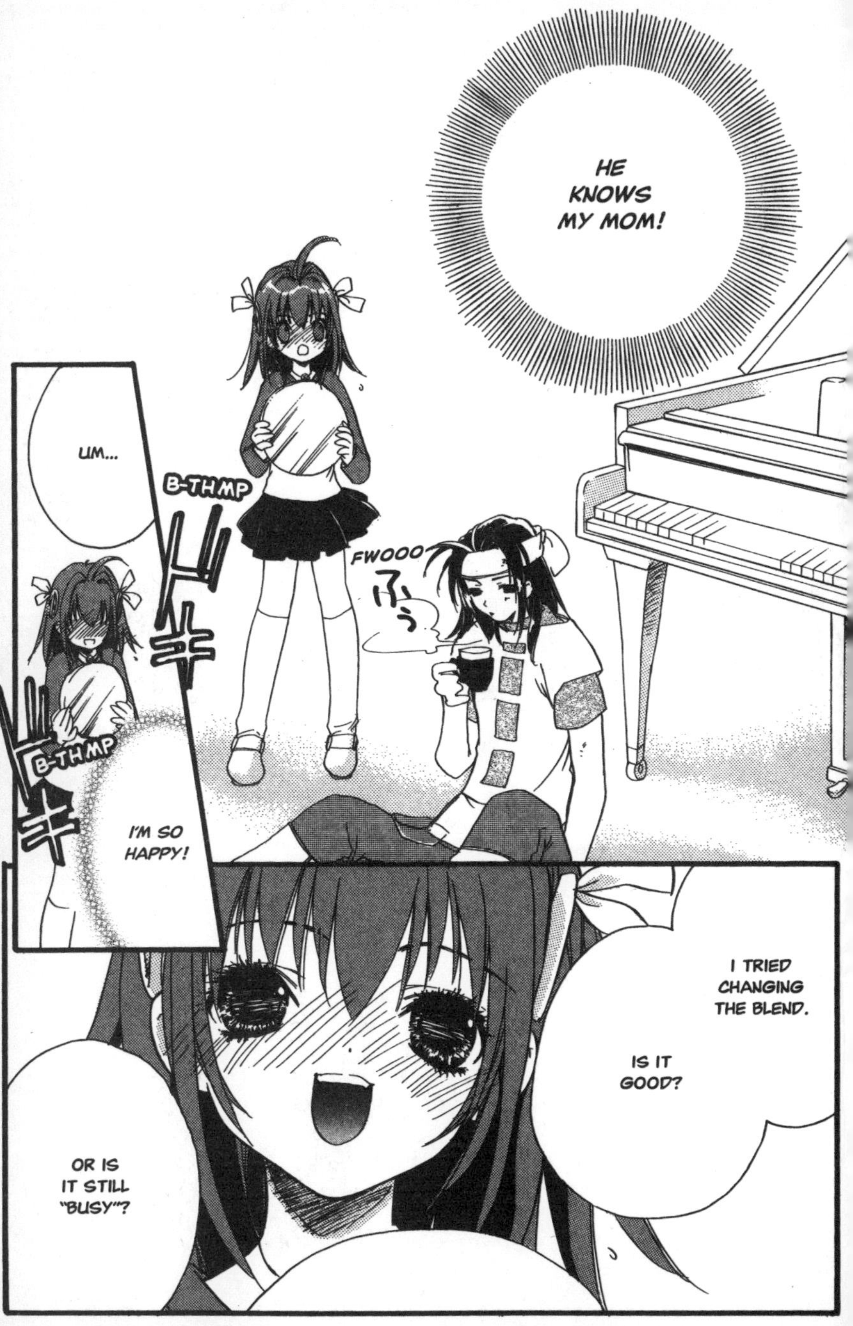
HE KNOWS MY MOM!
UM...
B-THMP
B-THMP
I'M SO HAPPY!
FWOOO
ふぅ
I TRIED CHANGING THE BLEND.
IS IT GOOD?
OR IS IT STILL "BUSY"?

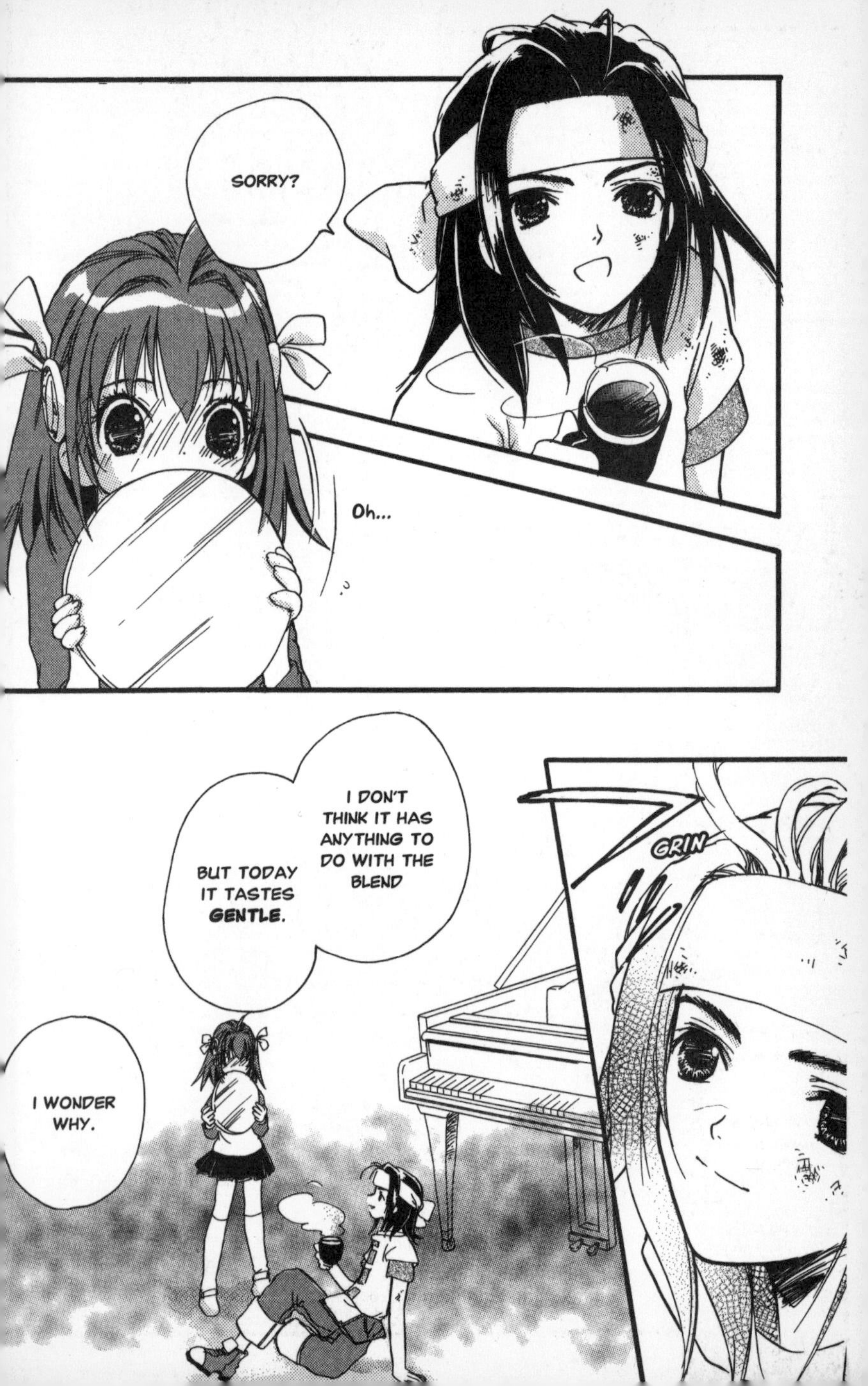
SORRY?
Oh...
I DON'T THINK IT HAS ANYTHING TO DO WITH THE BLEND
BUT TODAY IT TASTES GENTLE.
GRIN
I WONDER WHY.

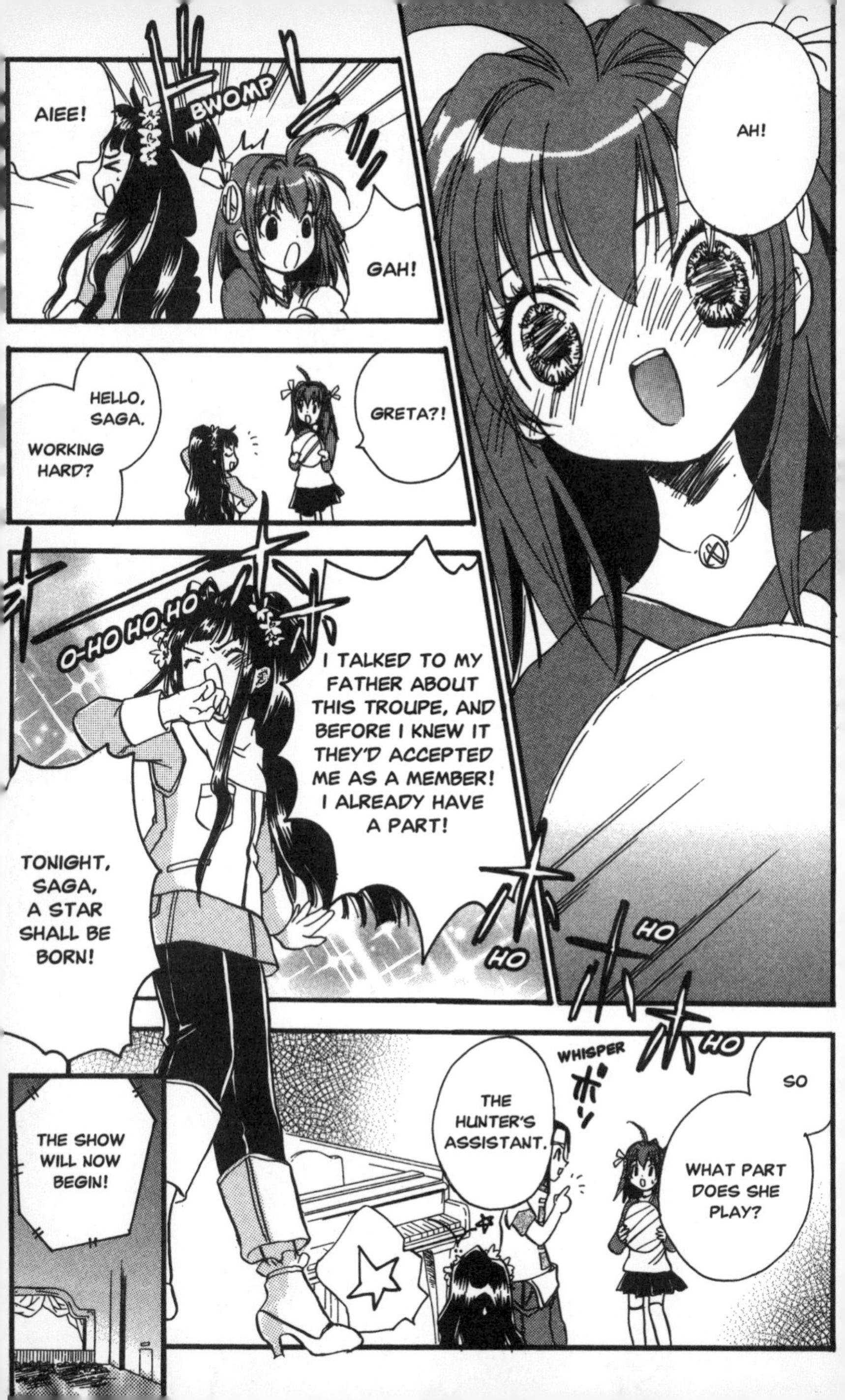
AH!
BWOMP
GAH!
AIEE!
GRETA?!
HELLO, SAGA.
WORKING HARD?
O-HO HO HO
I TALKED TO MY FATHER ABOUT THIS TROUPE, AND BEFORE I KNEW IT THEY'D ACCEPTED ME AS A MEMBER! I ALREADY HAVE A PART!
TONIGHT, SAGA, A STAR SHALL BE BORN!
HO
HO
HO
SO
WHAT PART DOES SHE PLAY?
WHISPER
THE HUNTER'S ASSISTANT.
THE SHOW WILL NOW BEGIN!

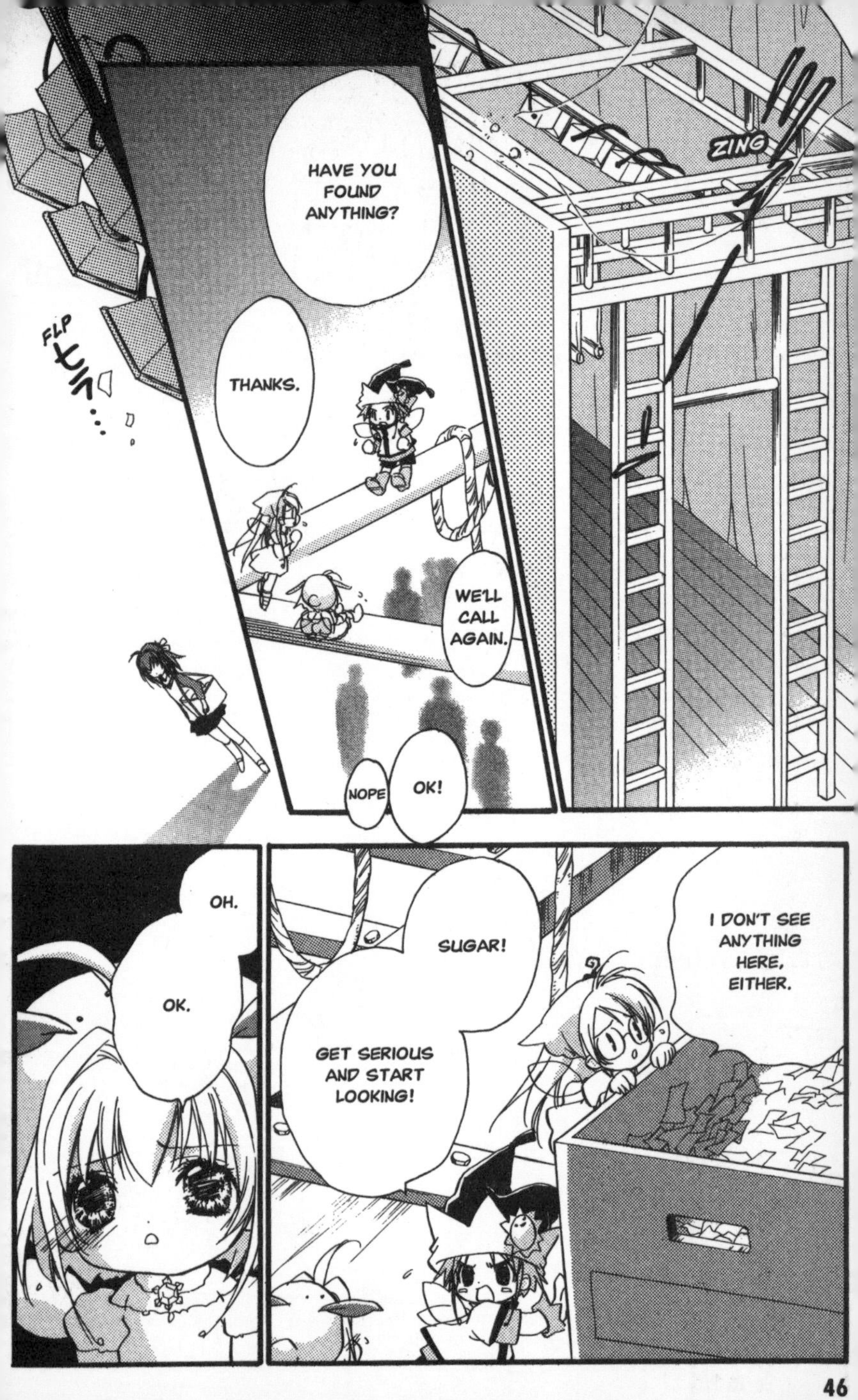
ZING
HAVE YOU FOUND ANYTHING?
THANKS.
WE'LL CALL AGAIN.
OK!
NOPE
FLP
I DON'T SEE ANYTHING HERE, EITHER.
SUGAR!
GET SERIOUS AND START LOOKING!
OH.
OK.

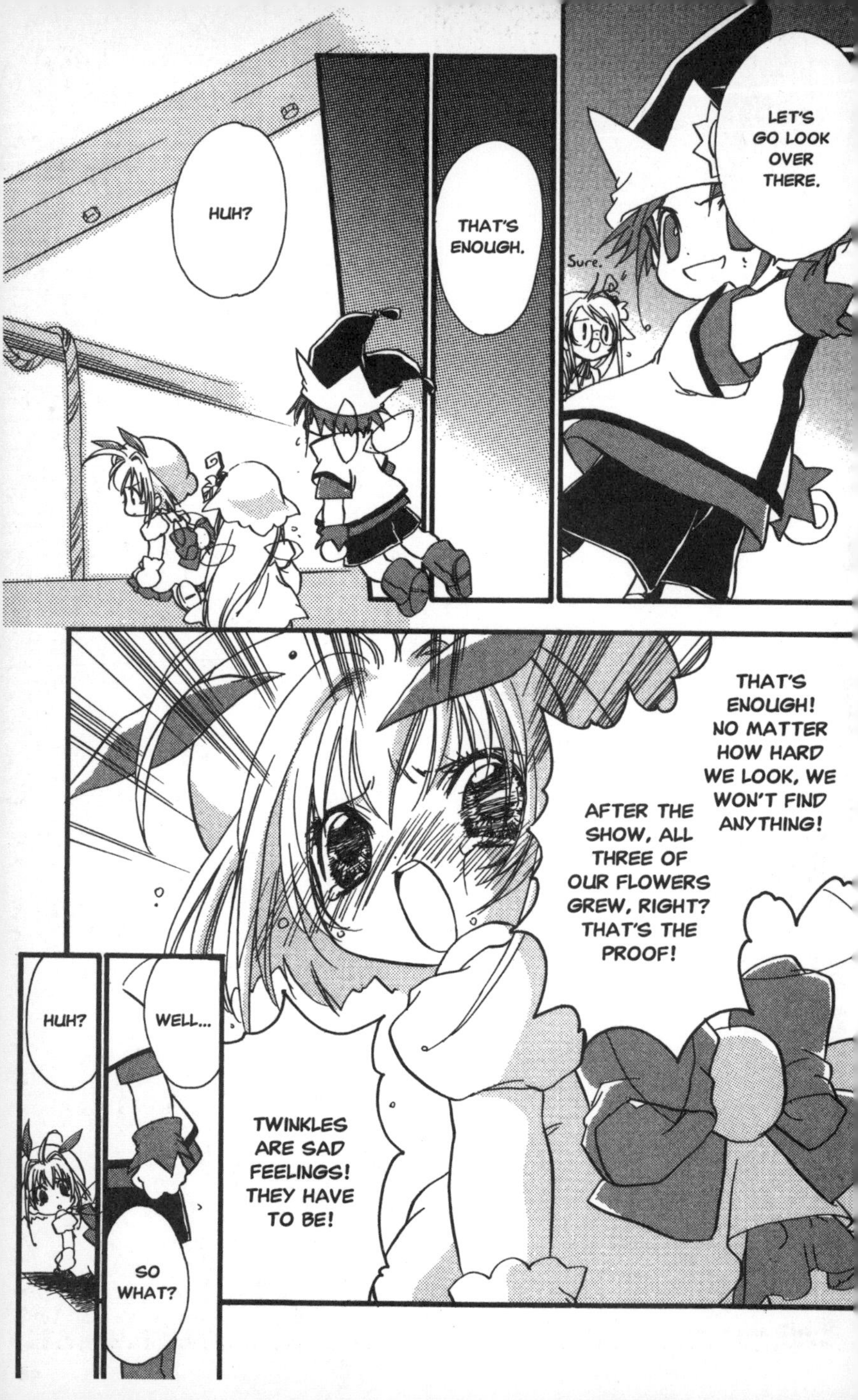
LET'S GO LOOK OVER THERE.
Sure.
THAT'S ENOUGH.
HUH?
THAT'S ENOUGH! NO MATTER HOW HARD WE LOOK, WE WON'T FIND ANYTHING!
AFTER THE SHOW, ALL THREE OF OUR FLOWERS GREW, RIGHT? THAT'S THE PROOF!
TWINKLES ARE SAD FEELINGS! THEY HAVE TO BE!
WELL...
SO WHAT?
HUH?

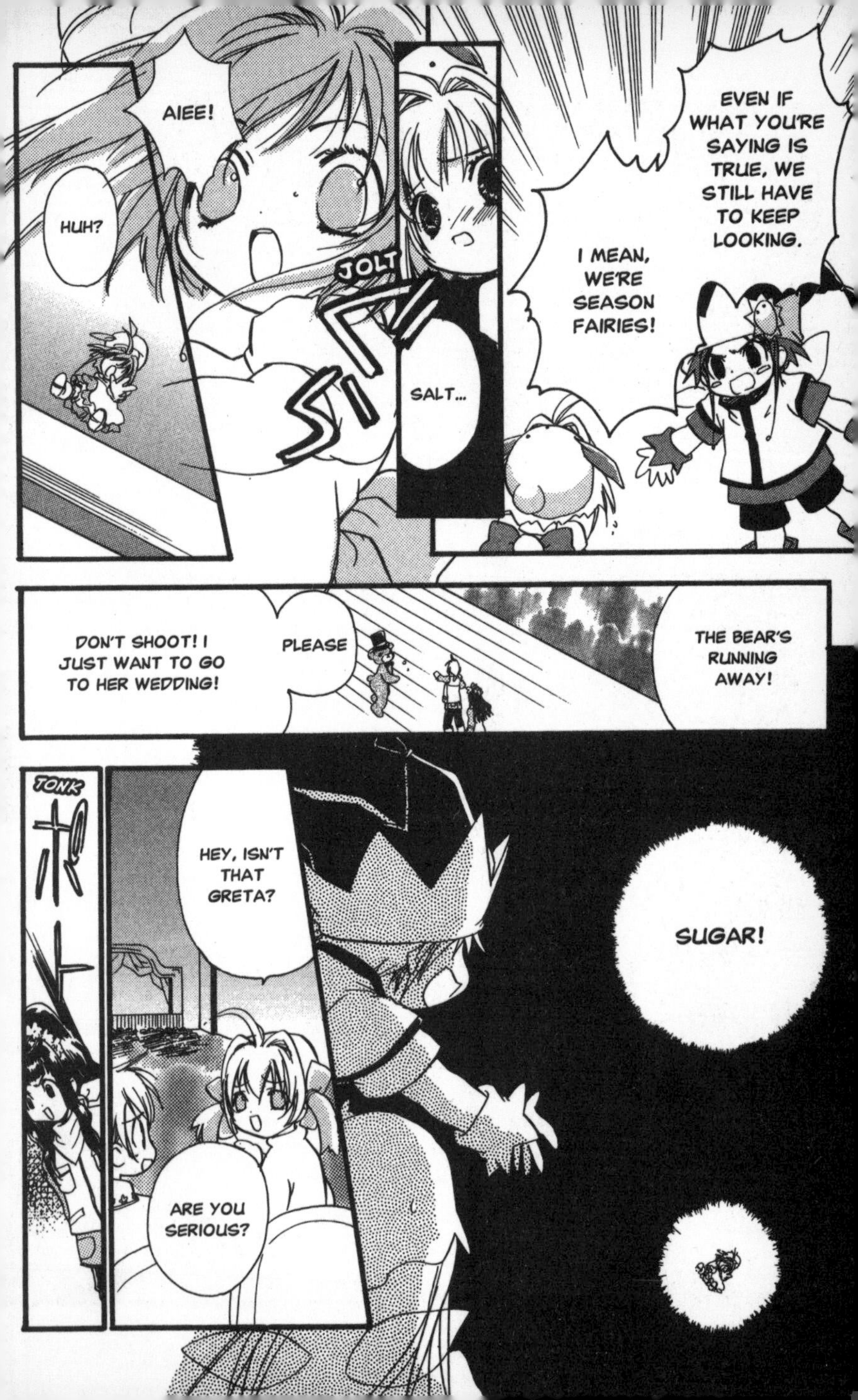
EVEN IF WHAT YOU'RE SAYING IS TRUE, WE STILL HAVE TO KEEP LOOKING.
I MEAN, WE'RE SEASON FAIRIES!
SALT...
JOLT
AIEE!
HUH?
THE BEAR'S RUNNING AWAY!
PLEASE
DON'T SHOOT! I JUST WANT TO GO TO HER WEDDING!
SUGAR!
HEY, ISN'T THAT GRETA?
ARE YOU SERIOUS?
TONK

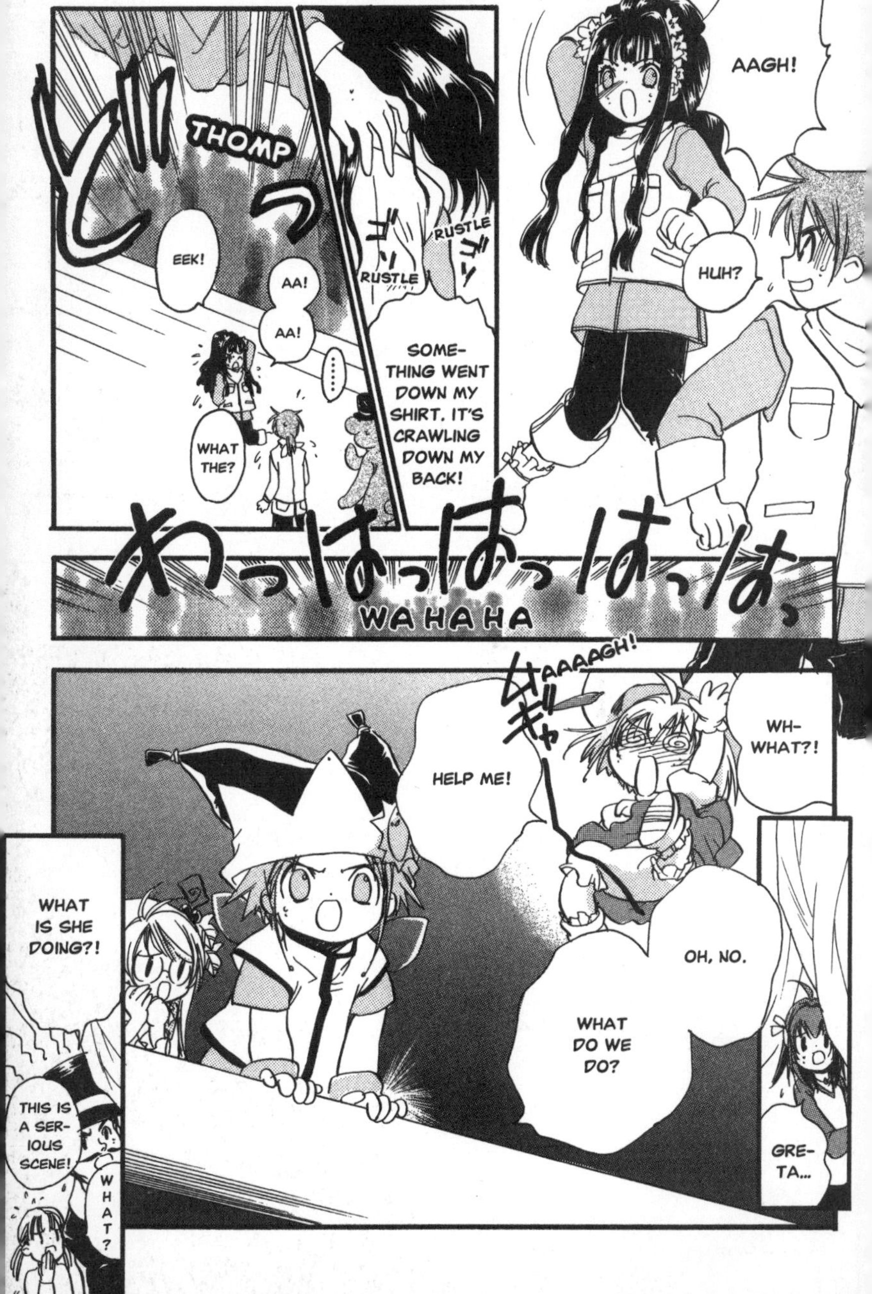
AAGH!
HUH?
RUSTLE
RUSTLE
SOME-THING WENT DOWN MY SHIRT. IT'S CRAWLING DOWN MY BACK!
THOMP
EEK!
AA!
AA!
......
WHAT THE?
WA HA HA
WH-WHAT?!
AAAAAGH!
HELP ME!
OH, NO.
WHAT DO WE DO?
GRE-TA...
WHAT IS SHE DOING?!
THIS IS A SER-IOUS SCENE!
WHAT?

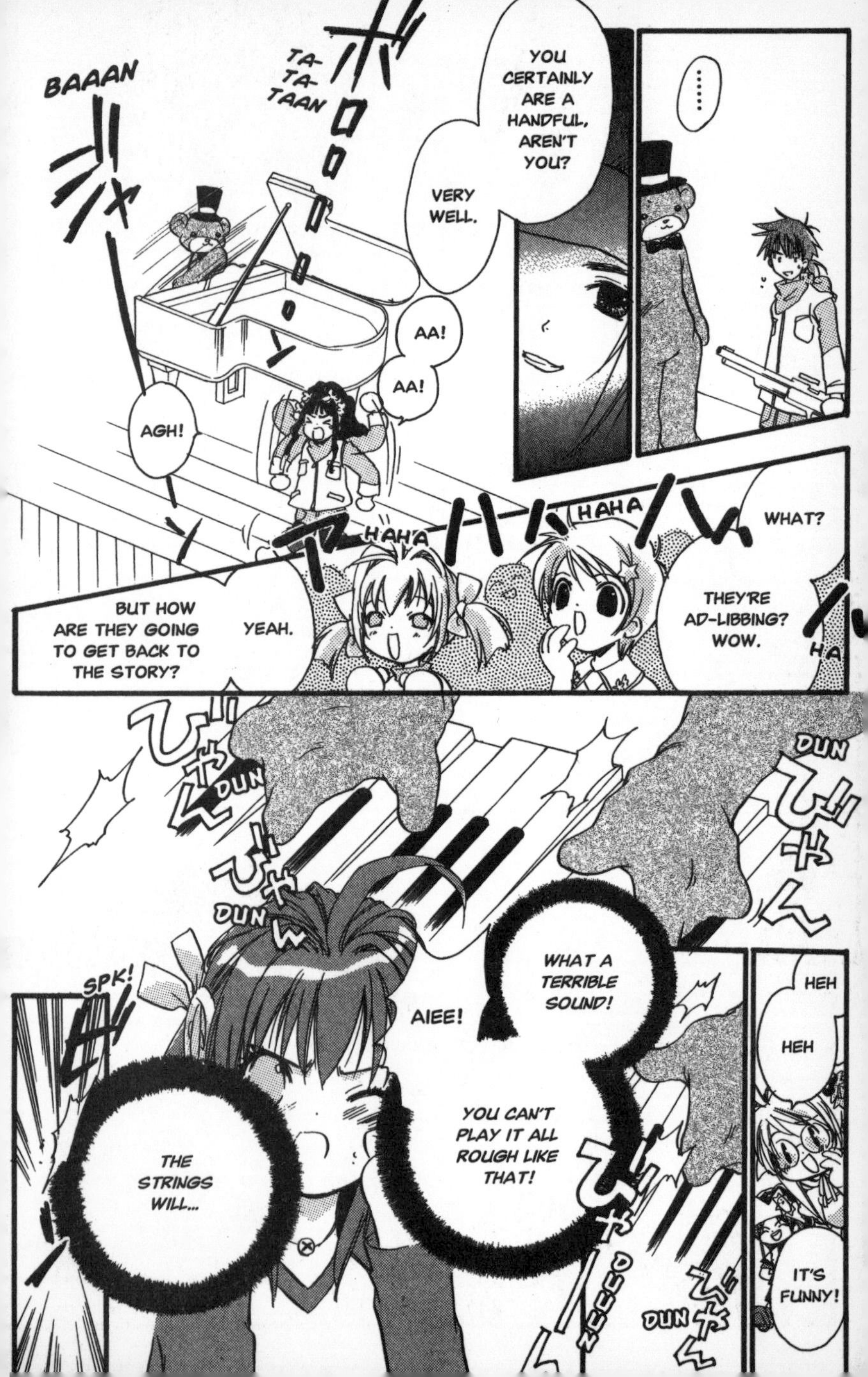
......
YOU CERTAINLY ARE A HANDFUL, AREN'T YOU?
VERY WELL.
TA-TA-TAAN
BAAAN
AA!
AA!
AGH!
WHAT?
HAHA
HAHA
THEY'RE AD-LIBBING? WOW.
HA
YEAH.
BUT HOW ARE THEY GOING TO GET BACK TO THE STORY?
DUN
DUN
DUN
HEH
HEH
IT'S FUNNY!
WHAT A TERRIBLE SOUND!
AIEE!
YOU CAN'T PLAY IT ALL ROUGH LIKE THAT!
SPK!
THE STRINGS WILL...
DUN

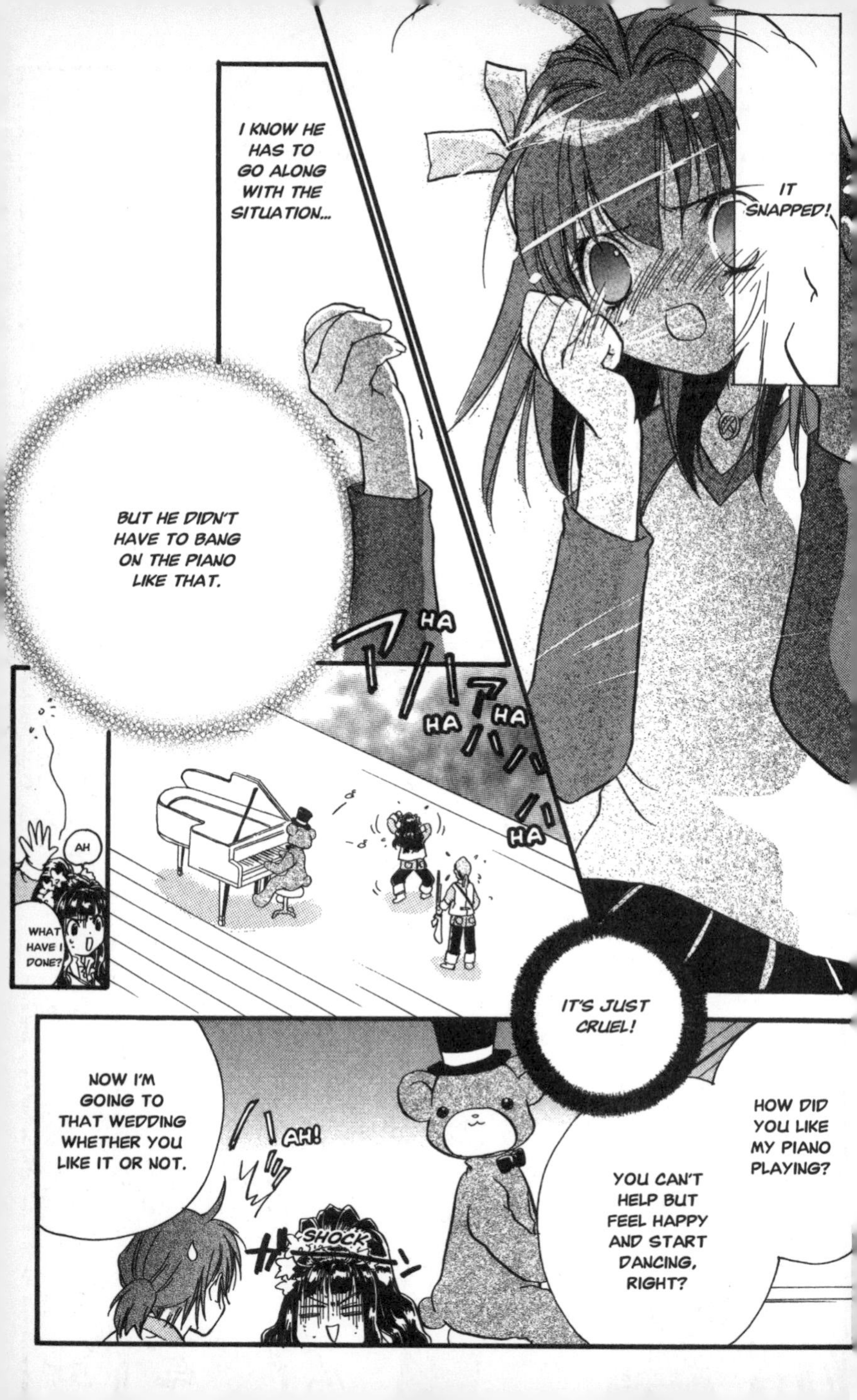
IT SNAPPED!
I KNOW HE HAS TO GO ALONG WITH THE SITUATION...
BUT HE DIDN'T HAVE TO BANG ON THE PIANO LIKE THAT.
HA
HA
HA
HA
IT'S JUST CRUEL!
AH
WHAT HAVE I DONE?
HOW DID YOU LIKE MY PIANO PLAYING?
YOU CAN'T HELP BUT FEEL HAPPY AND START DANCING, RIGHT?
AH!
SHOCK
NOW I'M GOING TO THAT WEDDING WHETHER YOU LIKE IT OR NOT.

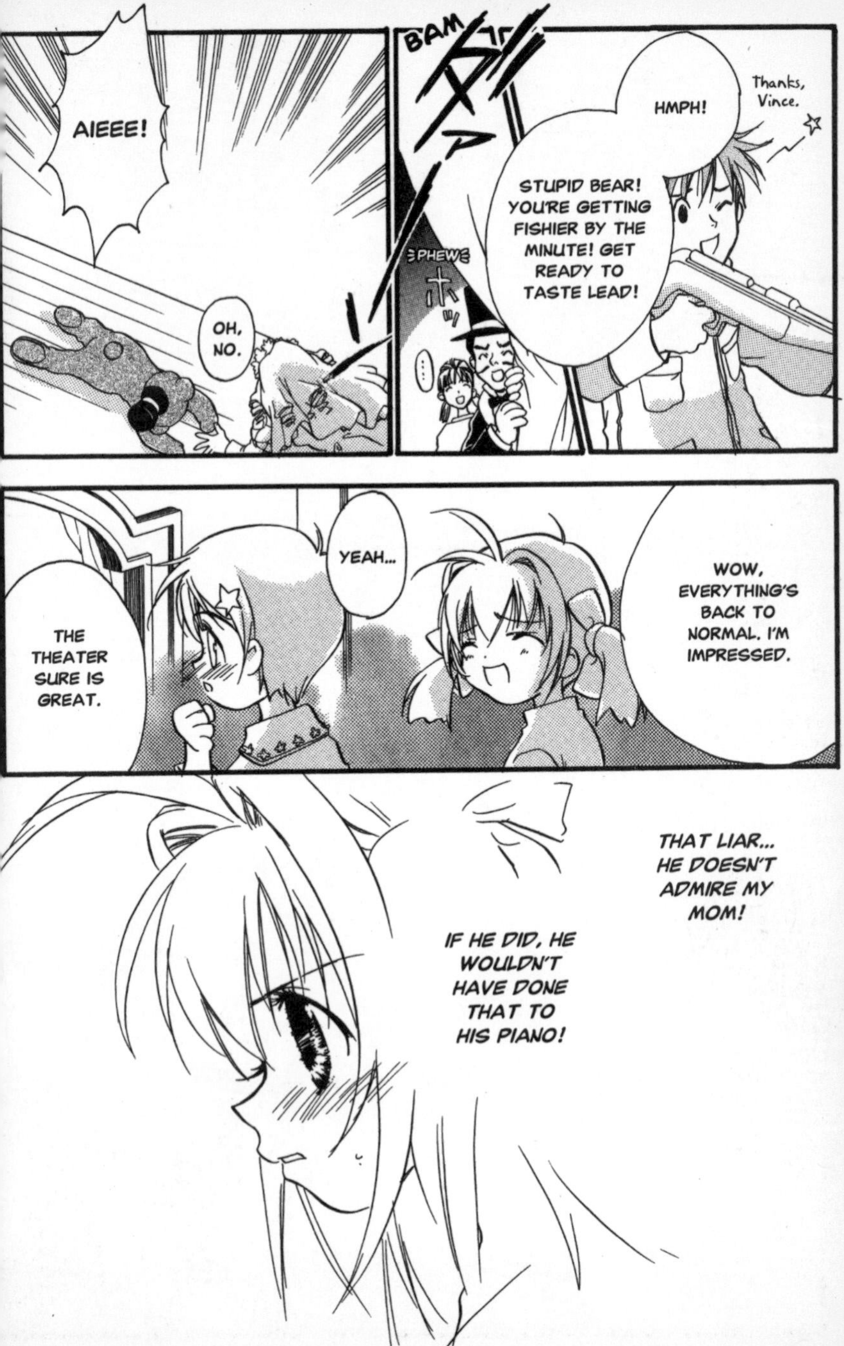
BAM
HMPH!
STUPID BEAR! YOU'RE GETTING FISHIER BY THE MINUTE! GET READY TO TASTE LEAD!
Thanks, Vince.
PHEW
...
AIEEE!
OH, NO.
WOW, EVERYTHING'S BACK TO NORMAL. I'M IMPRESSED.
YEAH...
THE THEATER SURE IS GREAT.
THAT LIAR... HE DOESN'T ADMIRE MY MOM!
IF HE DID, HE WOULDN'T HAVE DONE THAT TO HIS PIANO!

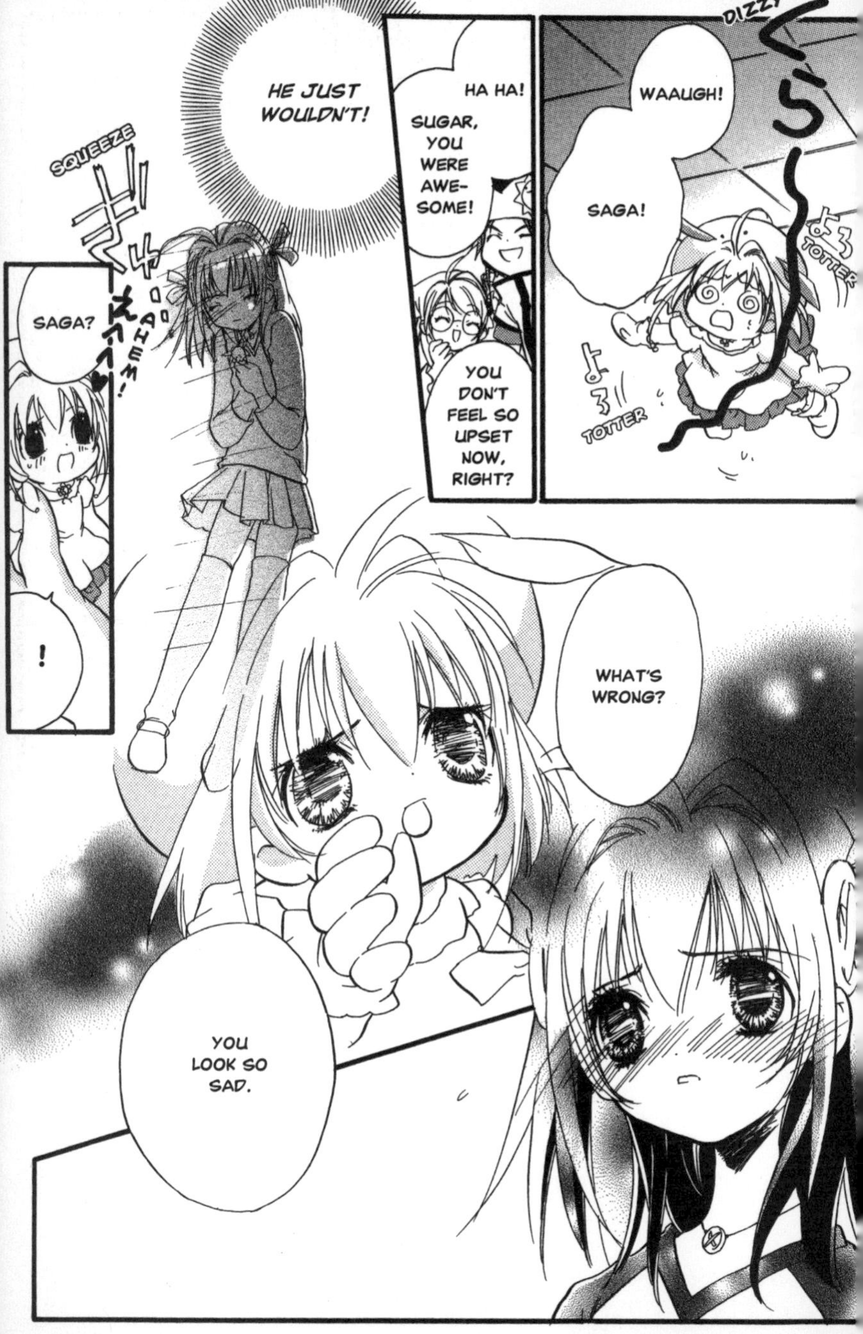
DIZZY
WAAUGH!
SAGA!
TOTTER
TOTTER
HA HA!
SUGAR, YOU WERE AWESOME!
YOU DON'T FEEL SO UPSET NOW, RIGHT?
HE JUST WOULDN'T!
SQUEEZE
AHEM!
SAGA?
!
WHAT'S WRONG?
YOU LOOK SO SAD.

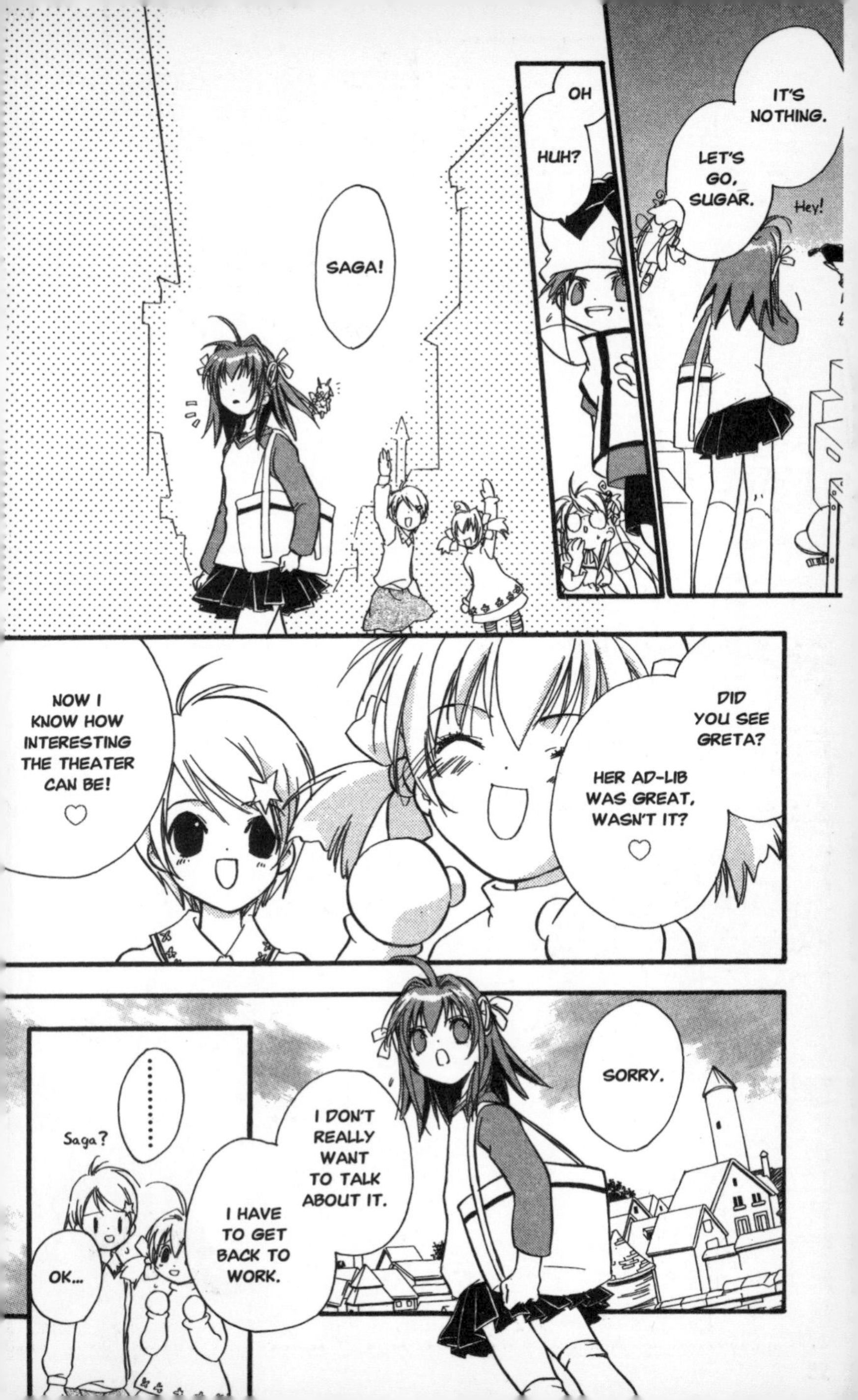
SAGA!
HUH?
OH
IT'S NOTHING.
LET'S GO, SUGAR.
Hey!
NOW I KNOW HOW INTERESTING THE THEATER CAN BE! ♡
DID YOU SEE GRETA?
HER AD-LIB WAS GREAT, WASN'T IT? ♡
SORRY.
I DON'T REALLY WANT TO TALK ABOUT IT.
I HAVE TO GET BACK TO WORK.
......
Saga?
OK...

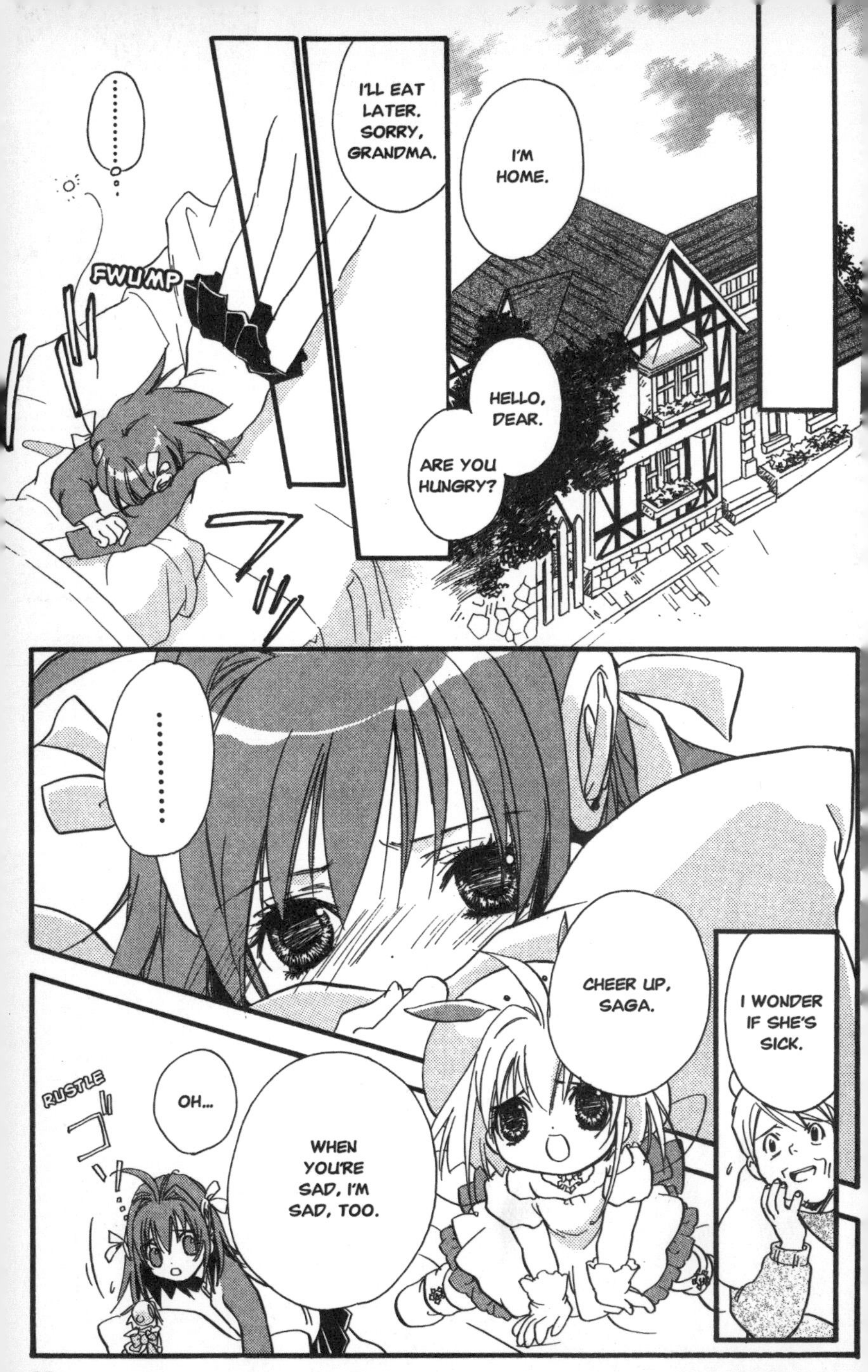
I'M HOME.
HELLO, DEAR.
ARE YOU HUNGRY?
I'LL EAT LATER. SORRY, GRANDMA.
FWUMP
......
......
I WONDER IF SHE'S SICK.
CHEER UP, SAGA.
WHEN YOU'RE SAD, I'M SAD, TOO.
OH...
RUSTLE

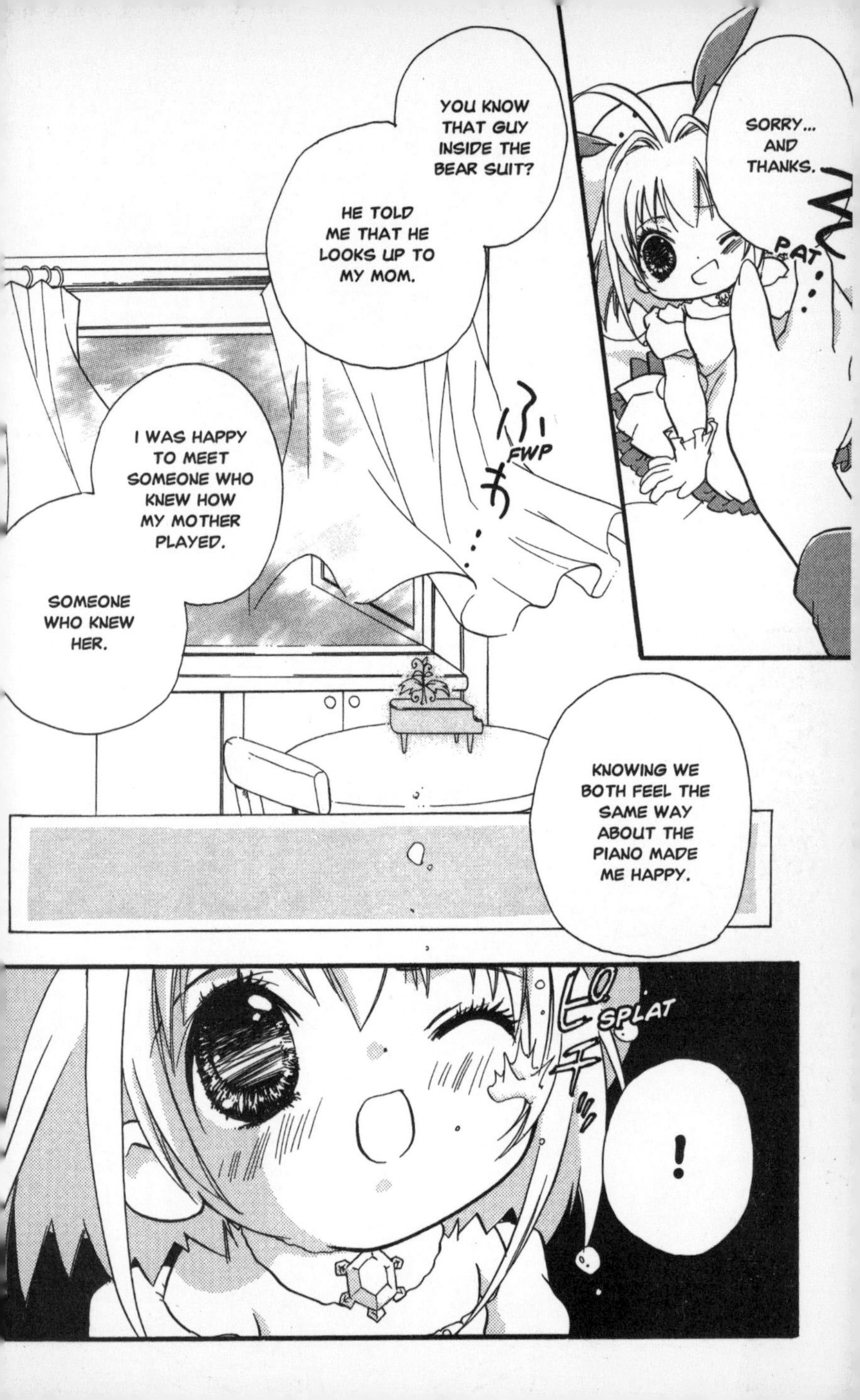
SORRY... AND THANKS.
PAT
YOU KNOW THAT GUY INSIDE THE BEAR SUIT?
HE TOLD ME THAT HE LOOKS UP TO MY MOM.
FWP
I WAS HAPPY TO MEET SOMEONE WHO KNEW HOW MY MOTHER PLAYED.
SOMEONE WHO KNEW HER.
KNOWING WE BOTH FEEL THE SAME WAY ABOUT THE PIANO MADE ME HAPPY.
SPLAT
!

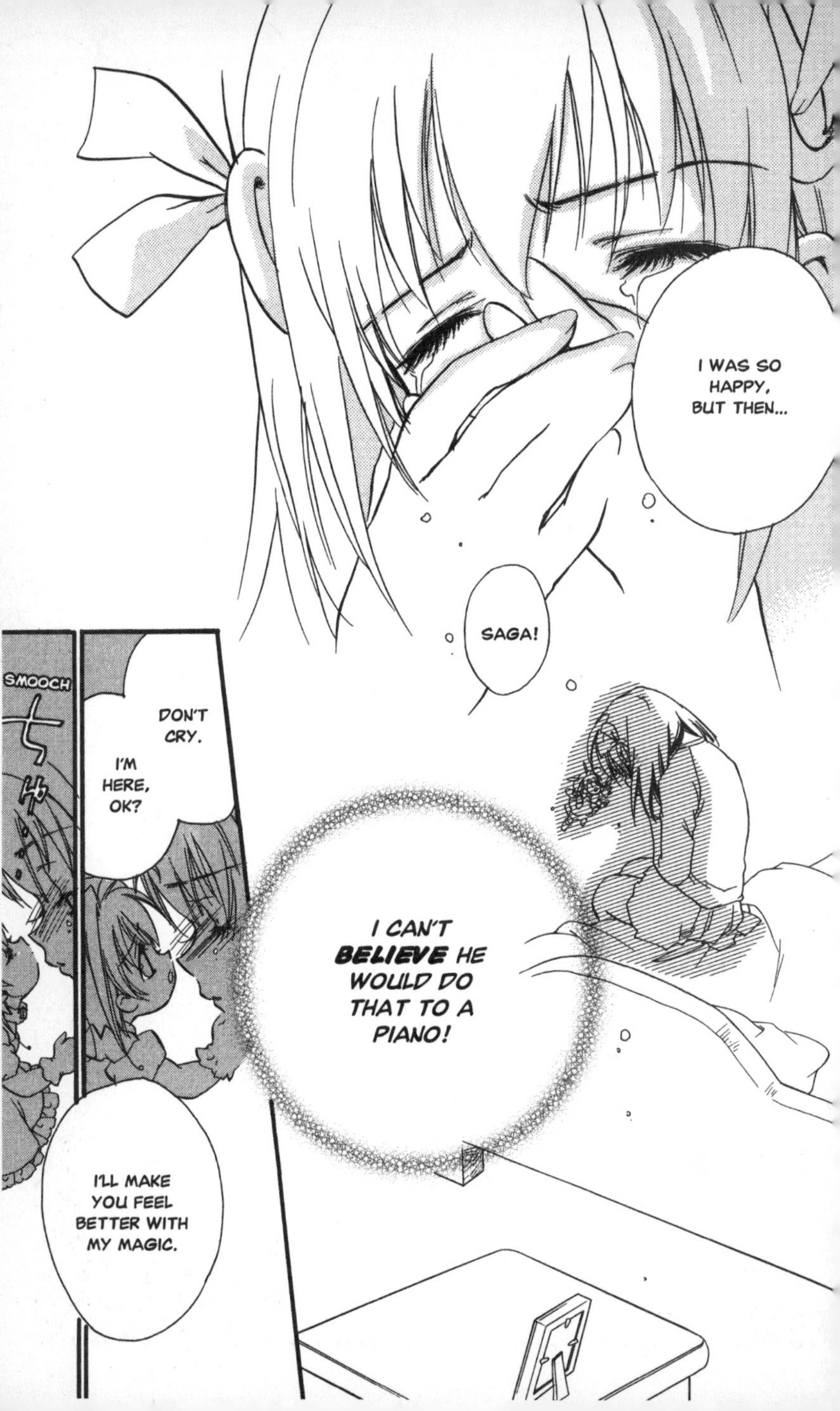
I WAS SO HAPPY, BUT THEN...
SAGA!
I CAN'T **BELIEVE** HE WOULD DO THAT TO A PIANO!
DON'T CRY.
I'M HERE, OK?
SMOOCH
I'LL MAKE YOU FEEL BETTER WITH MY MAGIC.

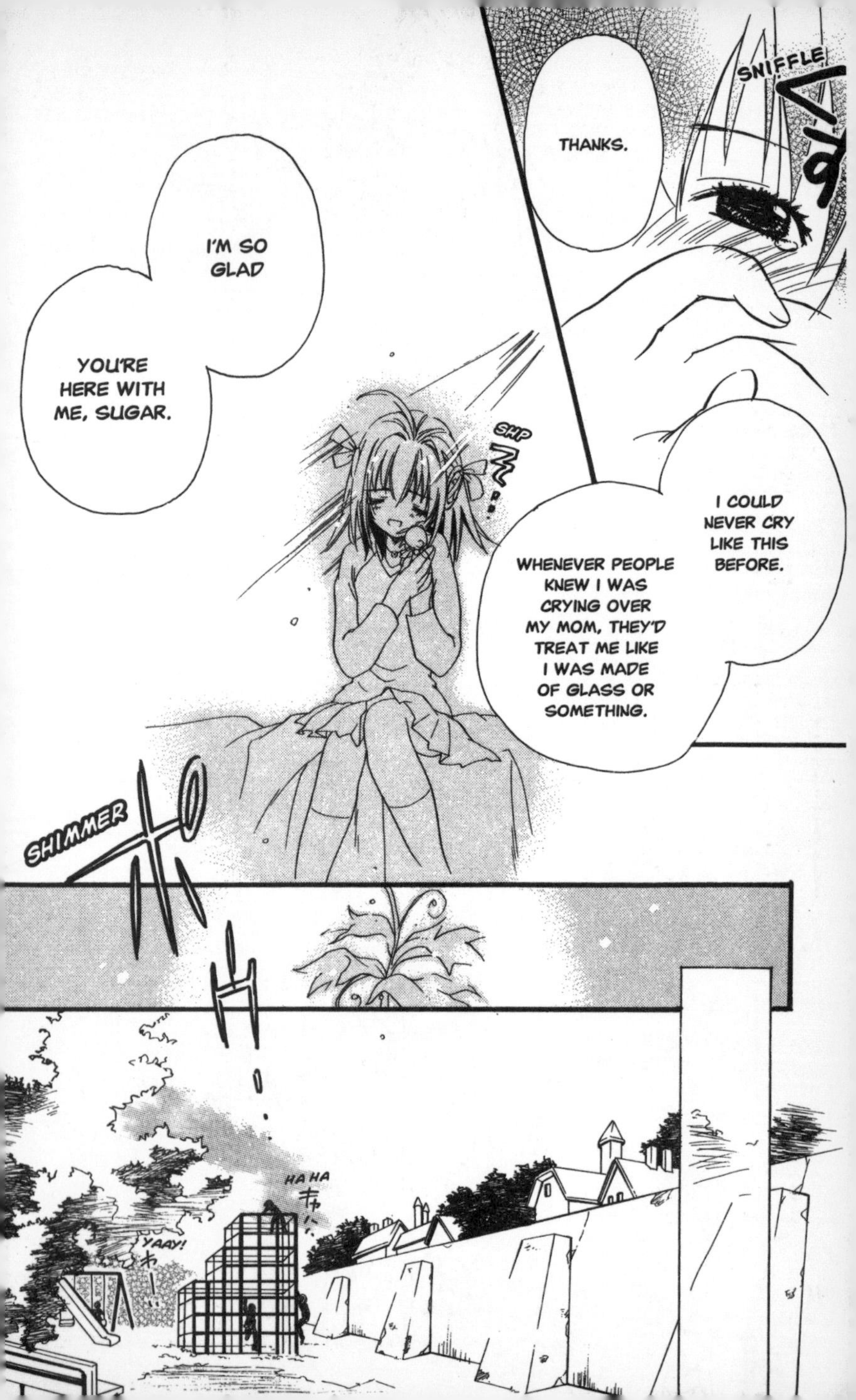
SNIFFLE
THANKS.
I COULD NEVER CRY LIKE THIS BEFORE.
WHENEVER PEOPLE KNEW I WAS CRYING OVER MY MOM, THEY'D TREAT ME LIKE I WAS MADE OF GLASS OR SOMETHING.
SHP
I'M SO GLAD
YOU'RE HERE WITH ME, SUGAR.
SHIMMER
HA HA
YAAY!

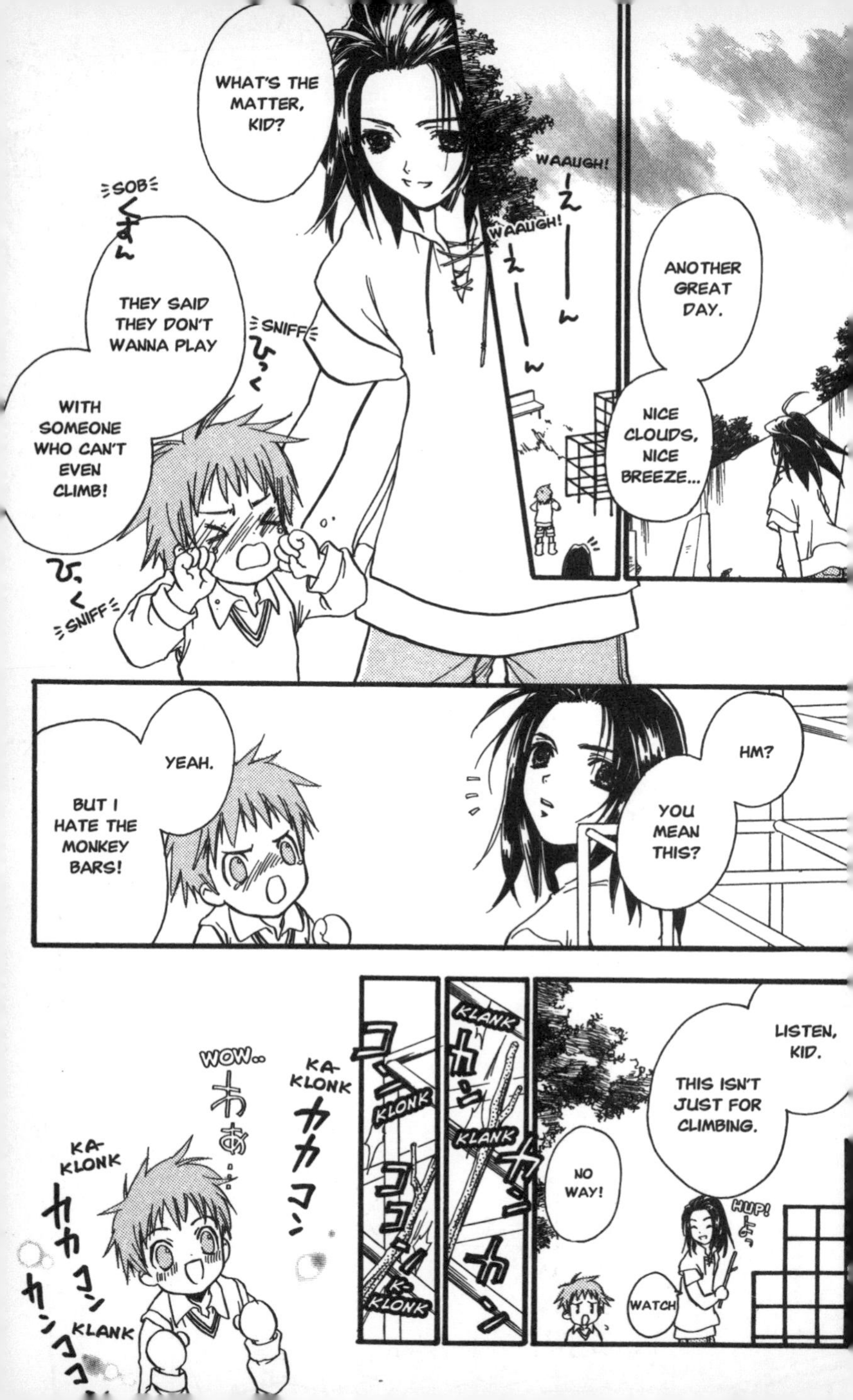
ANOTHER GREAT DAY.
NICE CLOUDS, NICE BREEZE...
WAAUGH!
WAAUGH!
WHAT'S THE MATTER, KID?
SOB
THEY SAID THEY DON'T WANNA PLAY
SNIFF
WITH SOMEONE WHO CAN'T EVEN CLIMB!
SNIFF
HM?
YOU MEAN THIS?
YEAH.
BUT I HATE THE MONKEY BARS!
LISTEN, KID.
THIS ISN'T JUST FOR CLIMBING.
NO WAY!
HUP!
WATCH
KLANK
KLANK
KLONK
K-KLONK
KA-KLONK
WOW..
KA-KLONK
KLANK

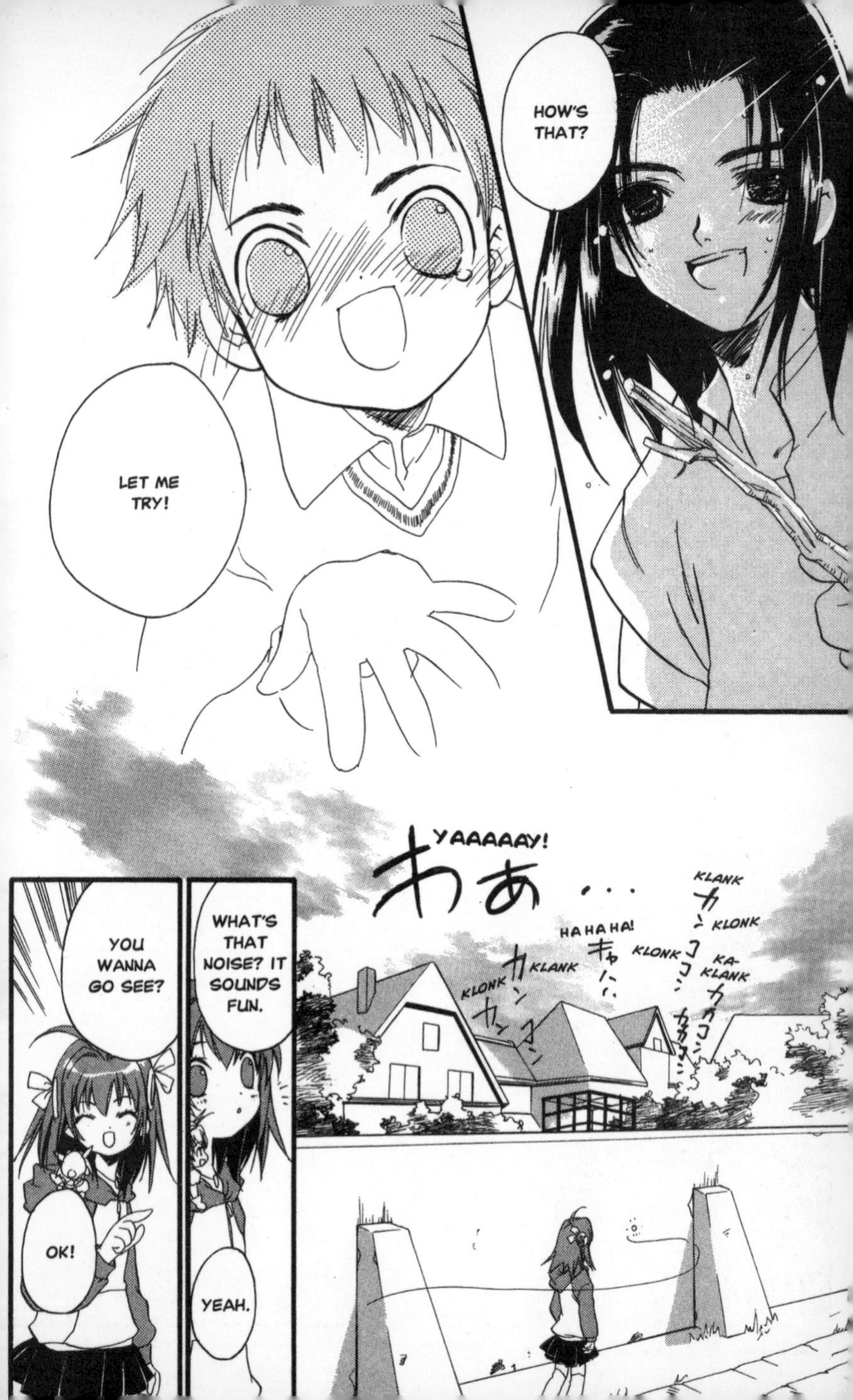
HOW'S THAT?
LET ME TRY!
YAAAAAY!
わぁ…
KLANK
KLONK
HAHAHA!
キャハハ
KLONK
KA-KLANK
KLANK
KLONK
WHAT'S THAT NOISE? IT SOUNDS FUN.
YOU WANNA GO SEE?
YEAH.
OK!

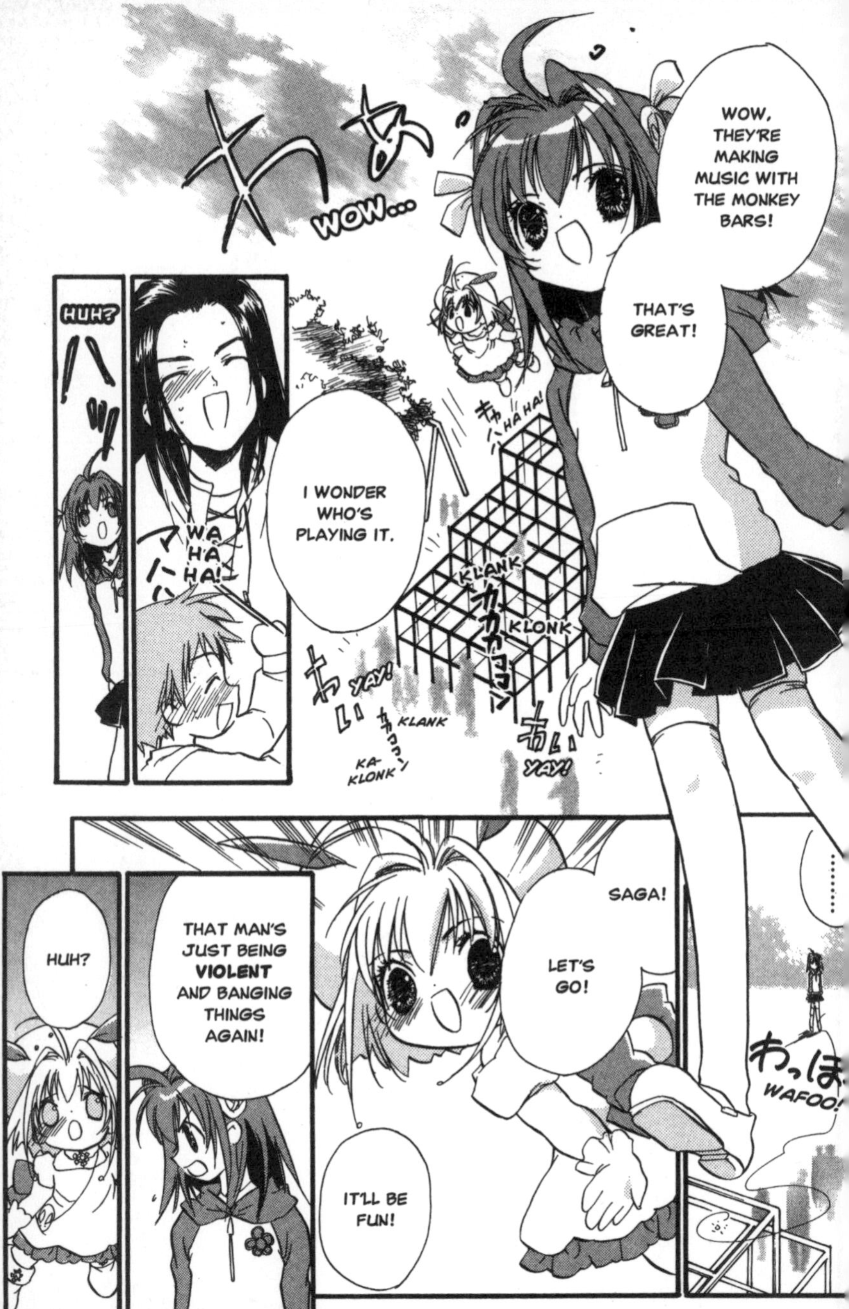
WOW, THEY'RE MAKING MUSIC WITH THE MONKEY BARS!
THAT'S GREAT!
WOW...
I WONDER WHO'S PLAYING IT.
HA HA!
KLANK
KLONK
YAY!
KLANK
KA-KLONK
YAY!
WA HA HA!
HUH?
......
WAFOO!
SAGA!
LET'S GO!
IT'LL BE FUN!
THAT MAN'S JUST BEING **VIOLENT** AND BANGING THINGS AGAIN!
HUH?

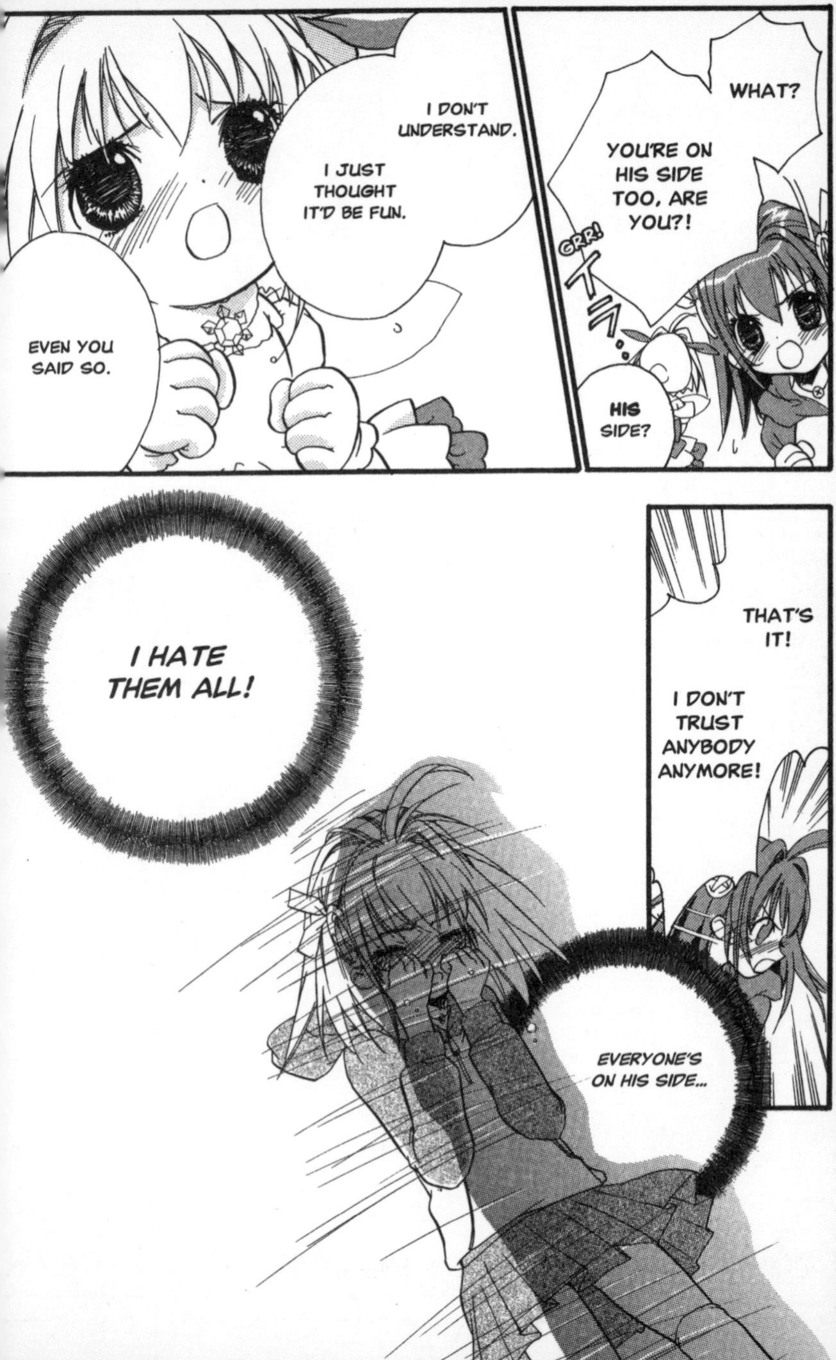
WHAT?
YOU'RE ON HIS SIDE TOO, ARE YOU?!
GRR!
HIS SIDE?
I DON'T UNDERSTAND.
I JUST THOUGHT IT'D BE FUN.
EVEN YOU SAID SO.
THAT'S IT!
I DON'T TRUST ANYBODY ANYMORE!
EVERYONE'S ON HIS SIDE...
I HATE THEM ALL!

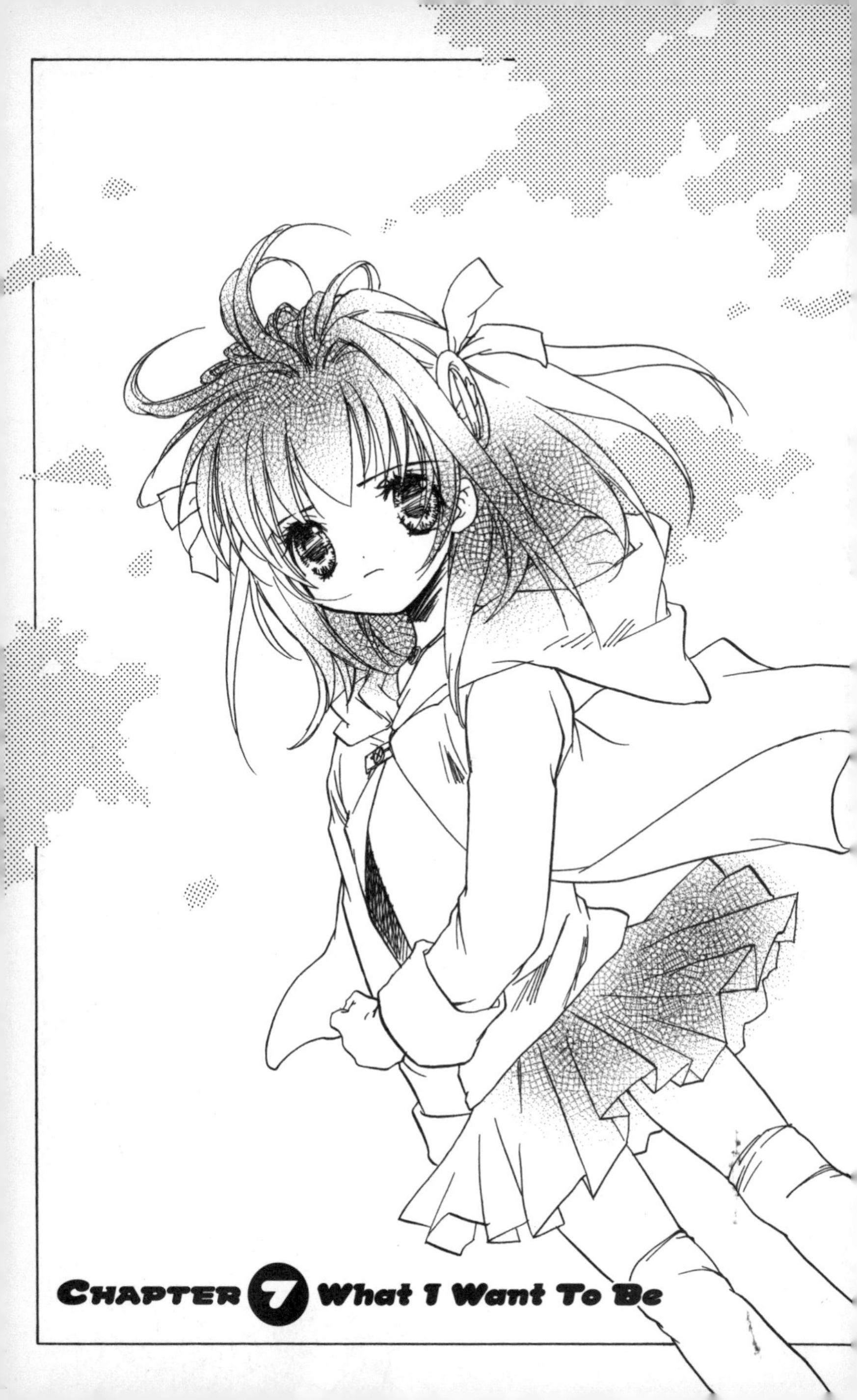

CHAPTER 7 What I Want To Be

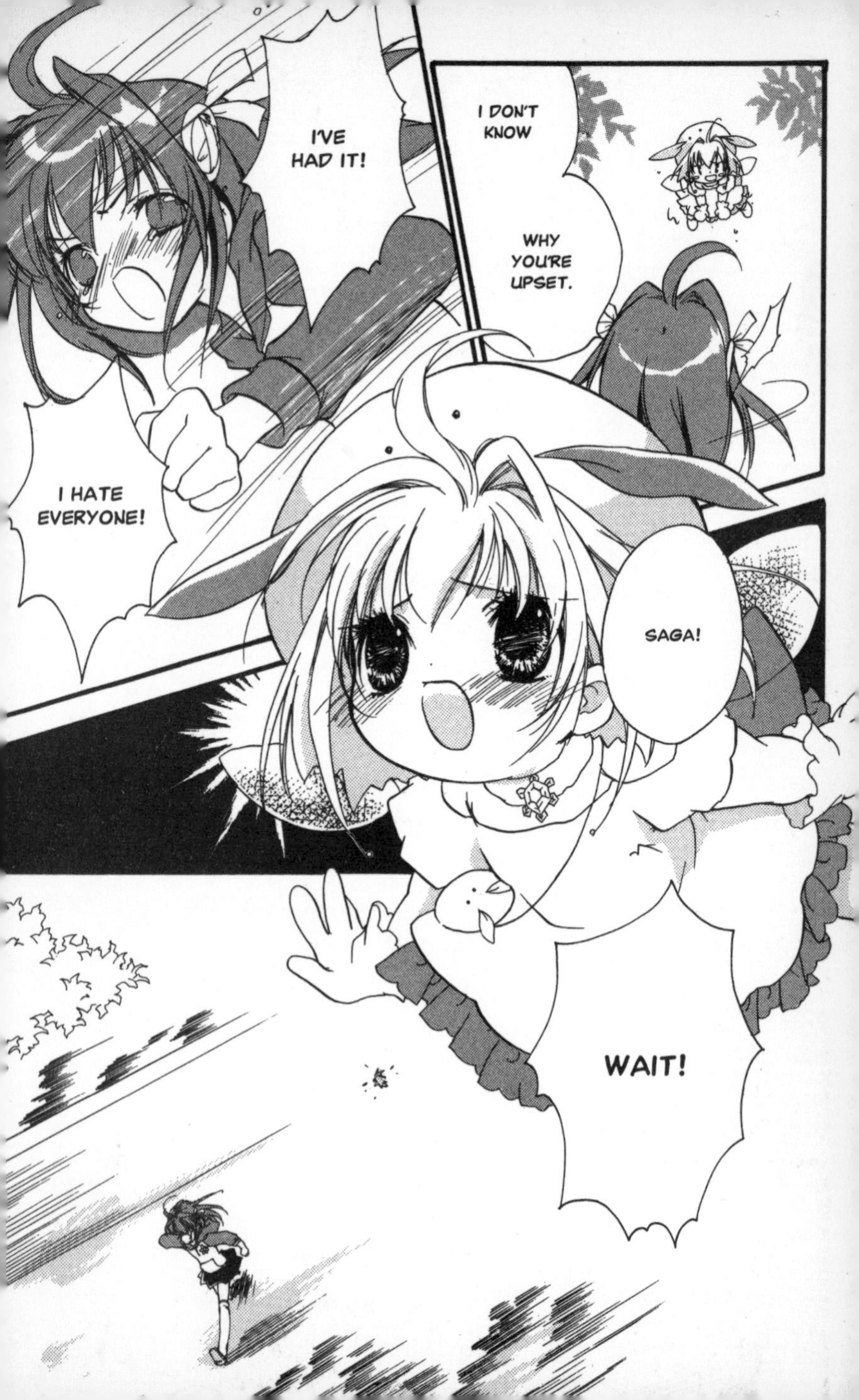
I DON'T KNOW
WHY YOU'RE UPSET.
I'VE HAD IT!
I HATE EVERYONE!
SAGA!
WAIT!

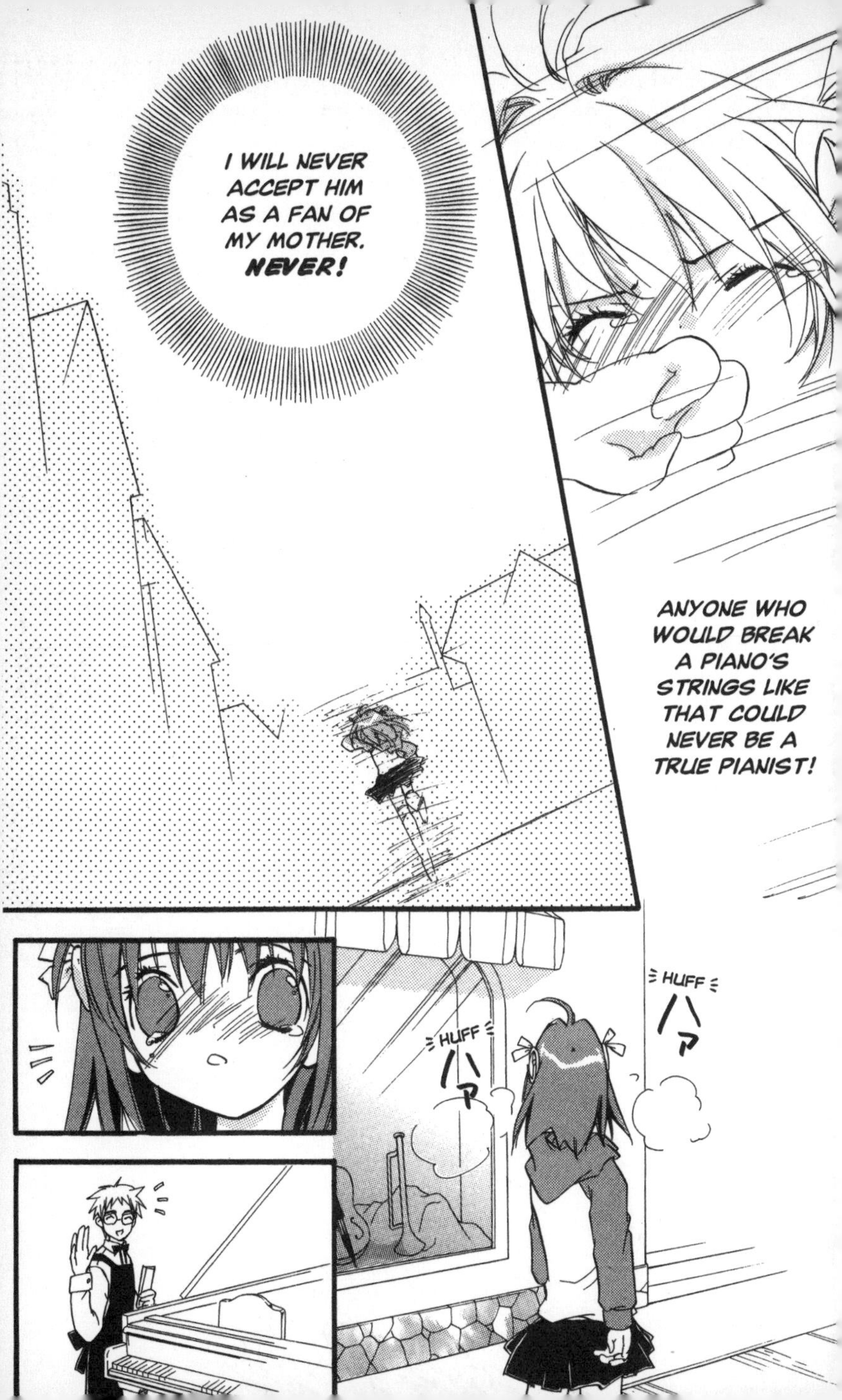

I WILL NEVER ACCEPT HIM AS A FAN OF MY MOTHER. NEVER!
ANYONE WHO WOULD BREAK A PIANO'S STRINGS LIKE THAT COULD NEVER BE A TRUE PIANIST!
HUFF ハァ
HUFF ハァ

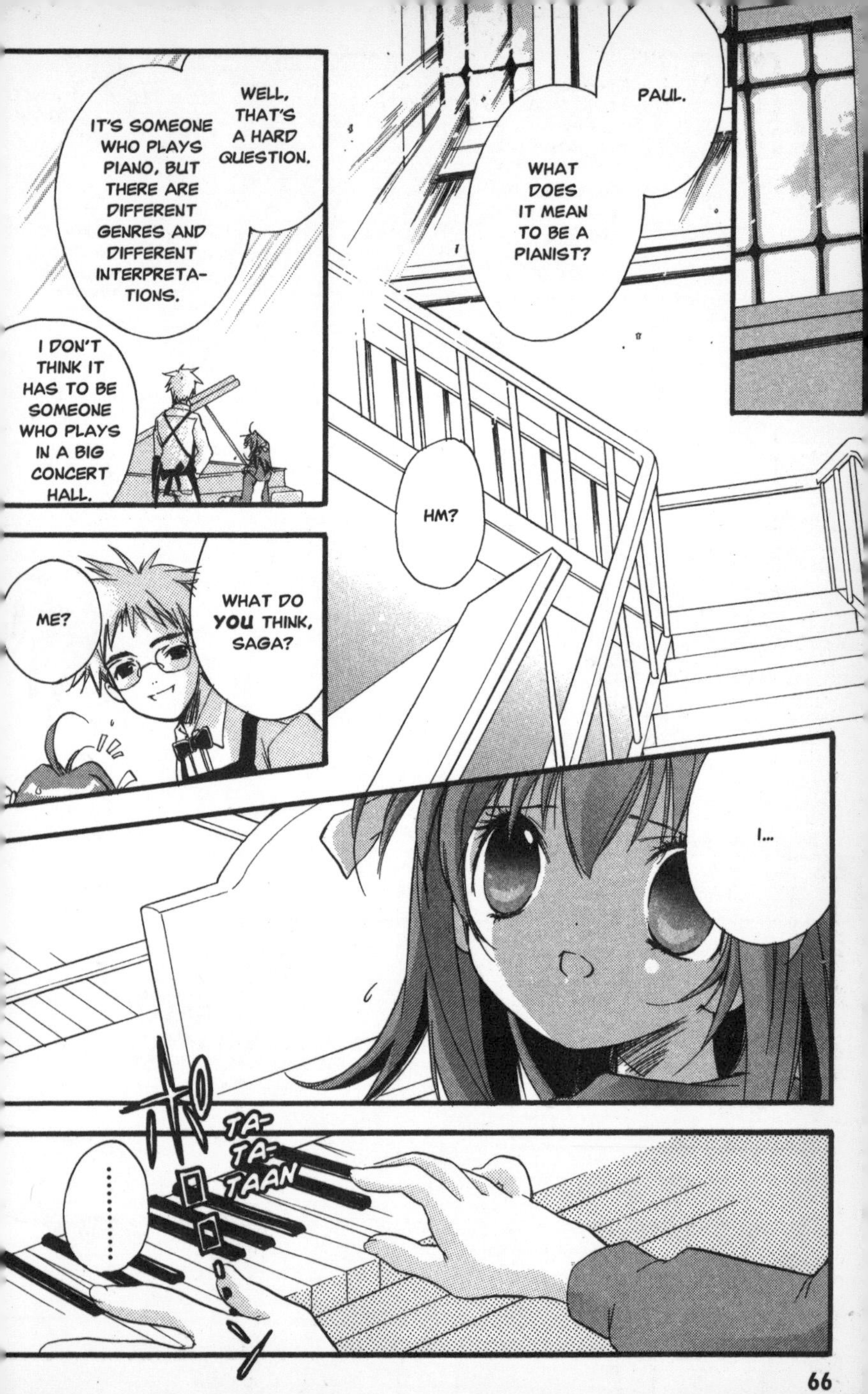
PAUL.
WHAT DOES IT MEAN TO BE A PIANIST?
HM?
WELL, THAT'S A HARD QUESTION.
IT'S SOMEONE WHO PLAYS PIANO, BUT THERE ARE DIFFERENT GENRES AND DIFFERENT INTERPRETA-TIONS.
I DON'T THINK IT HAS TO BE SOMEONE WHO PLAYS IN A BIG CONCERT HALL.
WHAT DO YOU THINK, SAGA?
ME?
I...
TA-TA-TAAN
......

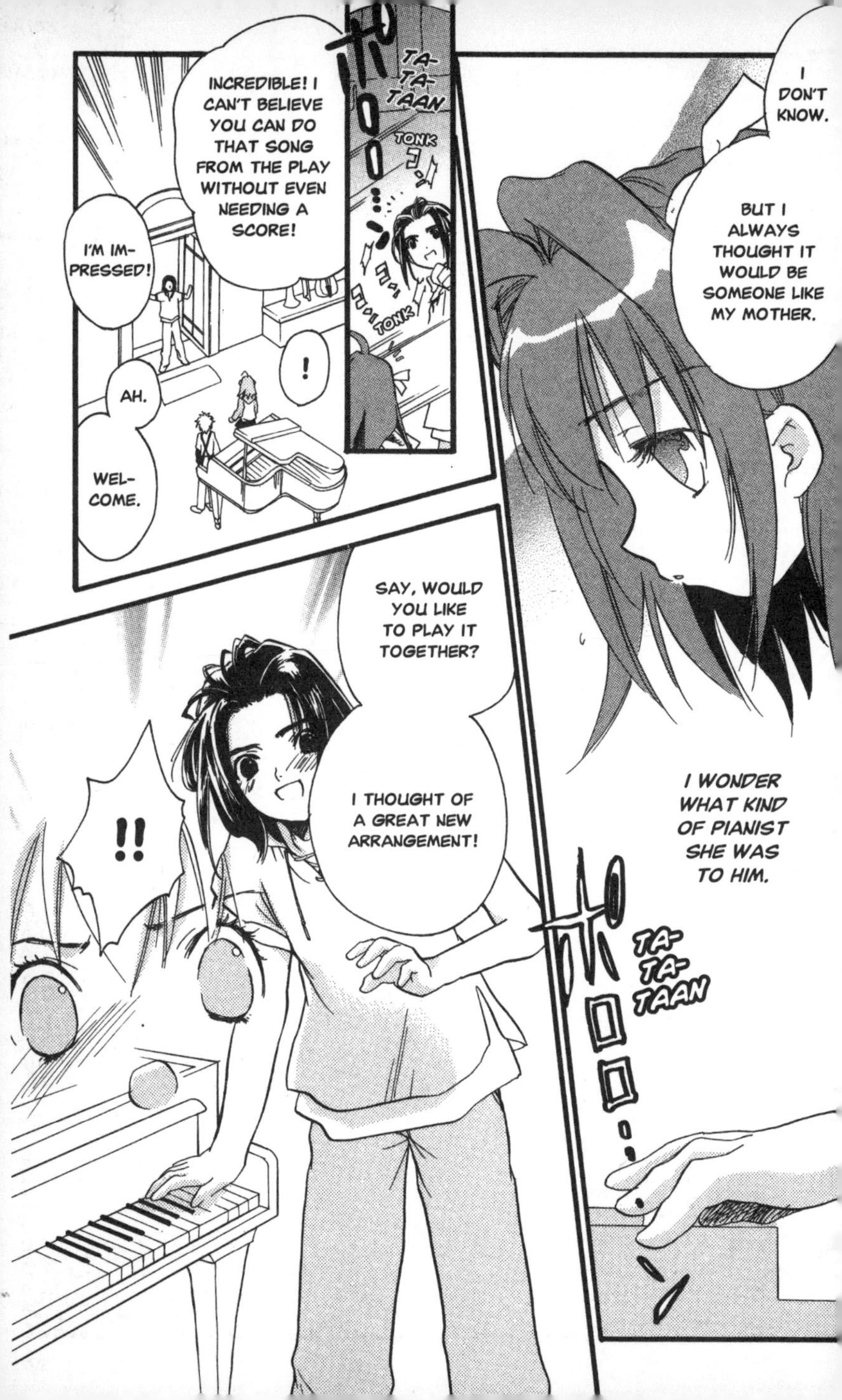
I DON'T KNOW.
BUT I ALWAYS THOUGHT IT WOULD BE SOMEONE LIKE MY MOTHER.
I WONDER WHAT KIND OF PIANIST SHE WAS TO HIM.
TA-TA-TAAN
TA-TA-TAAN
TONK
TONK
INCREDIBLE! I CAN'T BELIEVE YOU CAN DO THAT SONG FROM THE PLAY WITHOUT EVEN NEEDING A SCORE!
I'M IM-PRESSED!
!
AH.
WEL-COME.
SAY, WOULD YOU LIKE TO PLAY IT TOGETHER?
I THOUGHT OF A GREAT NEW ARRANGEMENT!
!!

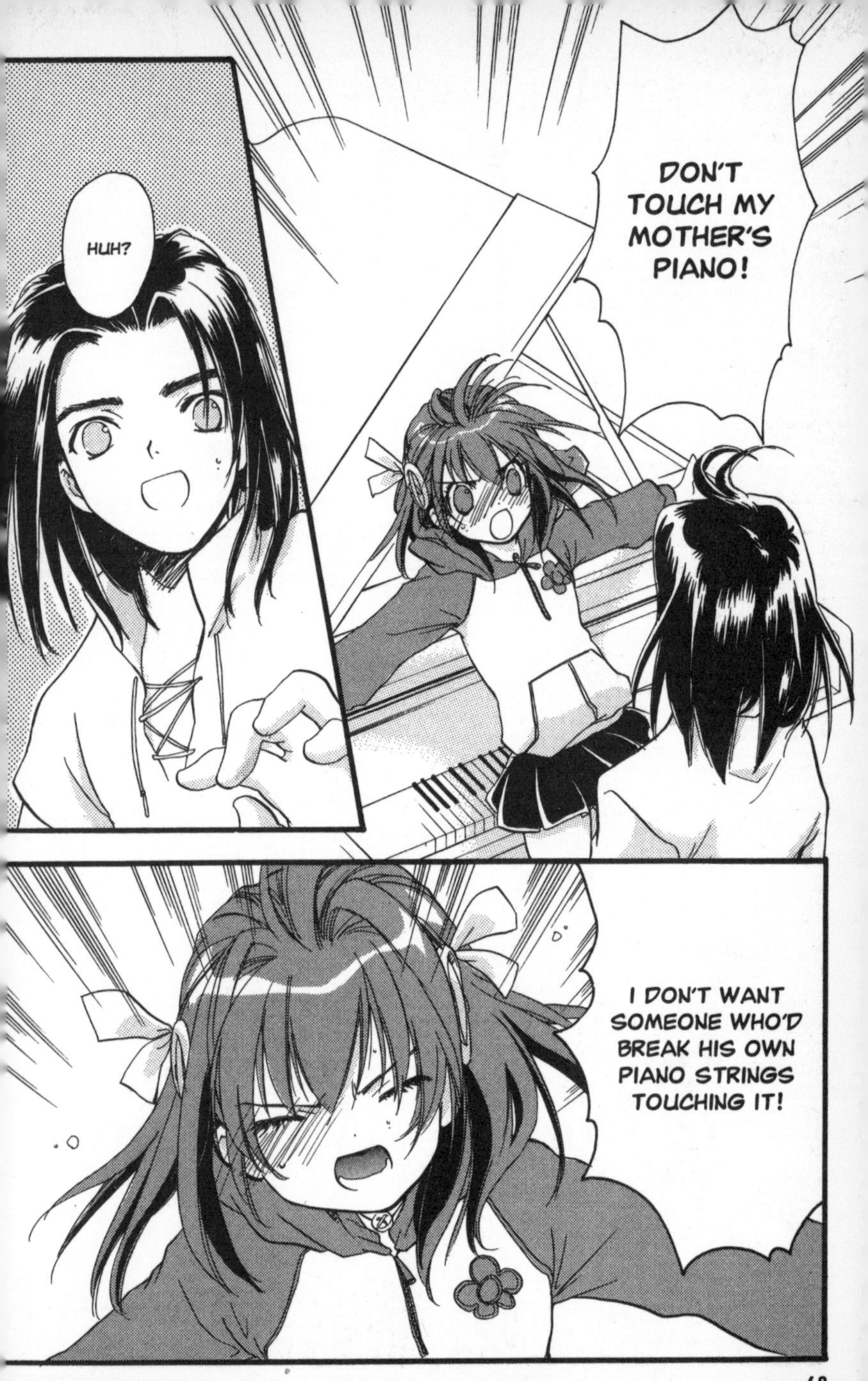
DON'T TOUCH MY MOTHER'S PIANO!
HUH?
I DON'T WANT SOMEONE WHO'D BREAK HIS OWN PIANO STRINGS TOUCHING IT!

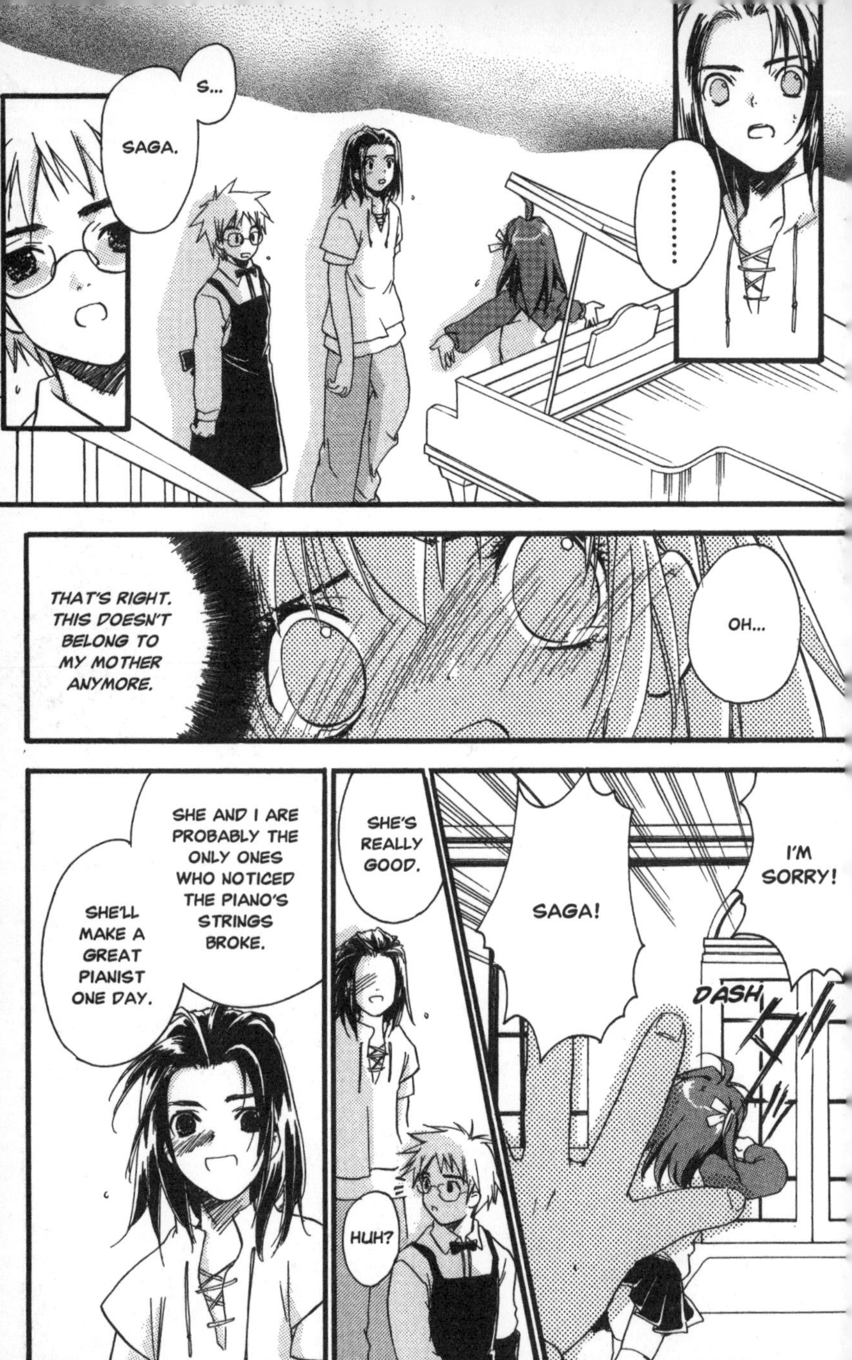
......
S...
SAGA.
OH...
THAT'S RIGHT. THIS DOESN'T BELONG TO MY MOTHER ANYMORE.
I'M SORRY!
SAGA!
DASH
SHE'S REALLY GOOD.
HUH?
SHE AND I ARE PROBABLY THE ONLY ONES WHO NOTICED THE PIANO'S STRINGS BROKE.
SHE'LL MAKE A GREAT PIANIST ONE DAY.

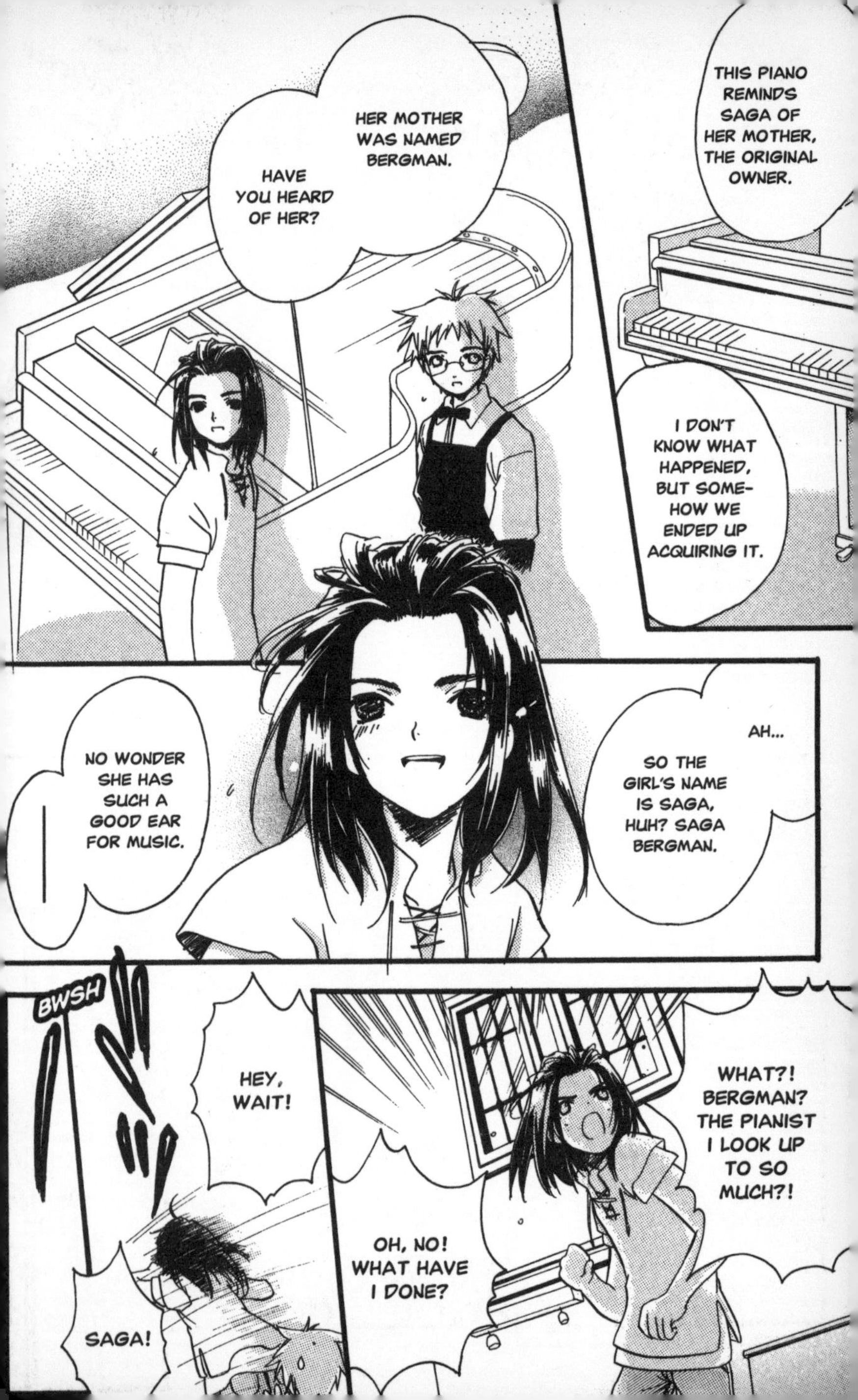
THIS PIANO REMINDS SAGA OF HER MOTHER, THE ORIGINAL OWNER.
I DON'T KNOW WHAT HAPPENED, BUT SOME-HOW WE ENDED UP ACQUIRING IT.
HER MOTHER WAS NAMED BERGMAN.
HAVE YOU HEARD OF HER?
AH...
SO THE GIRL'S NAME IS SAGA, HUH? SAGA BERGMAN.
NO WONDER SHE HAS SUCH A GOOD EAR FOR MUSIC.
WHAT?! BERGMAN? THE PIANIST I LOOK UP TO SO MUCH?!
OH, NO! WHAT HAVE I DONE?
HEY, WAIT!
BWSH
SAGA!

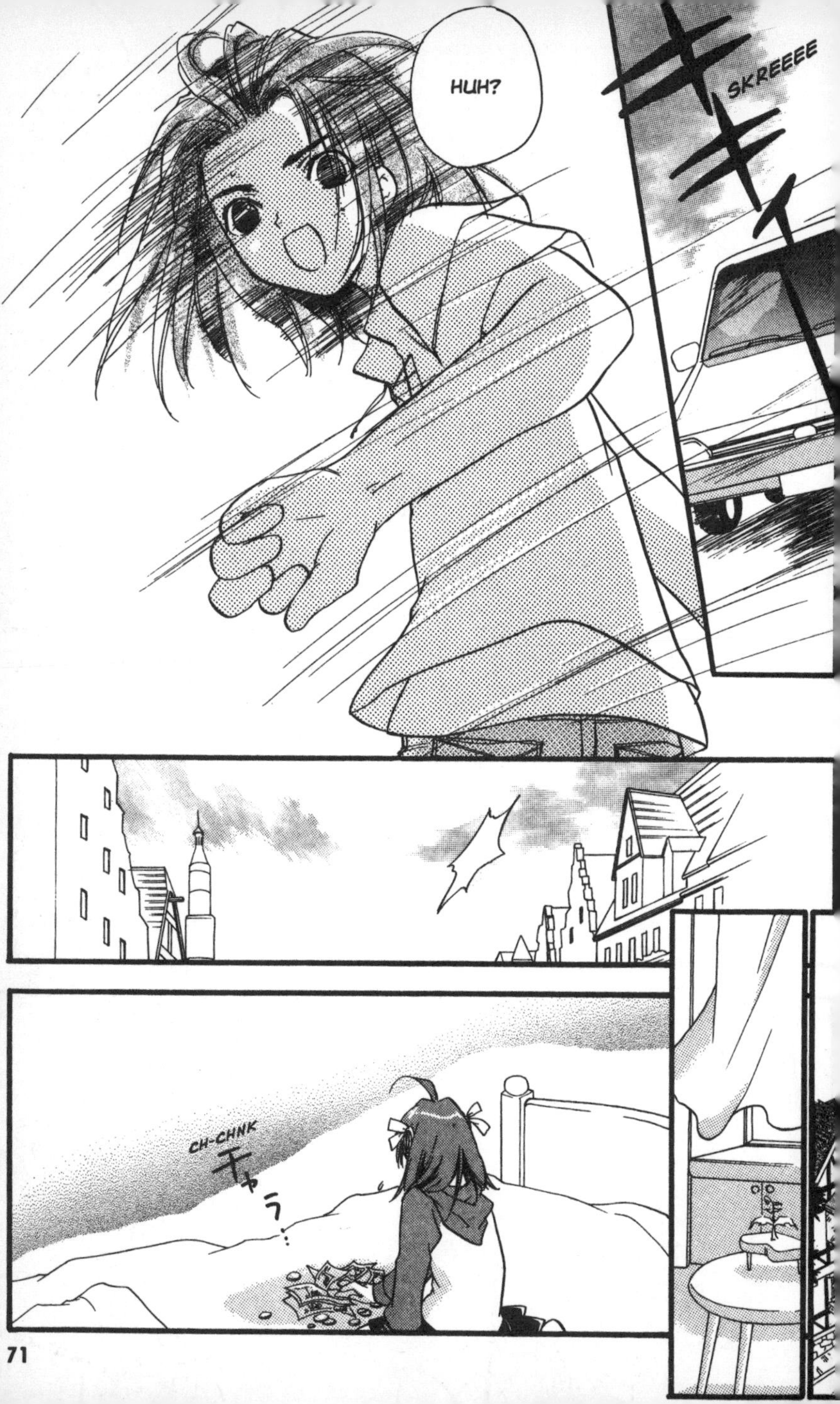
SKREEEE
キキイ
HUH?
CH-CHNK
チャラ…

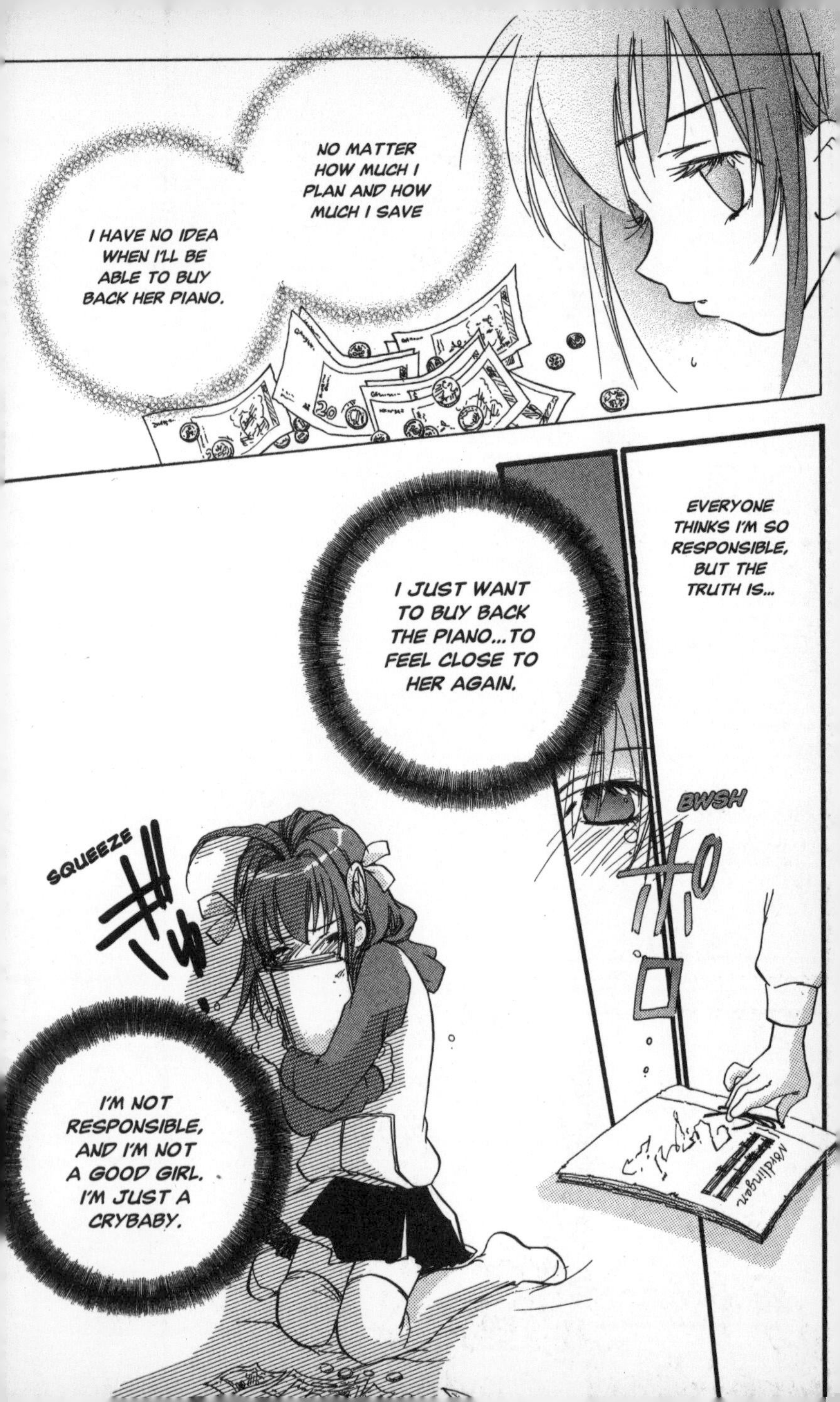

NO MATTER HOW MUCH I PLAN AND HOW MUCH I SAVE
I HAVE NO IDEA WHEN I'LL BE ABLE TO BUY BACK HER PIANO.
EVERYONE THINKS I'M SO RESPONSIBLE, BUT THE TRUTH IS...
I JUST WANT TO BUY BACK THE PIANO...TO FEEL CLOSE TO HER AGAIN.
BWSH
SQUEEZE
I'M NOT RESPONSIBLE, AND I'M NOT A GOOD GIRL. I'M JUST A CRYBABY.

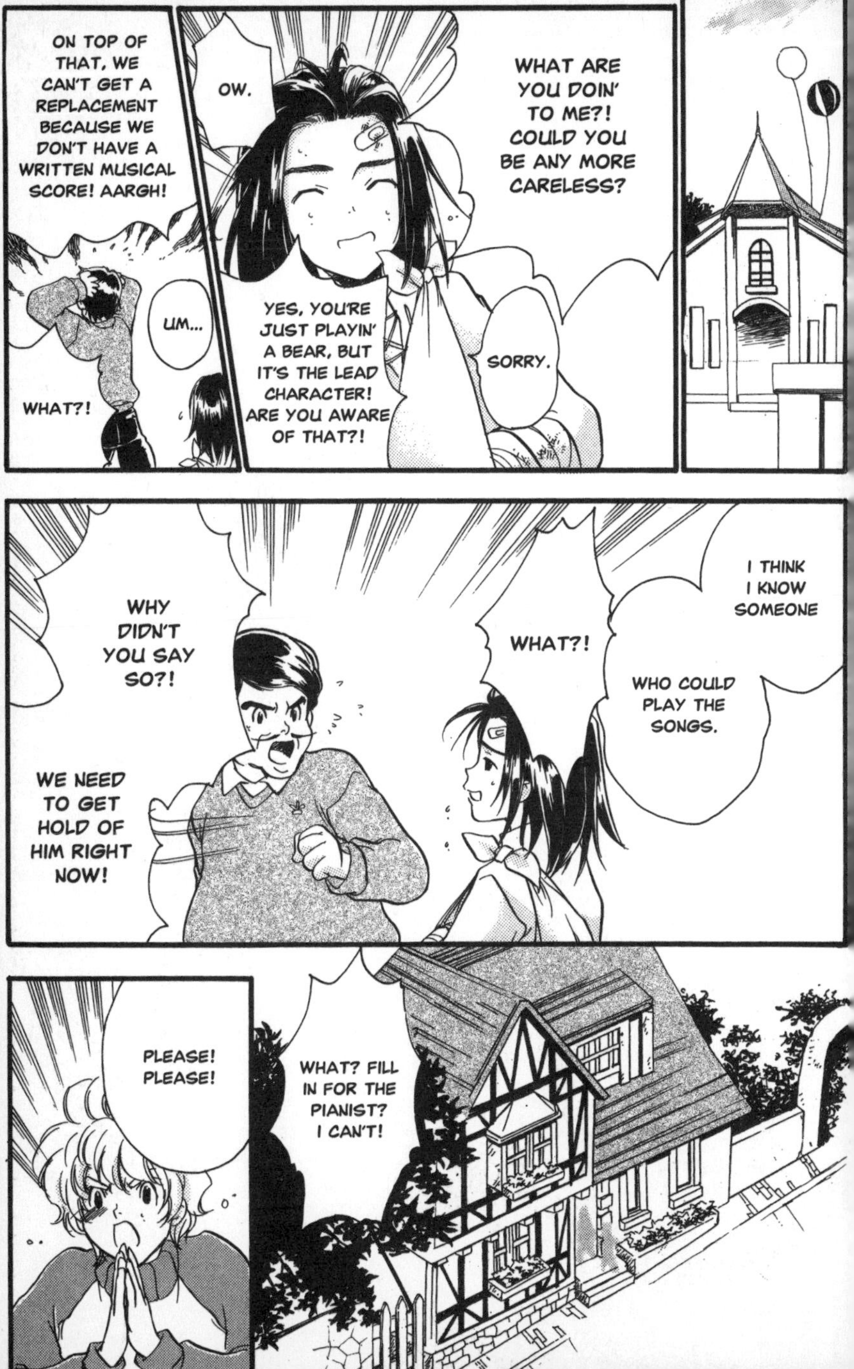
WHAT ARE YOU DOIN' TO ME?! COULD YOU BE ANY MORE CARELESS?
OW.
SORRY.
YES, YOU'RE JUST PLAYIN' A BEAR, BUT IT'S THE LEAD CHARACTER! ARE YOU AWARE OF THAT?!
ON TOP OF THAT, WE CAN'T GET A REPLACEMENT BECAUSE WE DON'T HAVE A WRITTEN MUSICAL SCORE! AARGH!
UM...
WHAT?!
I THINK I KNOW SOMEONE
WHO COULD PLAY THE SONGS.
WHAT?!
WHY DIDN'T YOU SAY SO?!
WE NEED TO GET HOLD OF HIM RIGHT NOW!
WHAT? FILL IN FOR THE PIANIST? I CAN'T!
PLEASE! PLEASE!

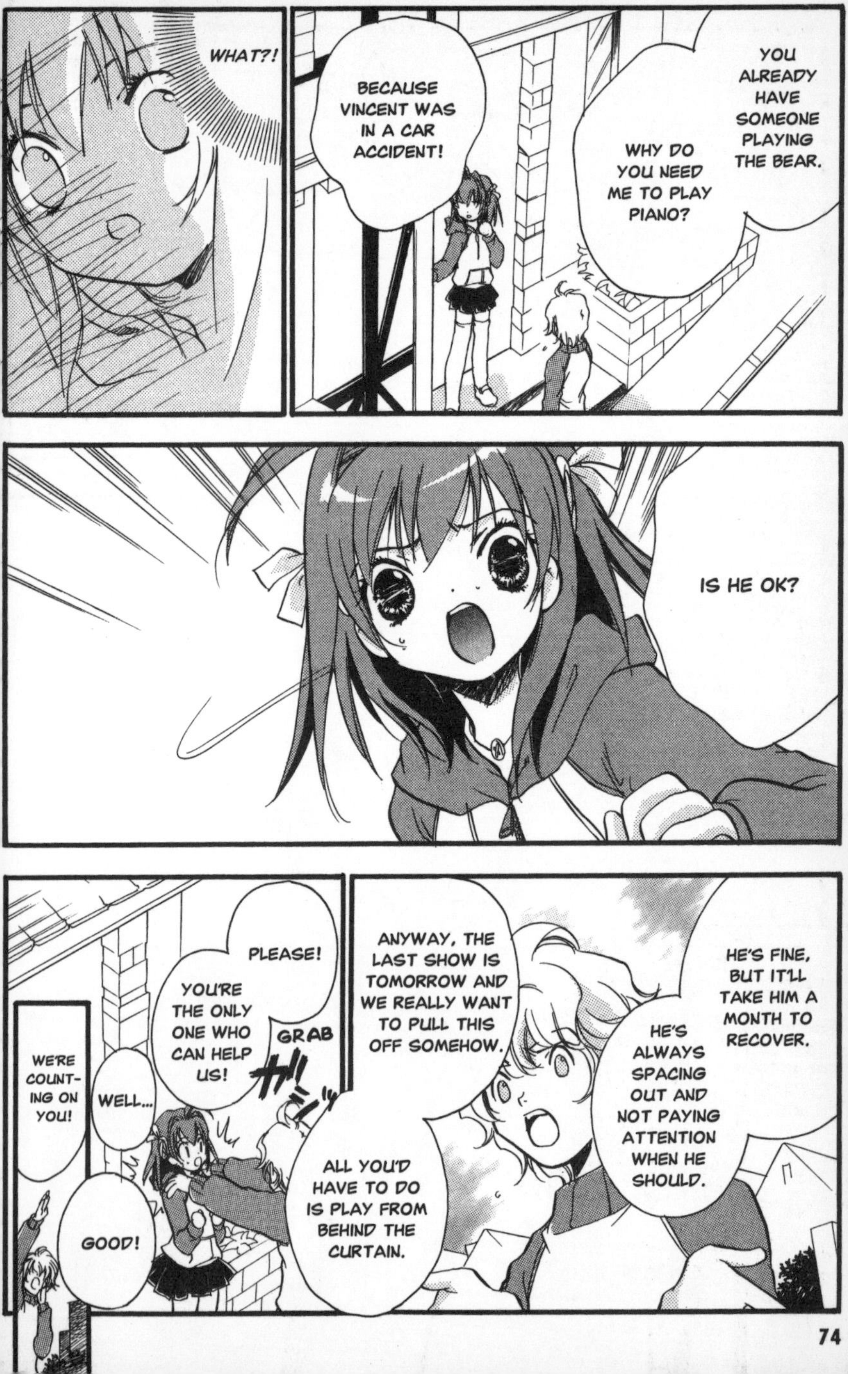
YOU ALREADY HAVE SOMEONE PLAYING THE BEAR.
WHY DO YOU NEED ME TO PLAY PIANO?
BECAUSE VINCENT WAS IN A CAR ACCIDENT!
WHAT?!
IS HE OK?
HE'S FINE, BUT IT'LL TAKE HIM A MONTH TO RECOVER.
HE'S ALWAYS SPACING OUT AND NOT PAYING ATTENTION WHEN HE SHOULD.
ANYWAY, THE LAST SHOW IS TOMORROW AND WE REALLY WANT TO PULL THIS OFF SOMEHOW.
ALL YOU'D HAVE TO DO IS PLAY FROM BEHIND THE CURTAIN.
PLEASE!
YOU'RE THE ONLY ONE WHO CAN HELP US!
GRAB
WELL...
WE'RE COUNTING ON YOU!
GOOD!

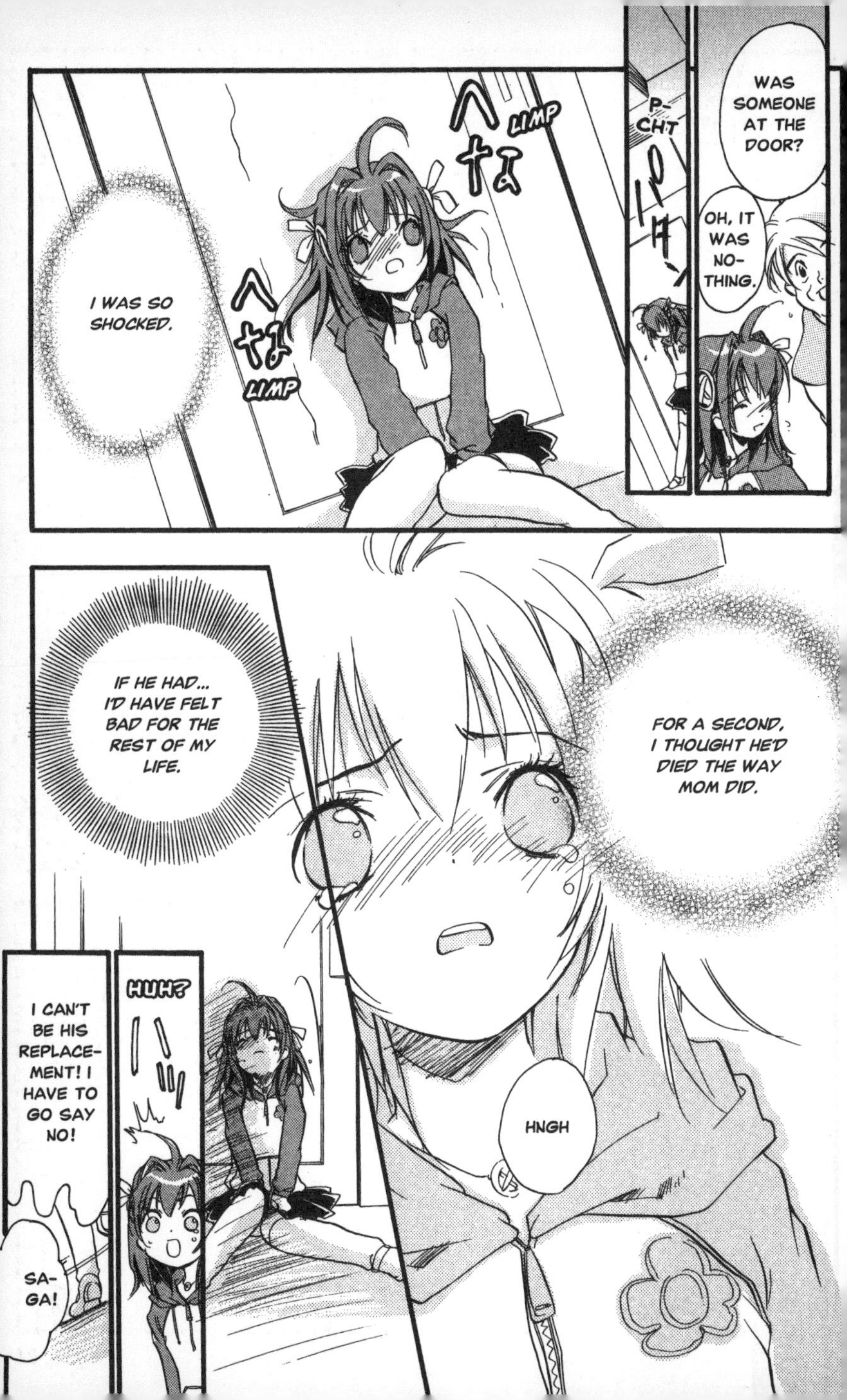
WAS SOMEONE AT THE DOOR?
P-CHT
OH, IT WAS NO-THING.
LIMP
LIMP
I WAS SO SHOCKED.
FOR A SECOND, I THOUGHT HE'D DIED THE WAY MOM DID.
IF HE HAD... I'D HAVE FELT BAD FOR THE REST OF MY LIFE.
HNGH
HUH?
I CAN'T BE HIS REPLACE-MENT! I HAVE TO GO SAY NO!
SA-GA!

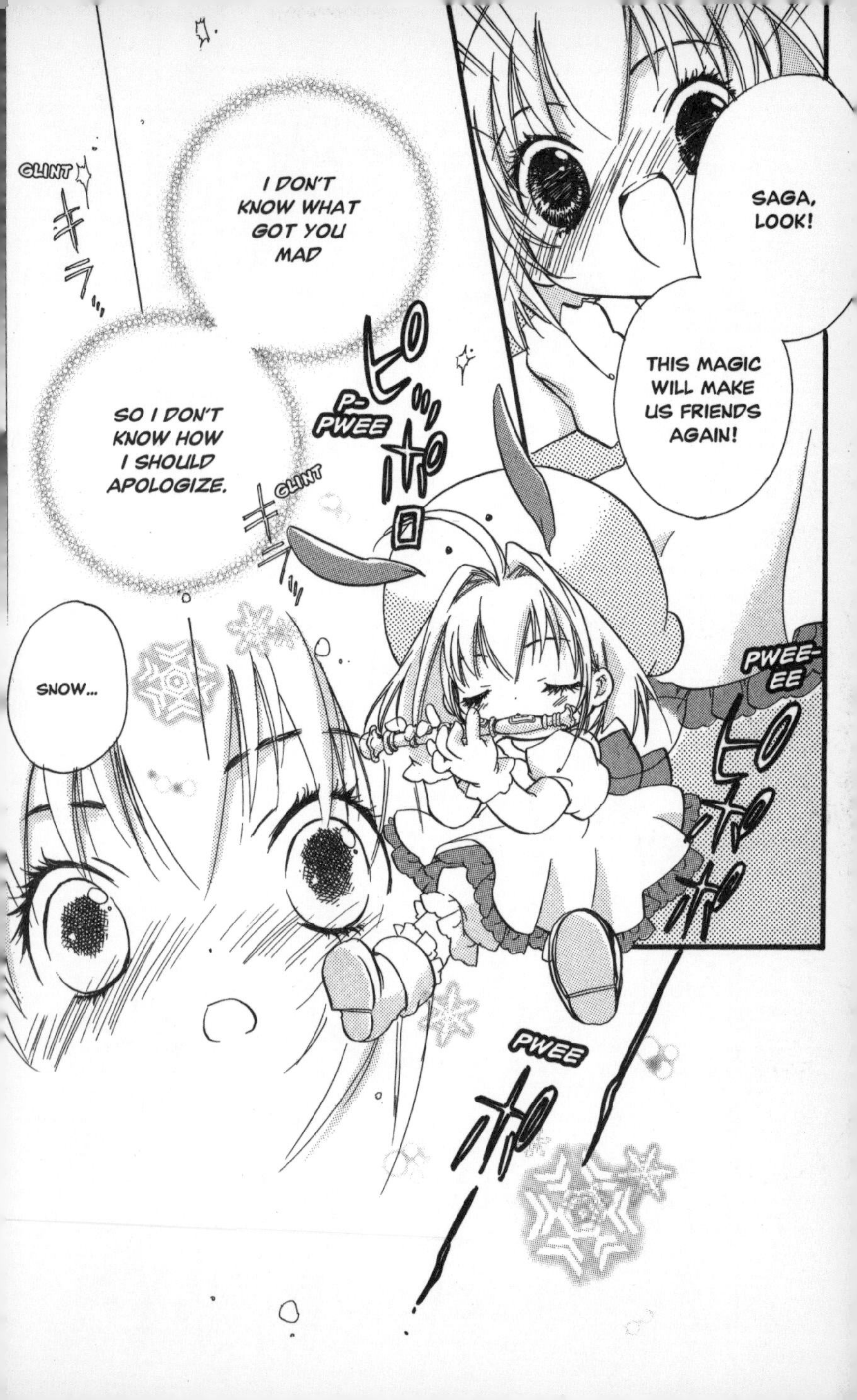
SAGA, LOOK!
THIS MAGIC WILL MAKE US FRIENDS AGAIN!
I DON'T KNOW WHAT GOT YOU MAD
SO I DON'T KNOW HOW I SHOULD APOLOGIZE.
GLINT
P-PWEE
GLINT
PWEE-EE
SNOW...
PWEE

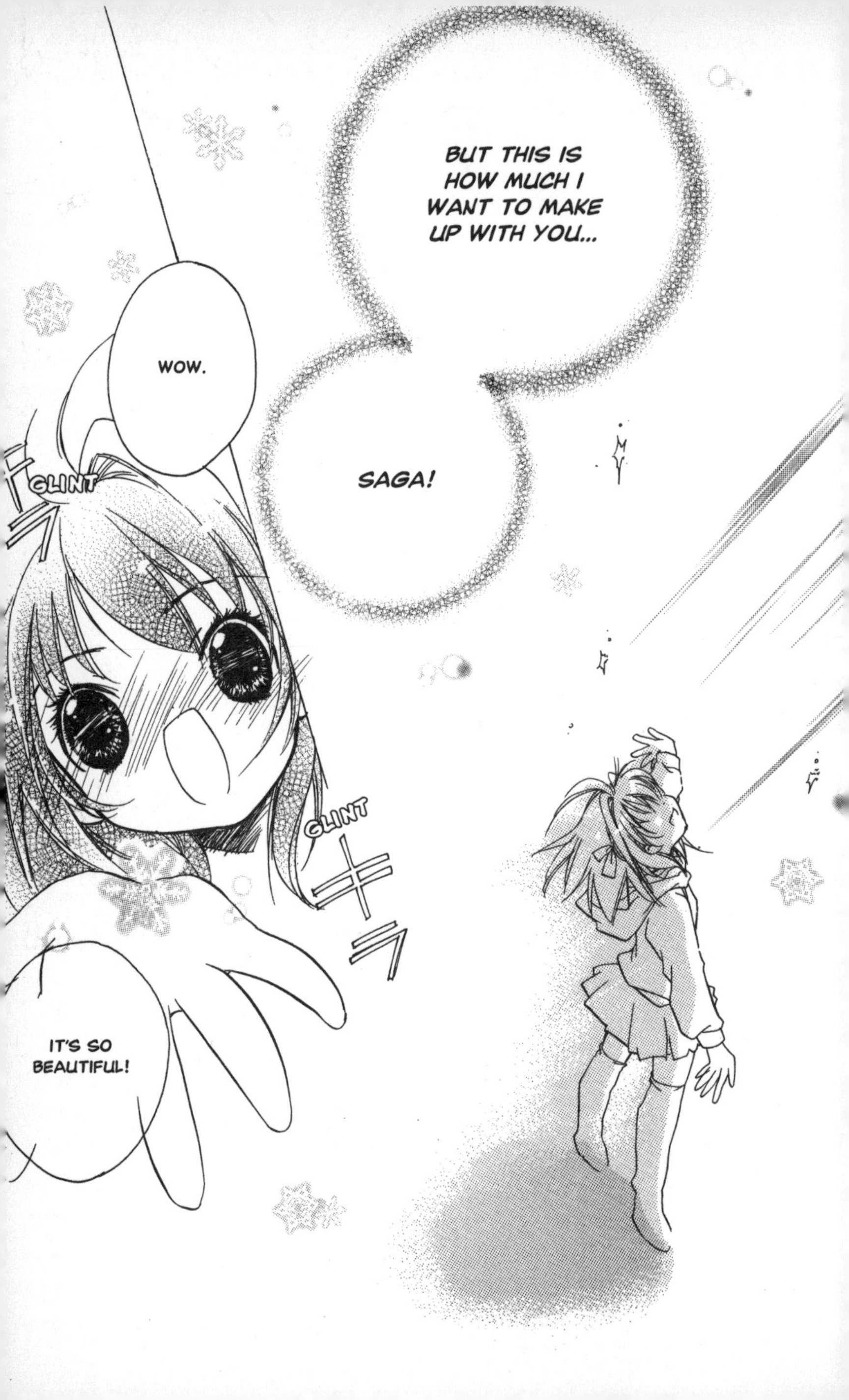
BUT THIS IS HOW MUCH I WANT TO MAKE UP WITH YOU...
SAGA!
WOW.
GLINT
GLINT
IT'S SO BEAUTIFUL!

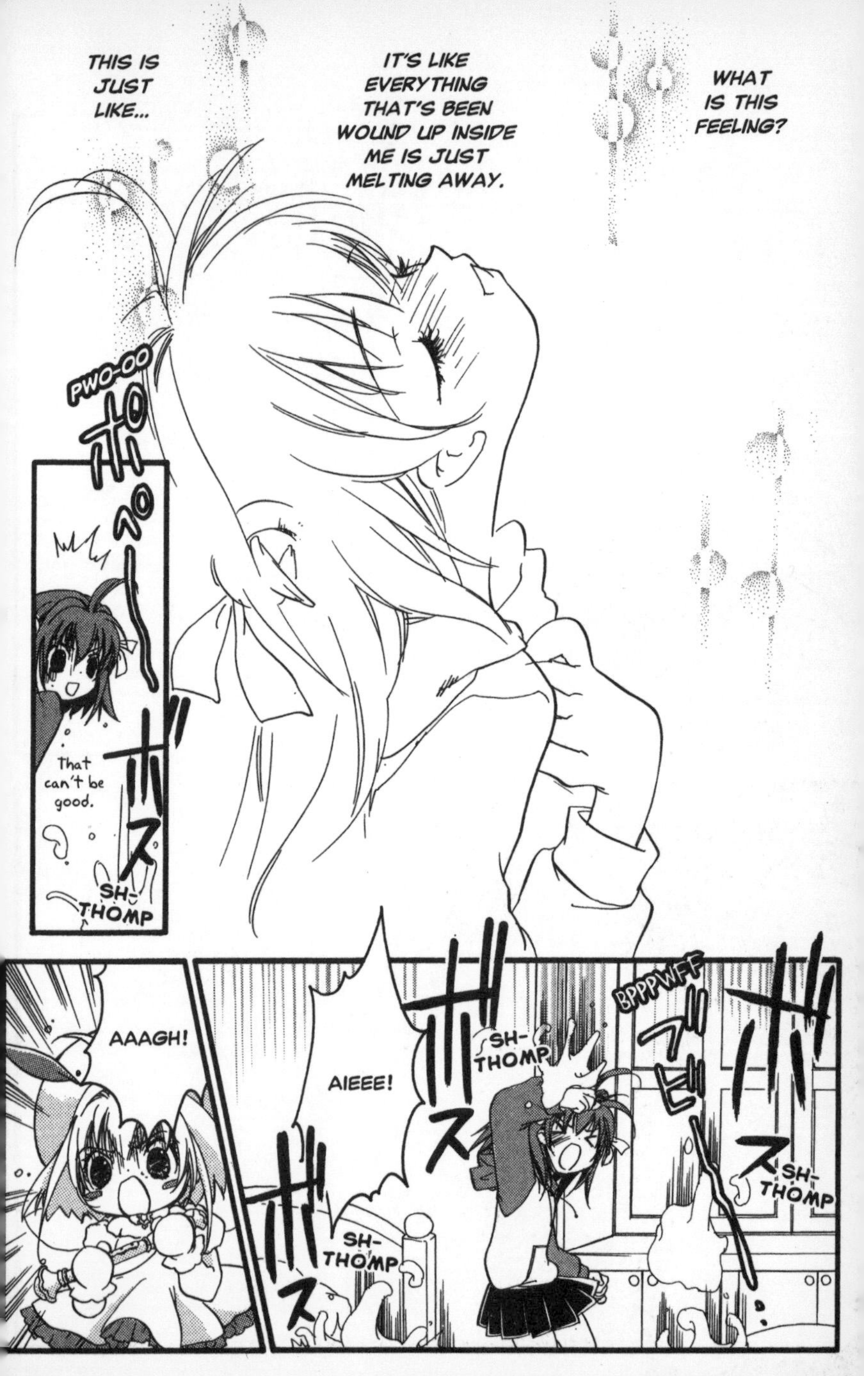
WHAT IS THIS FEELING?
IT'S LIKE EVERYTHING THAT'S BEEN WOUND UP INSIDE ME IS JUST MELTING AWAY.
THIS IS JUST LIKE...
PWO-OO
ポーッ
ボフ
That can't be good.
SH-THOMP
ボフ
SH-THOMP
BPPPWFF
ブビ
AIEEE!
ボフ
SH-THOMP
ボフ
SH-THOMP
AAAGH!

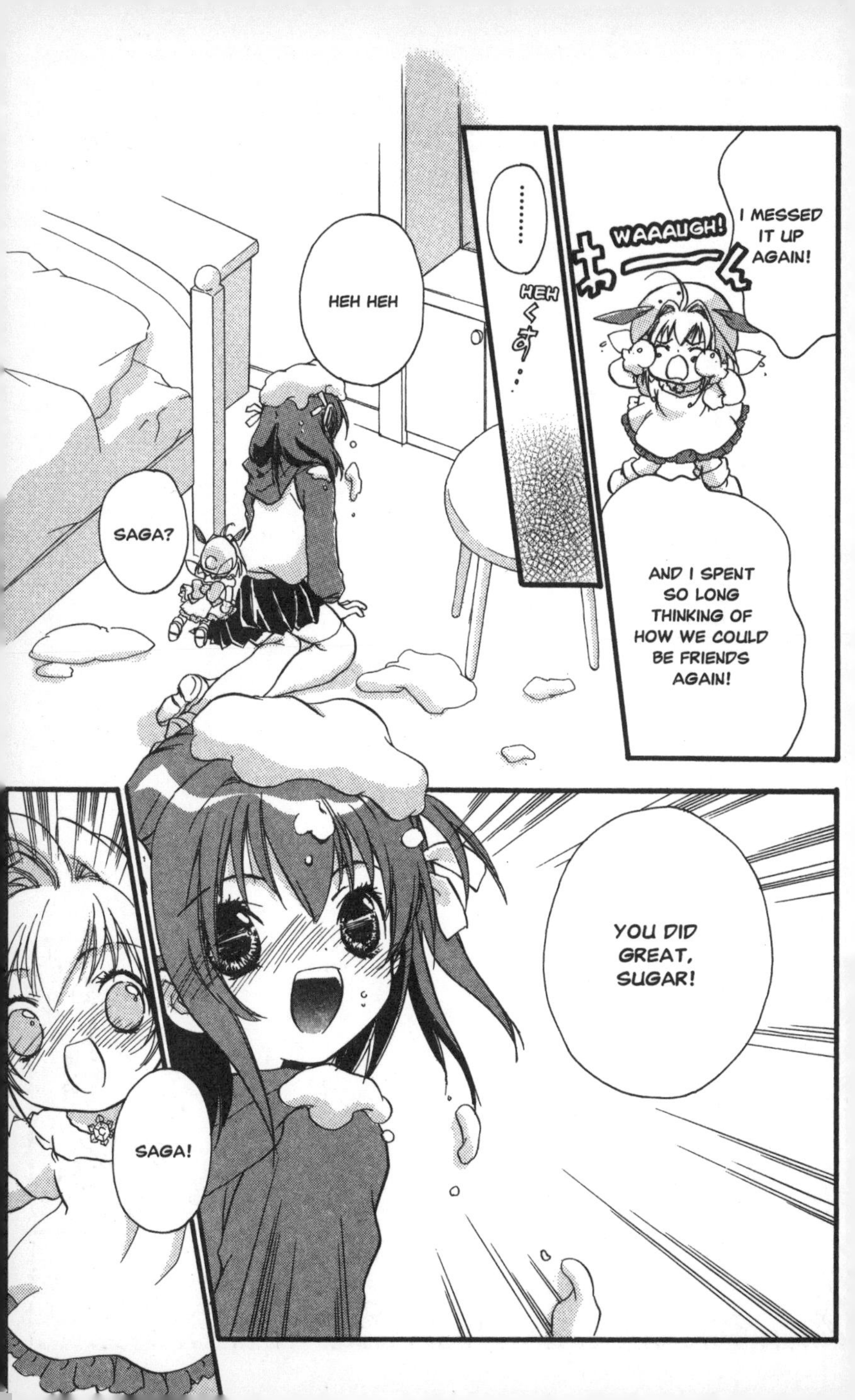
I MESSED IT UP AGAIN!
WAAAUGH!
AND I SPENT SO LONG THINKING OF HOW WE COULD BE FRIENDS AGAIN!
......
HEH
HEH HEH
SAGA?
YOU DID GREAT, SUGAR!
SAGA!

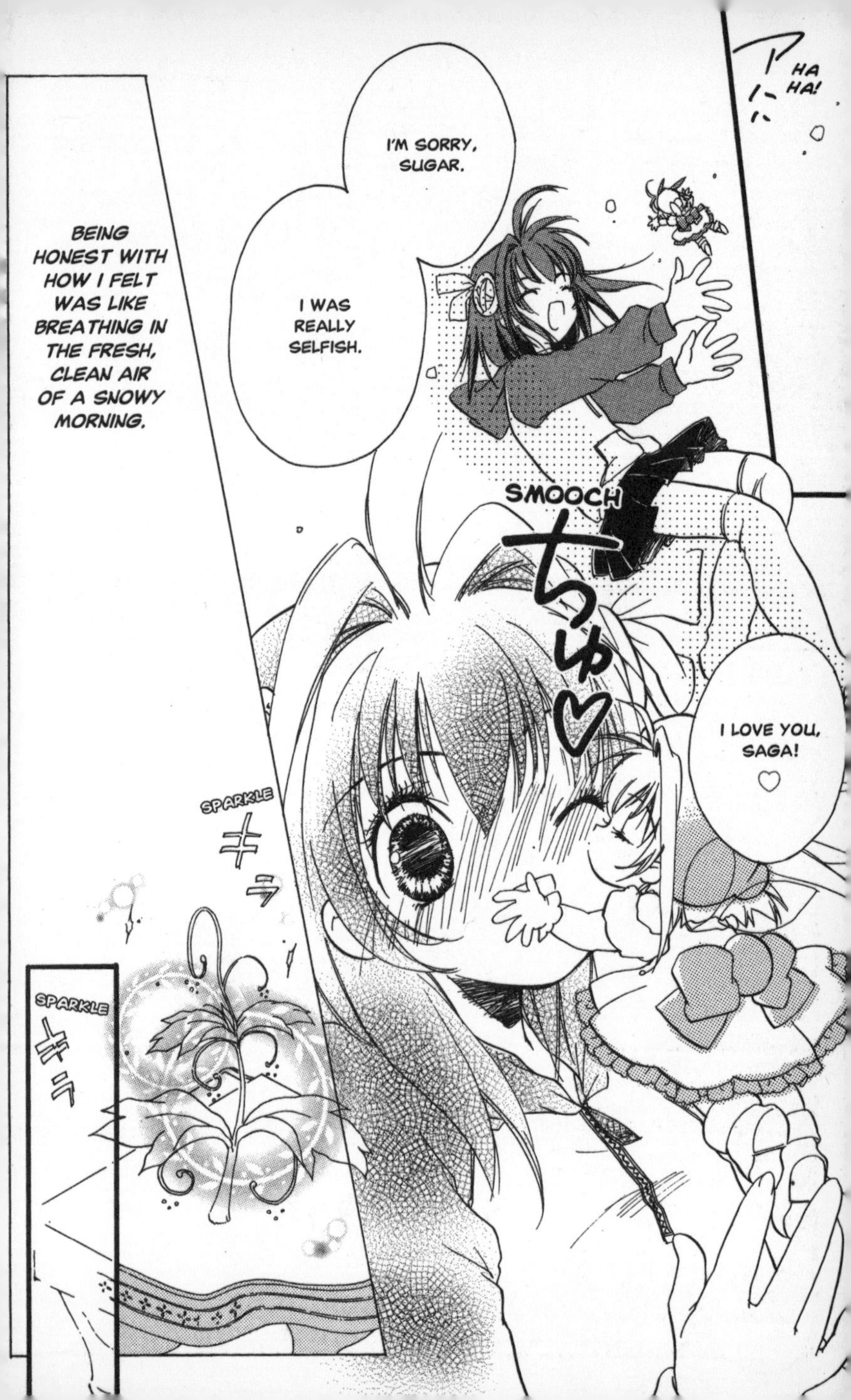
HA HA!
I'M SORRY, SUGAR.
I WAS REALLY SELFISH.
BEING HONEST WITH HOW I FELT WAS LIKE BREATHING IN THE FRESH, CLEAN AIR OF A SNOWY MORNING.
SMOOCH
ちゅ♡
I LOVE YOU, SAGA! ♡
SPARKLE
キラ
SPARKLE
キラ

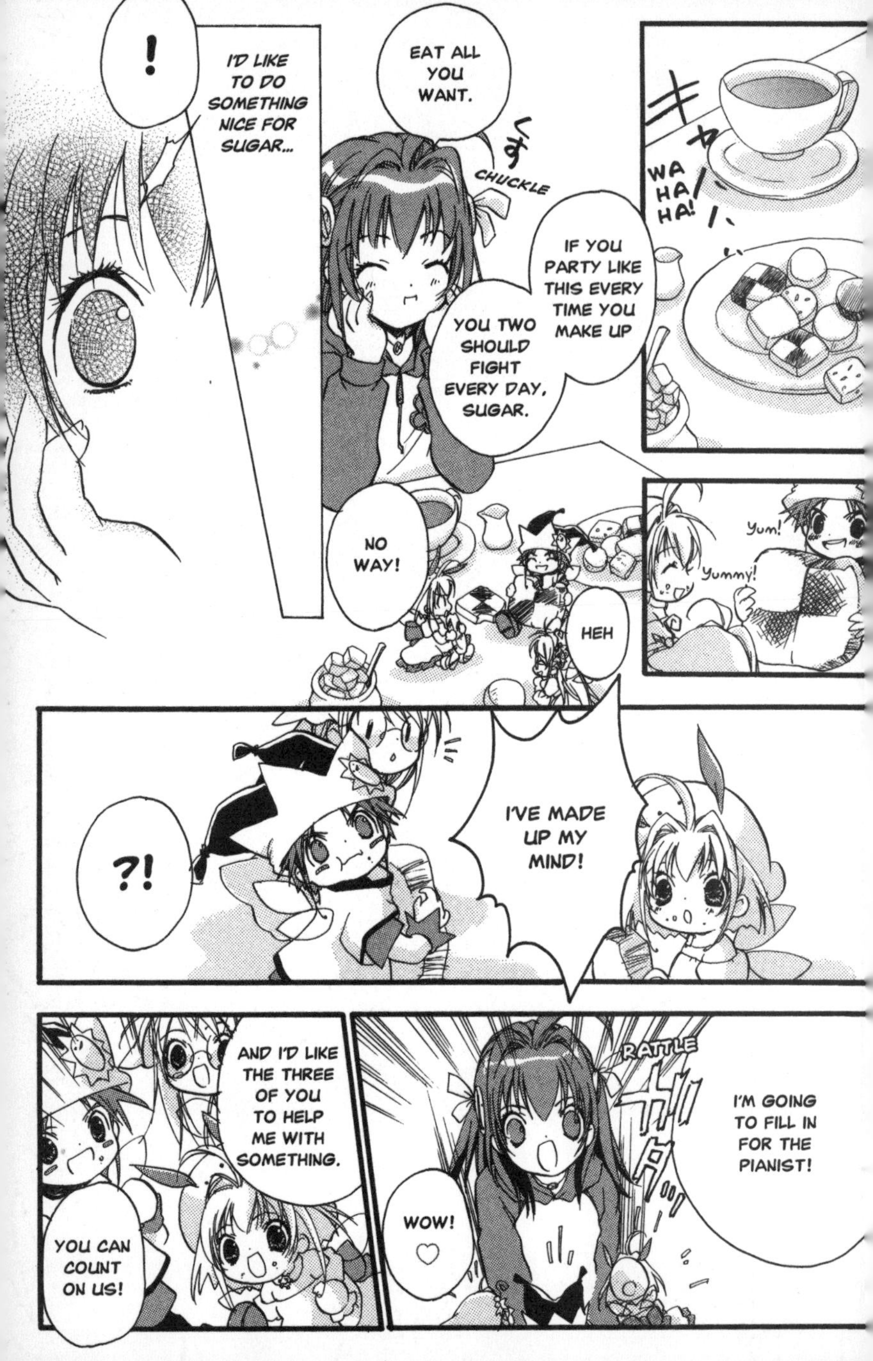
WA HA HA!
EAT ALL YOU WANT.
くす
CHUCKLE
IF YOU PARTY LIKE THIS EVERY TIME YOU MAKE UP
YOU TWO SHOULD FIGHT EVERY DAY, SUGAR.
!
I'D LIKE TO DO SOMETHING NICE FOR SUGAR...
Yum!
Yummy!
HEH
NO WAY!
I'VE MADE UP MY MIND!
?!
RATTLE
I'M GOING TO FILL IN FOR THE PIANIST!
WOW! ♡
AND I'D LIKE THE THREE OF YOU TO HELP ME WITH SOMETHING.
YOU CAN COUNT ON US!

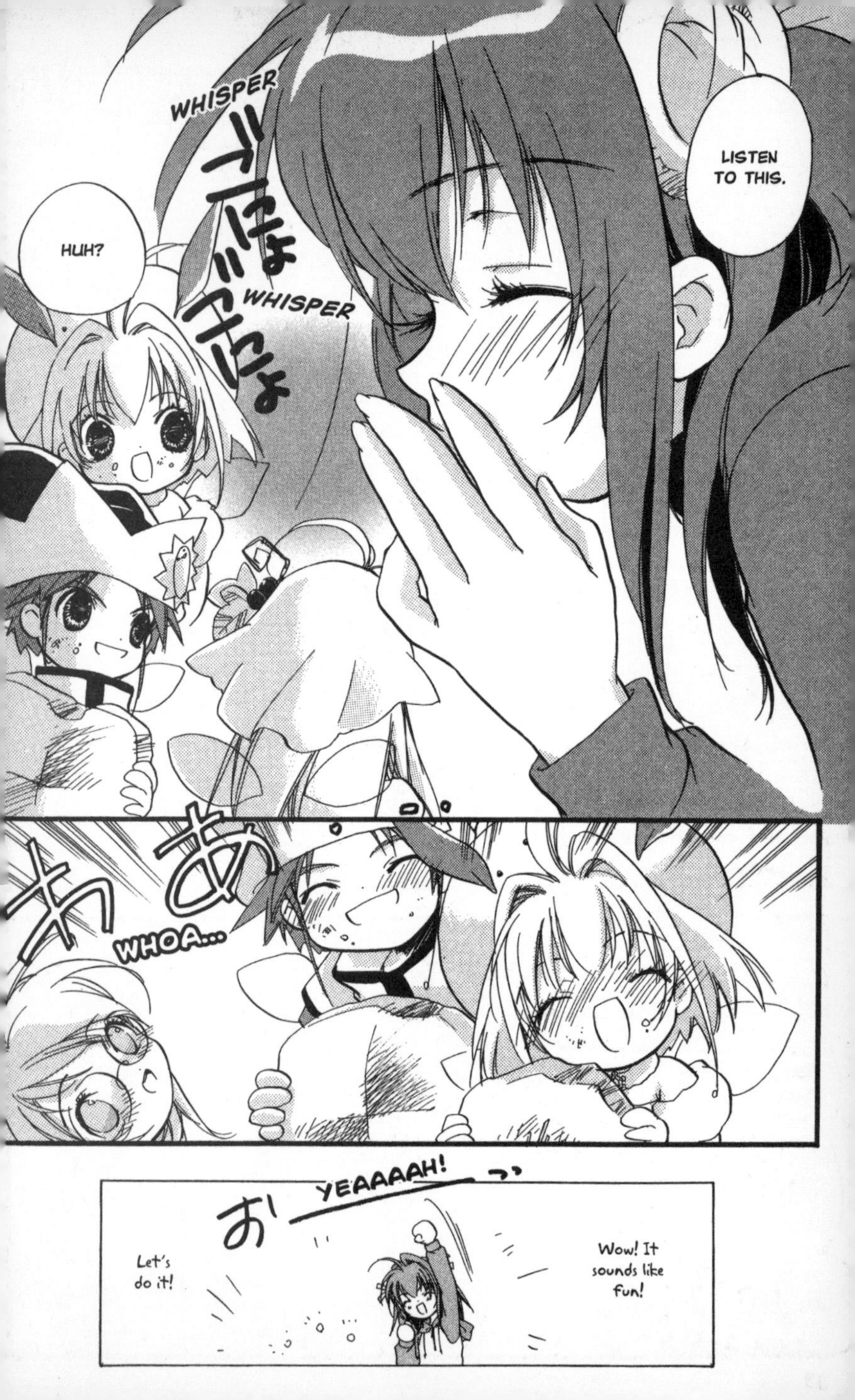

LISTEN TO THIS.
WHISPER
WHISPER
HUH?
わあ
WHOA...
YEAAAAH!
Wow! It sounds like fun!
Let's do it!

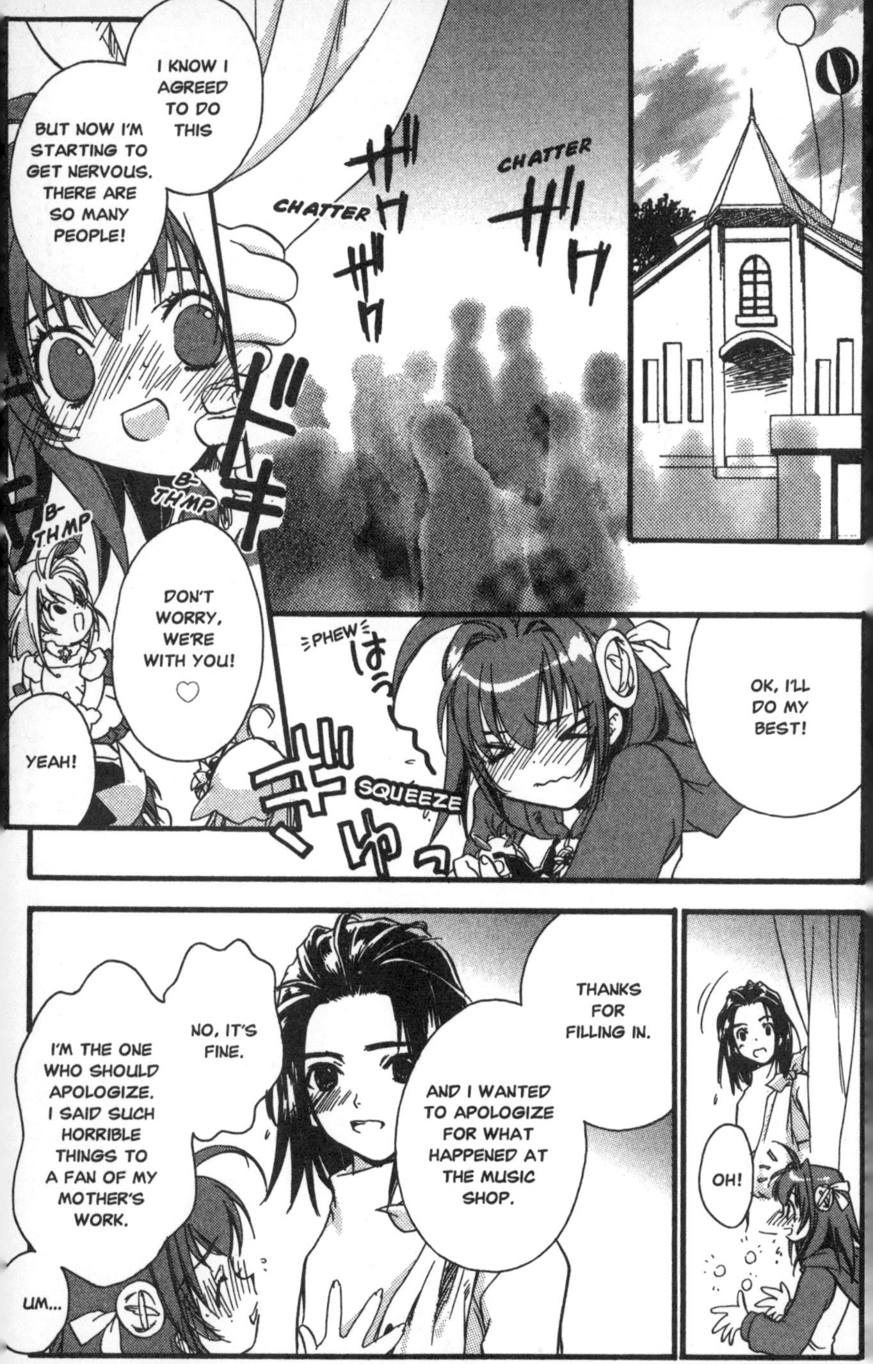
CHATTER
CHATTER
I KNOW I AGREED TO DO THIS
BUT NOW I'M STARTING TO GET NERVOUS. THERE ARE SO MANY PEOPLE!
B-THMP
B-THMP
DON'T WORRY, WE'RE WITH YOU! ♡
YEAH!
OK, I'LL DO MY BEST!
PHEW
SQUEEZE
OH!
THANKS FOR FILLING IN.
AND I WANTED TO APOLOGIZE FOR WHAT HAPPENED AT THE MUSIC SHOP.
NO, IT'S FINE.
I'M THE ONE WHO SHOULD APOLOGIZE. I SAID SUCH HORRIBLE THINGS TO A FAN OF MY MOTHER'S WORK.
UM...

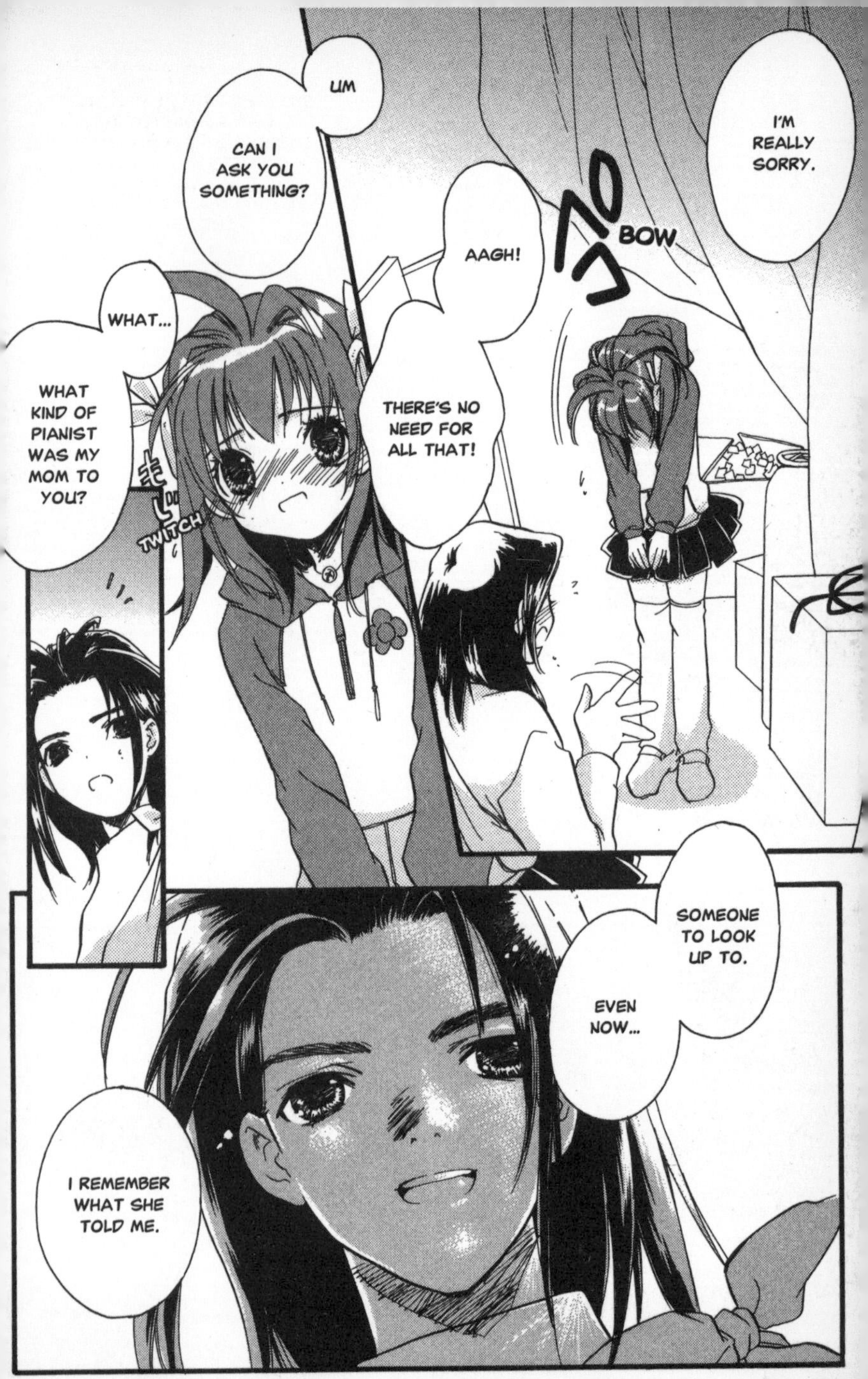
I'M REALLY SORRY.
BOW
AAGH!
THERE'S NO NEED FOR ALL THAT!
UM
CAN I ASK YOU SOMETHING?
WHAT...
WHAT KIND OF PIANIST WAS MY MOM TO YOU?
TWITCH
SOMEONE TO LOOK UP TO.
EVEN NOW...
I REMEMBER WHAT SHE TOLD ME.

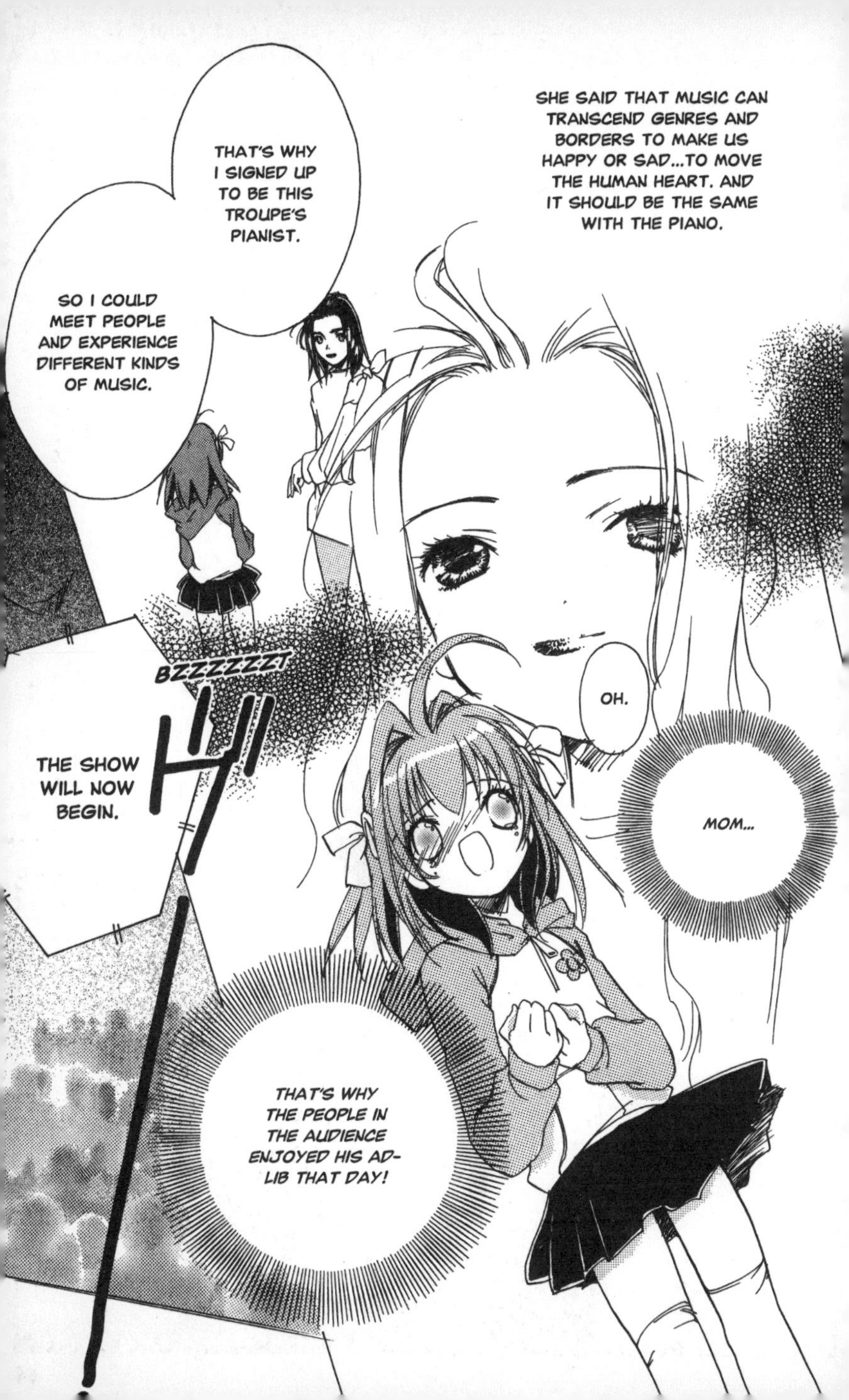
SHE SAID THAT MUSIC CAN TRANSCEND GENRES AND BORDERS TO MAKE US HAPPY OR SAD...TO MOVE THE HUMAN HEART. AND IT SHOULD BE THE SAME WITH THE PIANO.
THAT'S WHY I SIGNED UP TO BE THIS TROUPE'S PIANIST.
SO I COULD MEET PEOPLE AND EXPERIENCE DIFFERENT KINDS OF MUSIC.
OH.
MOM...
THE SHOW WILL NOW BEGIN.
BZZZZZZZT
THAT'S WHY THE PEOPLE IN THE AUDIENCE ENJOYED HIS AD-LIB THAT DAY!

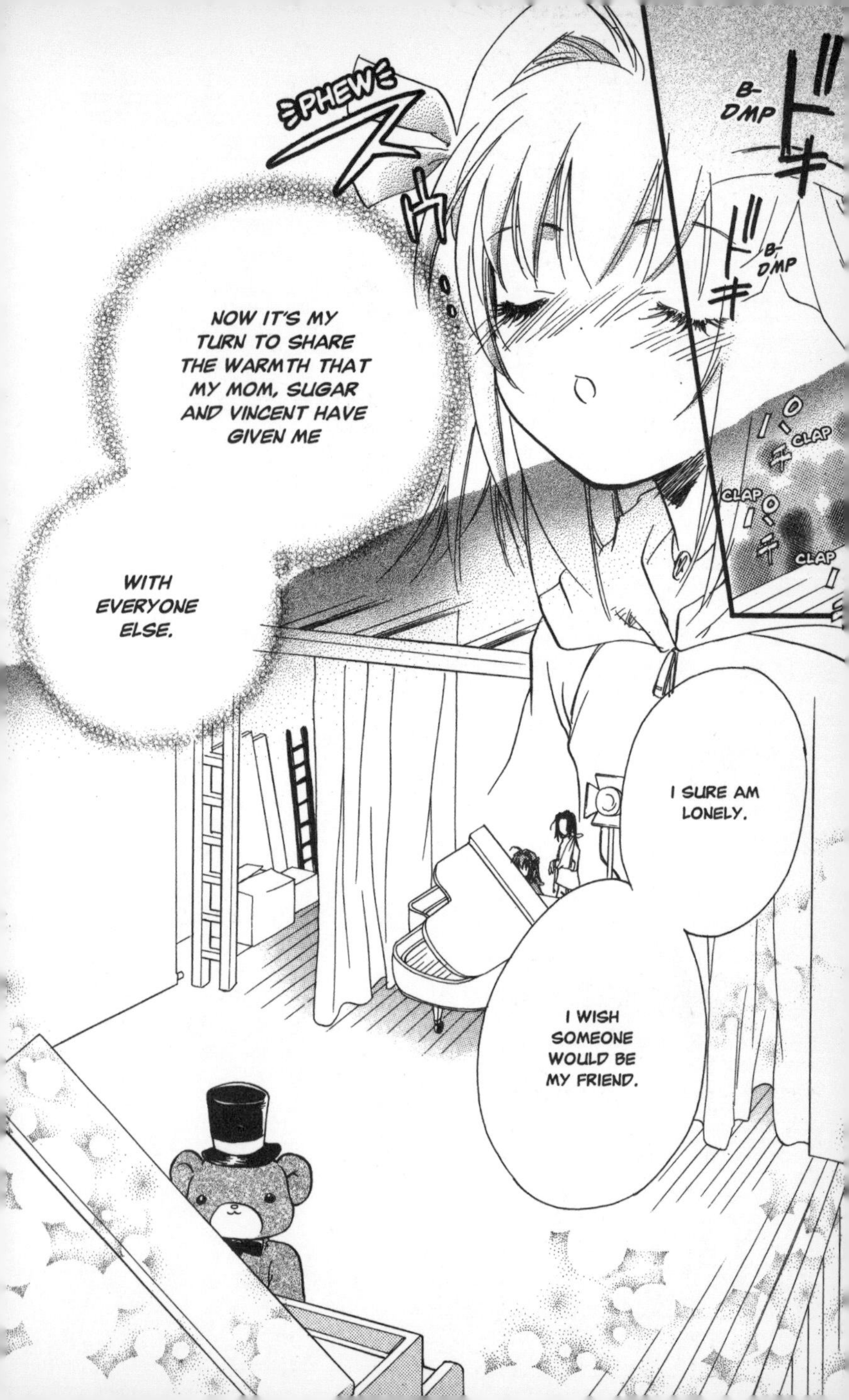
B-DMP
B-DMP
PHEW
CLAP
CLAP
CLAP
NOW IT'S MY TURN TO SHARE THE WARMTH THAT MY MOM, SUGAR AND VINCENT HAVE GIVEN ME
WITH EVERYONE ELSE.
I SURE AM LONELY.
I WISH SOMEONE WOULD BE MY FRIEND.

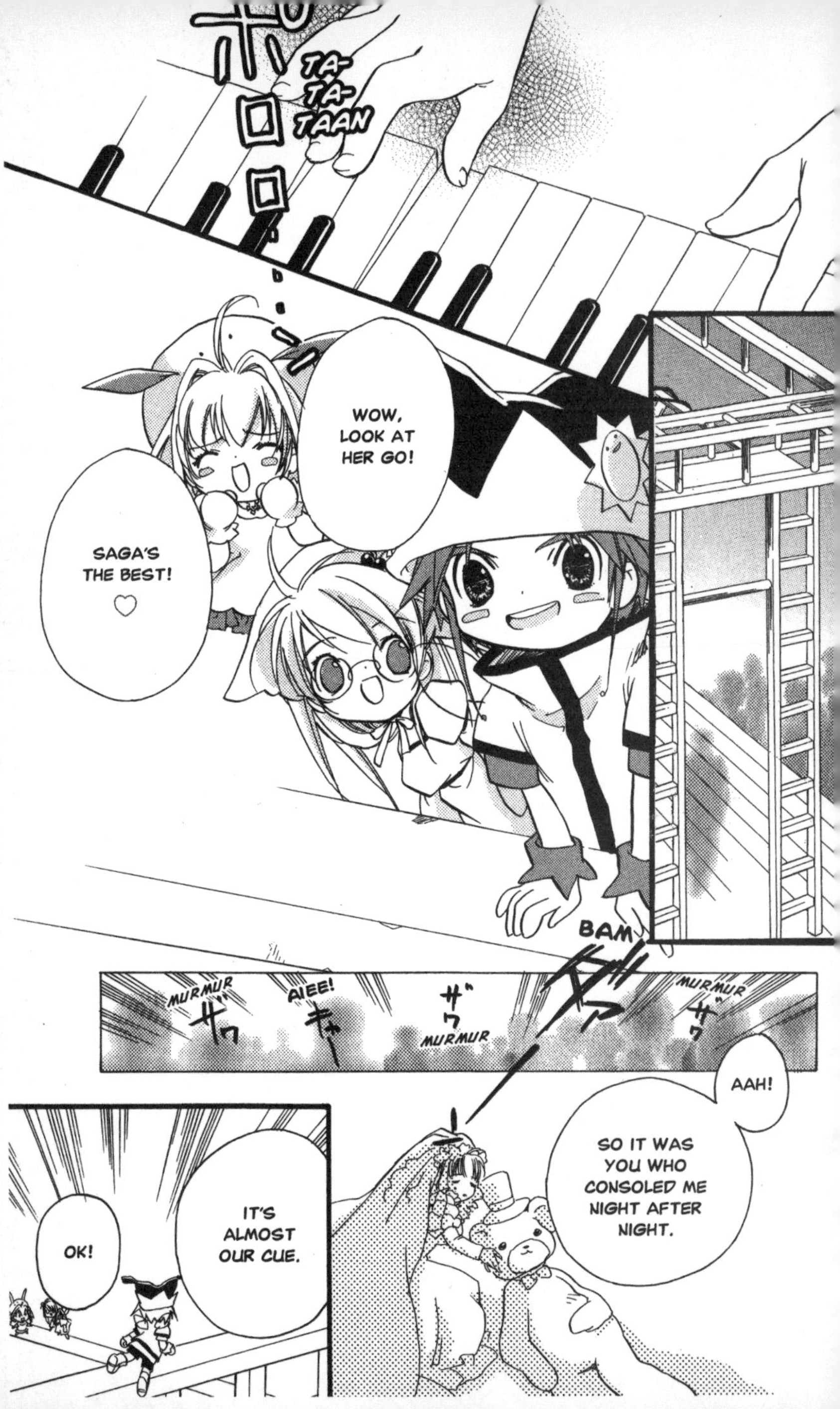
TA-TA-TAAN
WOW, LOOK AT HER GO!
SAGA'S THE BEST! ♡
BAM
MURMUR
MURMUR
AIEE!
MURMUR
AAH!
SO IT WAS YOU WHO CONSOLED ME NIGHT AFTER NIGHT.
IT'S ALMOST OUR CUE.
OK!

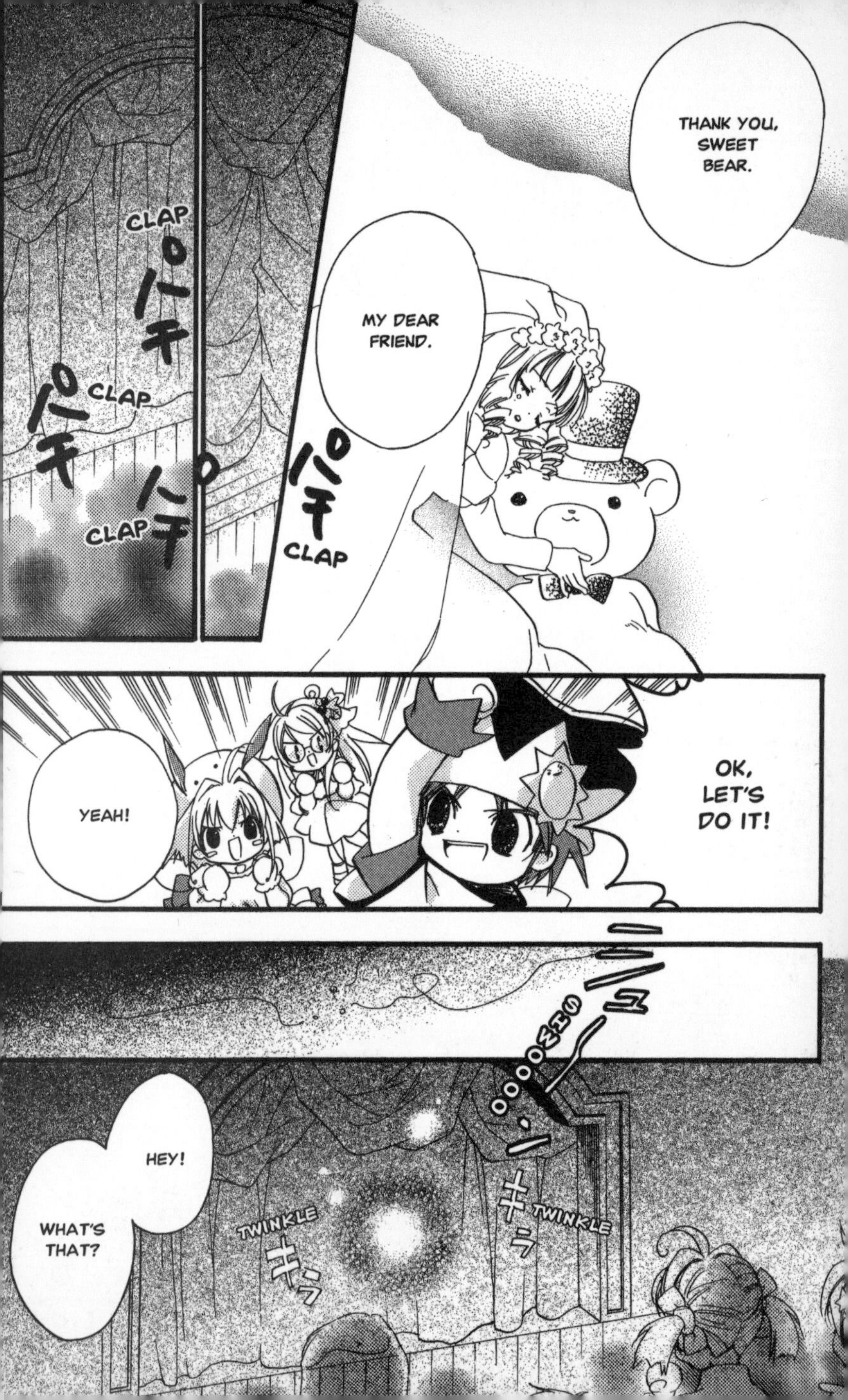
THANK YOU, SWEET BEAR.
MY DEAR FRIEND.
パチ
CLAP
パチ
CLAP
パチ
CLAP
パチ
CLAP
OK, LET'S DO IT!
YEAH!
SHOOOOO
キラ
TWINKLE
キラ
TWINKLE
HEY!
WHAT'S THAT?

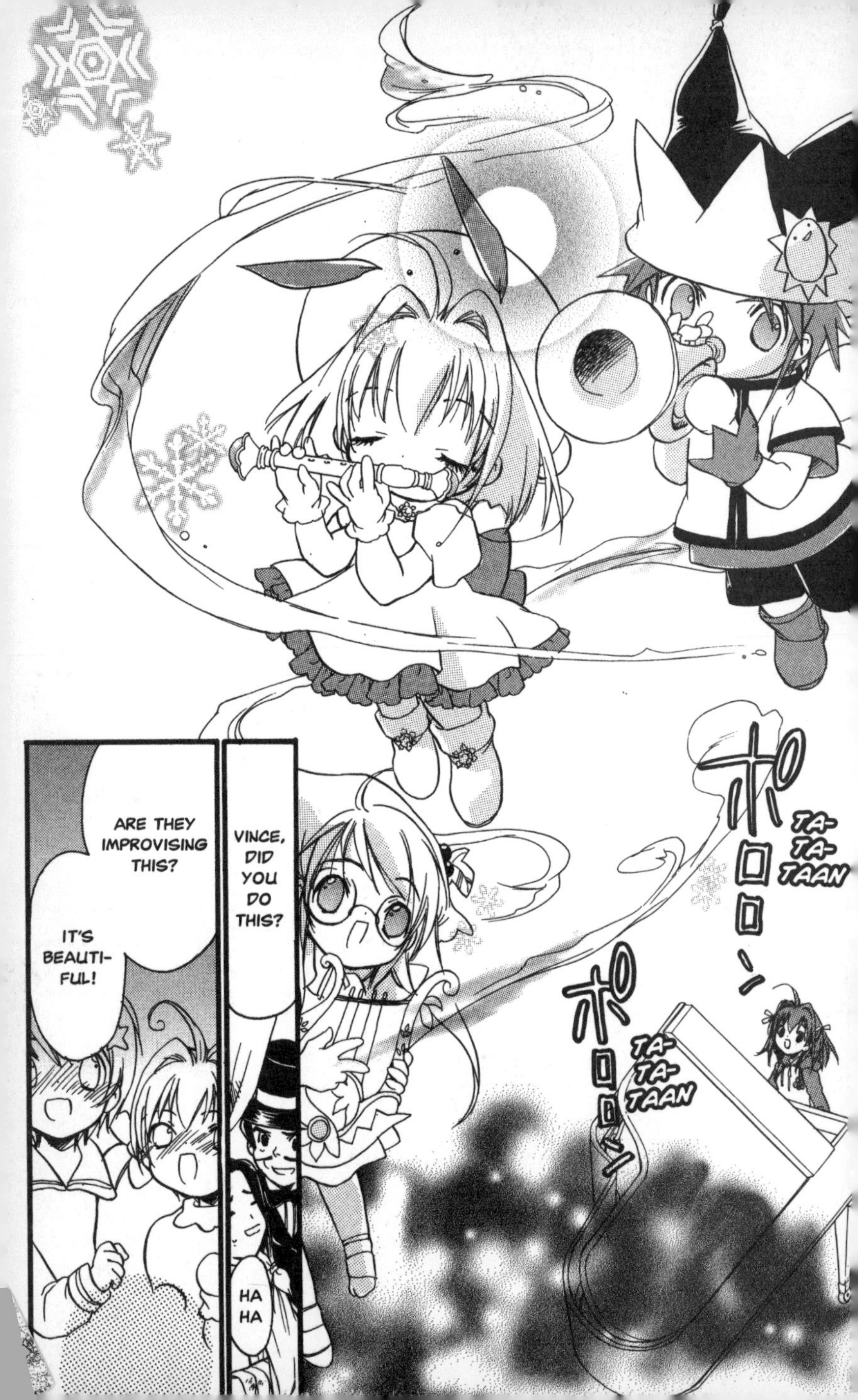
ポロローン
TA-TA-TAAN
ポロローン
TA-TA-TAAN
VINCE, DID YOU DO THIS?
HA HA
ARE THEY IMPROVISING THIS?
IT'S BEAUTI-FUL!

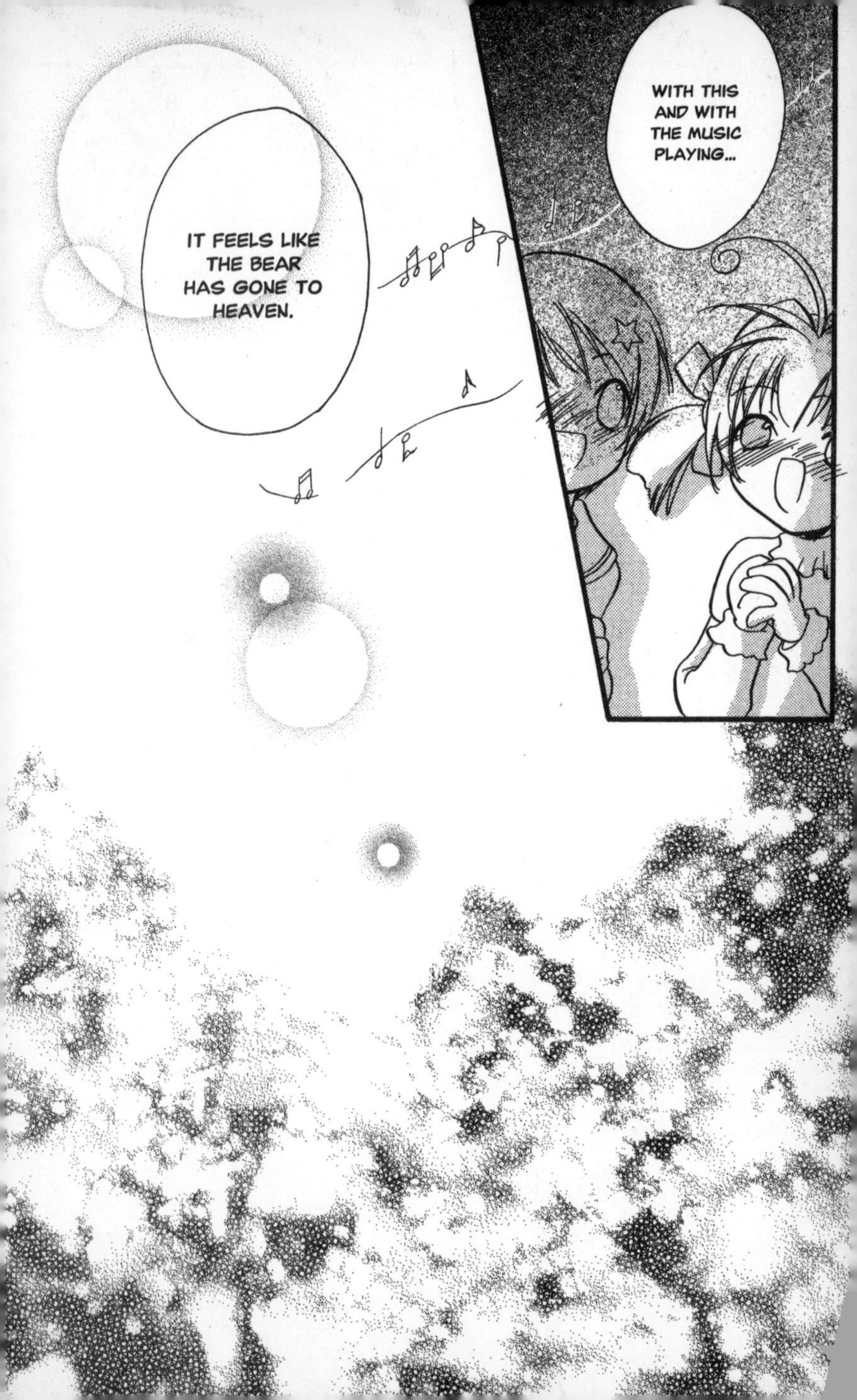
WITH THIS AND WITH THE MUSIC PLAYING...
IT FEELS LIKE THE BEAR HAS GONE TO HEAVEN.

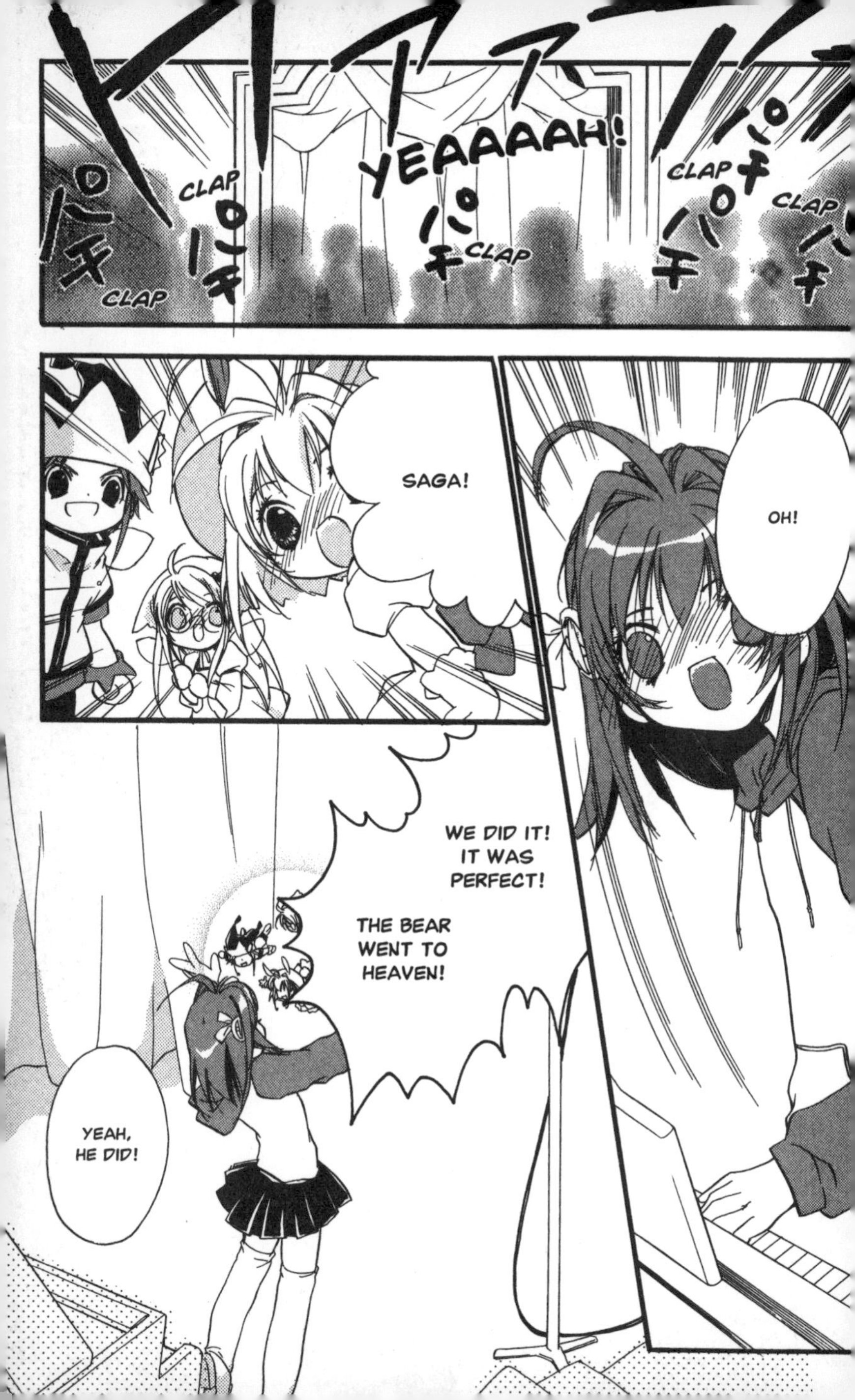
パチ
CLAP
パチ
CLAP
パチ
CLAP
YEAAAAH!
パチ
CLAP
パチ
CLAP
パチ
CLAP
OH!
SAGA!
WE DID IT! IT WAS PERFECT!
THE BEAR WENT TO HEAVEN!
YEAH, HE DID!

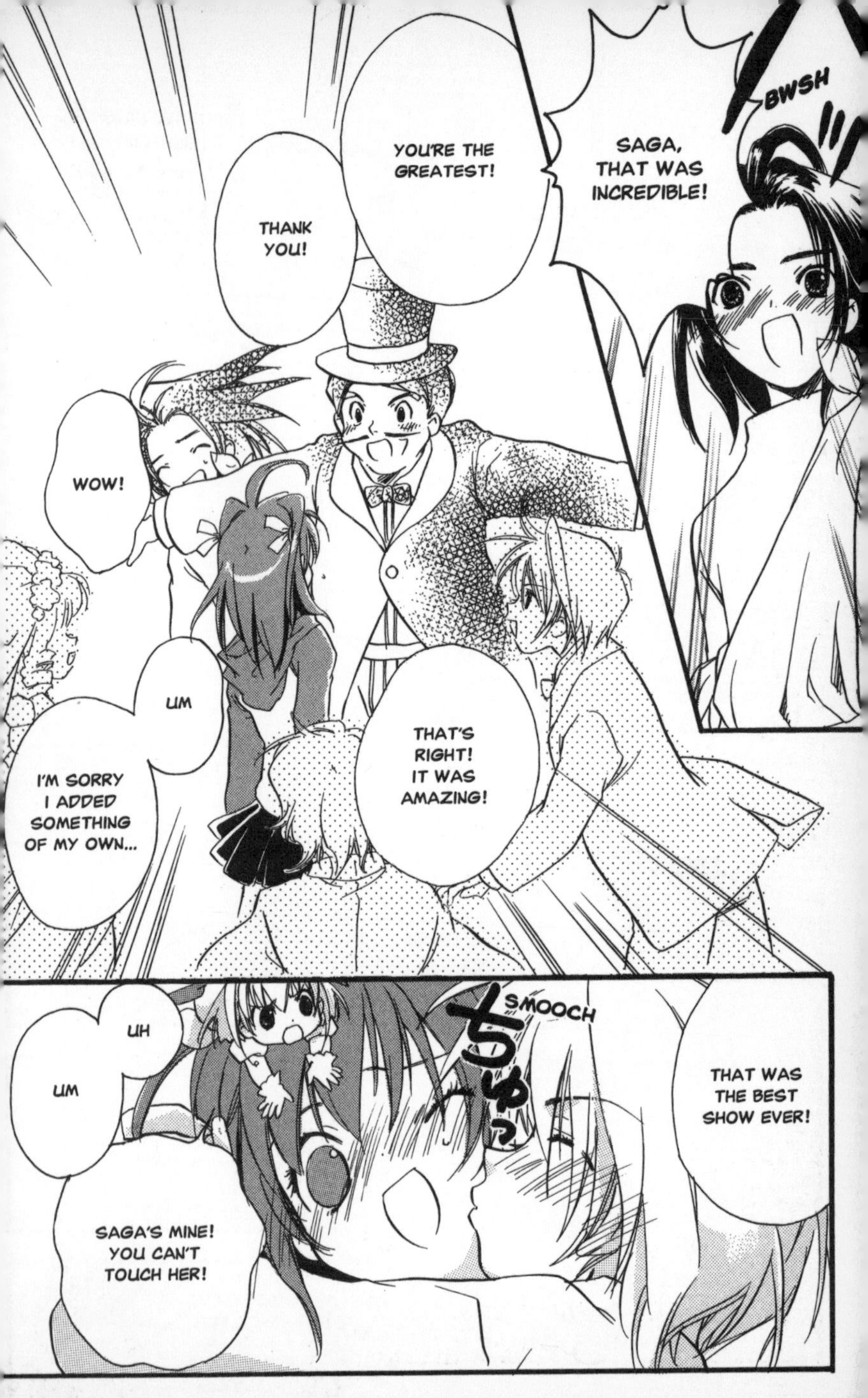
BWSH
SAGA, THAT WAS INCREDIBLE!
YOU'RE THE GREATEST!
THANK YOU!
WOW!
THAT'S RIGHT! IT WAS AMAZING!
UM
I'M SORRY I ADDED SOMETHING OF MY OWN...
THAT WAS THE BEST SHOW EVER!
ちゅっ
SMOOCH
UH
UM
SAGA'S MINE! YOU CAN'T TOUCH HER!

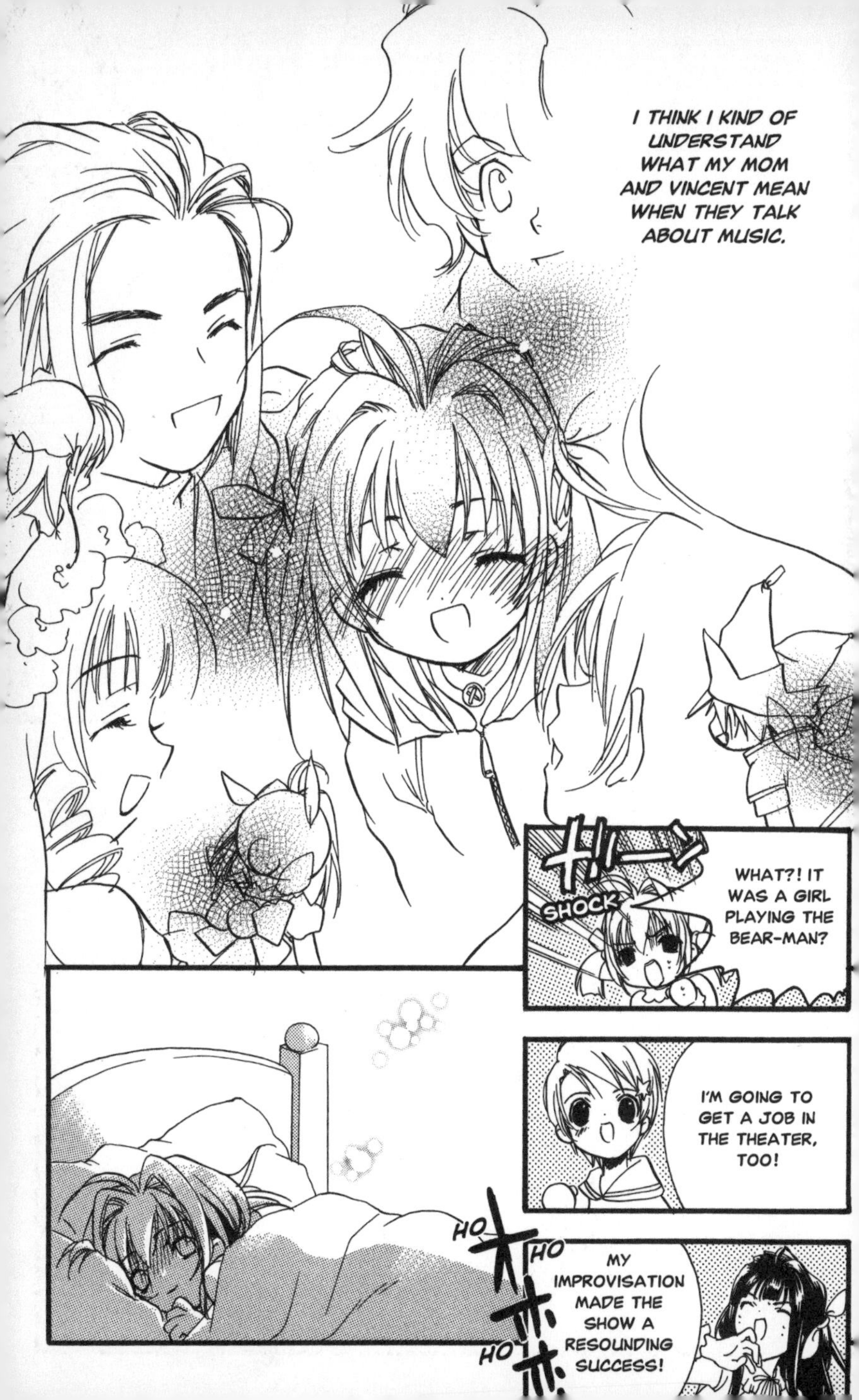
I THINK I KIND OF UNDERSTAND WHAT MY MOM AND VINCENT MEAN WHEN THEY TALK ABOUT MUSIC.
SHOCK
WHAT?! IT WAS A GIRL PLAYING THE BEAR-MAN?
I'M GOING TO GET A JOB IN THE THEATER, TOO!
HO HO HO
MY IMPROVISATION MADE THE SHOW A RESOUNDING SUCCESS!

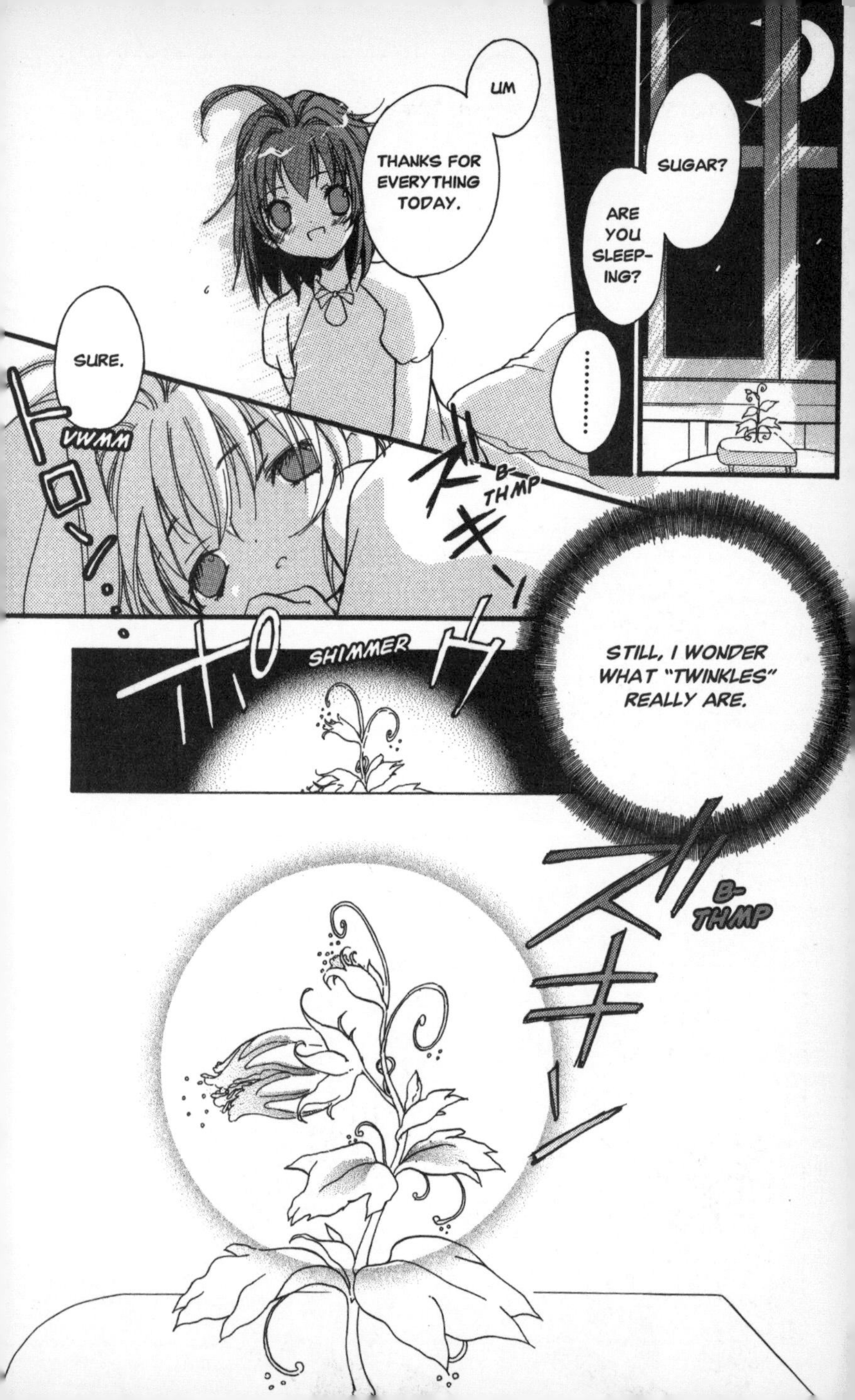
SUGAR?
ARE YOU SLEEP-ING?
UM
THANKS FOR EVERYTHING TODAY.
......
SURE.
VWMM
B-THMP
STILL, I WONDER WHAT "TWINKLES" REALLY ARE.
SHIMMER
B-THMP

CHAPTER 8 I've Decided

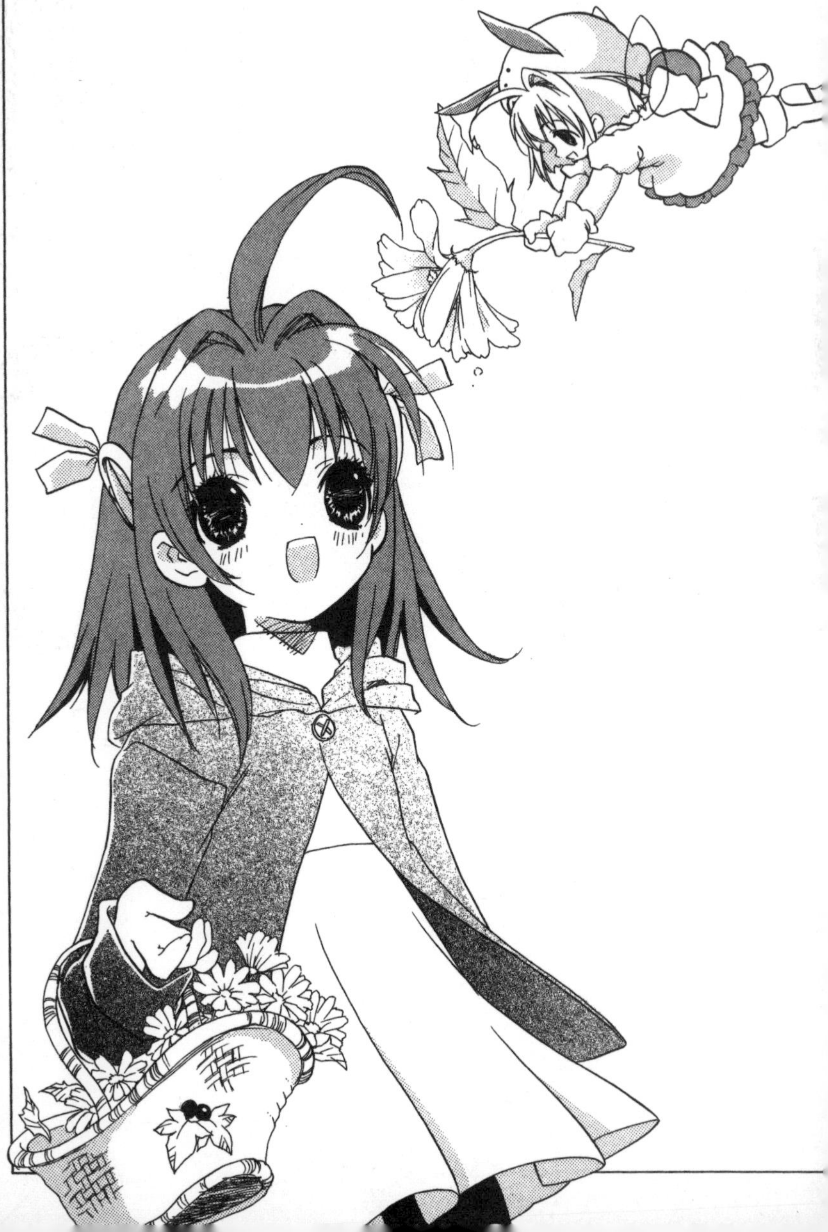

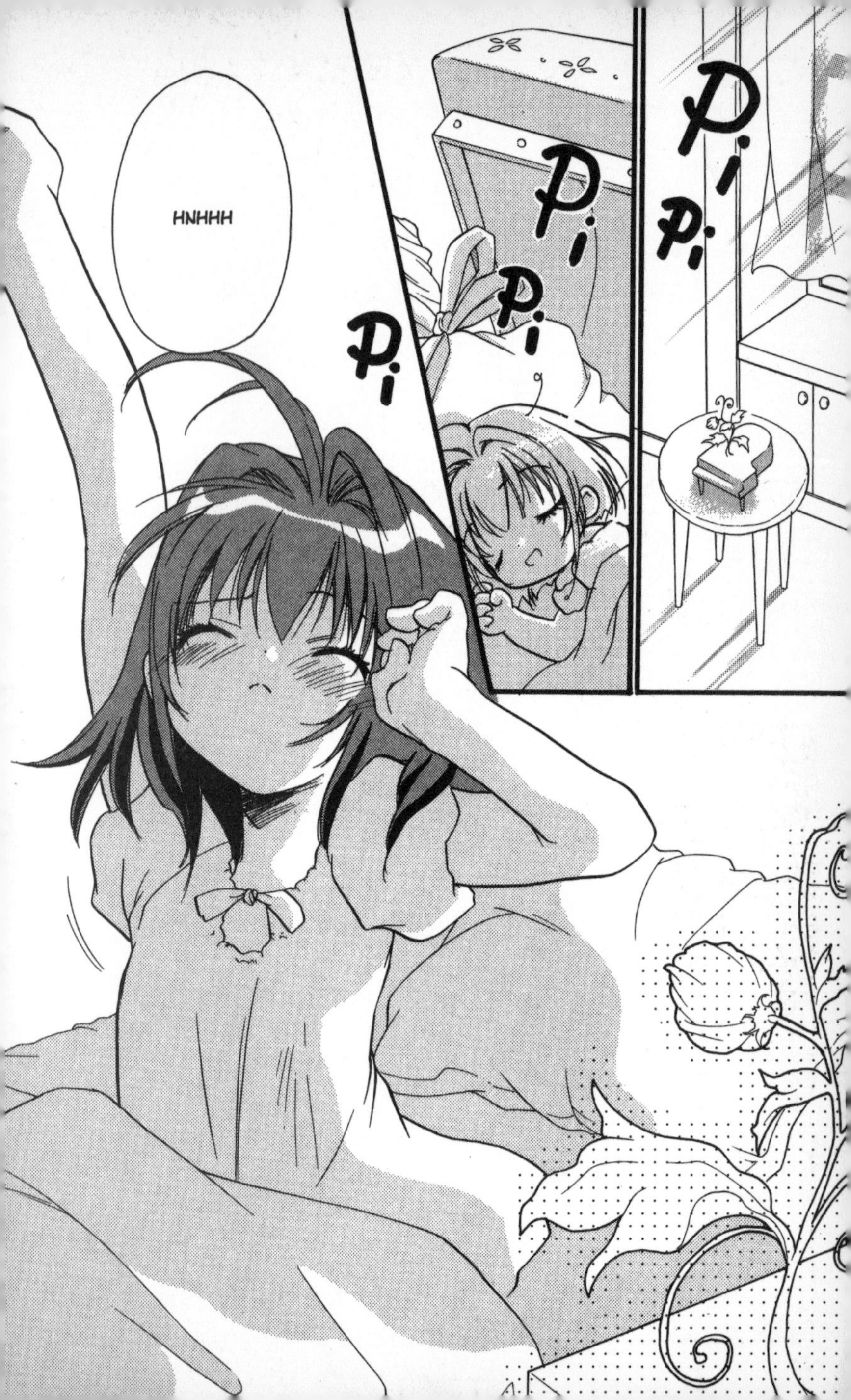
Pi
Pi
Pi
Pi
Pi
HNHHH

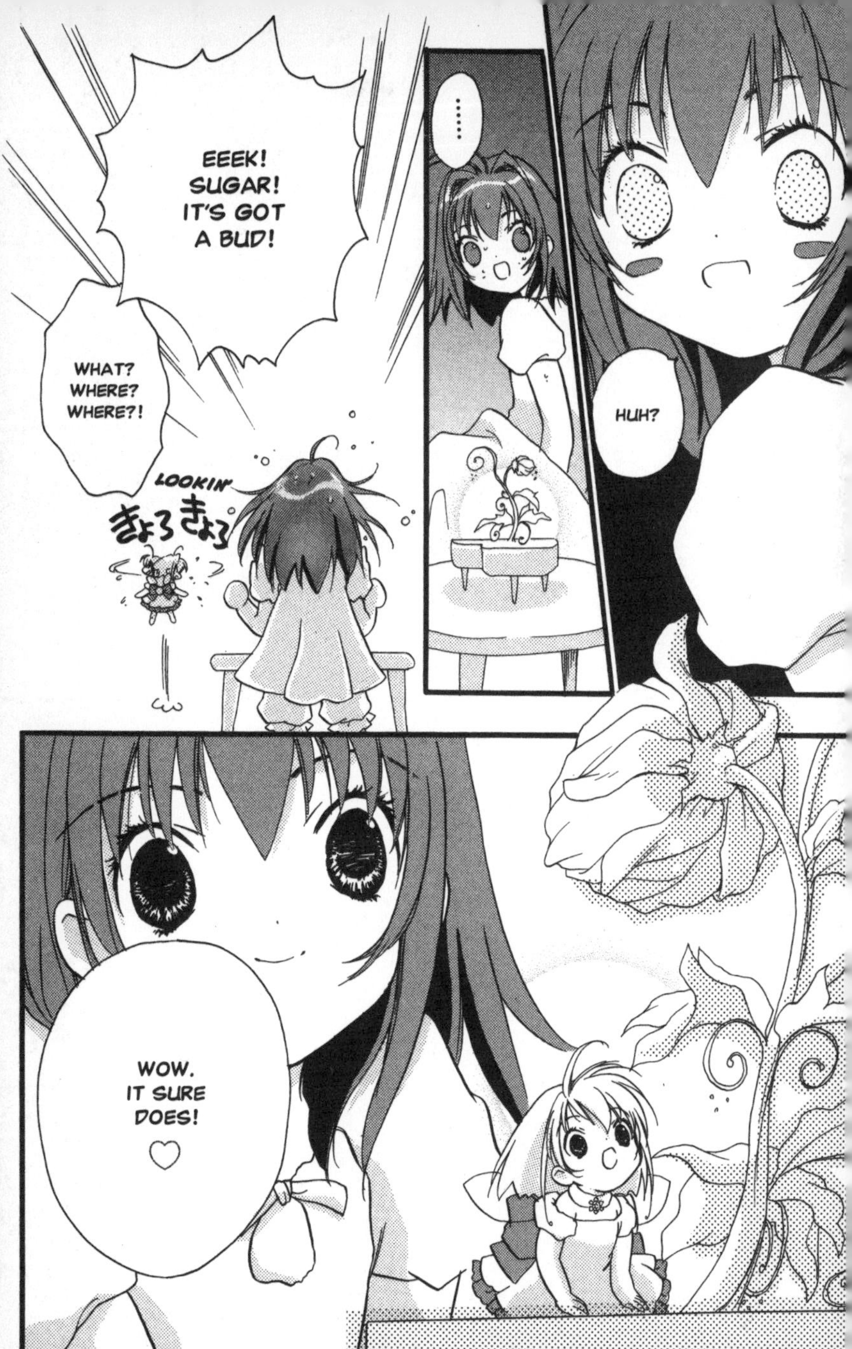
HUH?
......
EEEK! SUGAR! IT'S GOT A BUD!
WHAT? WHERE? WHERE?!
LOOKIN'
きょろきょろ
WOW. IT SURE DOES! ♡

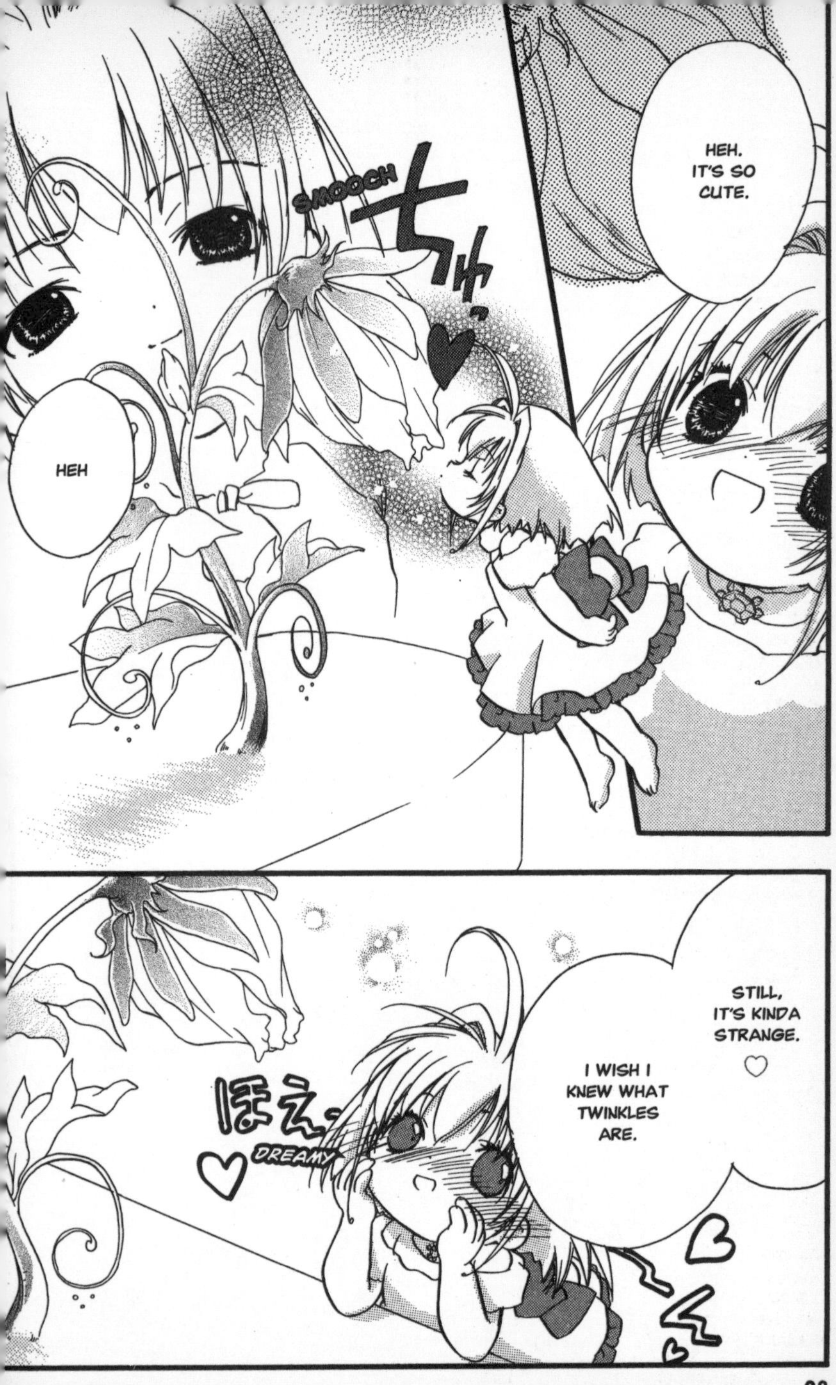
HEH. IT'S SO CUTE.
SMOOCH
ちゅ
HEH
STILL, IT'S KINDA STRANGE.
I WISH I KNEW WHAT TWINKLES ARE.
ほえ
DREAMY

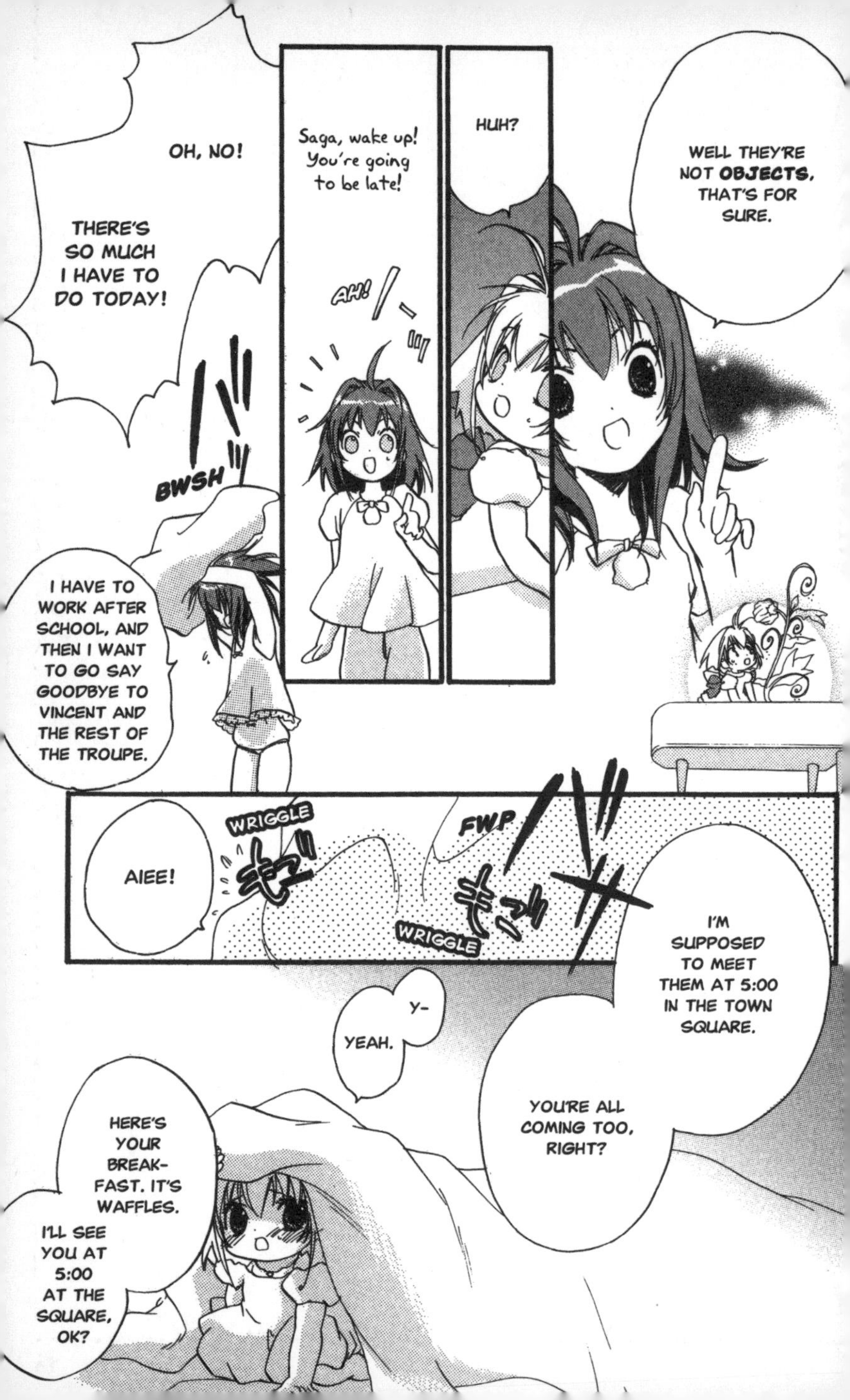
WELL THEY'RE NOT **OBJECTS**, THAT'S FOR SURE.
HUH?
Saga, wake up! You're going to be late!
AH!
OH, NO!
THERE'S SO MUCH I HAVE TO DO TODAY!
BWSH
I HAVE TO WORK AFTER SCHOOL, AND THEN I WANT TO GO SAY GOODBYE TO VINCENT AND THE REST OF THE TROUPE.
FWP
WRIGGLE
WRIGGLE
AIEE!
I'M SUPPOSED TO MEET THEM AT 5:00 IN THE TOWN SQUARE.
YOU'RE ALL COMING TOO, RIGHT?
Y- YEAH.
HERE'S YOUR BREAK-FAST. IT'S WAFFLES.
I'LL SEE YOU AT 5:00 AT THE SQUARE, OK?

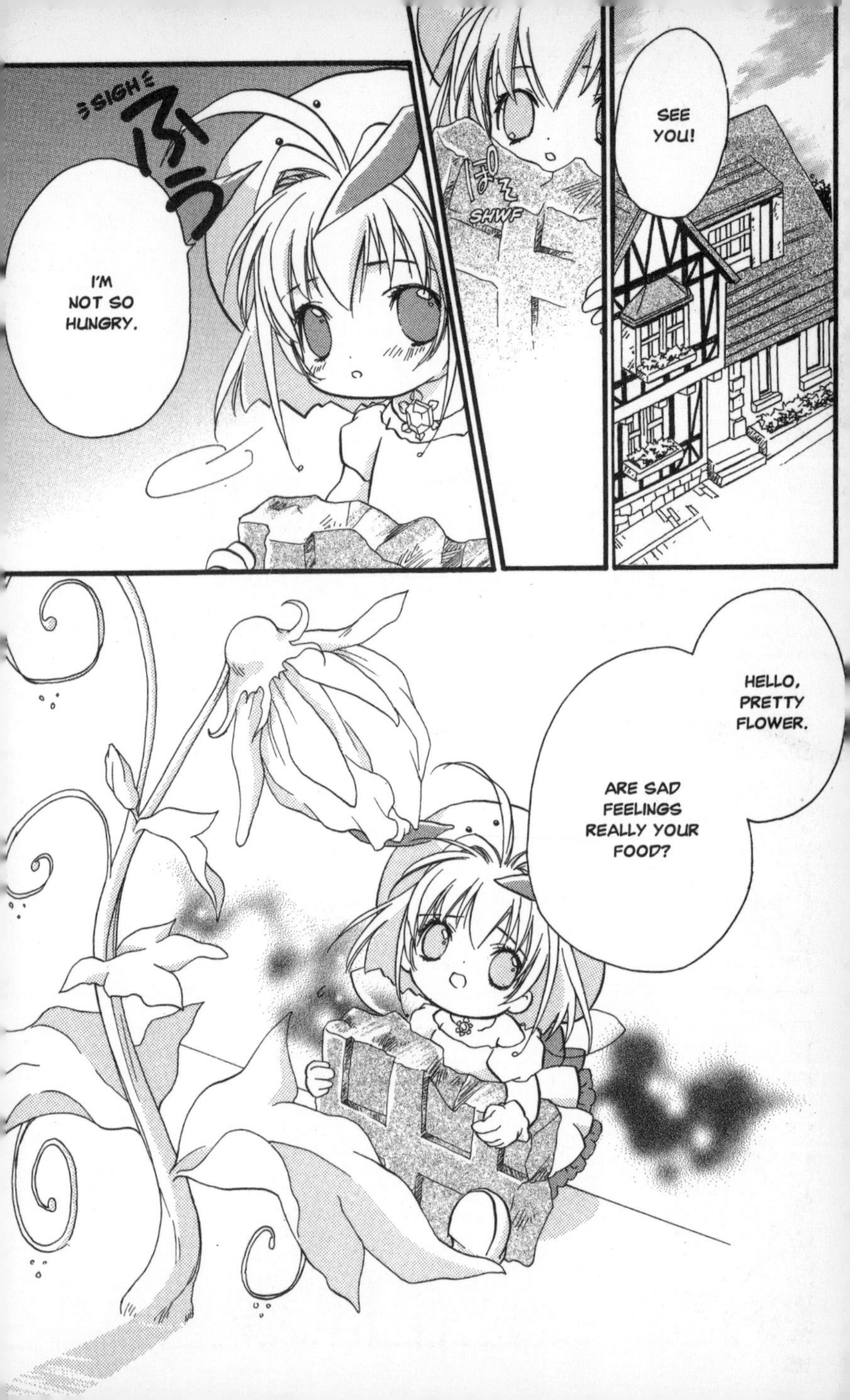
SEE YOU!
ぽそ
SHWF
ふう
SIGH
I'M NOT SO HUNGRY.
HELLO, PRETTY FLOWER.
ARE SAD FEELINGS REALLY YOUR FOOD?

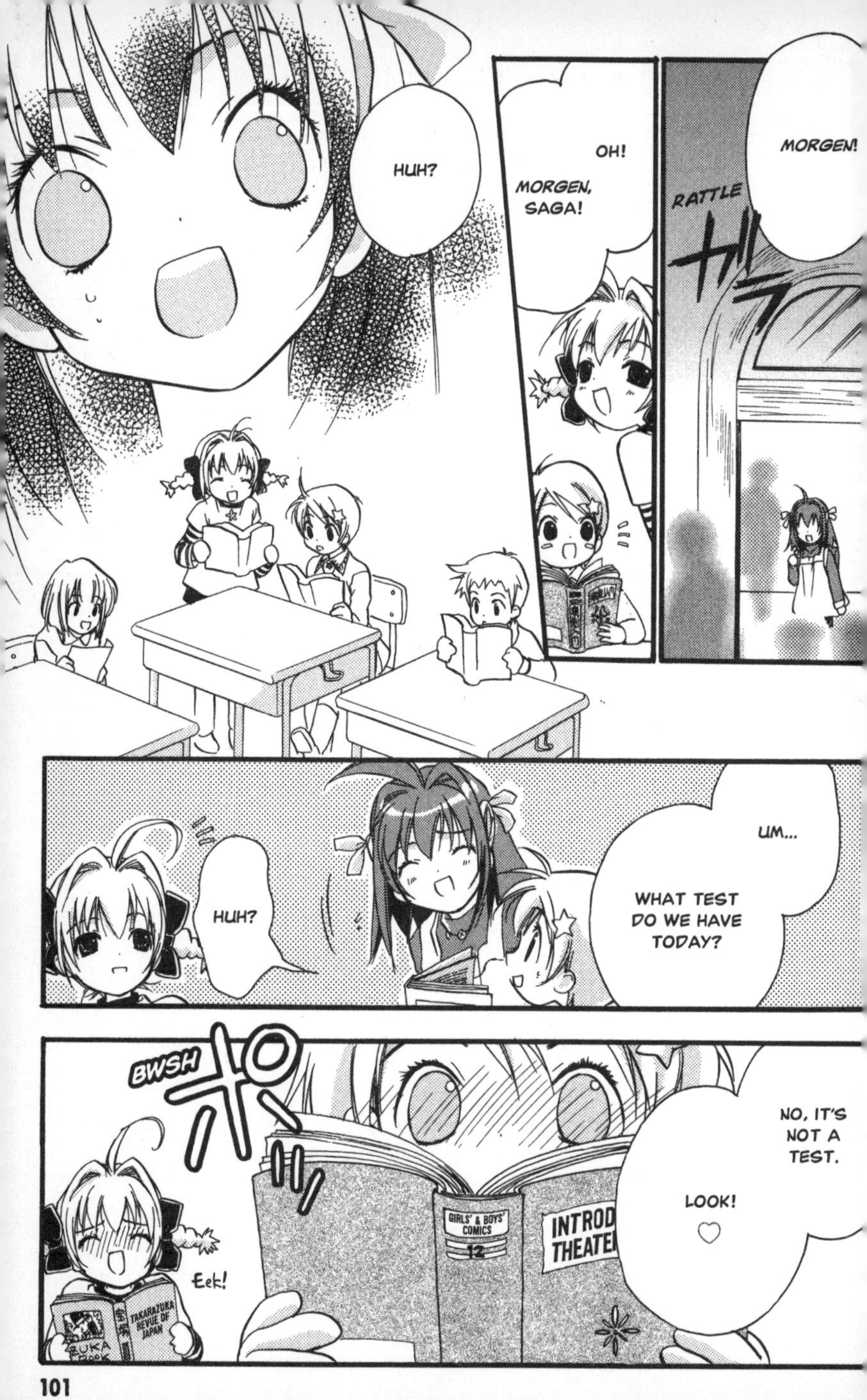
MORGEN!
RATTLE
OH!
MORGEN, SAGA!
HUH?
UM...
WHAT TEST DO WE HAVE TODAY?
HUH?
NO, IT'S NOT A TEST.
LOOK! ♡
GIRLS' & BOYS' COMICS 12
INTROD THEATER
BWSH
Eek!
TAKARAZUKA REVUE OF JAPAN

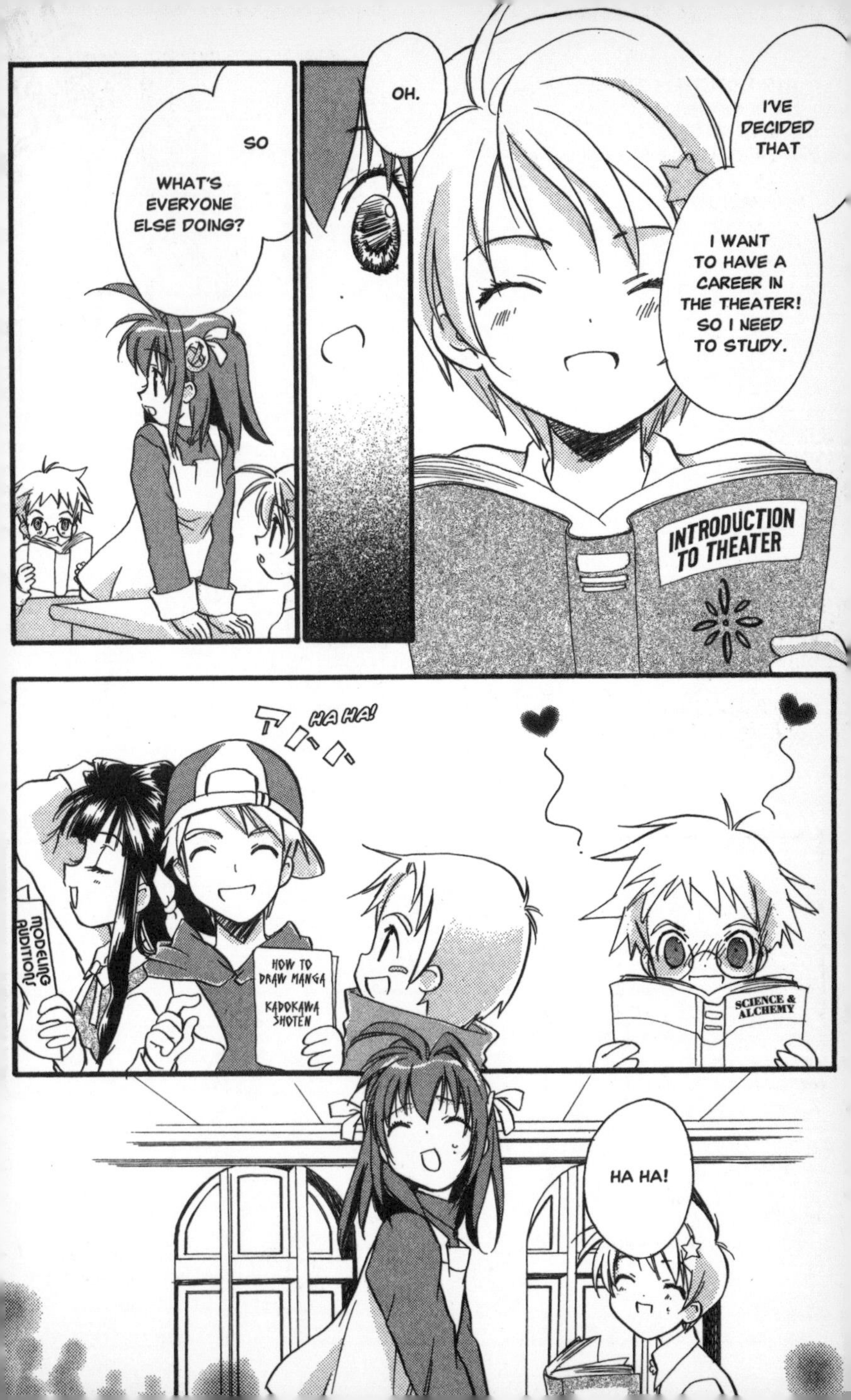
SO
WHAT'S EVERYONE ELSE DOING?
OH.
I'VE DECIDED THAT
I WANT TO HAVE A CAREER IN THE THEATER! SO I NEED TO STUDY.
INTRODUCTION TO THEATER
HA HA!
MODELING AUDITION!
HOW TO DRAW MANGA
KADOKAWA SHOTEN
SCIENCE & ALCHEMY
HA HA!

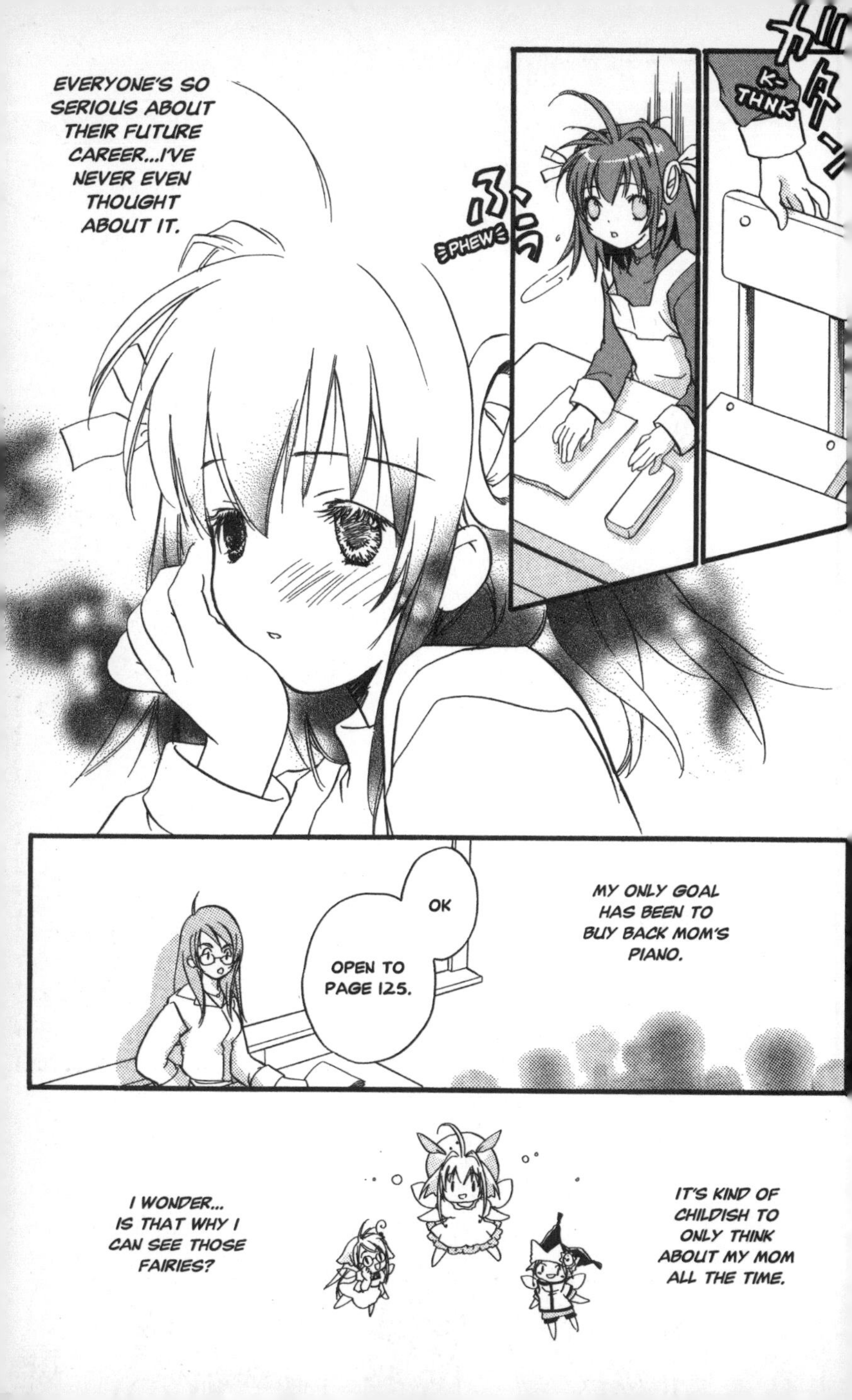
K-THNK
ふぅ
PHEW
EVERYONE'S SO SERIOUS ABOUT THEIR FUTURE CAREER...I'VE NEVER EVEN THOUGHT ABOUT IT.
MY ONLY GOAL HAS BEEN TO BUY BACK MOM'S PIANO.
OK
OPEN TO PAGE 125.
IT'S KIND OF CHILDISH TO ONLY THINK ABOUT MY MOM ALL THE TIME.
I WONDER... IS THAT WHY I CAN SEE THOSE FAIRIES?

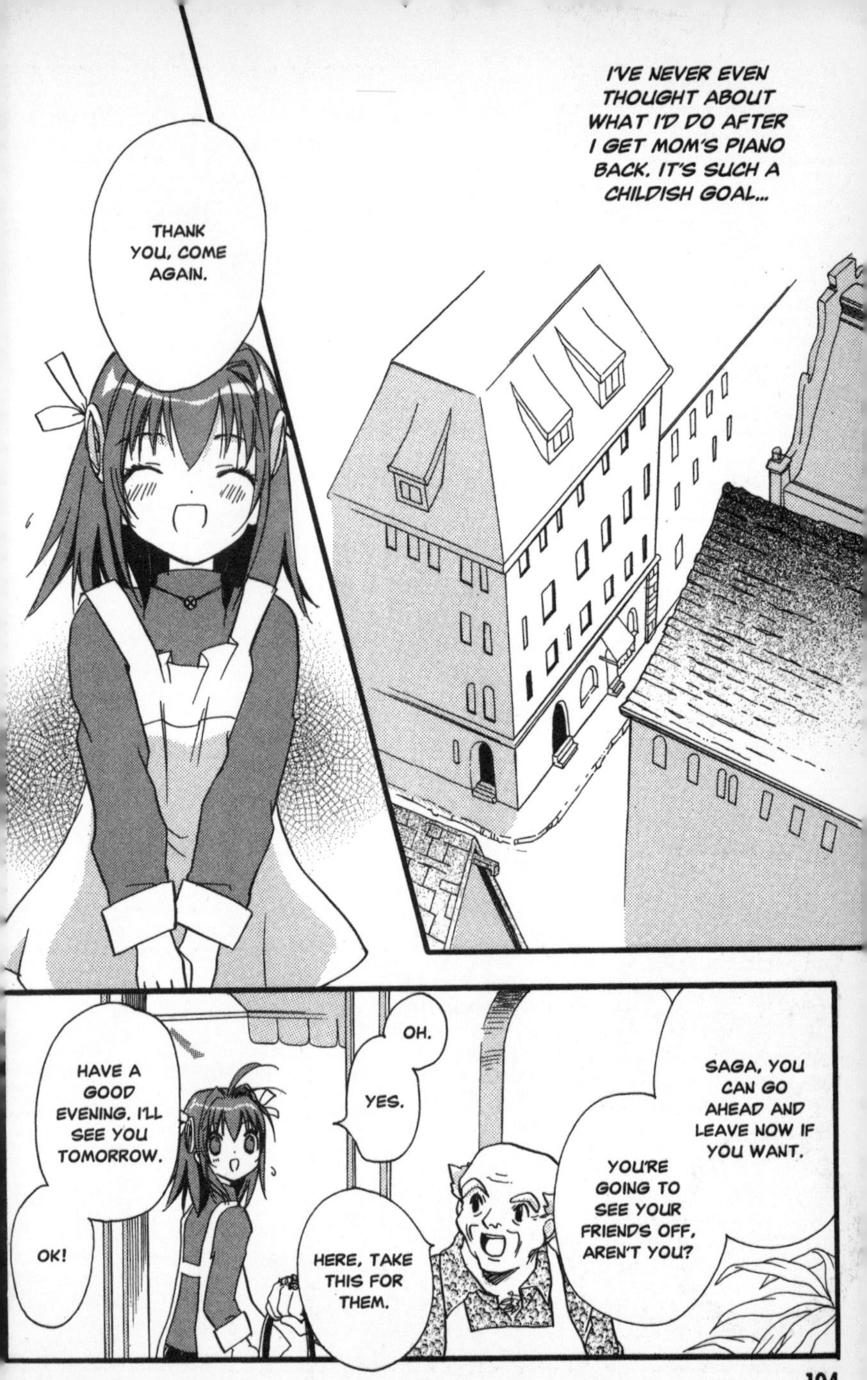
I'VE NEVER EVEN THOUGHT ABOUT WHAT I'D DO AFTER I GET MOM'S PIANO BACK. IT'S SUCH A CHILDISH GOAL...
THANK YOU, COME AGAIN.
SAGA, YOU CAN GO AHEAD AND LEAVE NOW IF YOU WANT.
YOU'RE GOING TO SEE YOUR FRIENDS OFF, AREN'T YOU?
OH.
YES.
HERE, TAKE THIS FOR THEM.
HAVE A GOOD EVENING. I'LL SEE YOU TOMORROW.
OK!

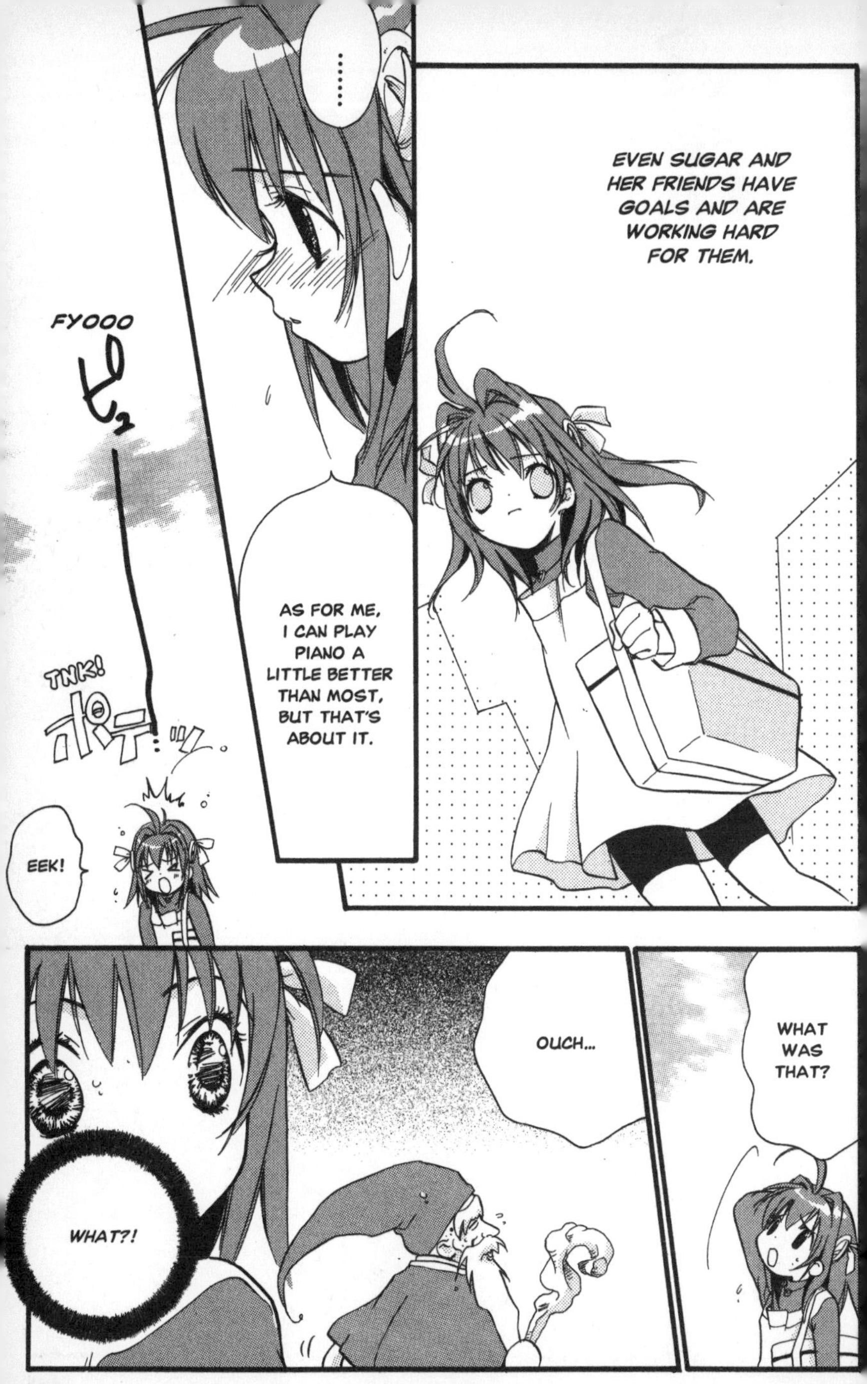
......
EVEN SUGAR AND HER FRIENDS HAVE GOALS AND ARE WORKING HARD FOR THEM.
AS FOR ME, I CAN PLAY PIANO A LITTLE BETTER THAN MOST, BUT THAT'S ABOUT IT.
FYOOO
TNK!
EEK!
WHAT WAS THAT?
OUCH...
WHAT?!

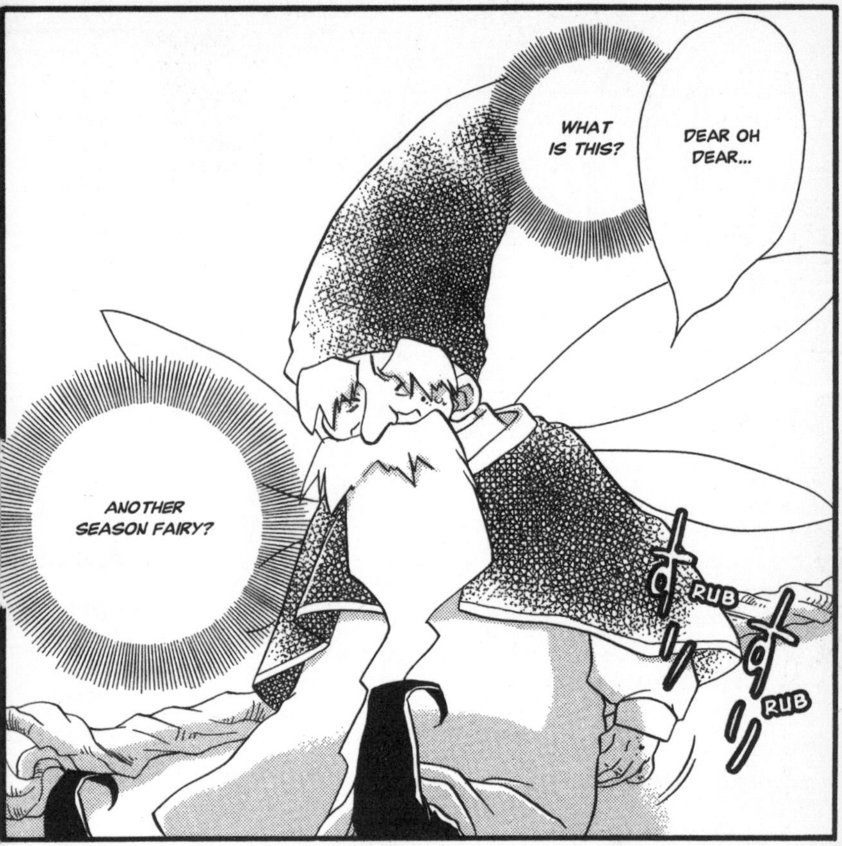
DEAR OH DEAR...
WHAT IS THIS?
ANOTHER SEASON FAIRY?
RUB
RUB

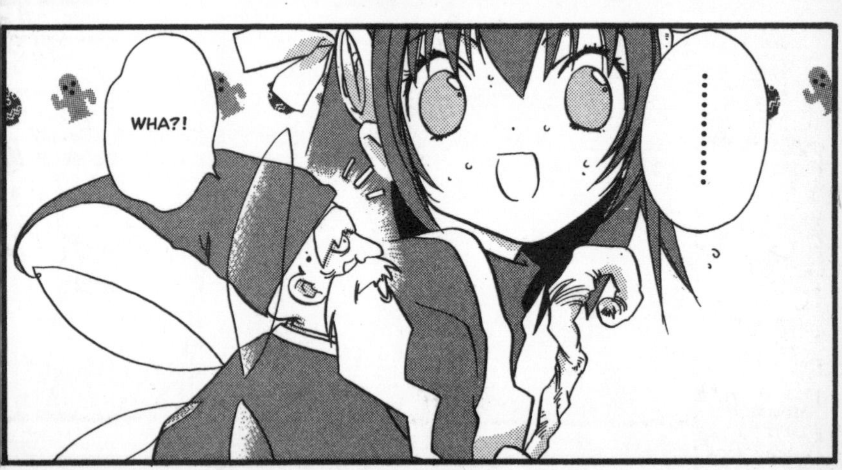
....
WHA?!

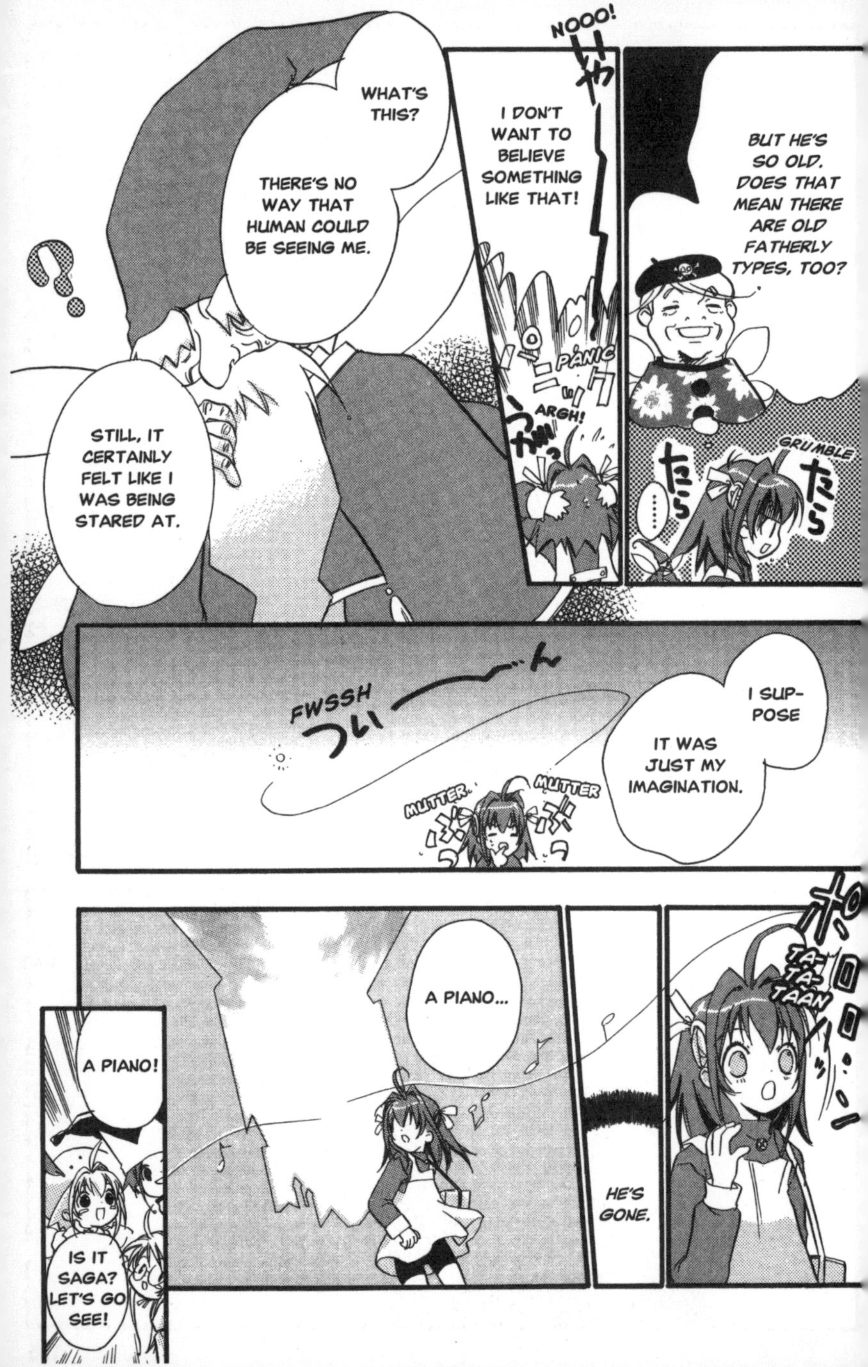
BUT HE'S SO OLD. DOES THAT MEAN THERE ARE OLD FATHERLY TYPES, TOO?
GRUMBLE
...
NOOO!
I DON'T WANT TO BELIEVE SOMETHING LIKE THAT!
PANIC
ARGH!
WHAT'S THIS?
THERE'S NO WAY THAT HUMAN COULD BE SEEING ME.
STILL, IT CERTAINLY FELT LIKE I WAS BEING STARED AT.
I SUP- POSE
IT WAS JUST MY IMAGINATION.
MUTTER
MUTTER
FWSSH
TA-TA-TAAN
HE'S GONE.
A PIANO...
A PIANO!
IS IT SAGA? LET'S GO SEE!

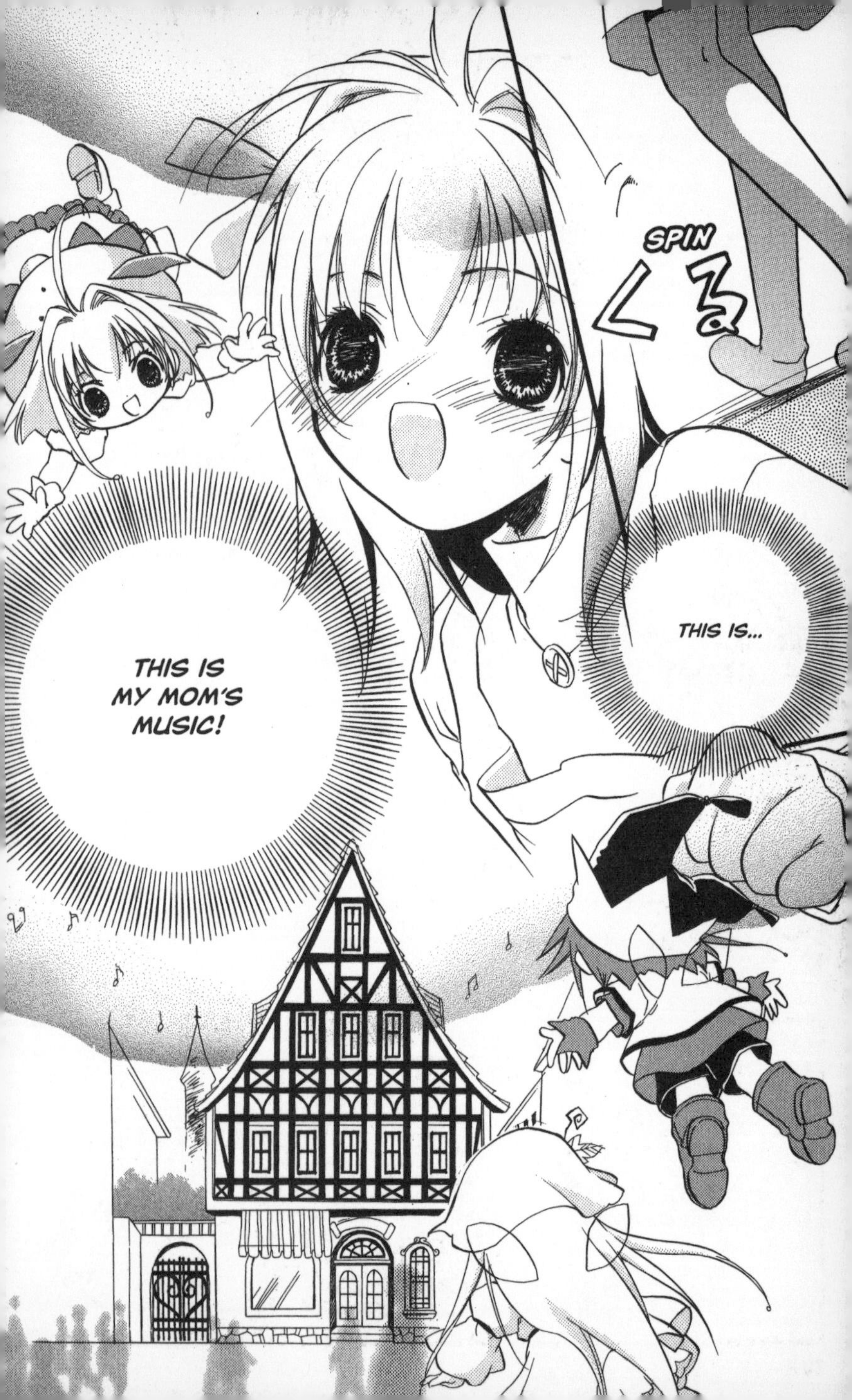
SPIN
くる
THIS IS...
THIS IS MY MOM'S MUSIC!

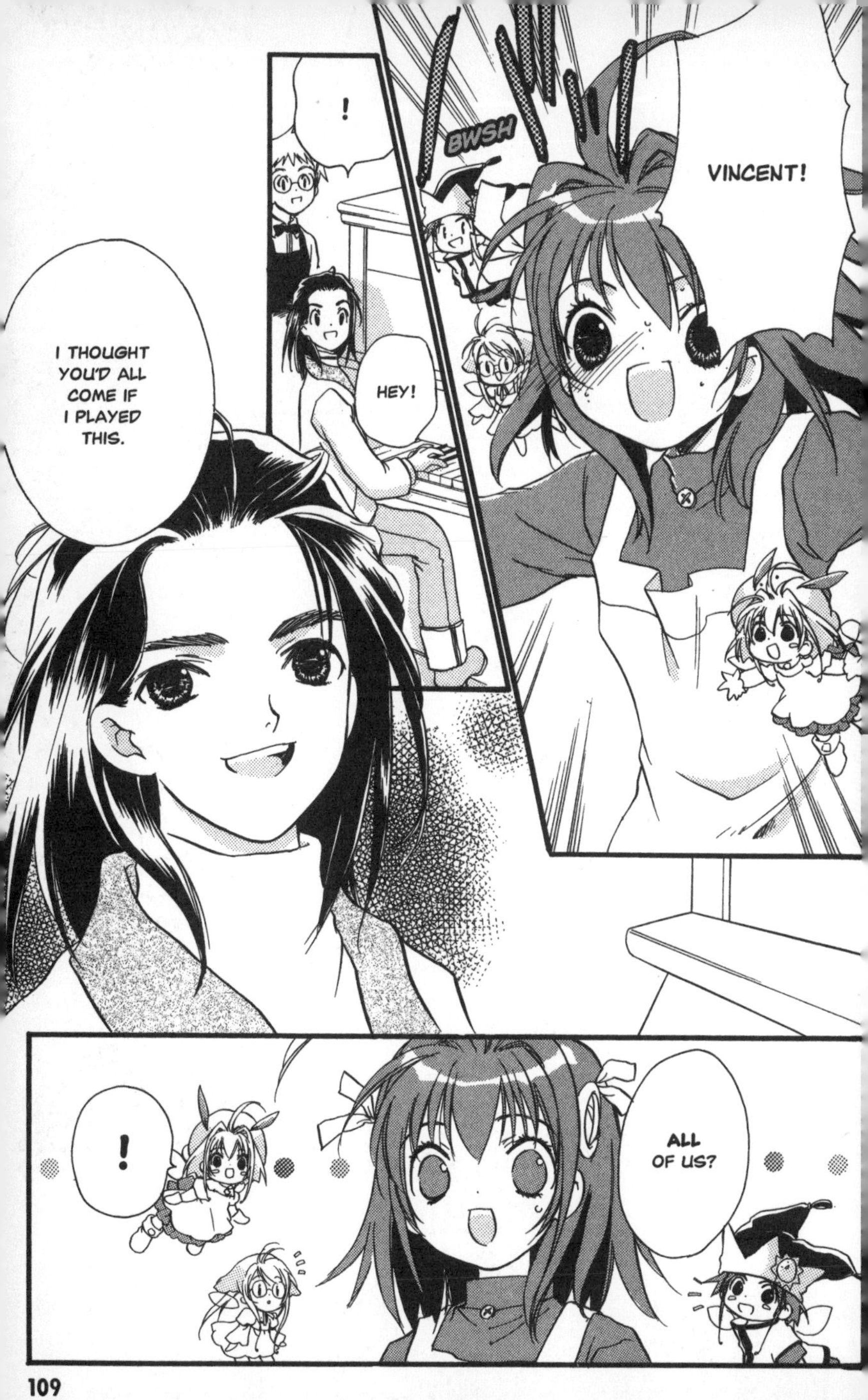
VINCENT!
BWSH
!
HEY!
I THOUGHT YOU'D ALL COME IF I PLAYED THIS.
ALL OF US?
!

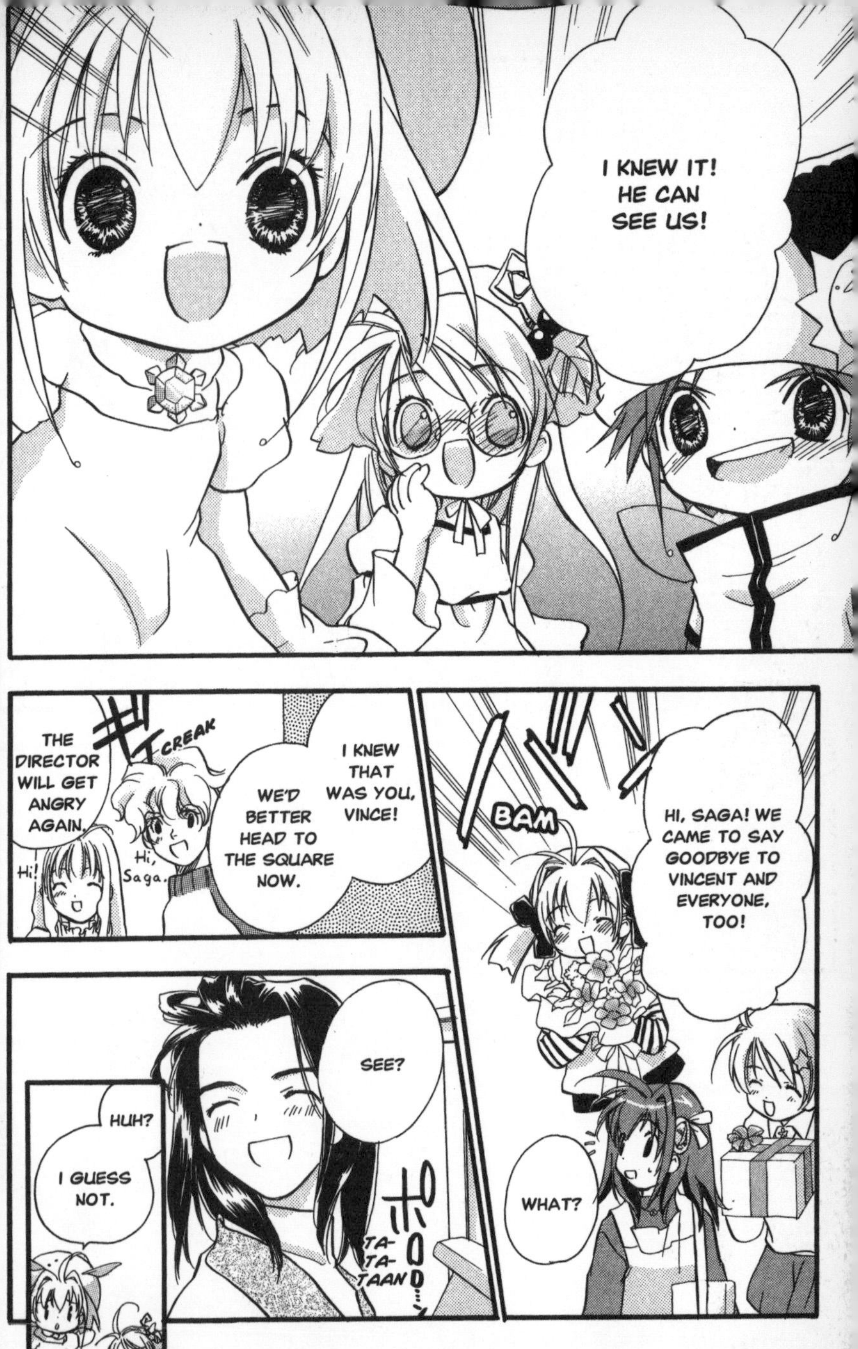
I KNEW IT! HE CAN SEE US!
BAM
HI, SAGA! WE CAME TO SAY GOODBYE TO VINCENT AND EVERYONE, TOO!
WHAT?
I KNEW THAT WAS YOU, VINCE!
WE'D BETTER HEAD TO THE SQUARE NOW.
CREAK
THE DIRECTOR WILL GET ANGRY AGAIN.
Hi, Saga.
Hi!
SEE?
TA-TA-TAAN
HUH?
I GUESS NOT.

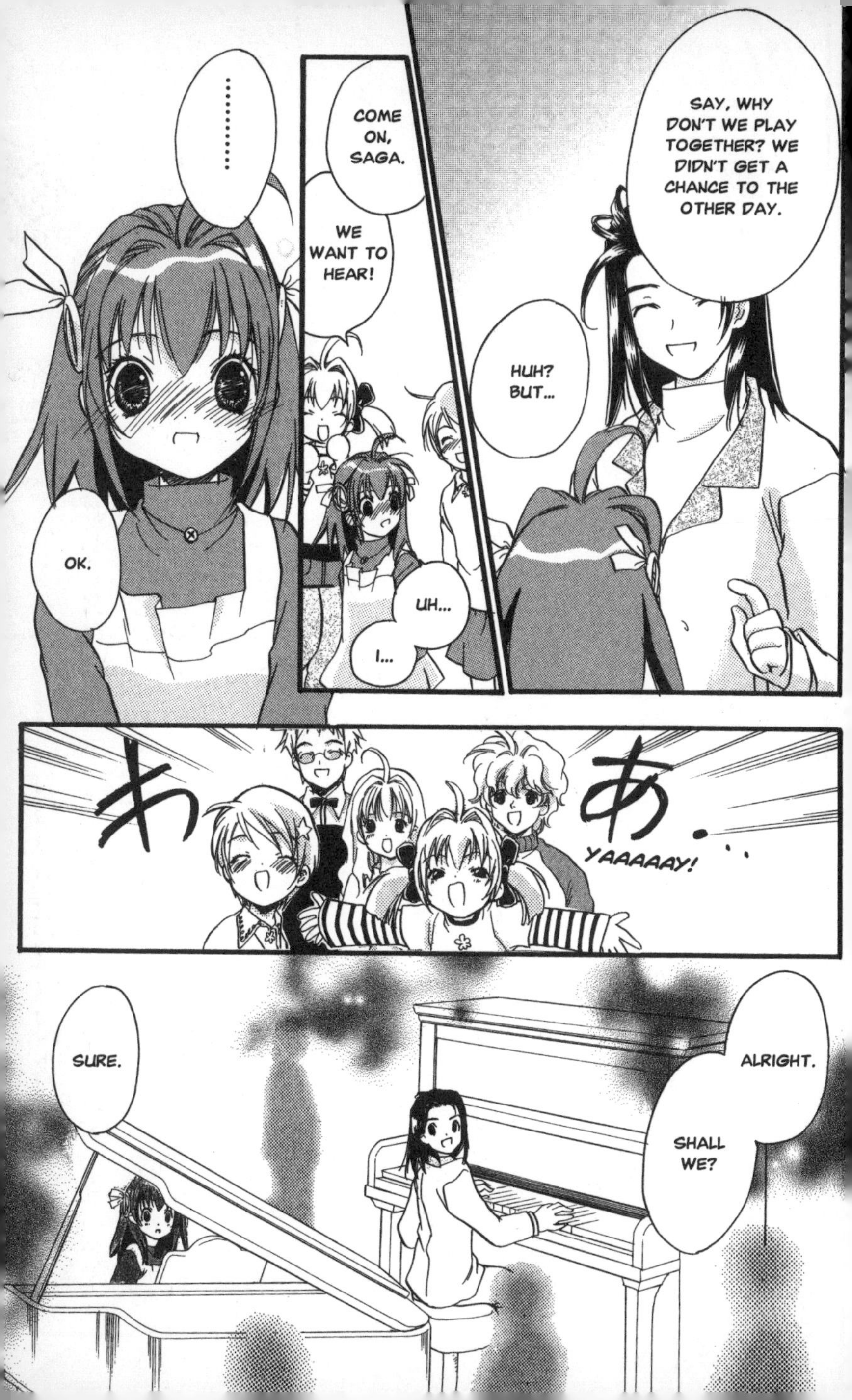
SAY, WHY DON'T WE PLAY TOGETHER? WE DIDN'T GET A CHANCE TO THE OTHER DAY.
HUH? BUT...
COME ON, SAGA.
WE WANT TO HEAR!
UH...
I...
......
OK.
わあ
YAAAAAY!
ALRIGHT.
SHALL WE?
SURE.

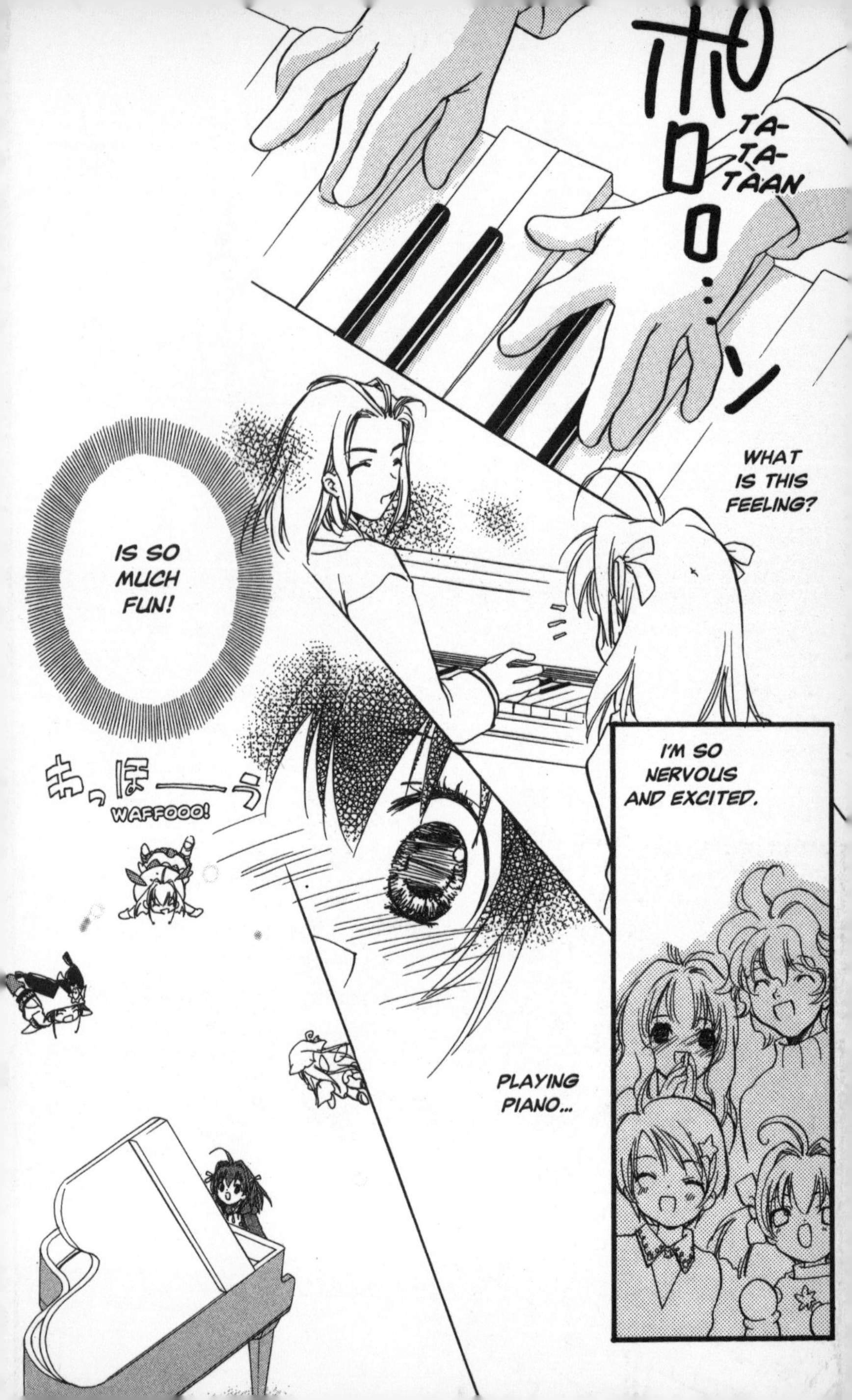

ポロロ…ン
TA-TA-TAAN
WHAT IS THIS FEELING?
I'M SO NERVOUS AND EXCITED.
PLAYING PIANO...
IS SO MUCH FUN!
わっほーう
WAFFOOO!

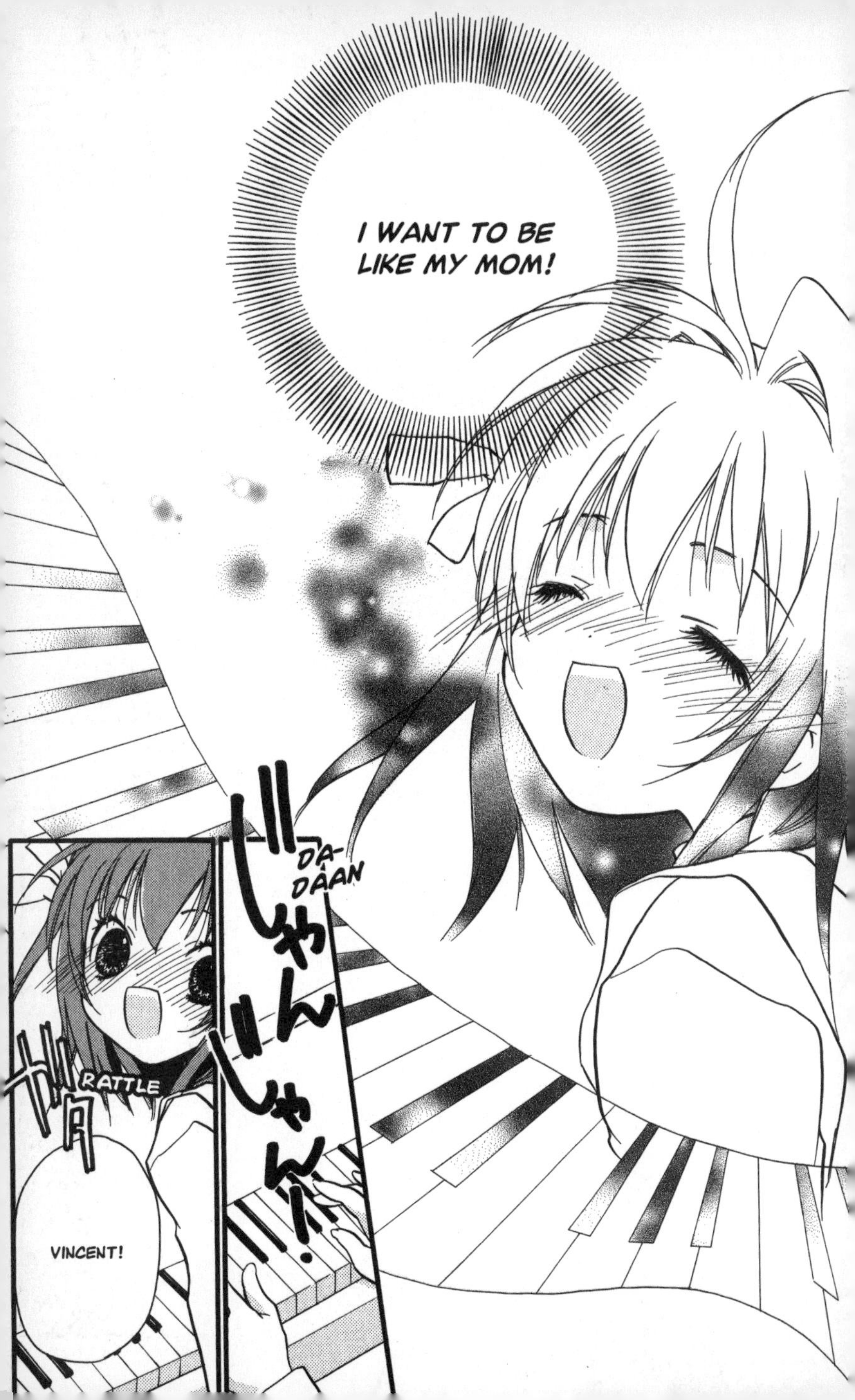
I WANT TO BE LIKE MY MOM!
じゃんじゃん!
DA-DAAN
RATTLE
VINCENT!

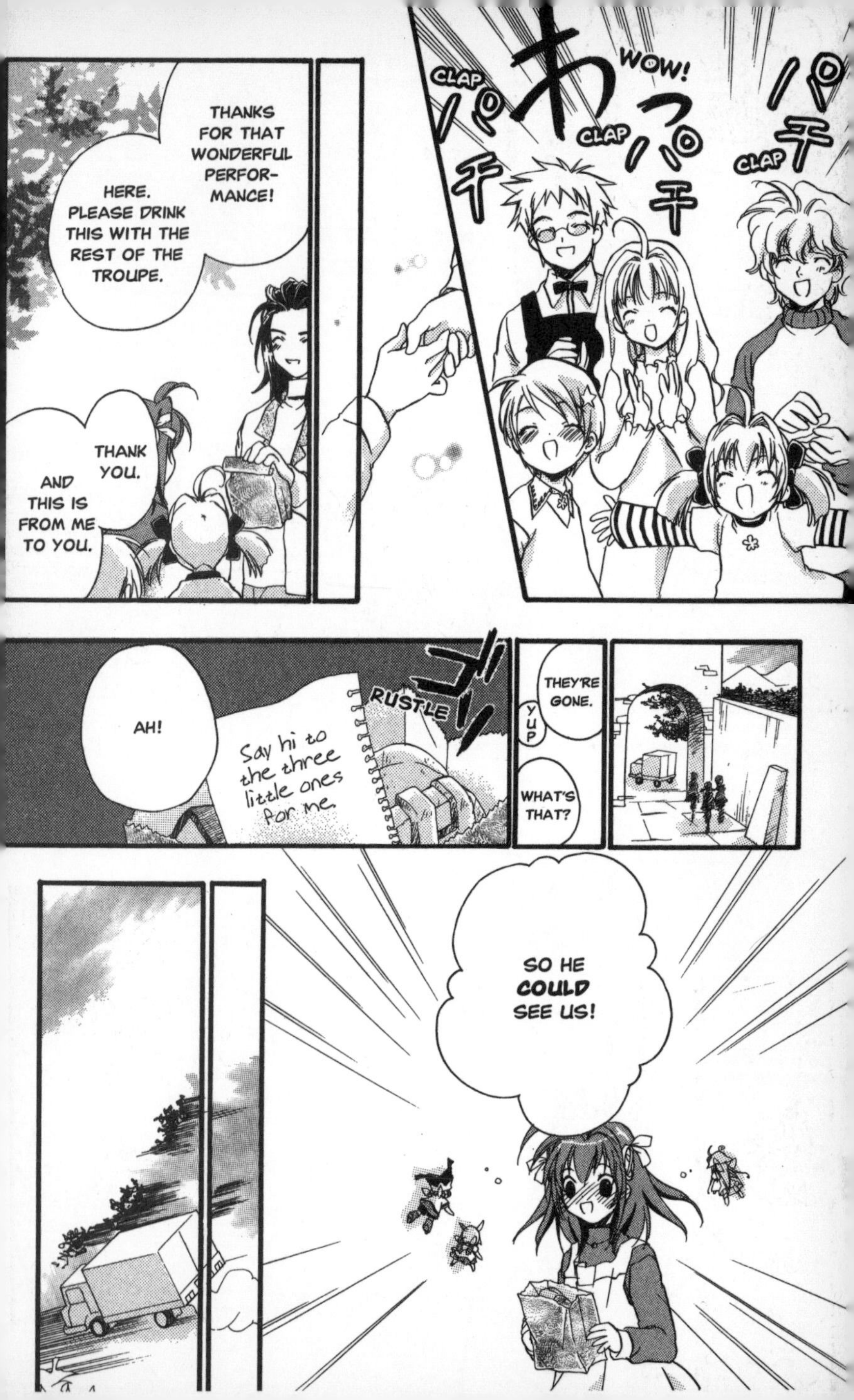
WOW!
CLAP
CLAP
CLAP
THANKS FOR THAT WONDERFUL PERFORMANCE!
HERE. PLEASE DRINK THIS WITH THE REST OF THE TROUPE.
THANK YOU.
AND THIS IS FROM ME TO YOU.
THEY'RE GONE.
YUP
WHAT'S THAT?
RUSTLE
Say hi to the three little ones for me.
AH!
SO HE **COULD** SEE US!

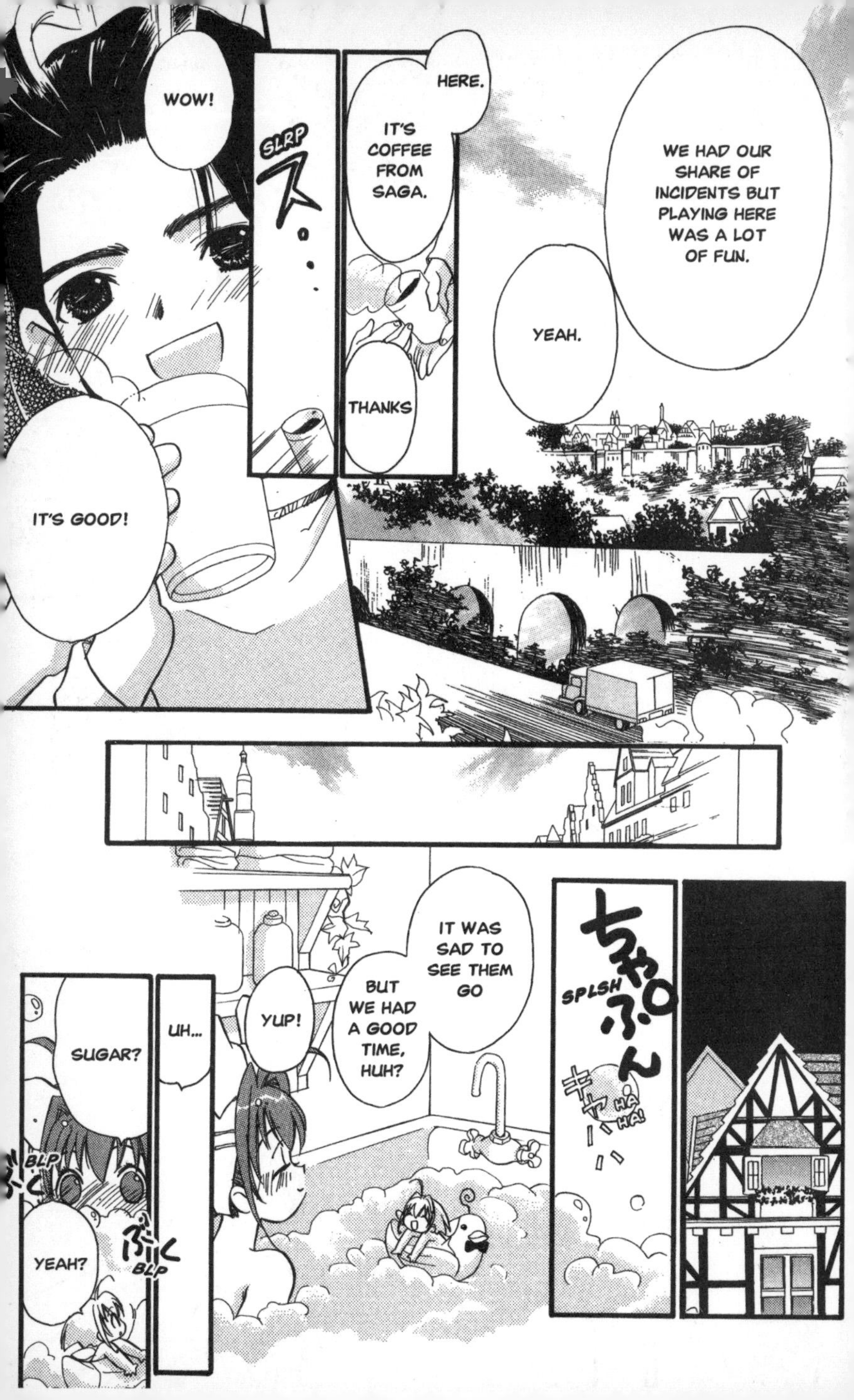
WE HAD OUR SHARE OF INCIDENTS BUT PLAYING HERE WAS A LOT OF FUN.
YEAH.
HERE.
IT'S COFFEE FROM SAGA.
THANKS
SLRP
ス
WOW!
IT'S GOOD!
ちゃぷん
SPLSH
キャ
HA HA!
IT WAS SAD TO SEE THEM GO
BUT WE HAD A GOOD TIME, HUH?
YUP!
UH...
SUGAR?
ぶく
BLP
YEAH?
ぶく
BLP

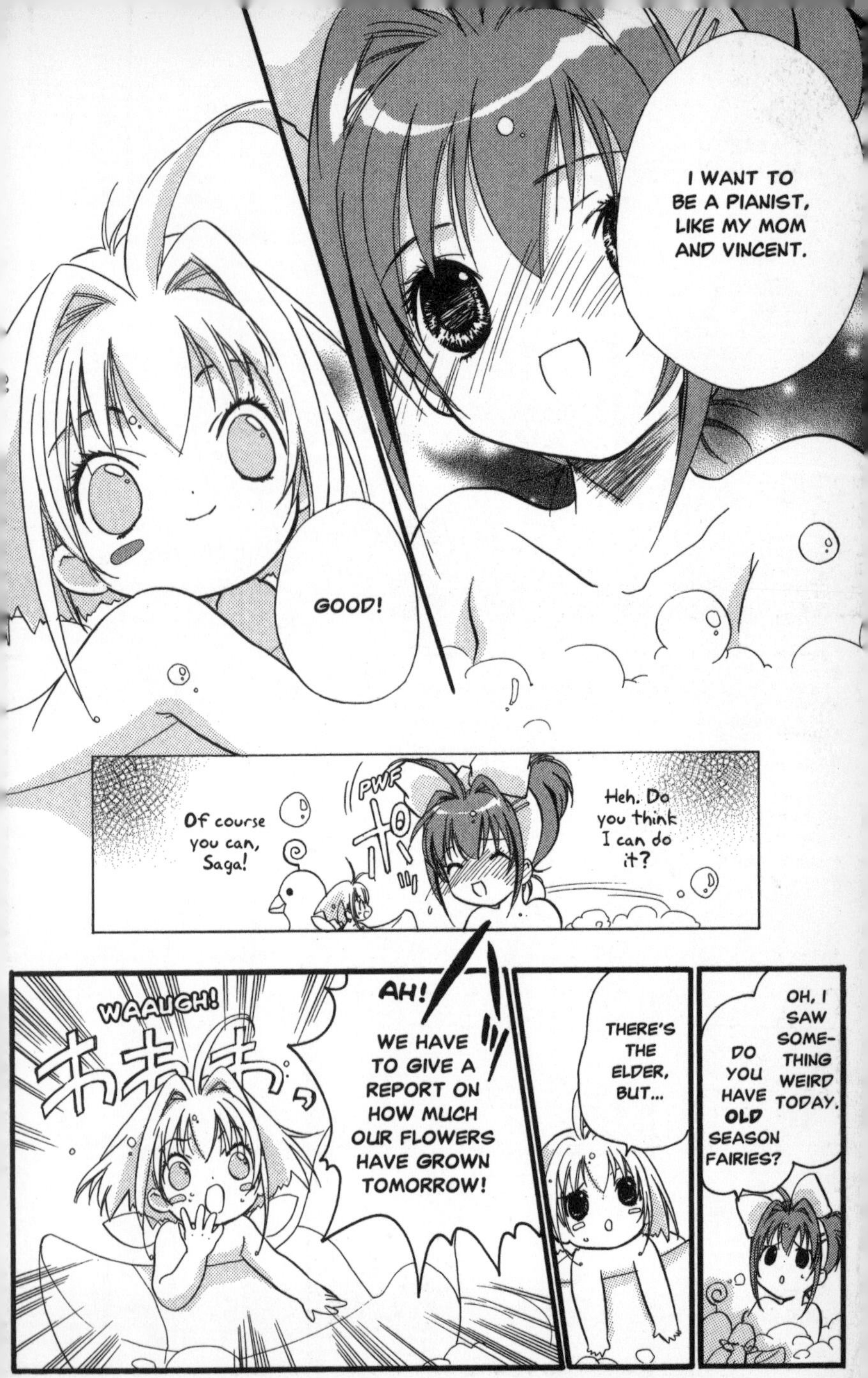
I WANT TO BE A PIANIST, LIKE MY MOM AND VINCENT.
GOOD!
Heh. Do you think I can do it?
PWF
Of course you can, Saga!
OH, I SAW SOMETHING WEIRD TODAY.
DO YOU HAVE OLD SEASON FAIRIES?
THERE'S THE ELDER, BUT...
AH!
WE HAVE TO GIVE A REPORT ON HOW MUCH OUR FLOWERS HAVE GROWN TOMORROW!
WAAUGH!

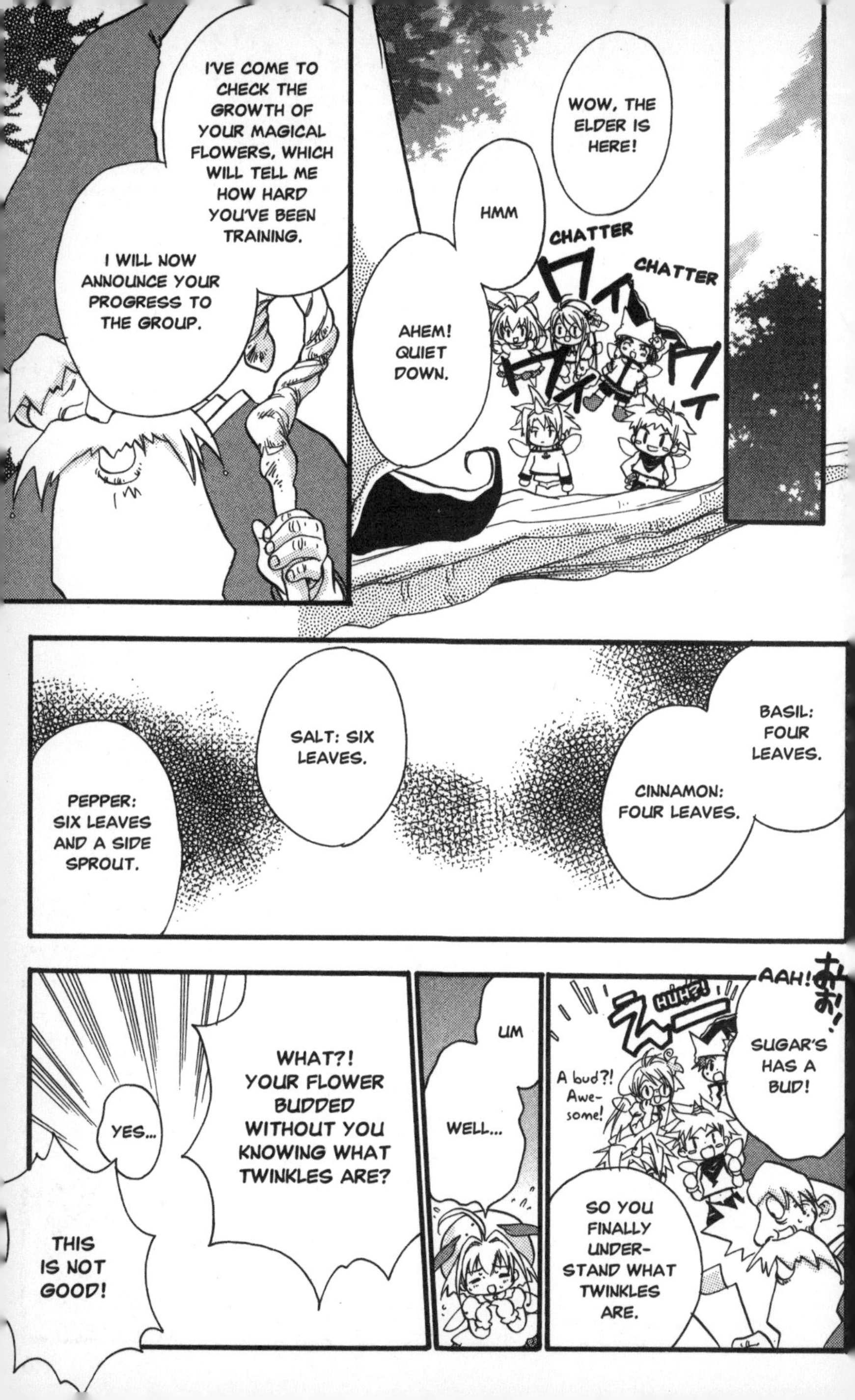
WOW, THE ELDER IS HERE!
CHATTER
CHATTER
HMM
AHEM! QUIET DOWN.
I'VE COME TO CHECK THE GROWTH OF YOUR MAGICAL FLOWERS, WHICH WILL TELL ME HOW HARD YOU'VE BEEN TRAINING.
I WILL NOW ANNOUNCE YOUR PROGRESS TO THE GROUP.
BASIL: FOUR LEAVES.
CINNAMON: FOUR LEAVES.
SALT: SIX LEAVES.
PEPPER: SIX LEAVES AND A SIDE SPROUT.
AAH!
HUH?!
SUGAR'S HAS A BUD!
A bud?! Awe-some!
SO YOU FINALLY UNDER-STAND WHAT TWINKLES ARE.
UM
WELL...
WHAT?! YOUR FLOWER BUDDED WITHOUT YOU KNOWING WHAT TWINKLES ARE?
YES...
THIS IS NOT GOOD!

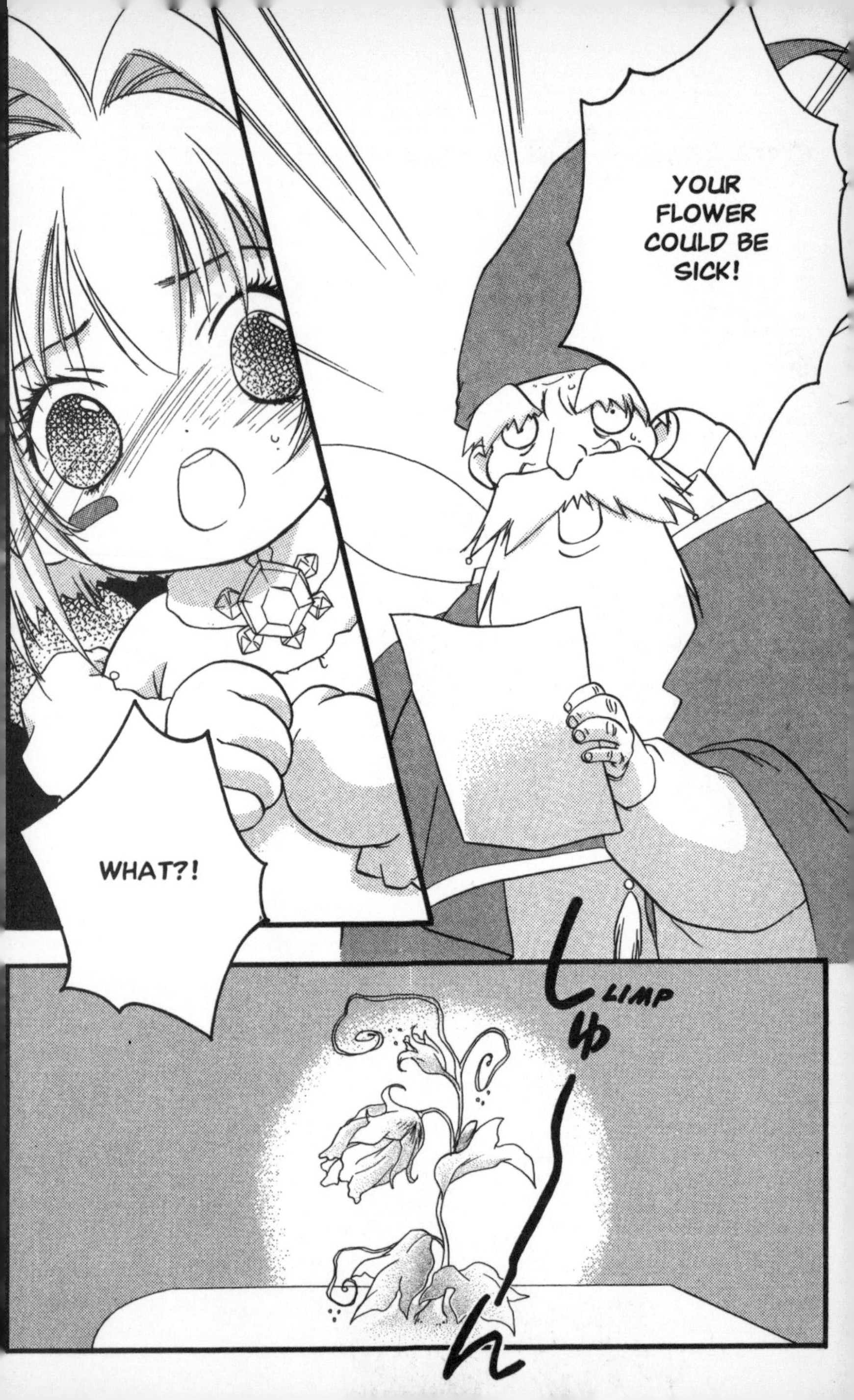
YOUR FLOWER COULD BE SICK!
WHAT?!
LIMP

CHAPTER 9 For Twinkles

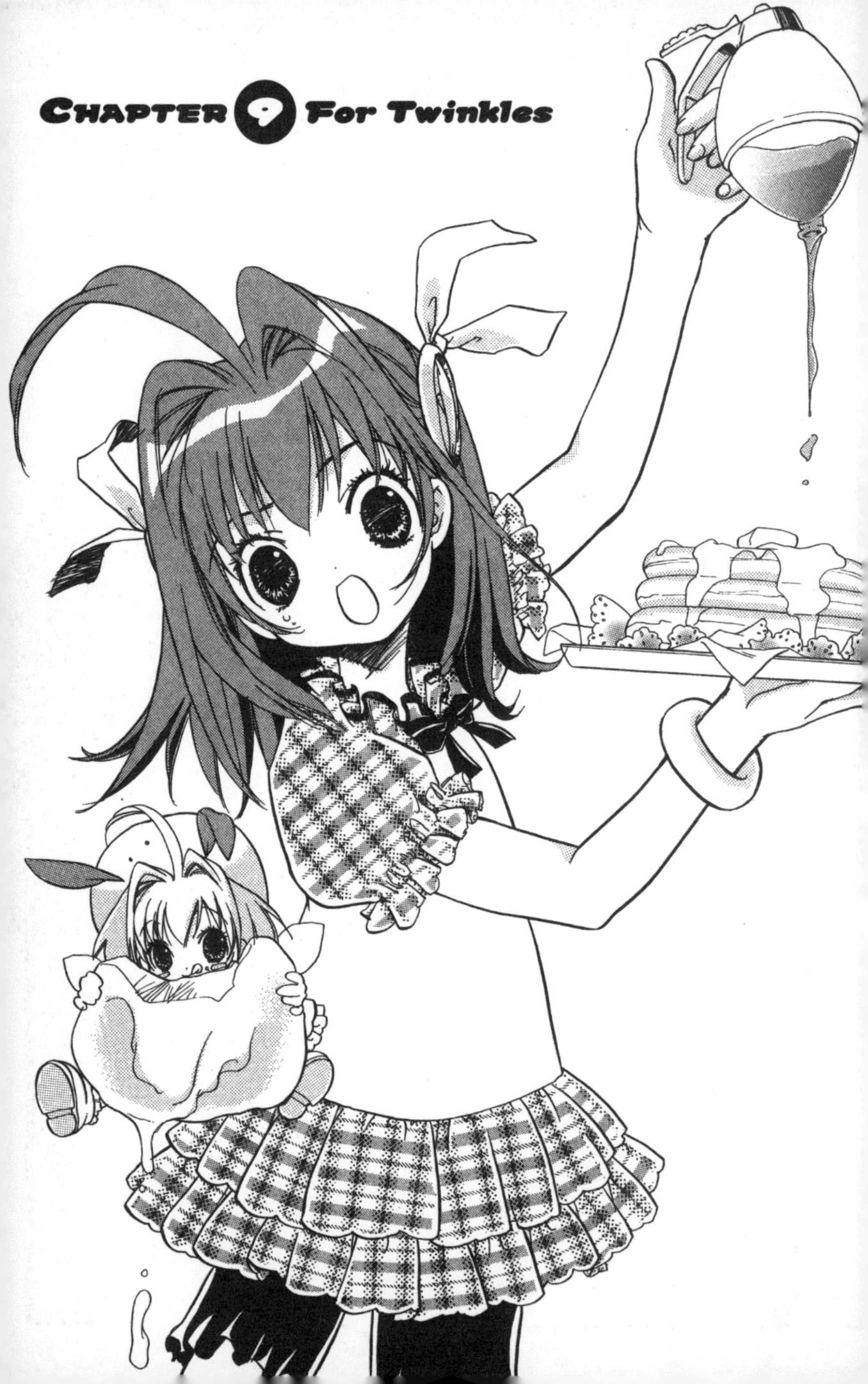

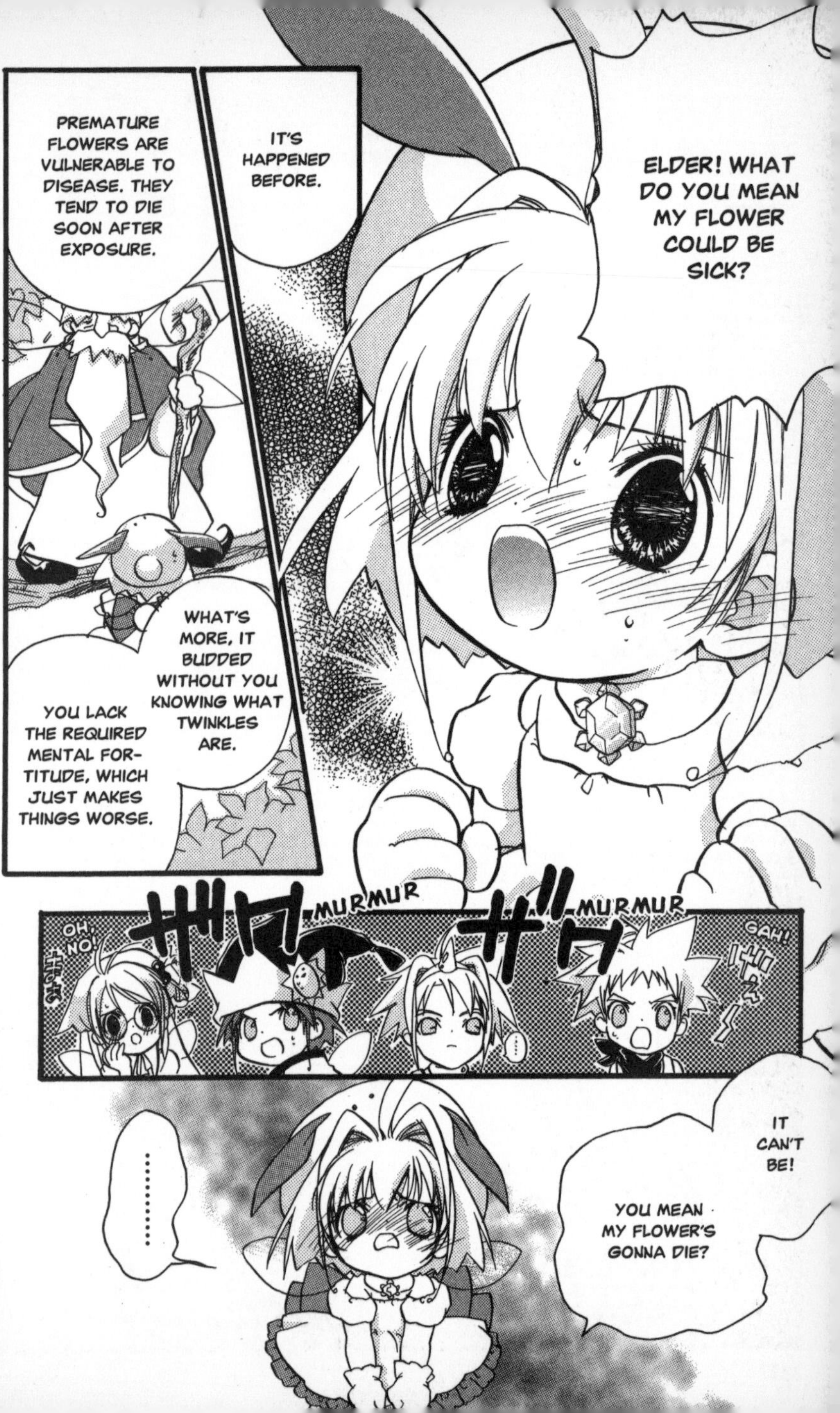
ELDER! WHAT DO YOU MEAN MY FLOWER COULD BE SICK?
IT'S HAPPENED BEFORE.
PREMATURE FLOWERS ARE VULNERABLE TO DISEASE. THEY TEND TO DIE SOON AFTER EXPOSURE.
WHAT'S MORE, IT BUDDED WITHOUT YOU KNOWING WHAT TWINKLES ARE.
YOU LACK THE REQUIRED MENTAL FOR-TITUDE, WHICH JUST MAKES THINGS WORSE.
MURMUR
MURMUR
GAH!
OH, NO!
...
IT CAN'T BE!
YOU MEAN MY FLOWER'S GONNA DIE?
....

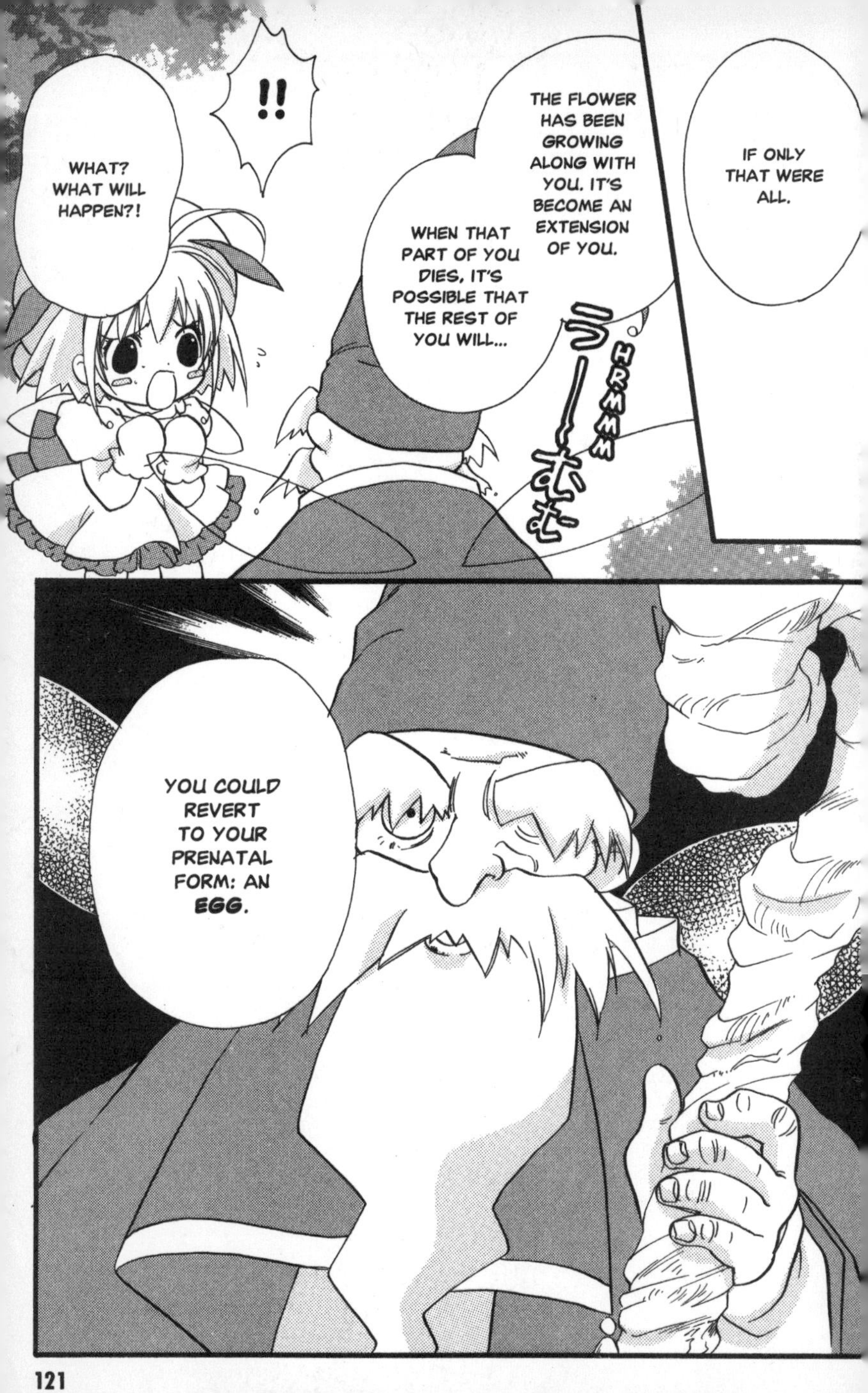
THE FLOWER HAS BEEN GROWING ALONG WITH YOU. IT'S BECOME AN EXTENSION OF YOU.
WHEN THAT PART OF YOU DIES, IT'S POSSIBLE THAT THE REST OF YOU WILL...
HRMMM
!!
WHAT? WHAT WILL HAPPEN?!
IF ONLY THAT WERE ALL.
YOU COULD REVERT TO YOUR PRENATAL FORM: AN EGG.

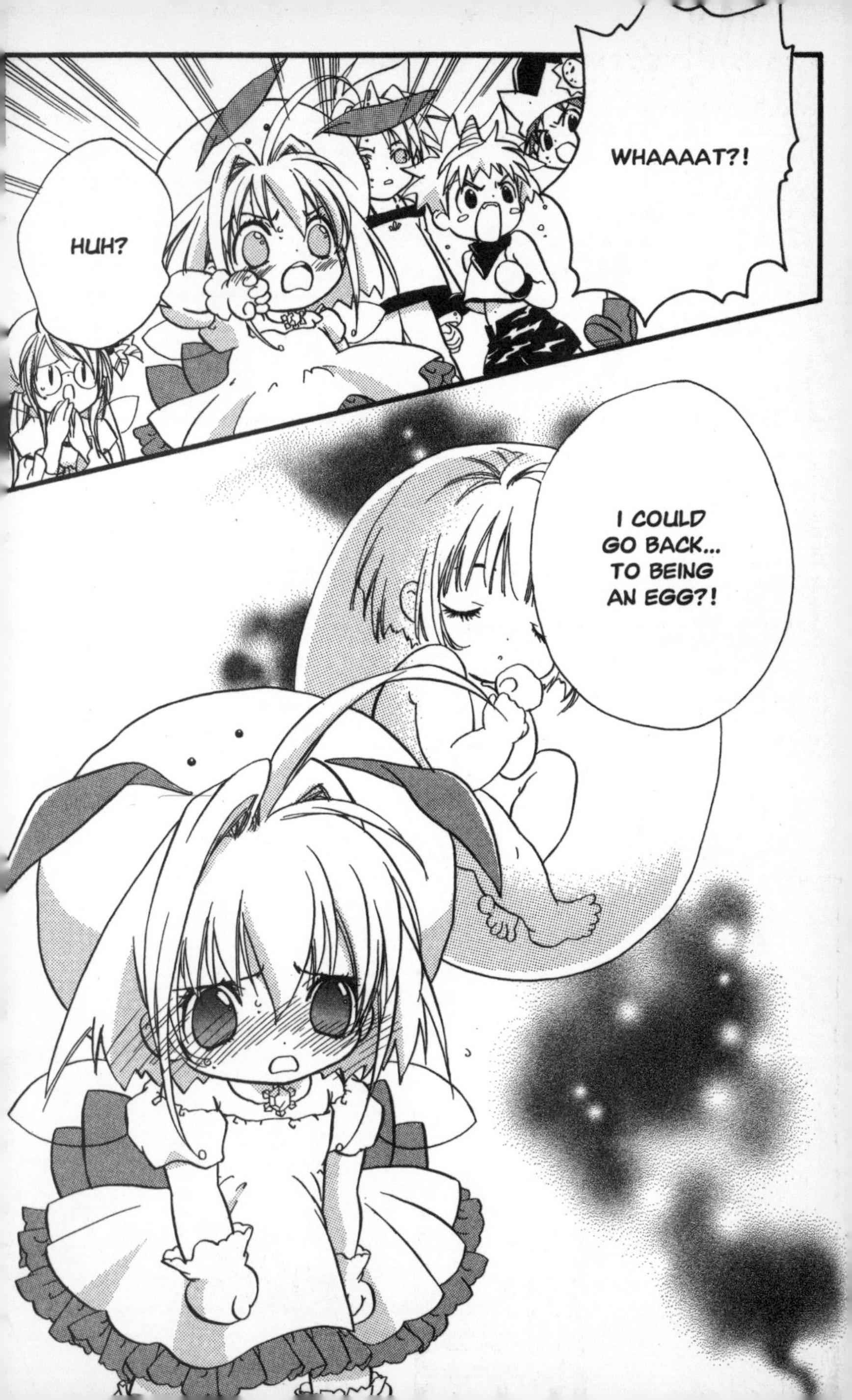
WHAAAAT?!
HUH?
I COULD GO BACK... TO BEING AN EGG?!

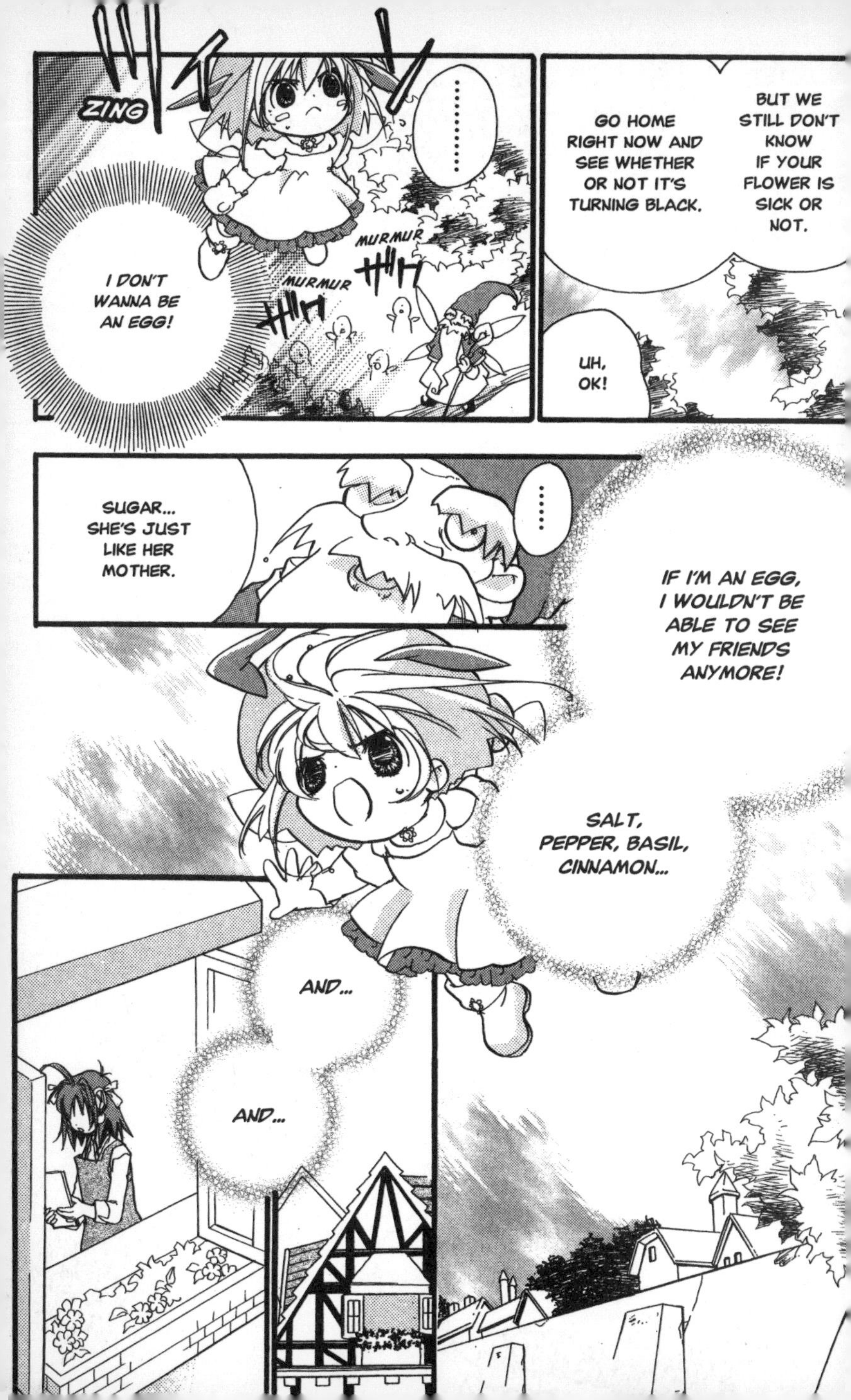
BUT WE STILL DON'T KNOW IF YOUR FLOWER IS SICK OR NOT.
GO HOME RIGHT NOW AND SEE WHETHER OR NOT IT'S TURNING BLACK.
UH, OK!
......
ZING
I DON'T WANNA BE AN EGG!
MURMUR
MURMUR
......
SUGAR... SHE'S JUST LIKE HER MOTHER.
IF I'M AN EGG, I WOULDN'T BE ABLE TO SEE MY FRIENDS ANYMORE!
SALT, PEPPER, BASIL, CINNAMON...
AND...
AND...

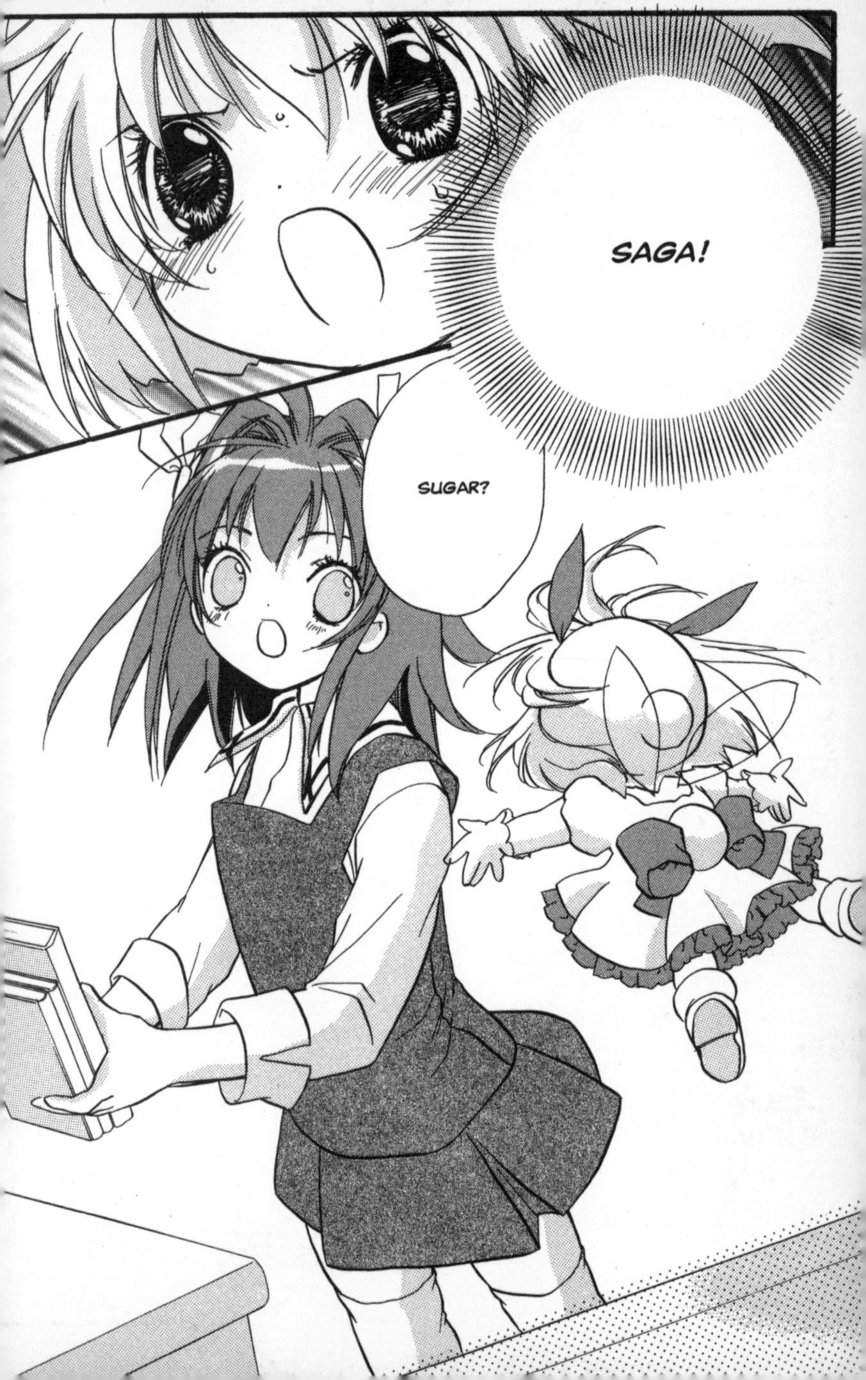
SAGA!
SUGAR?

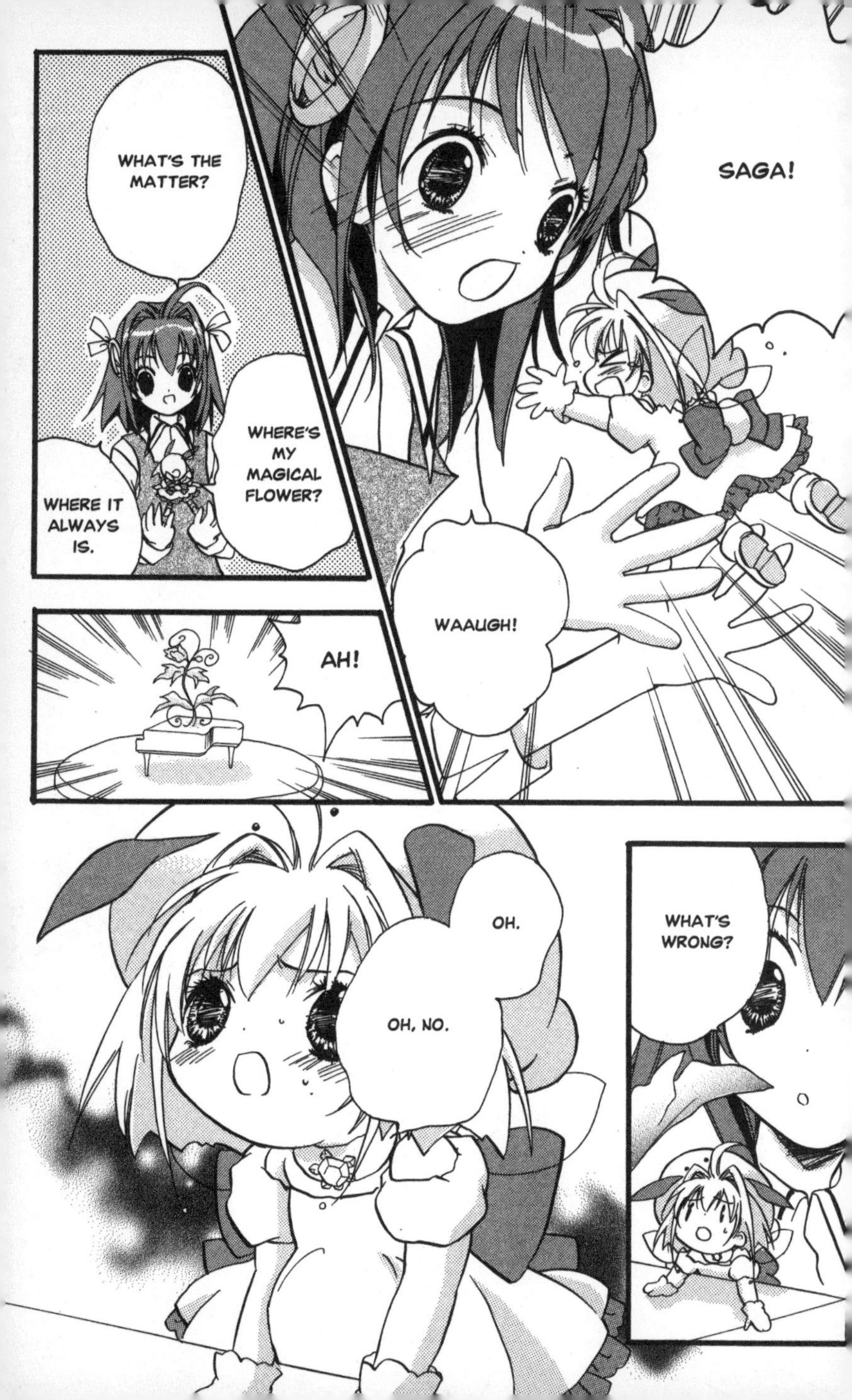

WHAT'S THE MATTER?
WHERE'S MY MAGICAL FLOWER?
WHERE IT ALWAYS IS.
AH!
SAGA!
WAAUGH!
WHAT'S WRONG?
OH.
OH, NO.

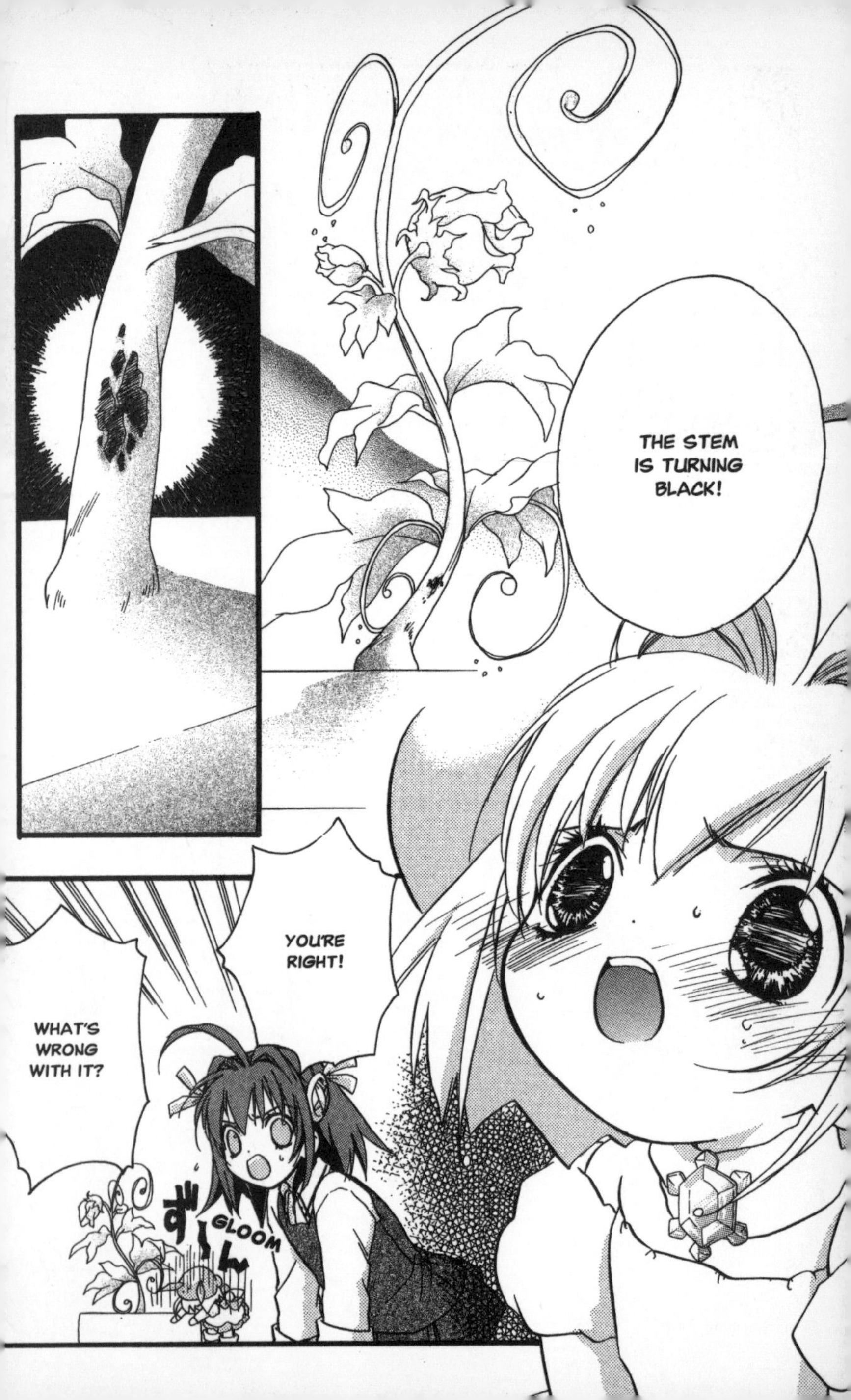
THE STEM IS TURNING BLACK!
YOU'RE RIGHT!
WHAT'S WRONG WITH IT?
ずーん
GLOOM

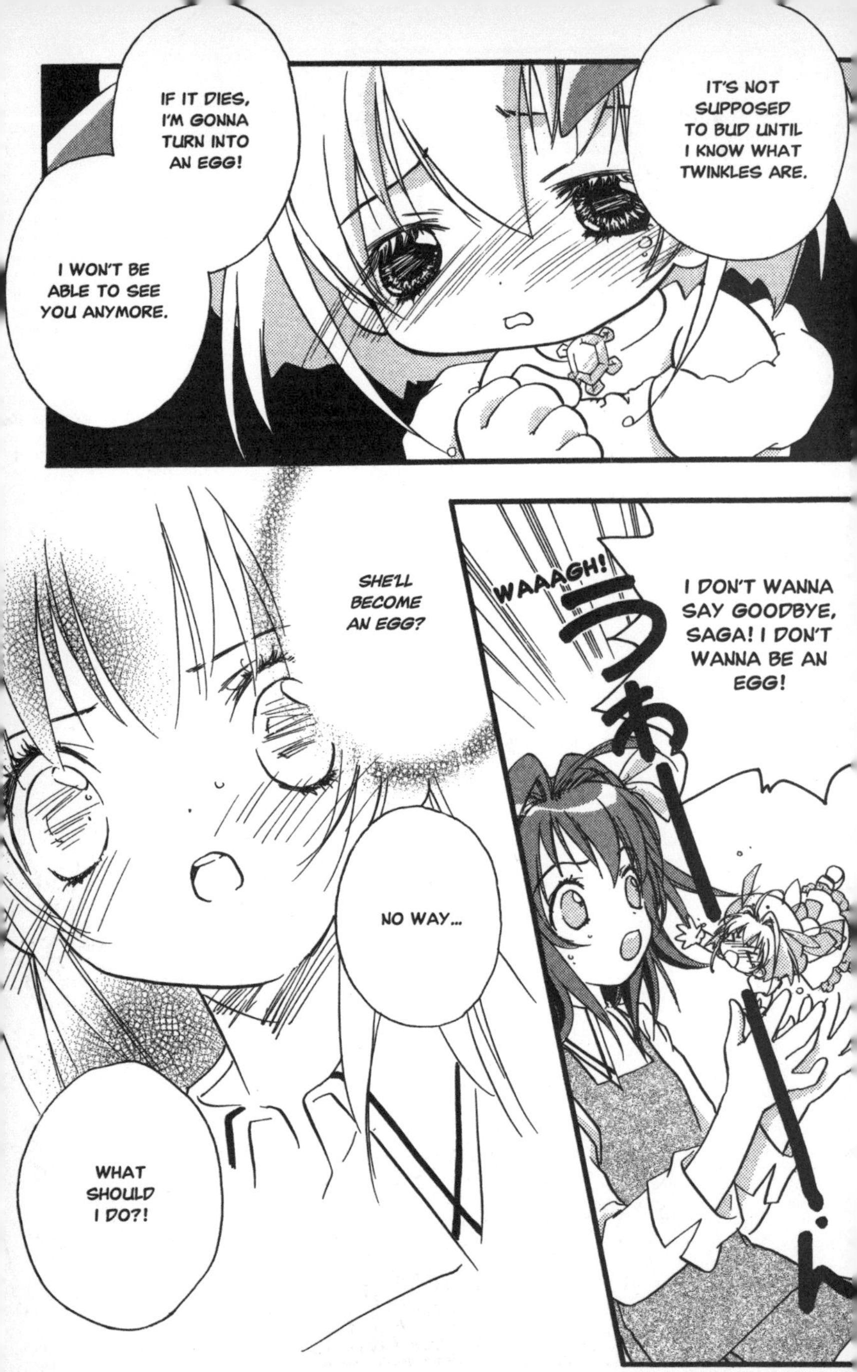

IT'S NOT SUPPOSED TO BUD UNTIL I KNOW WHAT TWINKLES ARE.
IF IT DIES, I'M GONNA TURN INTO AN EGG!
I WON'T BE ABLE TO SEE YOU ANYMORE.
WAAAGH!
I DON'T WANNA SAY GOODBYE, SAGA! I DON'T WANNA BE AN EGG!
SHE'LL BECOME AN EGG?
NO WAY...
WHAT SHOULD I DO?!

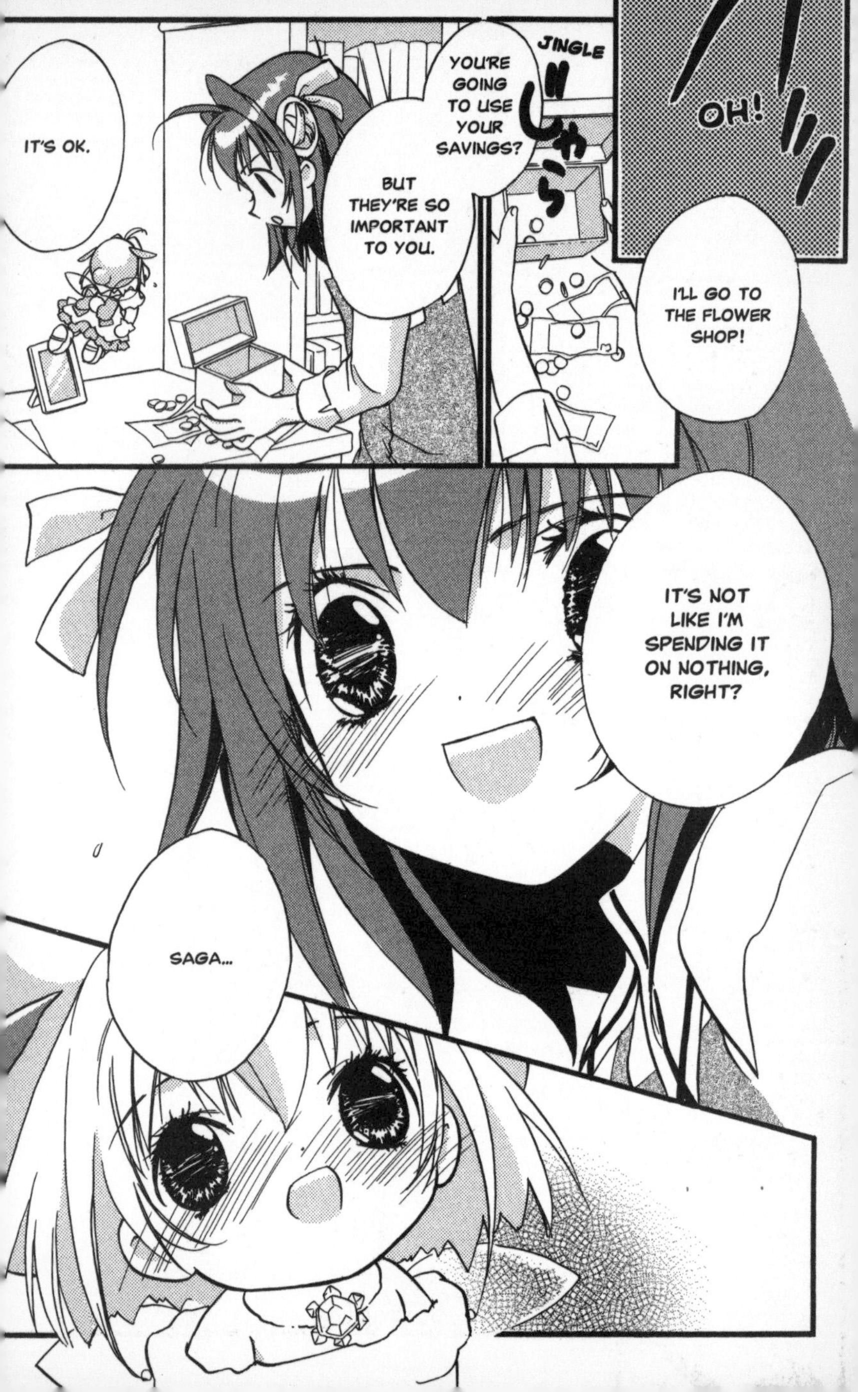
OH!
I'LL GO TO THE FLOWER SHOP!
JINGLE
しゃら
YOU'RE GOING TO USE YOUR SAVINGS?
BUT THEY'RE SO IMPORTANT TO YOU.
IT'S OK.
IT'S NOT LIKE I'M SPENDING IT ON NOTHING, RIGHT?
SAGA...

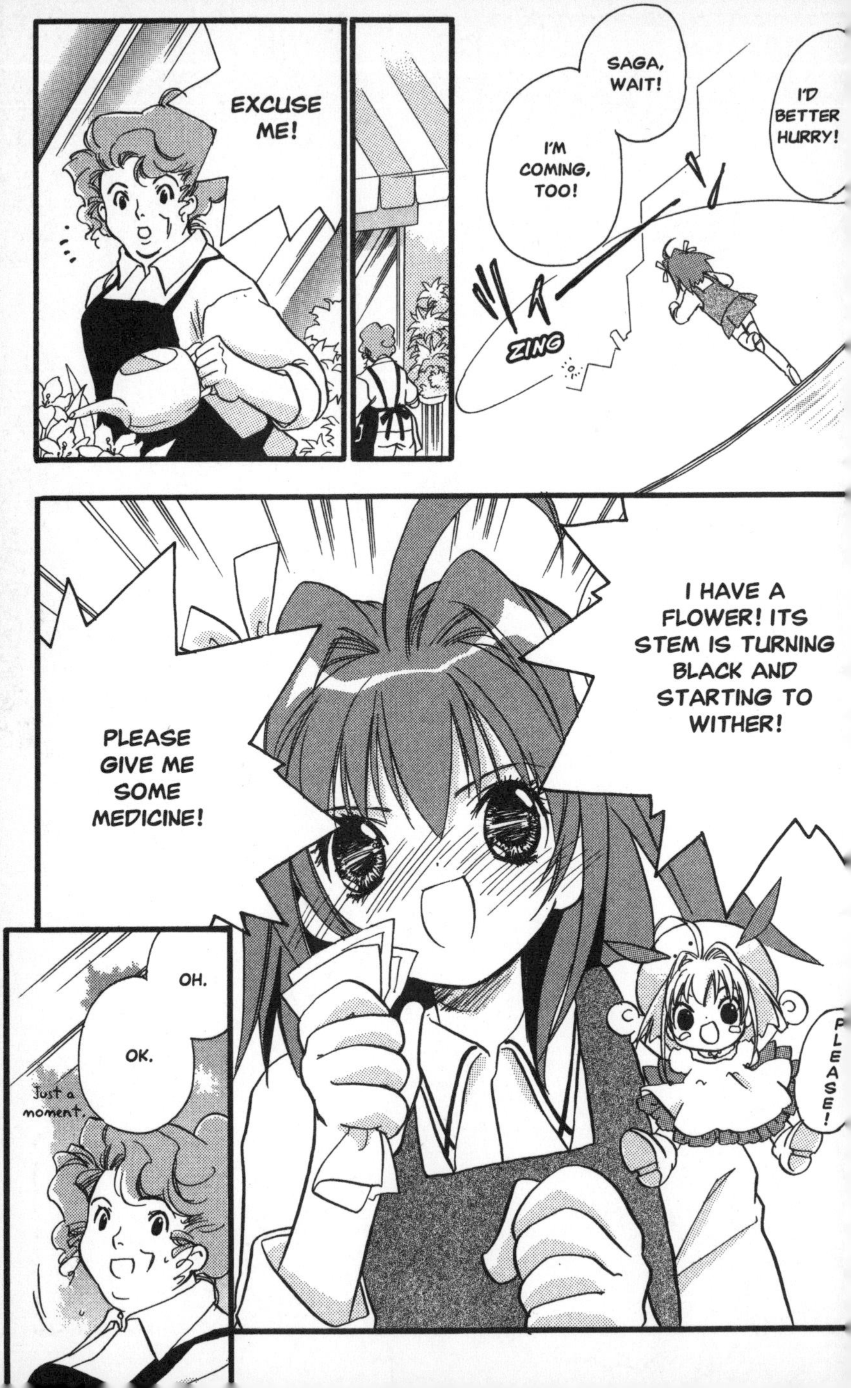
I'D BETTER HURRY!
SAGA, WAIT!
I'M COMING, TOO!
ZING
EXCUSE ME!
I HAVE A FLOWER! ITS STEM IS TURNING BLACK AND STARTING TO WITHER!
PLEASE GIVE ME SOME MEDICINE!
PLEASE!
OH.
OK.
Just a moment.

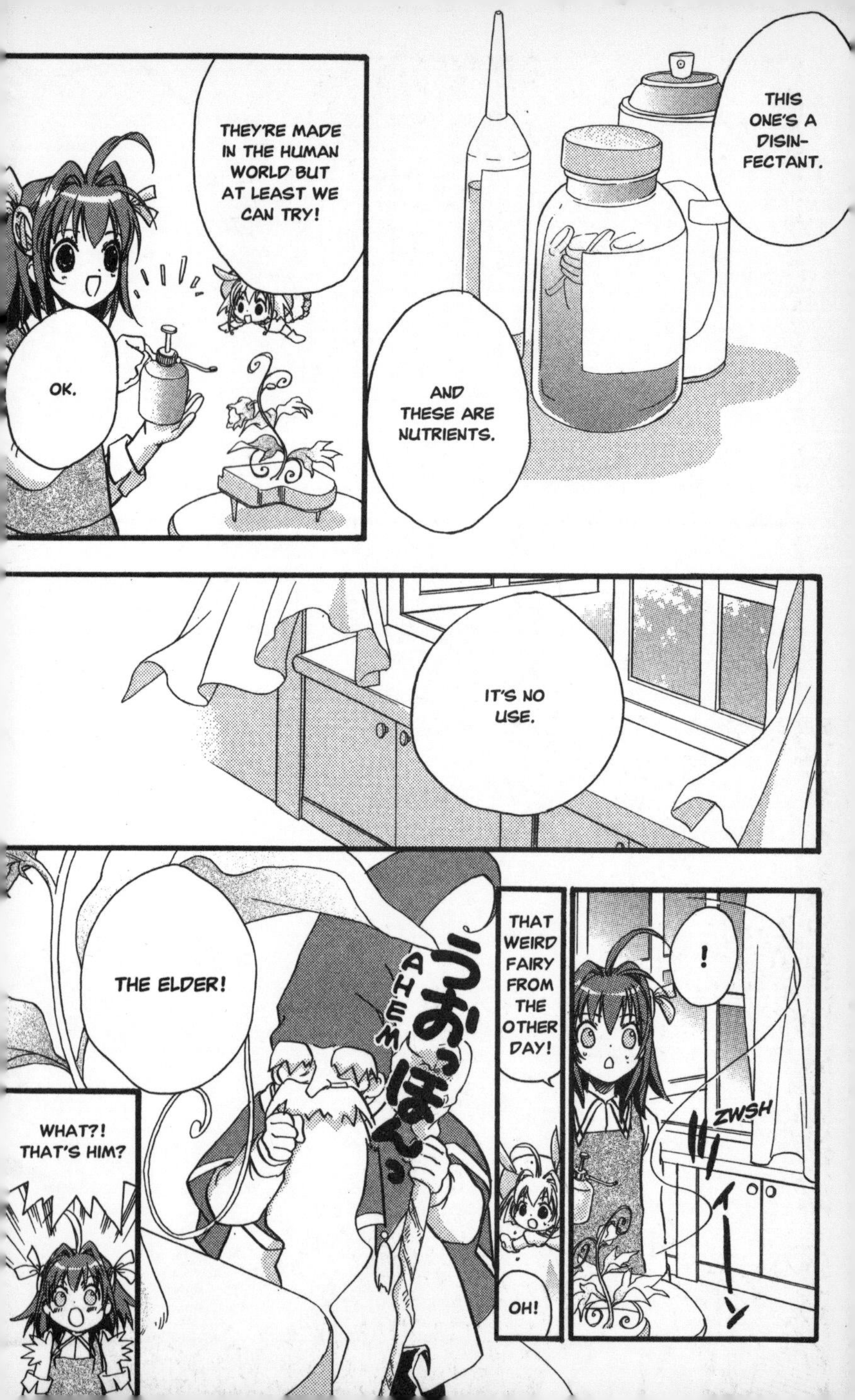
THIS ONE'S A DISIN- FECTANT.
AND THESE ARE NUTRIENTS.
THEY'RE MADE IN THE HUMAN WORLD BUT AT LEAST WE CAN TRY!
OK.
IT'S NO USE.
!
ZWSH
OH!
THAT WEIRD FAIRY FROM THE OTHER DAY!
AHEM
THE ELDER!
WHAT?! THAT'S HIM?

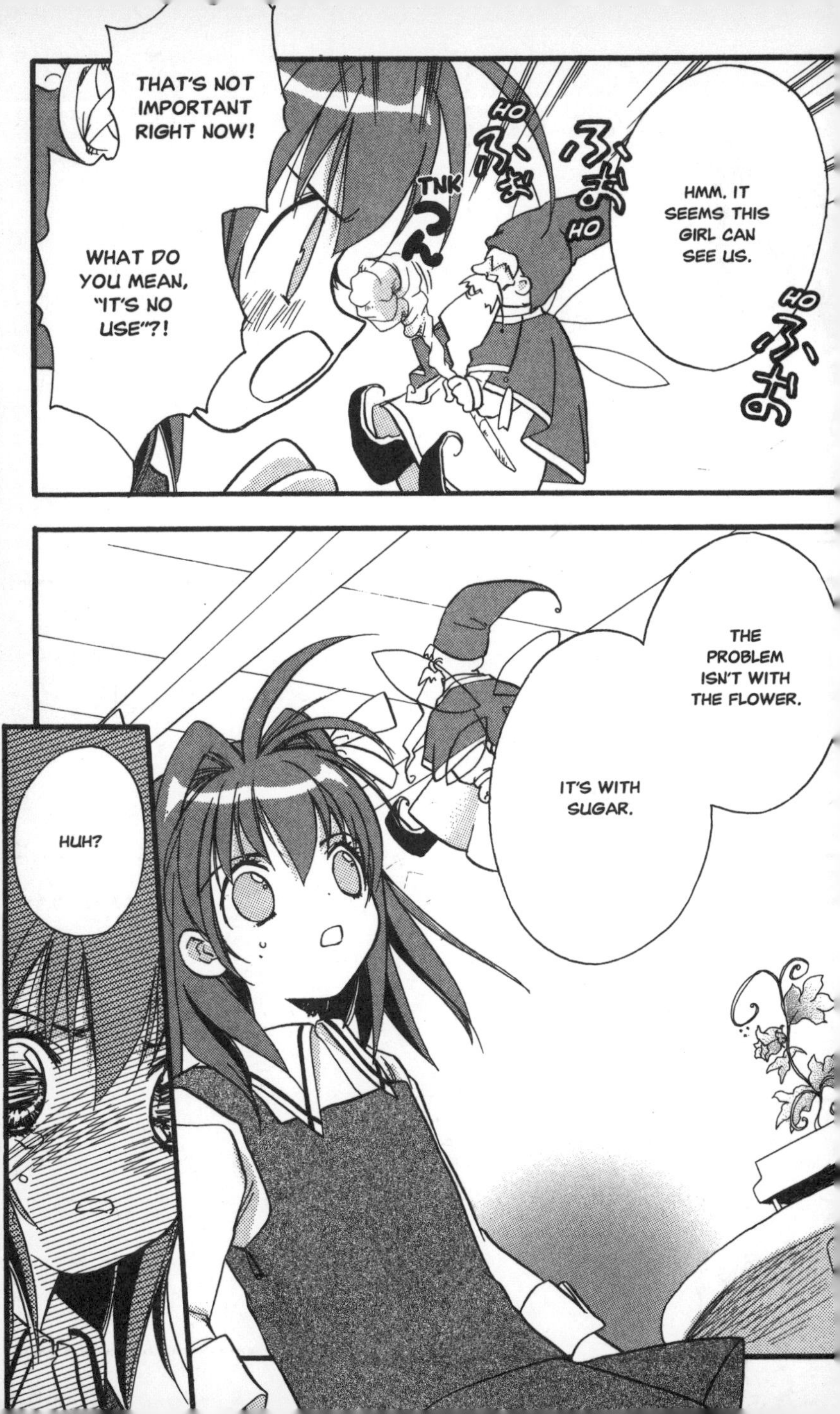
THAT'S NOT IMPORTANT RIGHT NOW!
WHAT DO YOU MEAN, "IT'S NO USE"?!
HO
HO
TNK
HMM. IT SEEMS THIS GIRL CAN SEE US.
HO
THE PROBLEM ISN'T WITH THE FLOWER.
IT'S WITH SUGAR.
HUH?

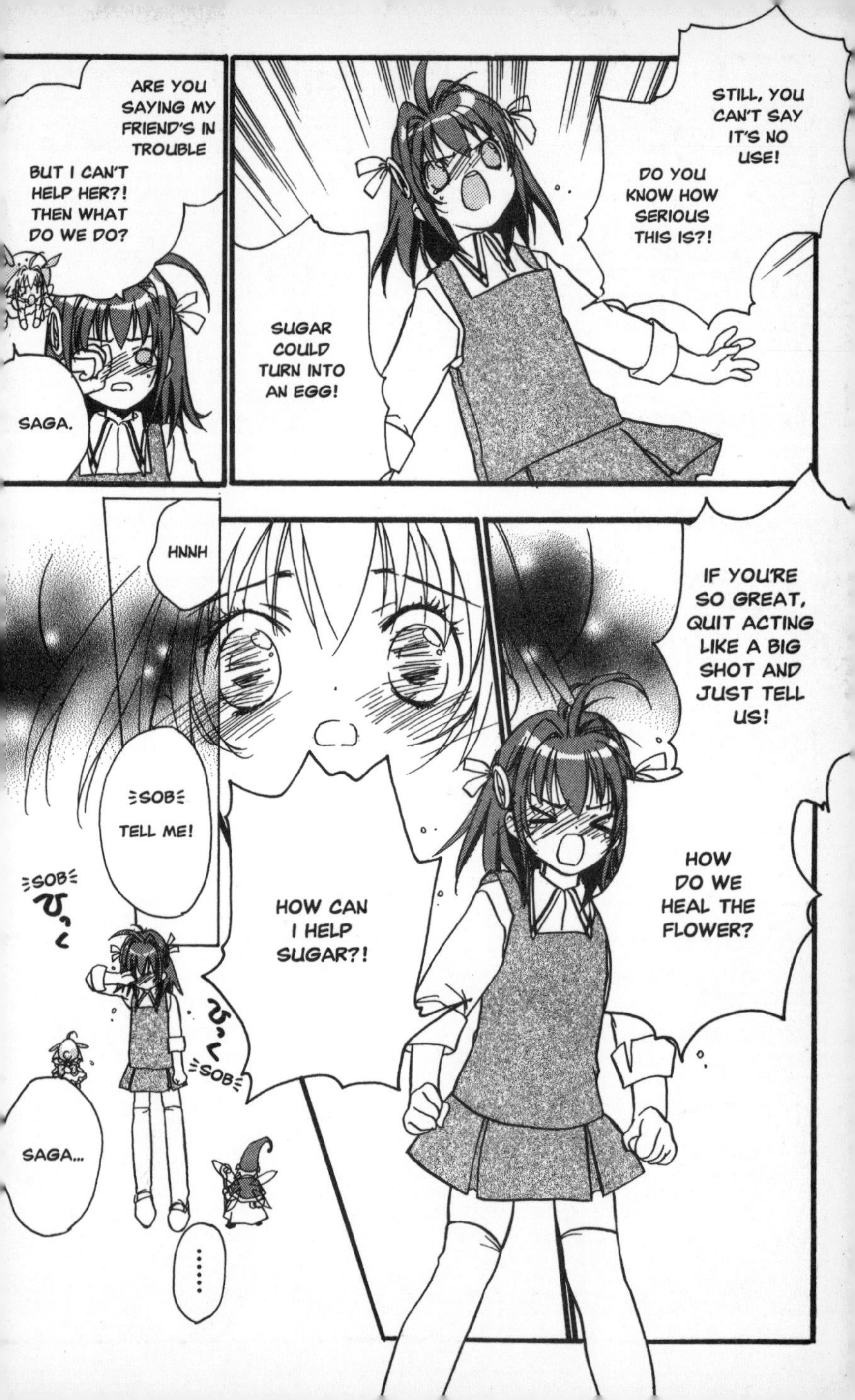

STILL, YOU CAN'T SAY IT'S NO USE!
DO YOU KNOW HOW SERIOUS THIS IS?!
SUGAR COULD TURN INTO AN EGG!
ARE YOU SAYING MY FRIEND'S IN TROUBLE
BUT I CAN'T HELP HER?! THEN WHAT DO WE DO?
SAGA.
IF YOU'RE SO GREAT, QUIT ACTING LIKE A BIG SHOT AND JUST TELL US!
HOW DO WE HEAL THE FLOWER?
HNNH
HOW CAN I HELP SUGAR?!
SOB
ひっく
SOB
TELL ME!
SOB
ひっく
SAGA...
......

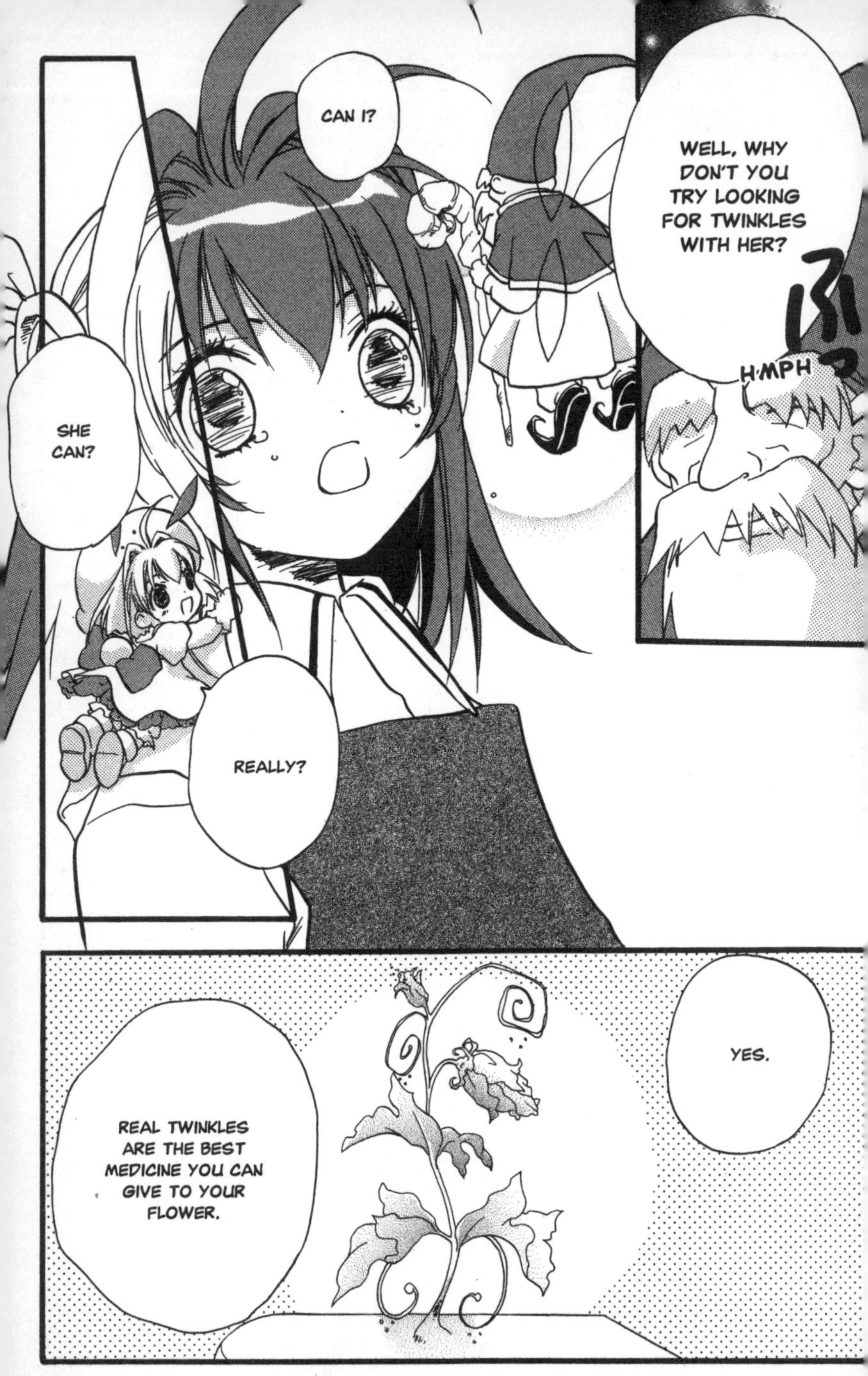
WELL, WHY DON'T YOU TRY LOOKING FOR TWINKLES WITH HER?
ふっ
HMPH
CAN I?
SHE CAN?
REALLY?
YES.
REAL TWINKLES ARE THE BEST MEDICINE YOU CAN GIVE TO YOUR FLOWER.

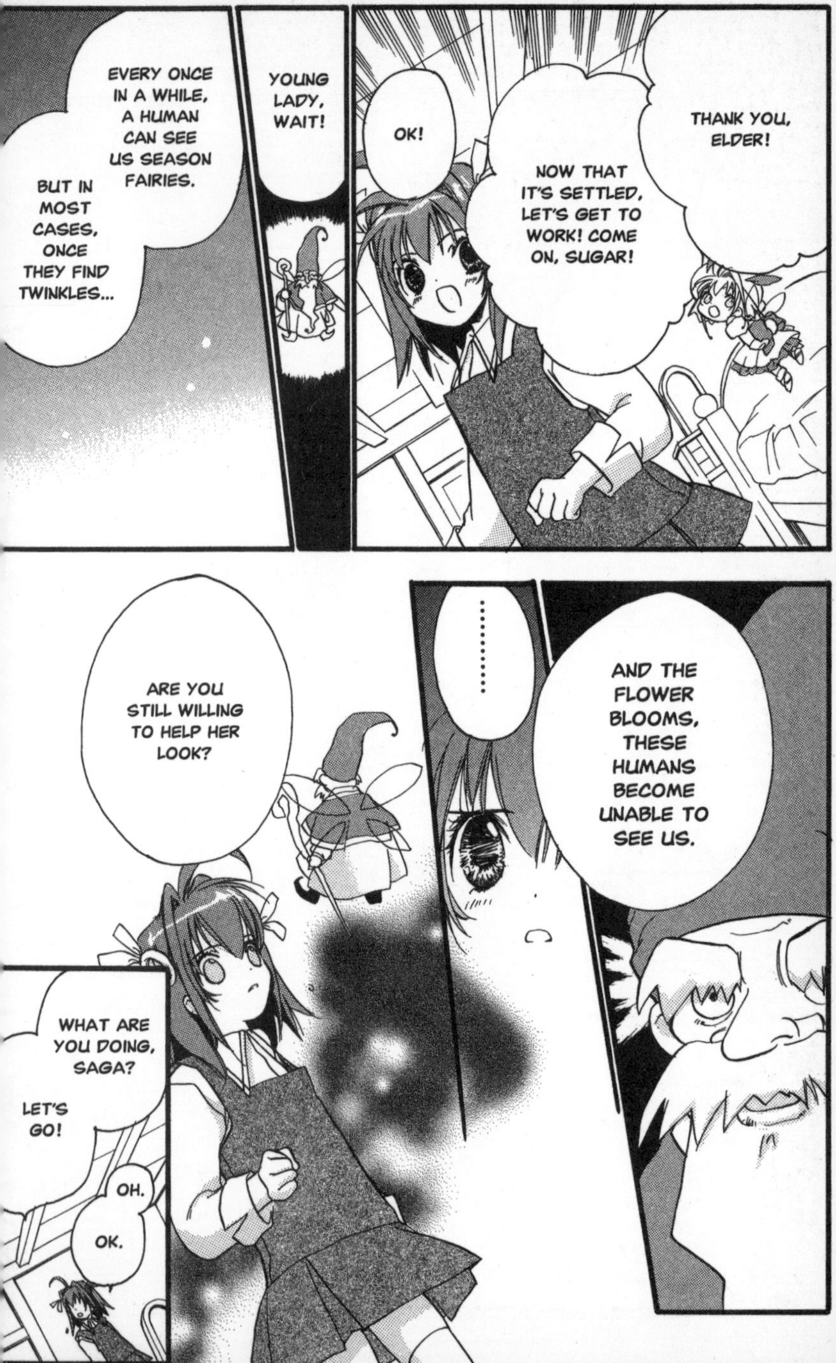
THANK YOU, ELDER!
NOW THAT IT'S SETTLED, LET'S GET TO WORK! COME ON, SUGAR!
OK!
YOUNG LADY, WAIT!
EVERY ONCE IN A WHILE, A HUMAN CAN SEE US SEASON FAIRIES.
BUT IN MOST CASES, ONCE THEY FIND TWINKLES...
AND THE FLOWER BLOOMS, THESE HUMANS BECOME UNABLE TO SEE US.
....
ARE YOU STILL WILLING TO HELP HER LOOK?
WHAT ARE YOU DOING, SAGA?
LET'S GO!
OH.
OK.

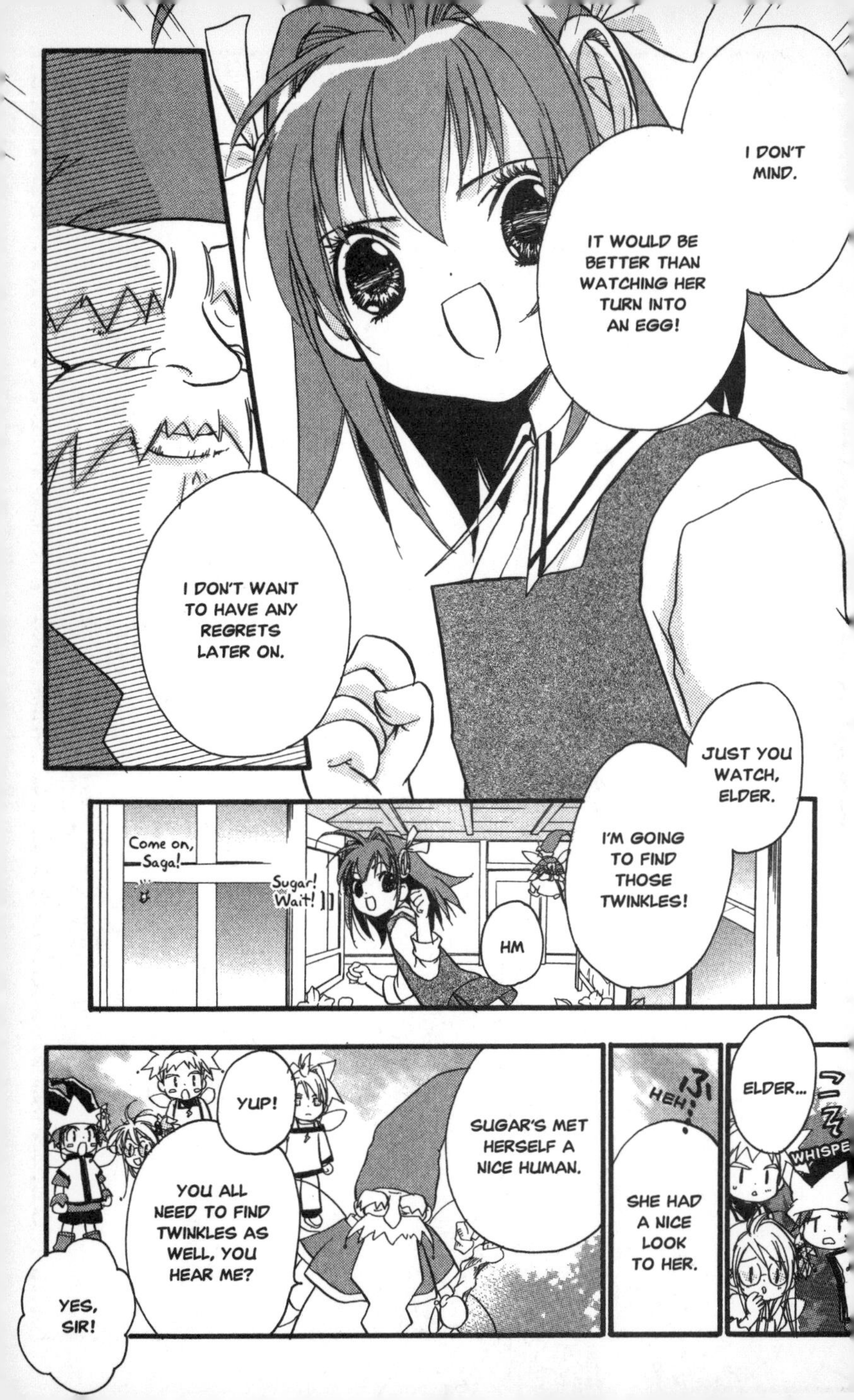

I DON'T MIND.
IT WOULD BE BETTER THAN WATCHING HER TURN INTO AN EGG!
I DON'T WANT TO HAVE ANY REGRETS LATER ON.
JUST YOU WATCH, ELDER.
I'M GOING TO FIND THOSE TWINKLES!
HM
Sugar! Wait!
Come on, Saga!
ELDER...
WHISPE
HEH
SHE HAD A NICE LOOK TO HER.
SUGAR'S MET HERSELF A NICE HUMAN.
YUP!
YOU ALL NEED TO FIND TWINKLES AS WELL, YOU HEAR ME?
YES, SIR!

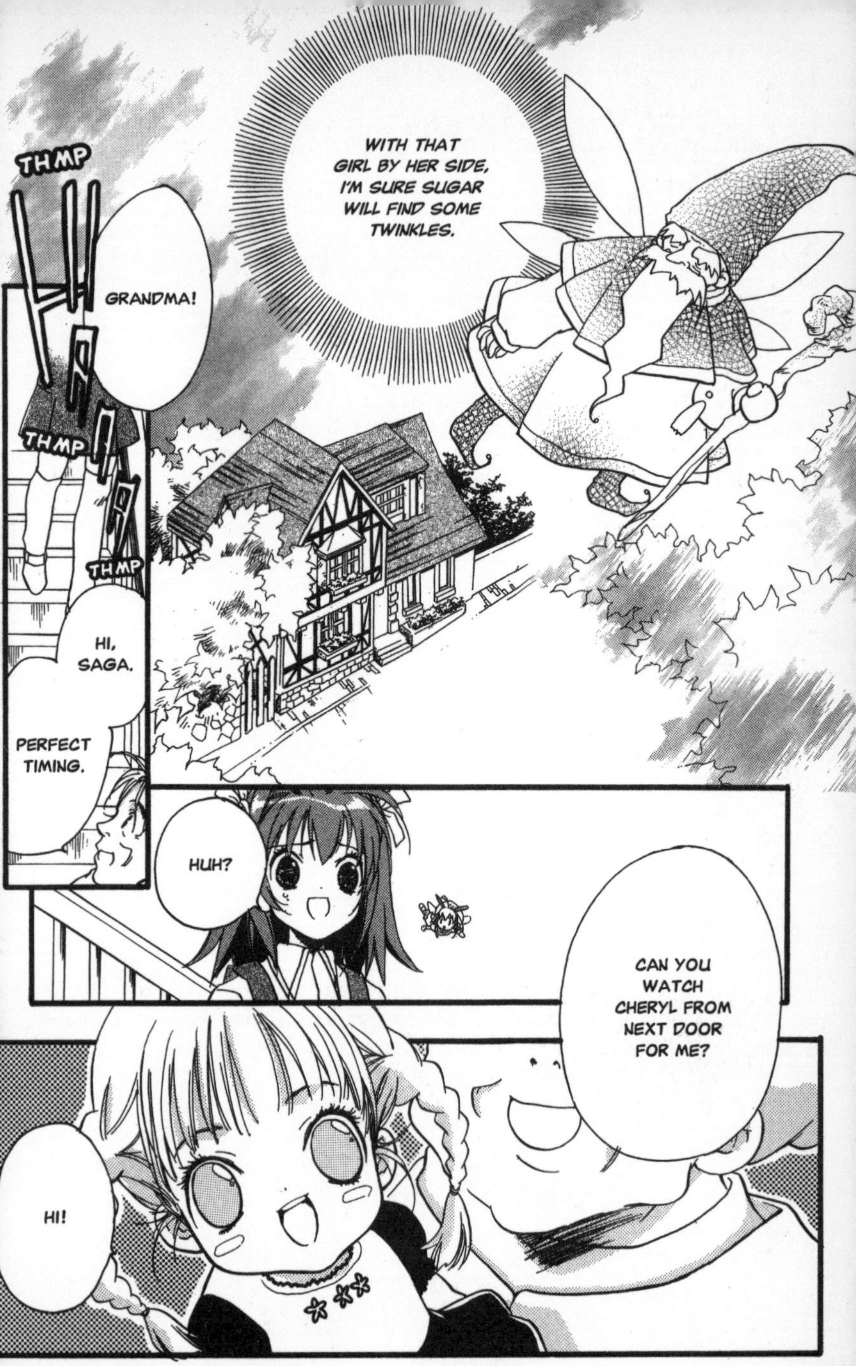
WITH THAT GIRL BY HER SIDE, I'M SURE SUGAR WILL FIND SOME TWINKLES.
THMP
GRANDMA!
THMP
THMP
HI, SAGA.
PERFECT TIMING.
HUH?
CAN YOU WATCH CHERYL FROM NEXT DOOR FOR ME?
HI!

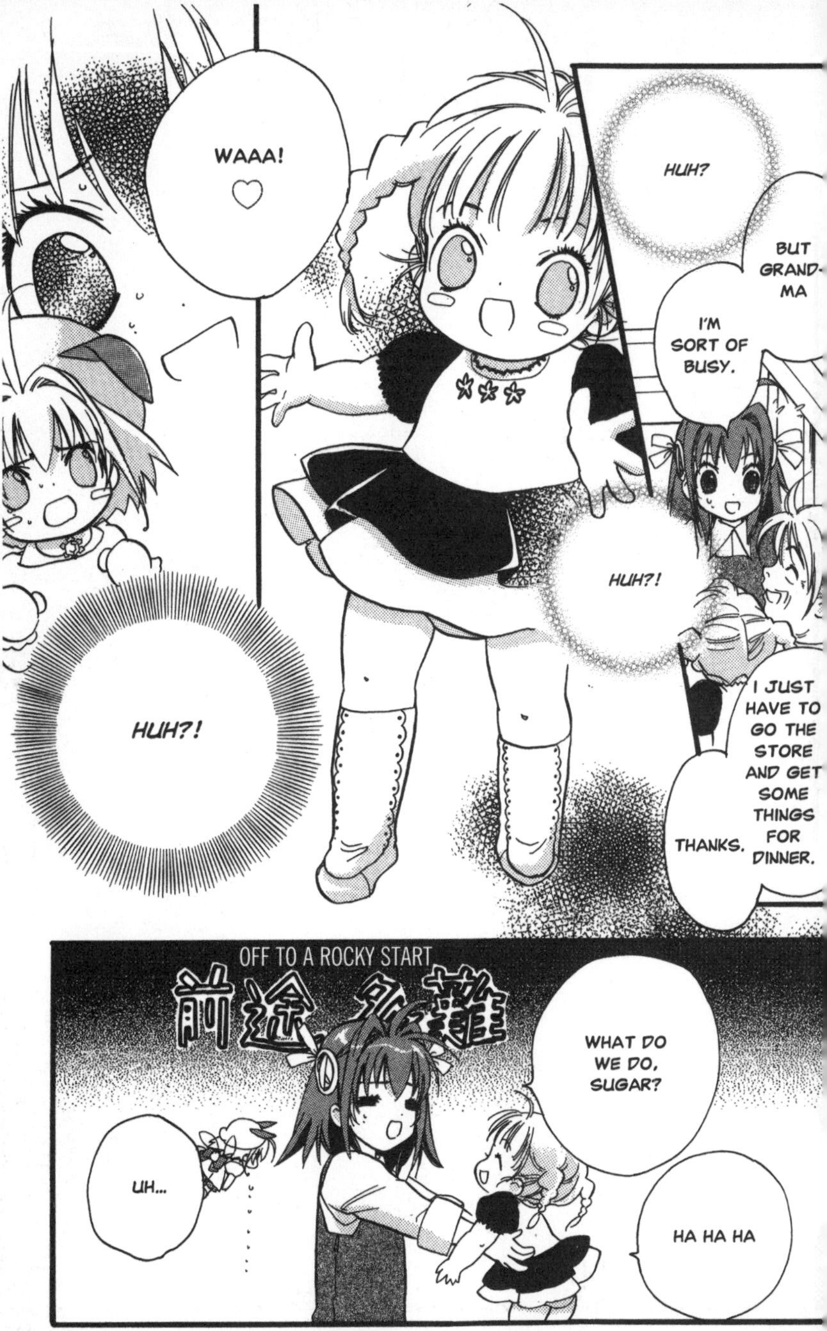
HUH?
BUT GRANDMA
I'M SORT OF BUSY.
HUH?!
I JUST HAVE TO GO THE STORE AND GET SOME THINGS FOR DINNER.
THANKS.
WAAA! ♡
HUH?!
OFF TO A ROCKY START
前途多難
WHAT DO WE DO, SUGAR?
HA HA HA
UH...

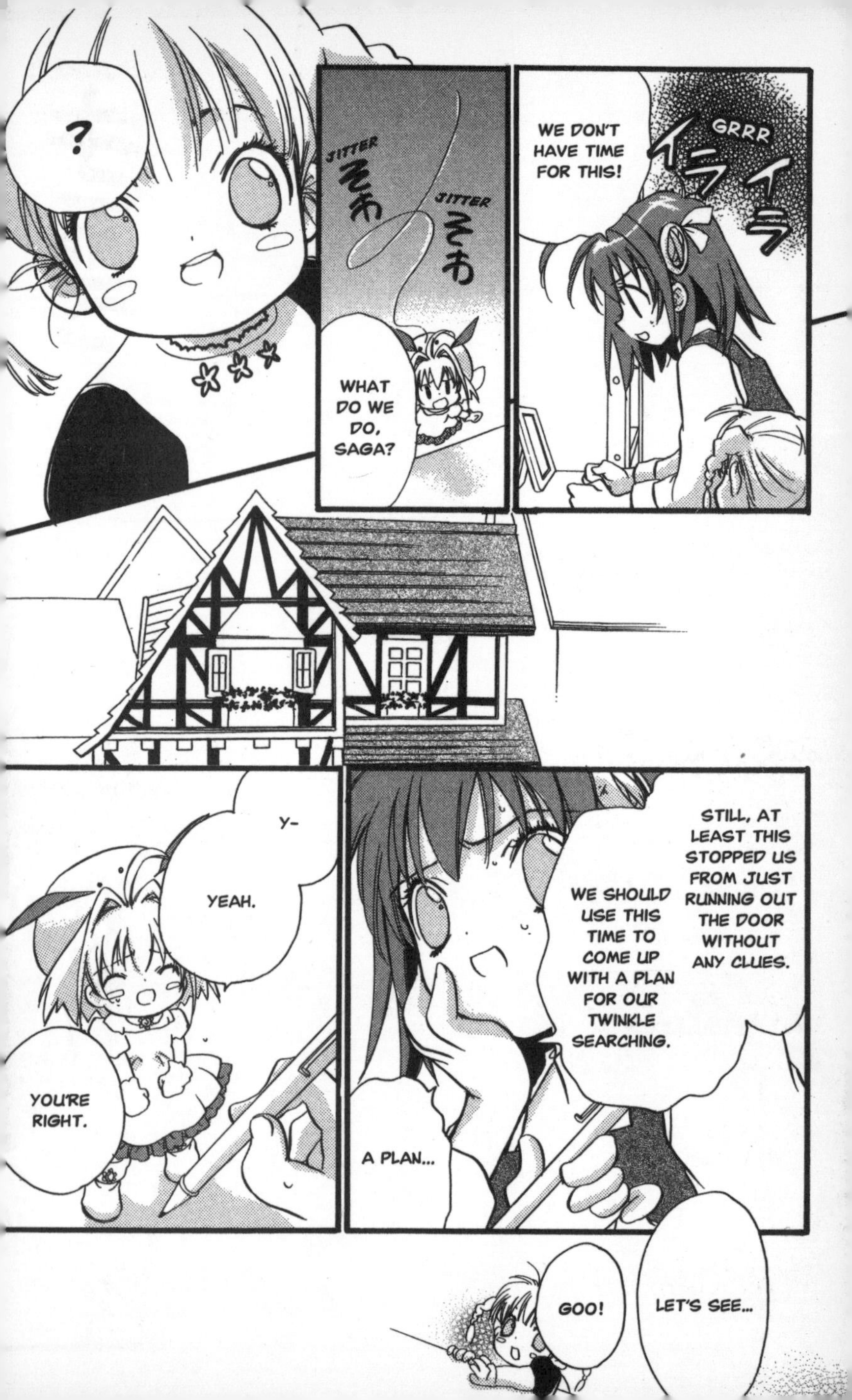

GRRR
イライラ
WE DON'T HAVE TIME FOR THIS!
JITTER
そわ
JITTER
そわ
WHAT DO WE DO, SAGA?
?
STILL, AT LEAST THIS STOPPED US FROM JUST RUNNING OUT THE DOOR WITHOUT ANY CLUES.
WE SHOULD USE THIS TIME TO COME UP WITH A PLAN FOR OUR TWINKLE SEARCHING.
A PLAN...
Y-
YEAH.
YOU'RE RIGHT.
LET'S SEE...
GOO!

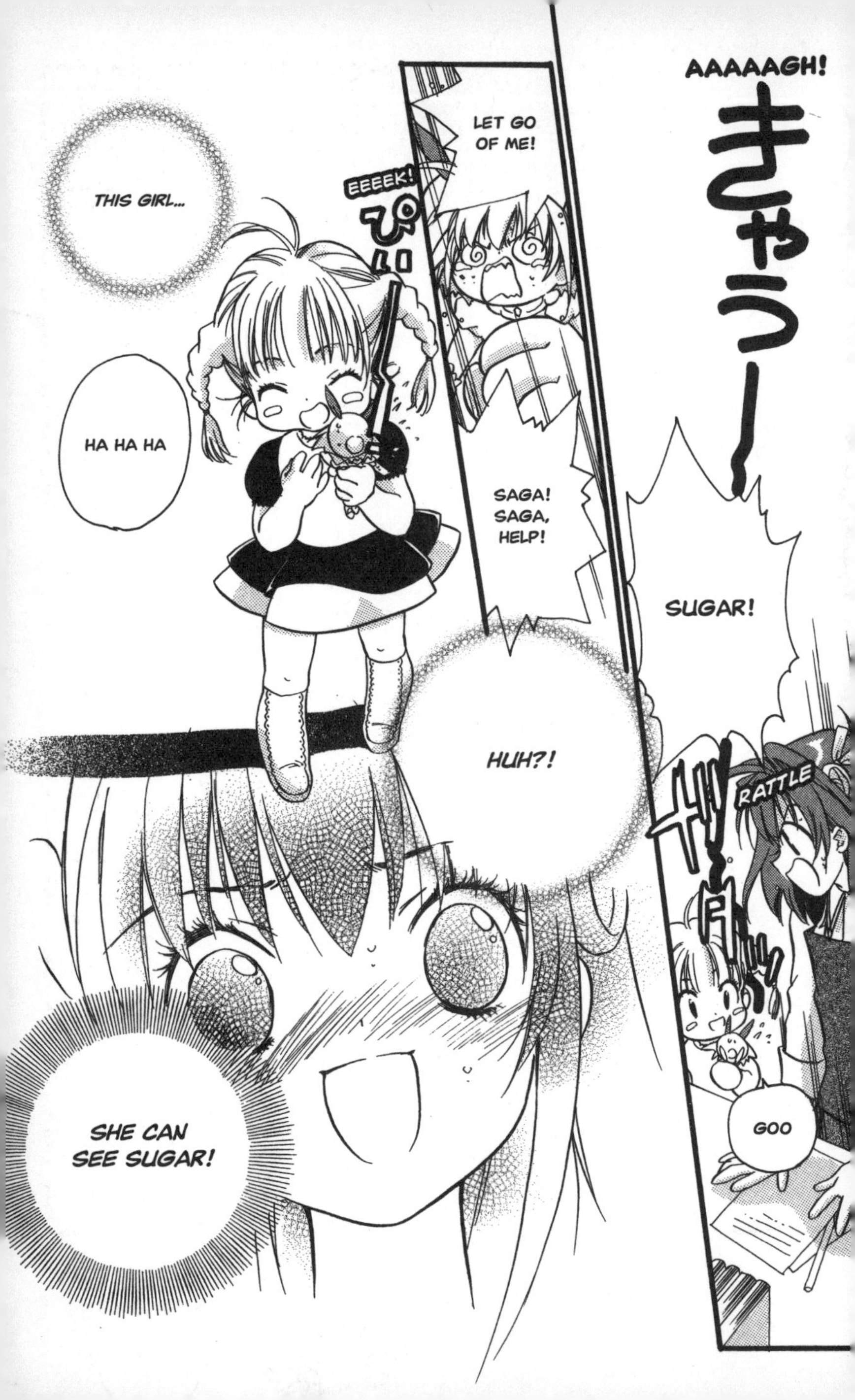

AAAAAGH!
きゃうー
SUGAR!
RATTLE
GOO
LET GO OF ME!
SAGA! SAGA, HELP!
HUH?!
EEEEK!
THIS GIRL...
HA HA HA
SHE CAN SEE SUGAR!

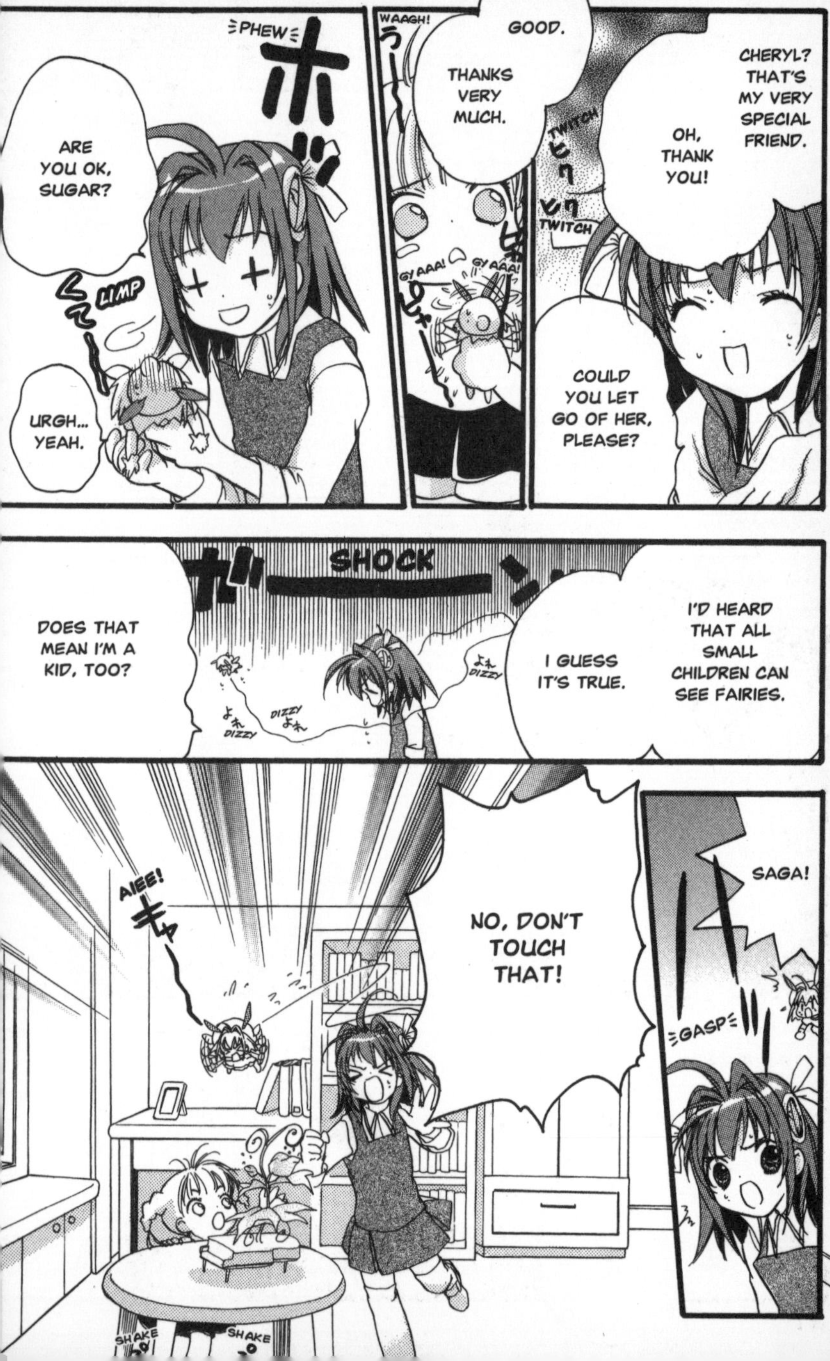
CHERYL? THAT'S MY VERY SPECIAL FRIEND.
OH, THANK YOU!
TWITCH
TWITCH
COULD YOU LET GO OF HER, PLEASE?
WAAGH!
GOOD.
THANKS VERY MUCH.
GYAAA!
GYAAA!
PHEW
ARE YOU OK, SUGAR?
LIMP
URGH... YEAH.
I'D HEARD THAT ALL SMALL CHILDREN CAN SEE FAIRIES.
I GUESS IT'S TRUE.
SHOCK
DIZZY
DIZZY
DIZZY
DOES THAT MEAN I'M A KID, TOO?
SAGA!
GASP
NO, DON'T TOUCH THAT!
AIEE!
SHAKE
SHAKE

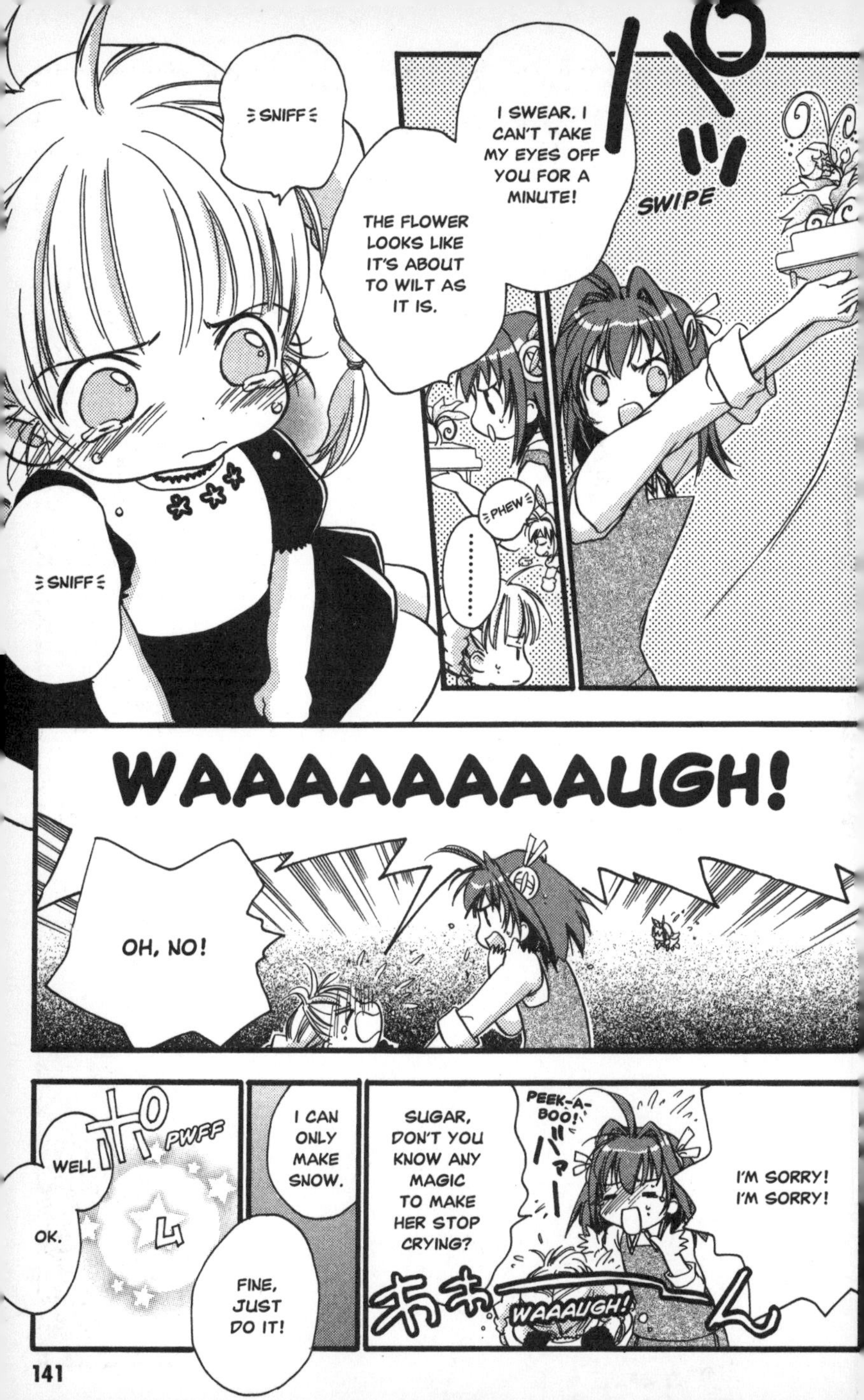
SWIPE
I SWEAR. I CAN'T TAKE MY EYES OFF YOU FOR A MINUTE!
THE FLOWER LOOKS LIKE IT'S ABOUT TO WILT AS IT IS.
PHEW
......
SNIFF
SNIFF
WAAAAAAAAAUGH!
OH, NO!
I'M SORRY! I'M SORRY!
PEEK-A-BOO!
WAAAUGH!
SUGAR, DON'T YOU KNOW ANY MAGIC TO MAKE HER STOP CRYING?
I CAN ONLY MAKE SNOW.
FINE, JUST DO IT!
WELL OK.
PWFF

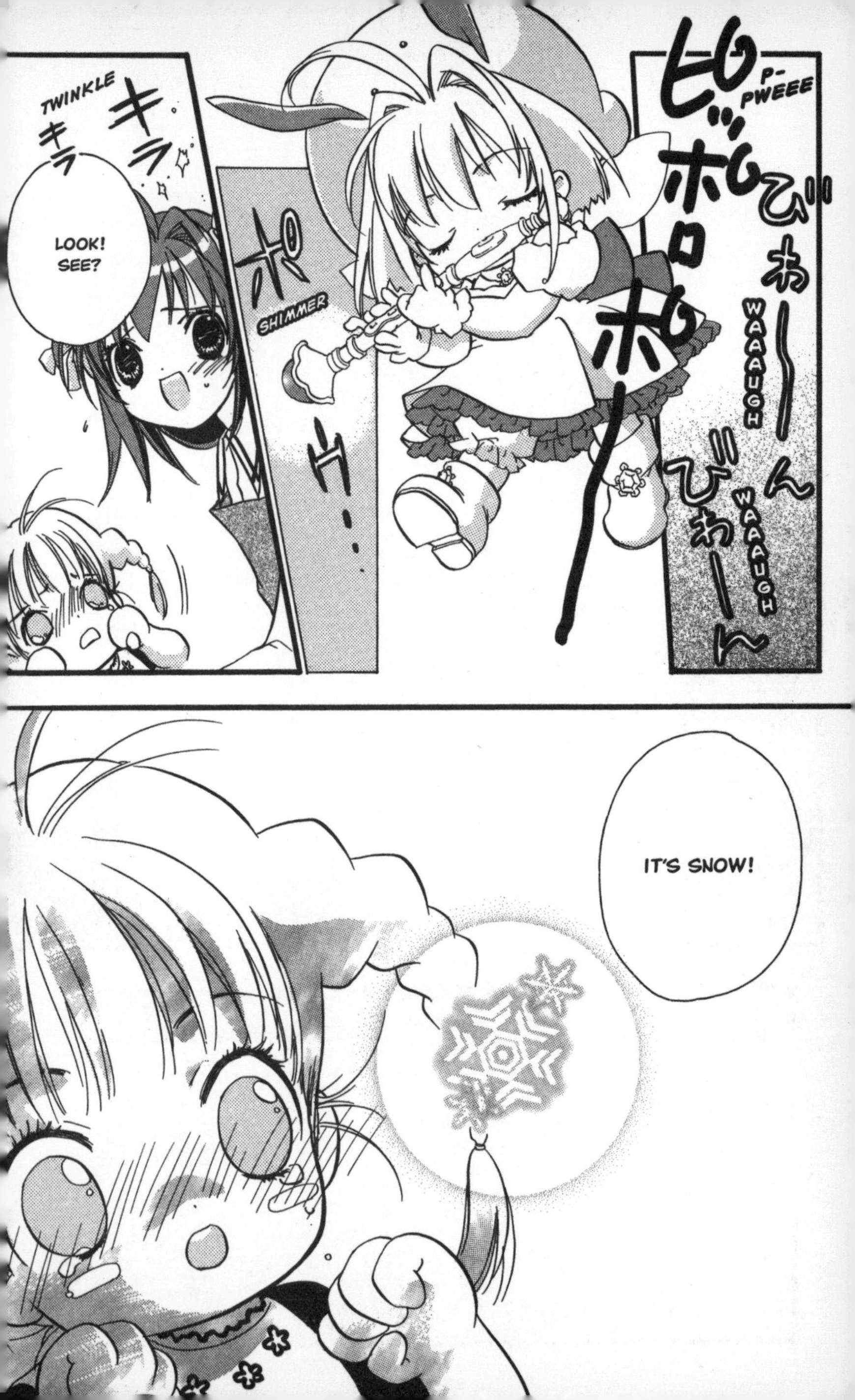
P-PWEEE
WAAAUGH
WAAAUGH
SHIMMER
キラ キラ
TWINKLE
LOOK! SEE?
IT'S SNOW!

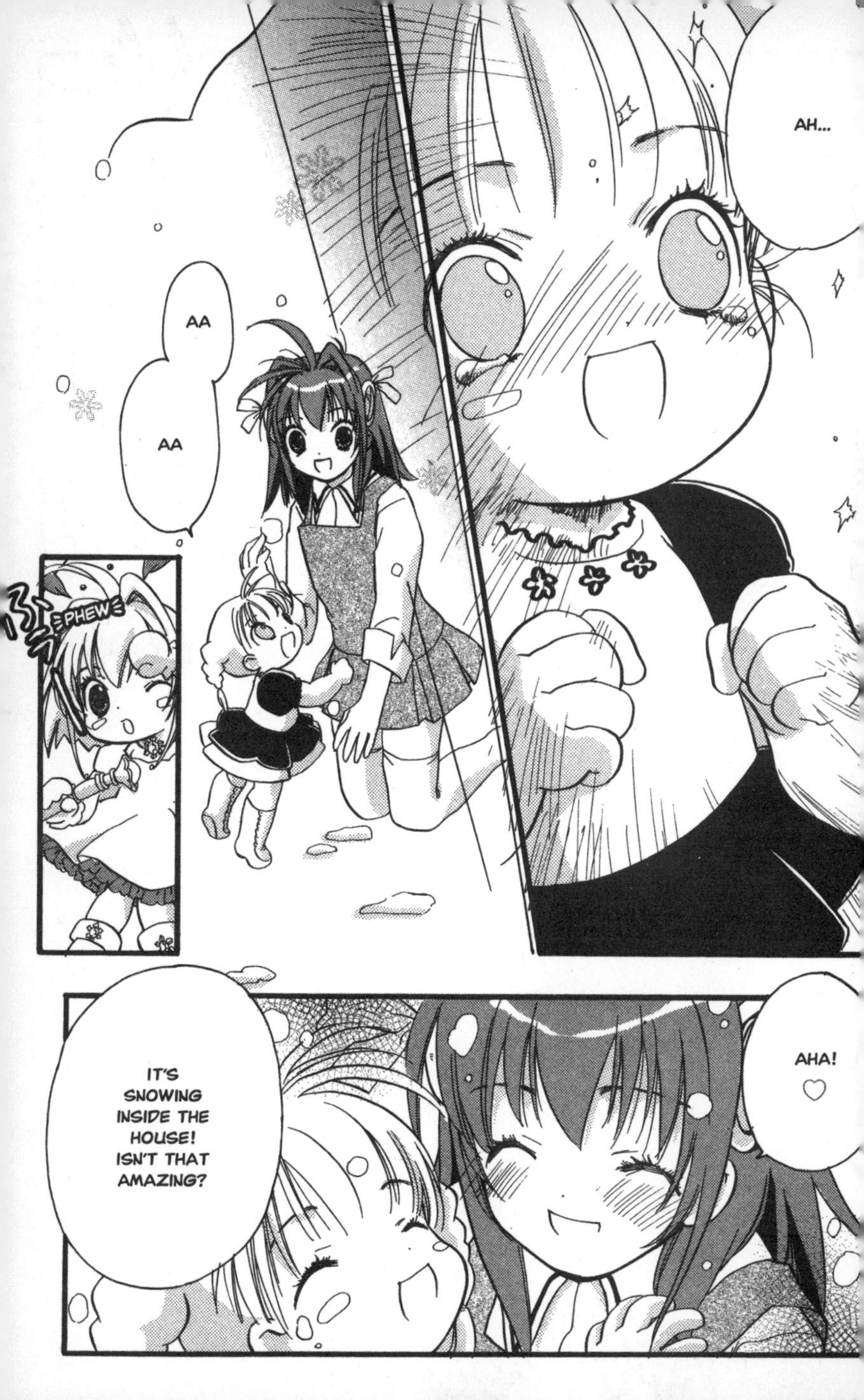
AH...
AA
AA
PHEW
AHA! ♡
IT'S SNOWING INSIDE THE HOUSE! ISN'T THAT AMAZING?

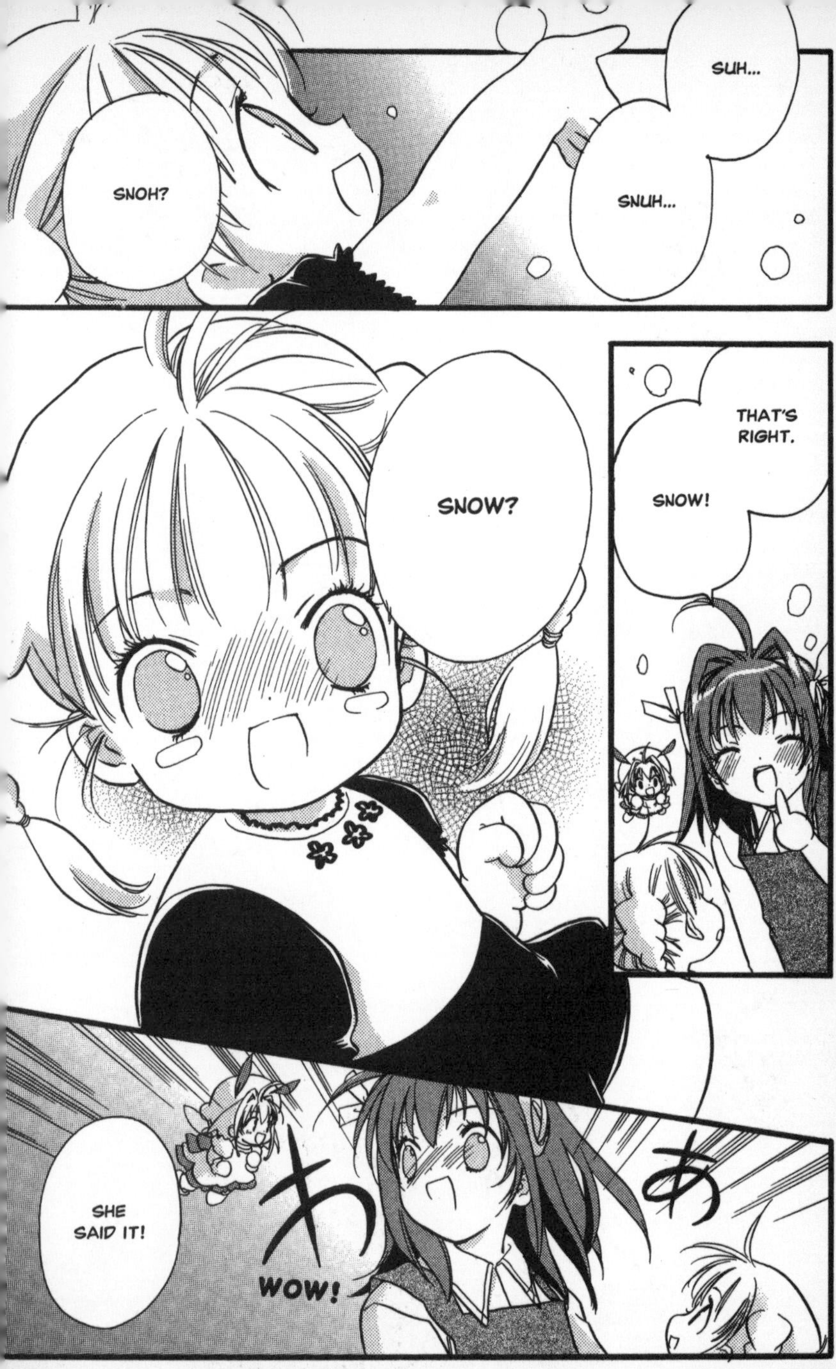
SUH...
SNUH...
SNOH?
THAT'S RIGHT.
SNOW!
SNOW?
あ
わ
WOW!
SHE SAID IT!

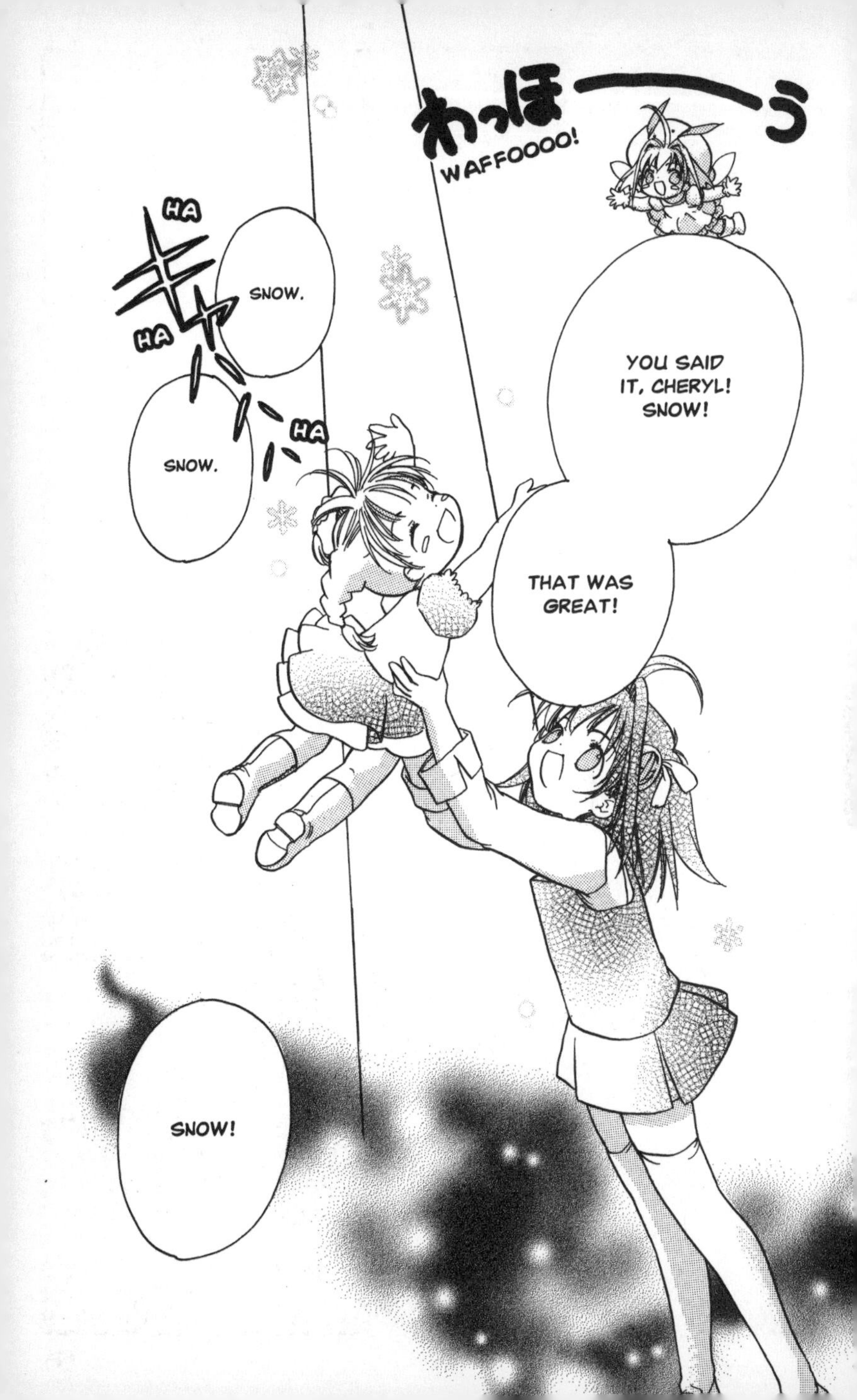

わっほーーーう
WAFFOOOO!
YOU SAID IT, CHERYL! SNOW!
THAT WAS GREAT!
HA
HA
HA
SNOW.
SNOW.
SNOW!

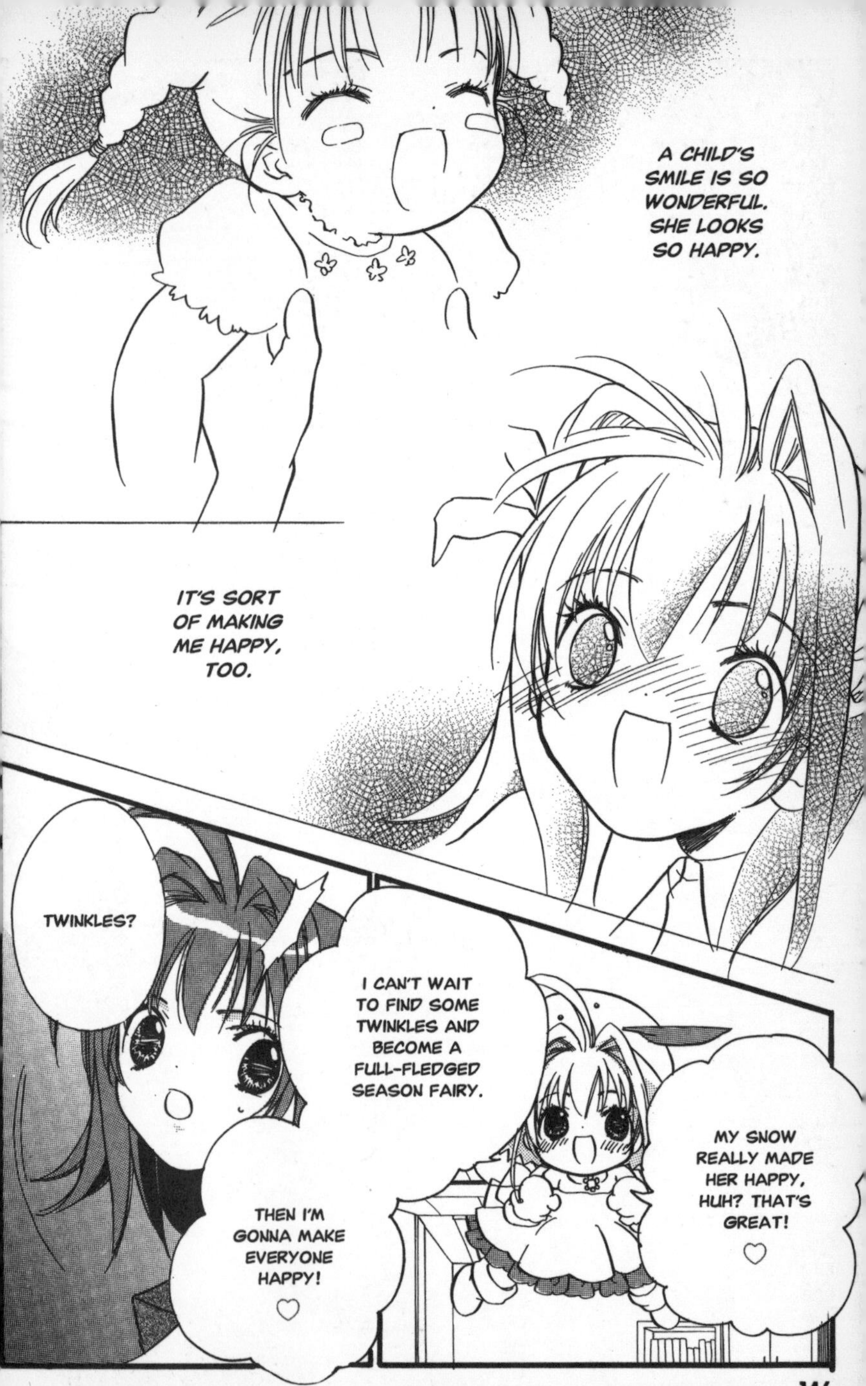
A CHILD'S SMILE IS SO WONDERFUL. SHE LOOKS SO HAPPY.
IT'S SORT OF MAKING ME HAPPY, TOO.
MY SNOW REALLY MADE HER HAPPY, HUH? THAT'S GREAT! ♡
I CAN'T WAIT TO FIND SOME TWINKLES AND BECOME A FULL-FLEDGED SEASON FAIRY.
THEN I'M GONNA MAKE EVERYONE HAPPY! ♡
TWINKLES?

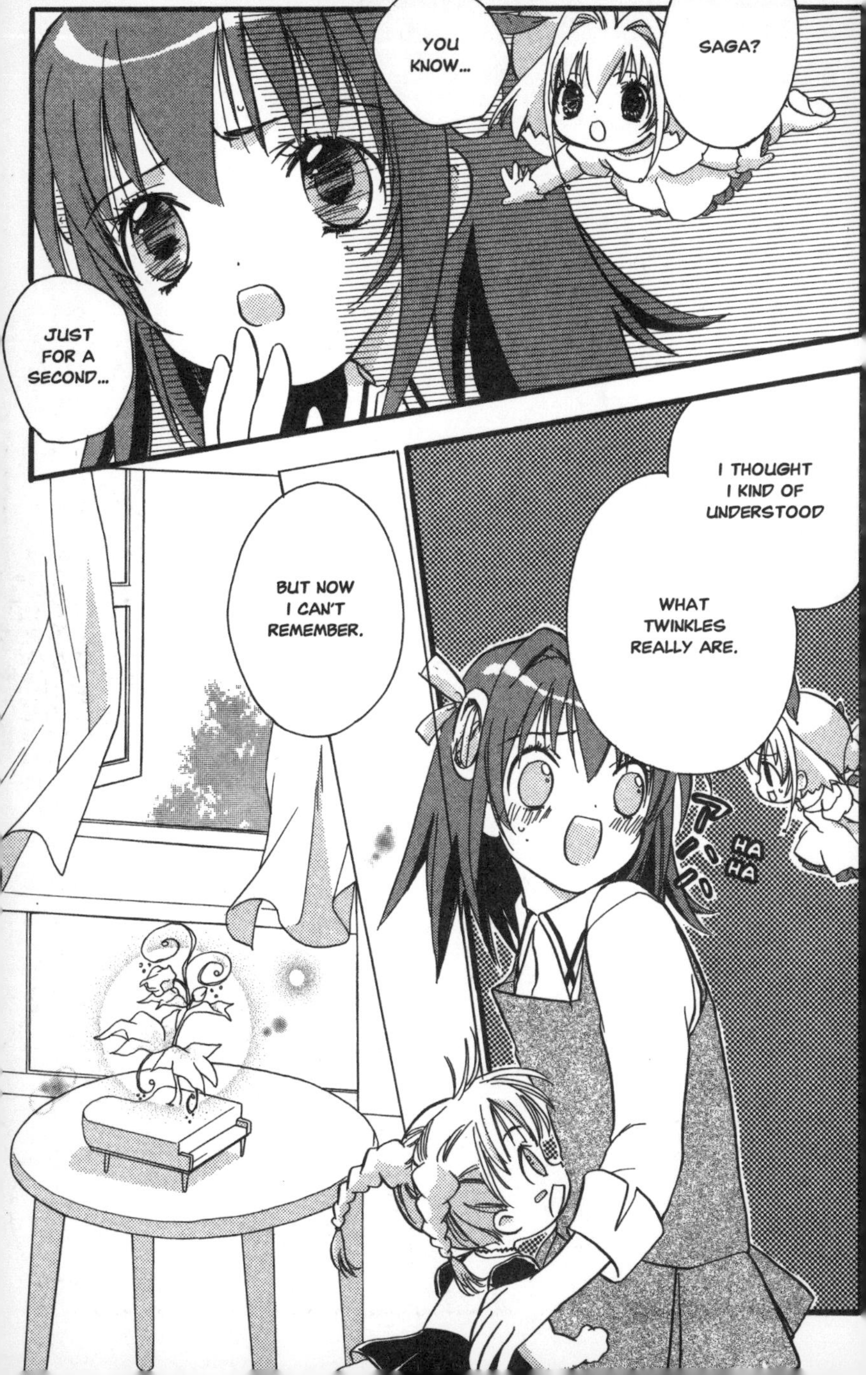
SAGA?
YOU KNOW...
JUST FOR A SECOND...
I THOUGHT I KIND OF UNDERSTOOD
WHAT TWINKLES REALLY ARE.
HA HA
BUT NOW I CAN'T REMEMBER.

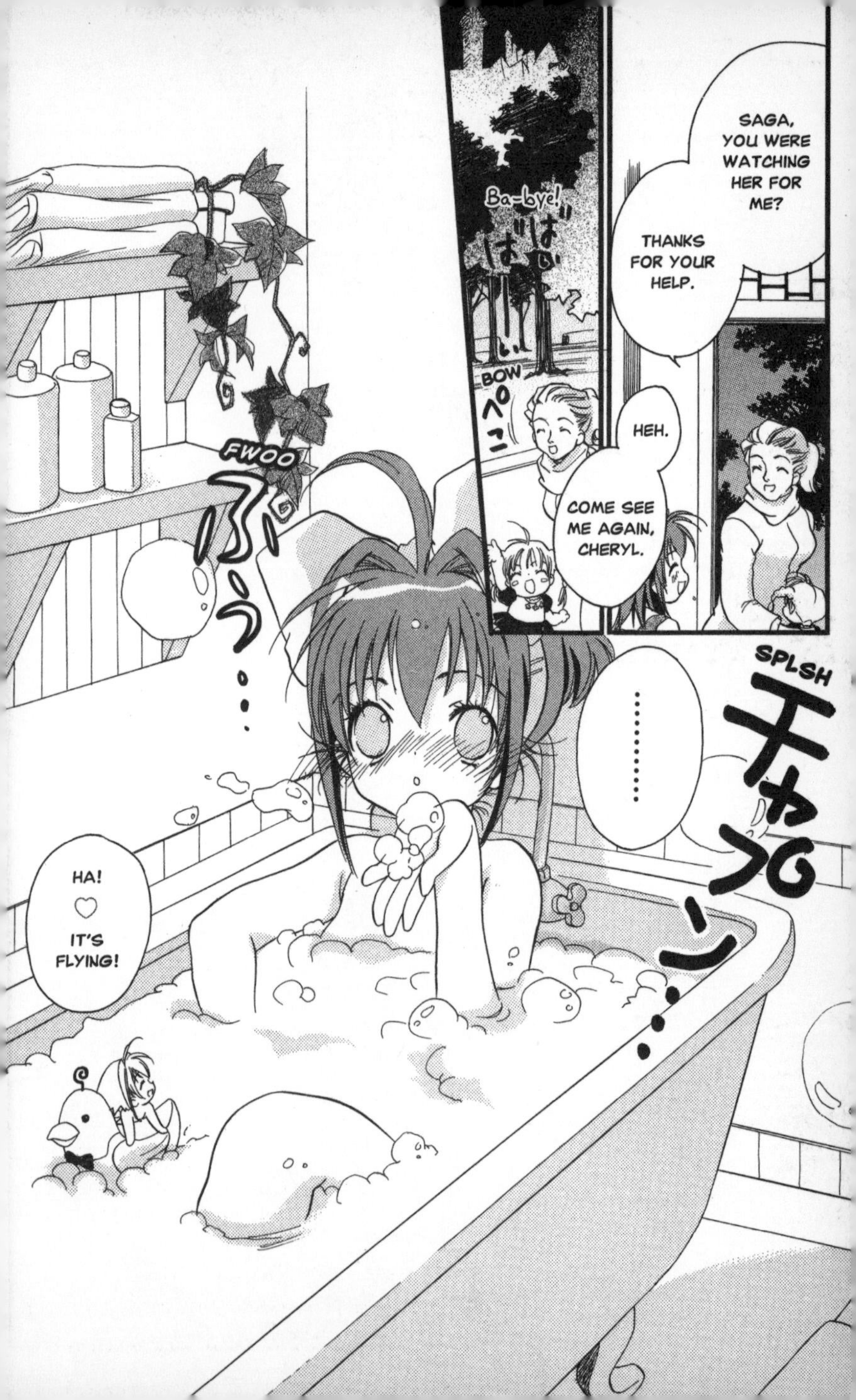
SAGA, YOU WERE WATCHING HER FOR ME?
THANKS FOR YOUR HELP.
HEH.
COME SEE ME AGAIN, CHERYL.
Ba-bye!
ばいばい
BOW
ぺこ
SPLSH
チャプン…
……………
FWOO
ふう…
HA! ♡ IT'S FLYING!

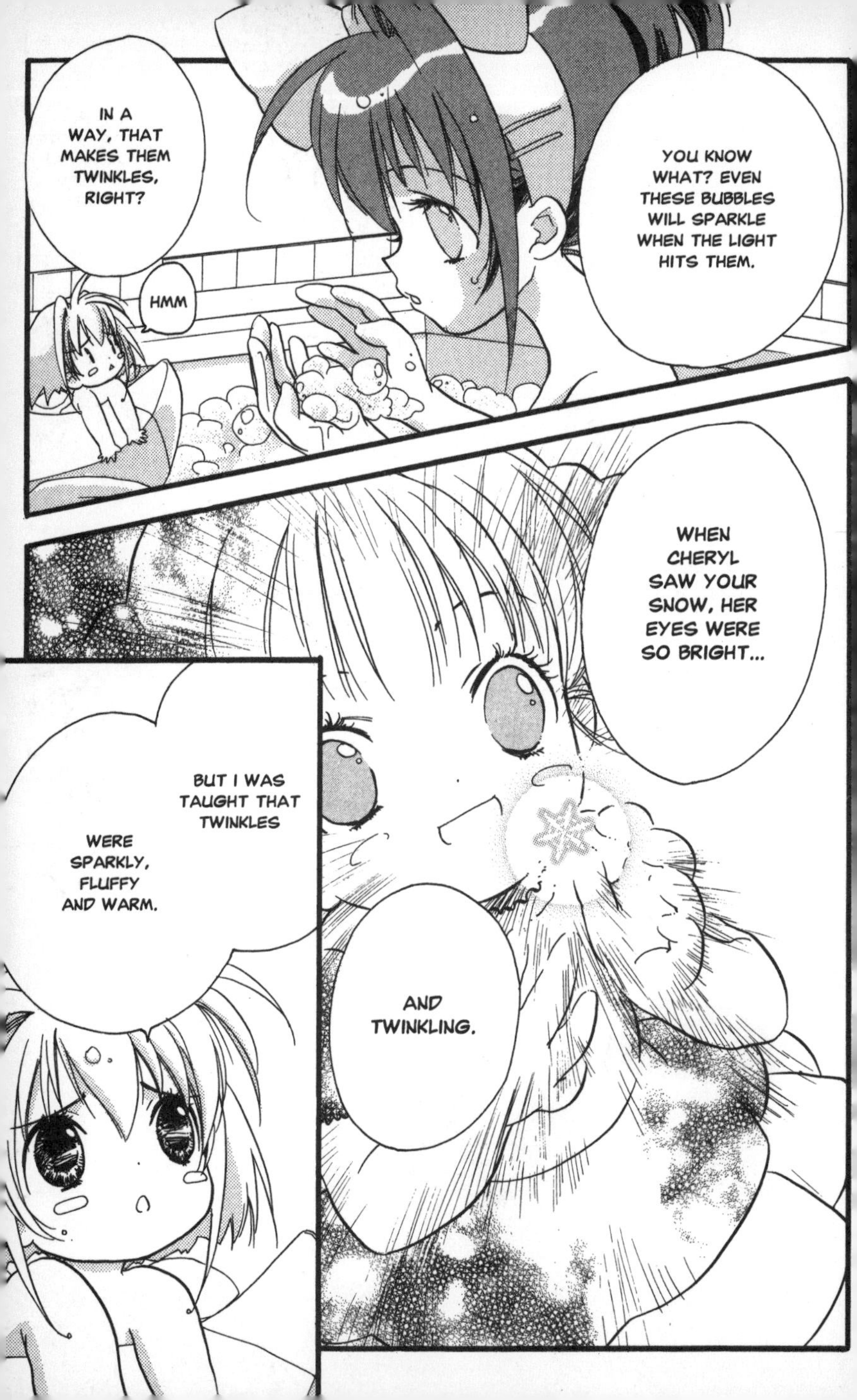
YOU KNOW WHAT? EVEN THESE BUBBLES WILL SPARKLE WHEN THE LIGHT HITS THEM.
IN A WAY, THAT MAKES THEM TWINKLES, RIGHT?
HMM
WHEN CHERYL SAW YOUR SNOW, HER EYES WERE SO BRIGHT...
AND TWINKLING.
BUT I WAS TAUGHT THAT TWINKLES WERE SPARKLY, FLUFFY AND WARM.

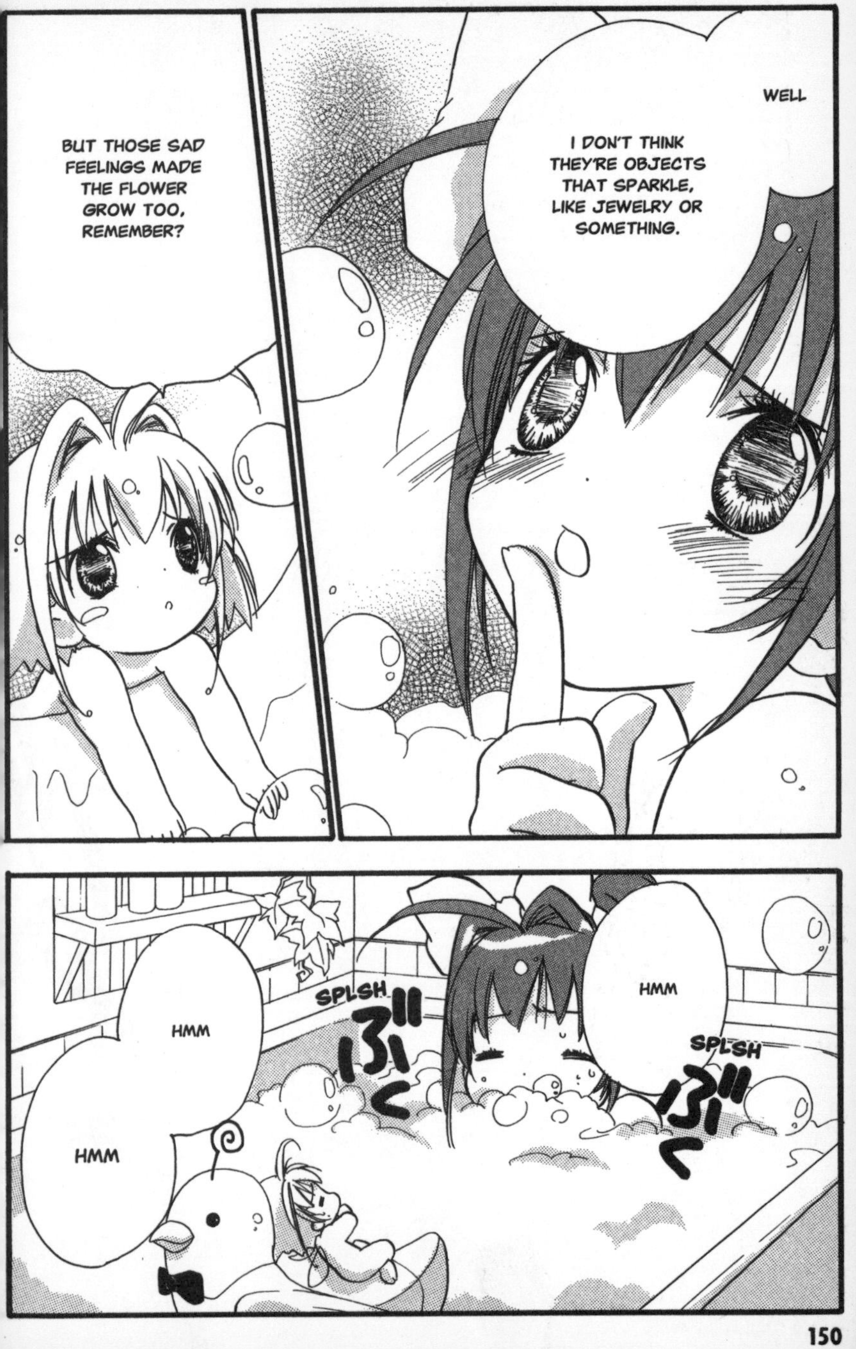
WELL
I DON'T THINK THEY'RE OBJECTS THAT SPARKLE, LIKE JEWELRY OR SOMETHING.
BUT THOSE SAD FEELINGS MADE THE FLOWER GROW TOO, REMEMBER?
HMM
SPLSH
ぶく
SPLSH
ぶく
HMM
HMM

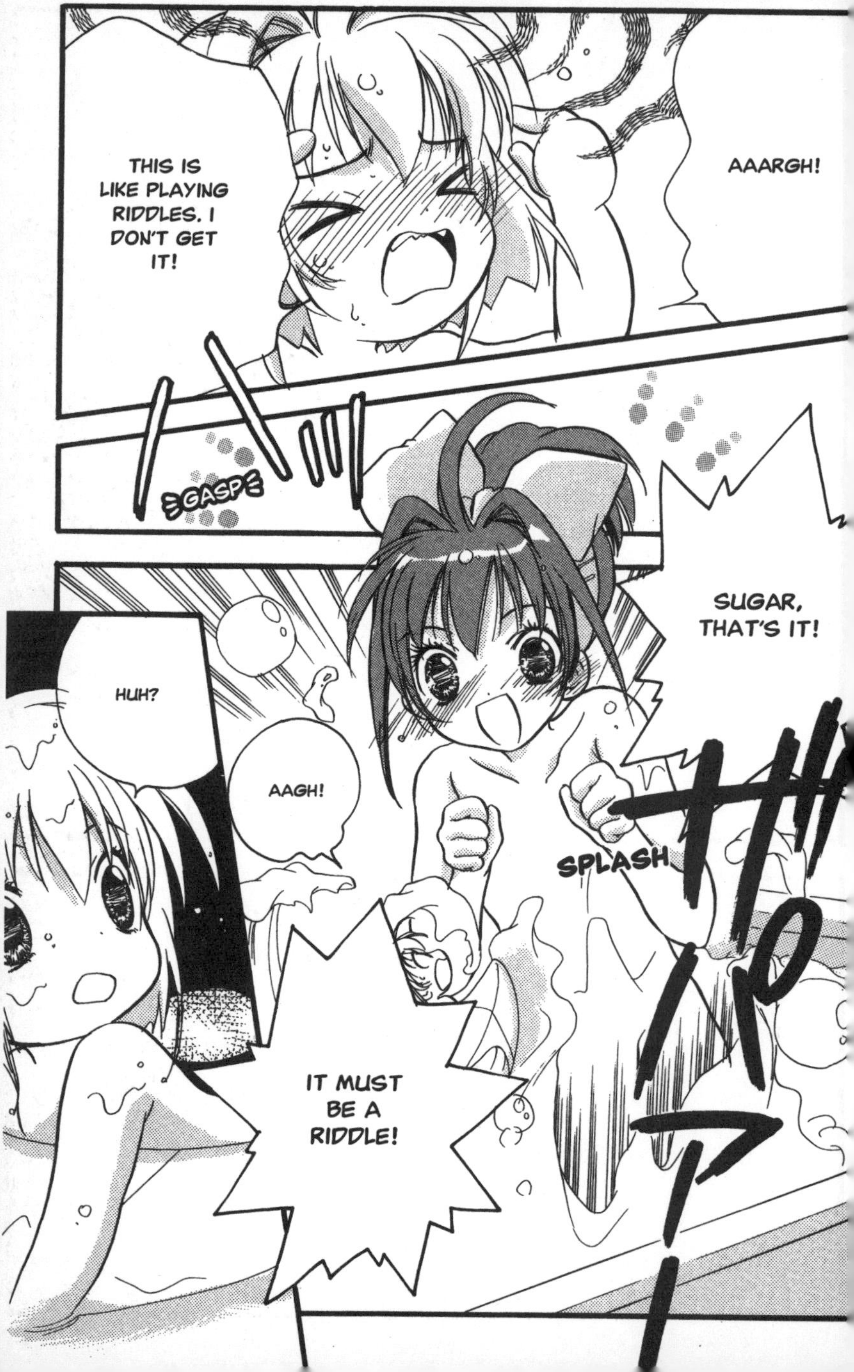
AAARGH!
THIS IS LIKE PLAYING RIDDLES. I DON'T GET IT!
GASP
SUGAR, THAT'S IT!
SPLASH
AAGH!
HUH?
IT MUST BE A RIDDLE!

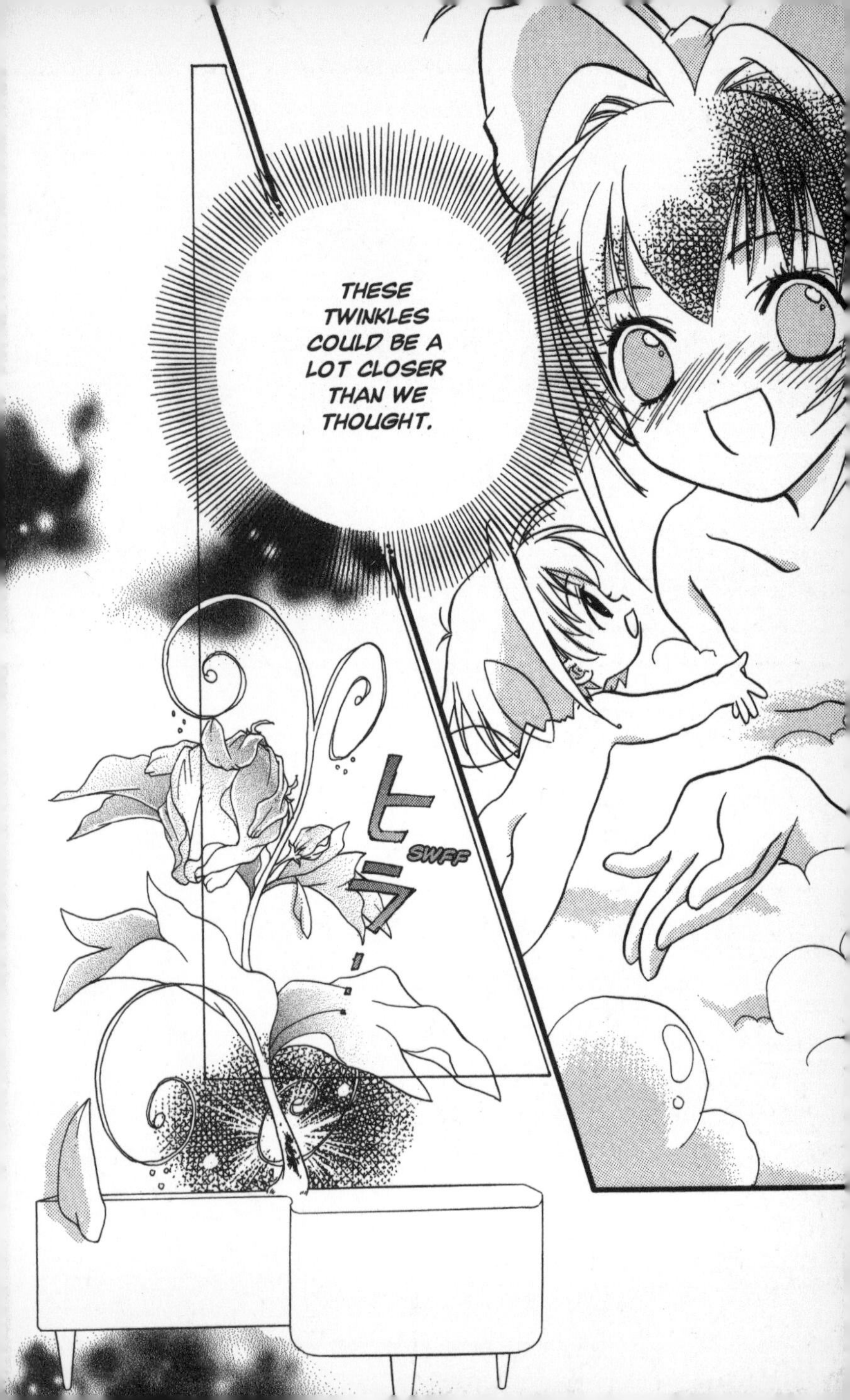
THESE TWINKLES COULD BE A LOT CLOSER THAN WE THOUGHT.
ヒラ
SWFF

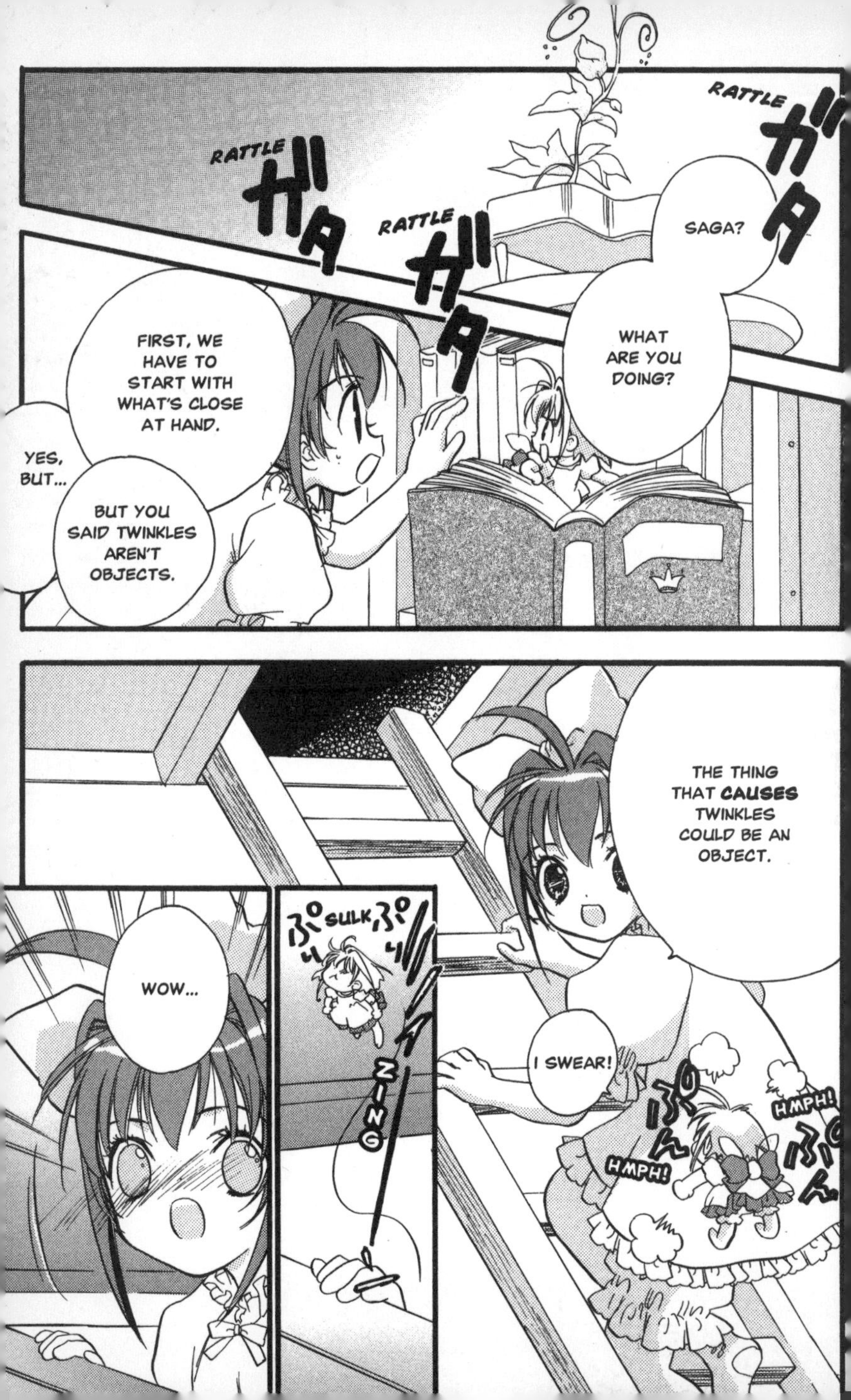
RATTLE
ガタ
SAGA?
WHAT ARE YOU DOING?
RATTLE
ガタ
RATTLE
ガタ
FIRST, WE HAVE TO START WITH WHAT'S CLOSE AT HAND.
YES, BUT...
BUT YOU SAID TWINKLES AREN'T OBJECTS.
THE THING THAT **CAUSES** TWINKLES COULD BE AN OBJECT.
I SWEAR!
HMPH!
ぷん
HMPH!
ぷん
SULK
ぷい
ぷい
ZING
WOW...

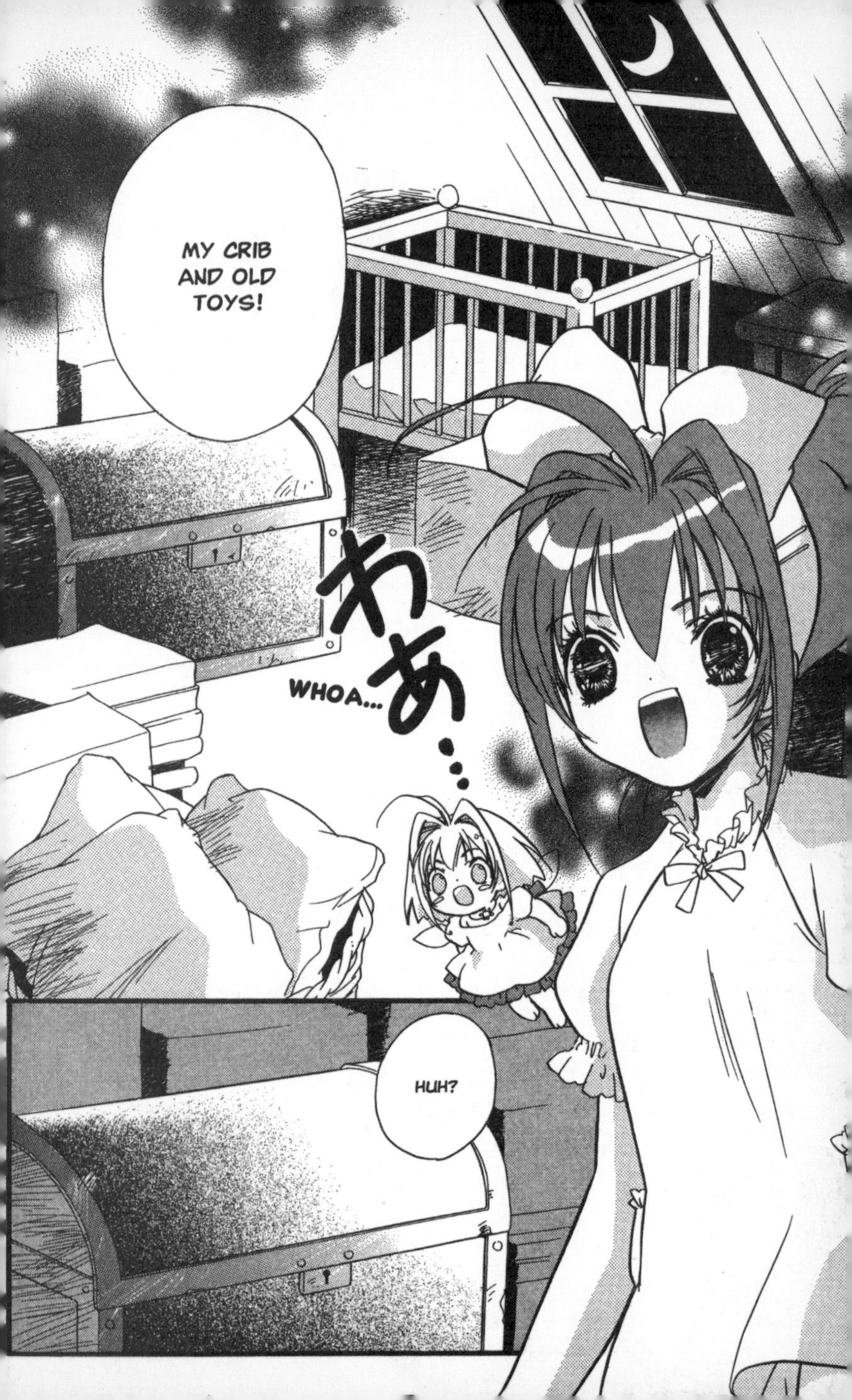
MY CRIB AND OLD TOYS!
わあ…
WHOA...
HUH?

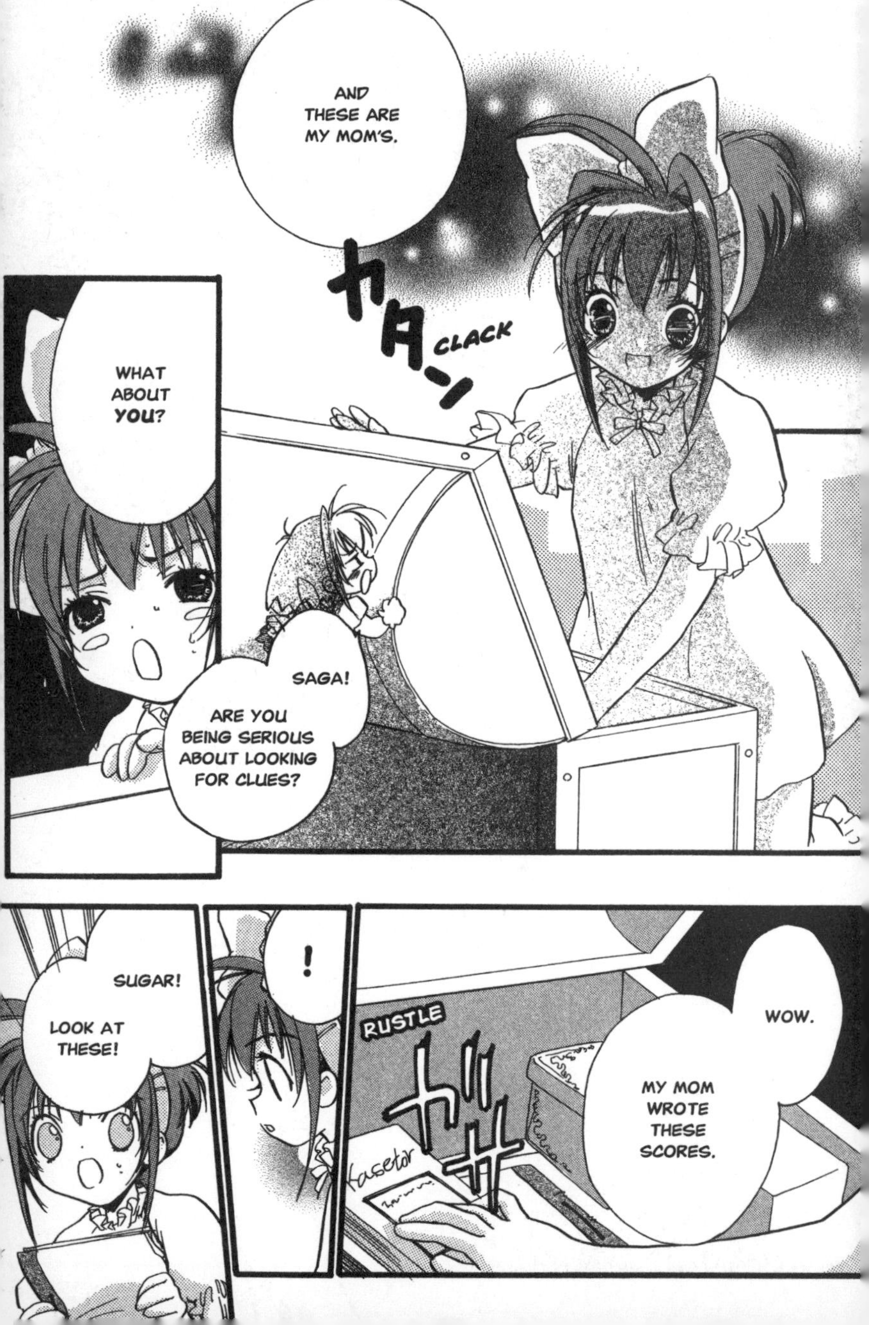
AND THESE ARE MY MOM'S.
CLACK
WHAT ABOUT YOU?
SAGA!
ARE YOU BEING SERIOUS ABOUT LOOKING FOR CLUES?
WOW.
MY MOM WROTE THESE SCORES.
RUSTLE
!
SUGAR!
LOOK AT THESE!

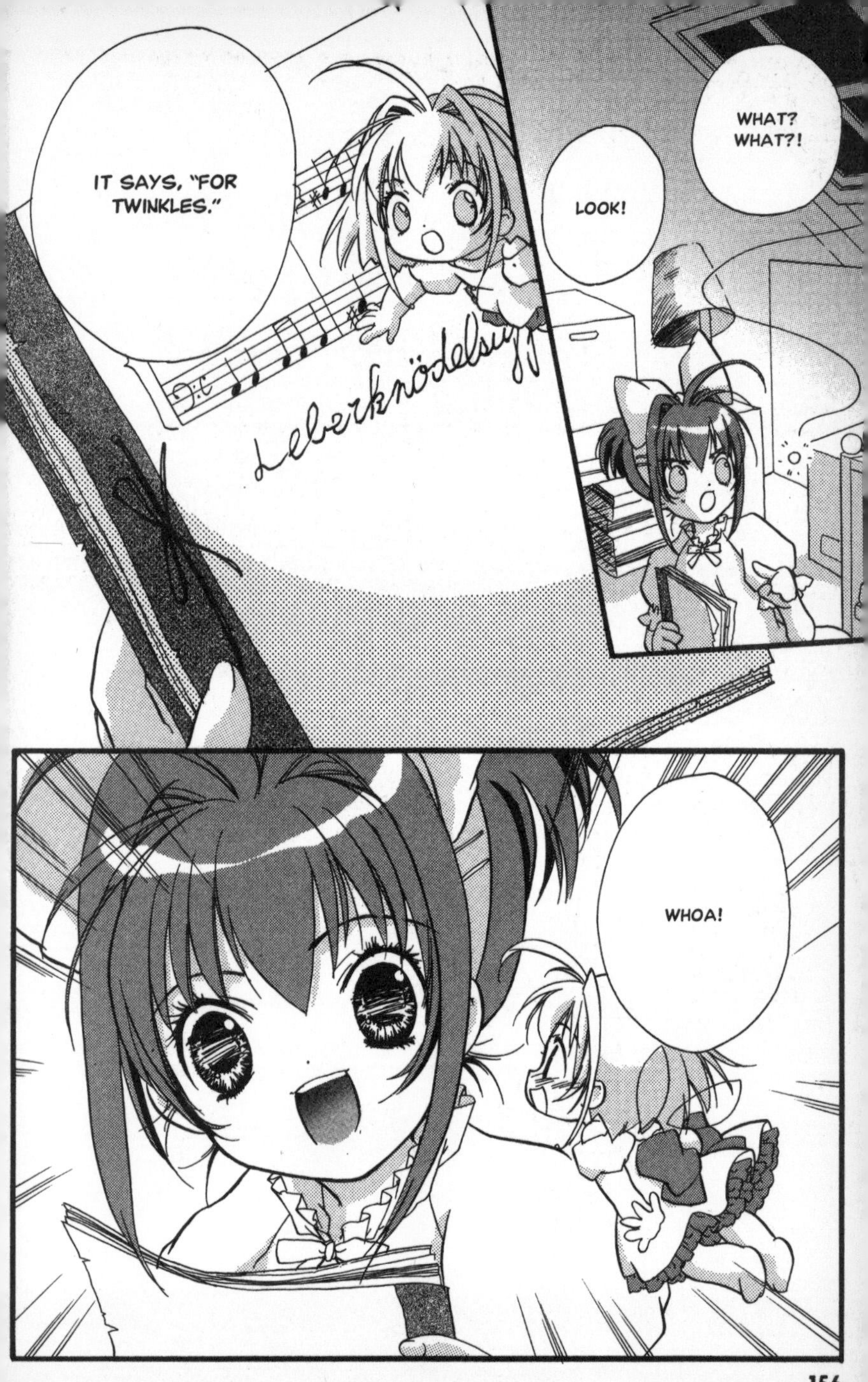
WHAT? WHAT?!
LOOK!
IT SAYS, "FOR TWINKLES."
Leberknödelsu
WHOA!

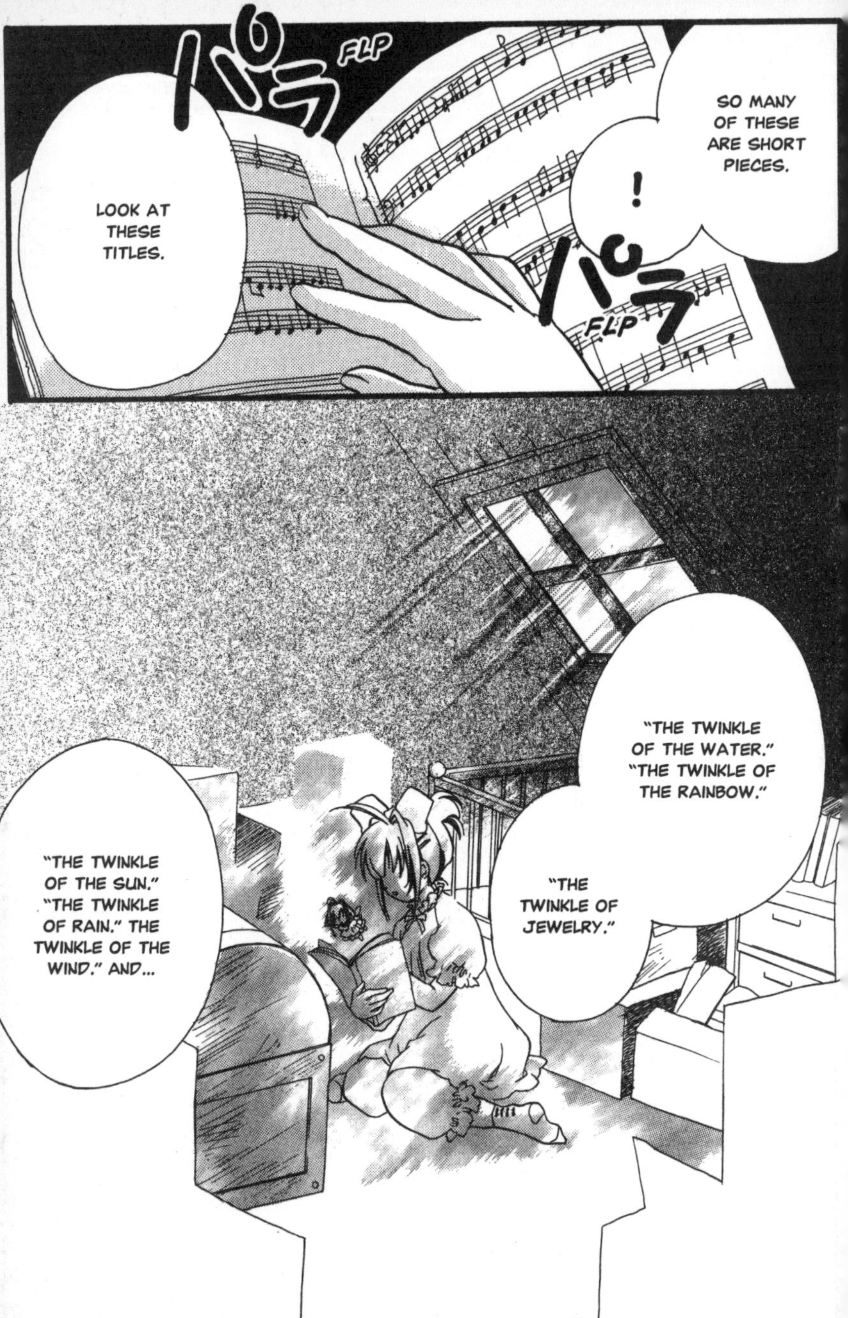
SO MANY OF THESE ARE SHORT PIECES.
!
パラ
FLP
パラ
FLP
LOOK AT THESE TITLES.
"THE TWINKLE OF THE WATER." "THE TWINKLE OF THE RAINBOW."
"THE TWINKLE OF JEWELRY."
"THE TWINKLE OF THE SUN." "THE TWINKLE OF RAIN." THE TWINKLE OF THE WIND." AND...

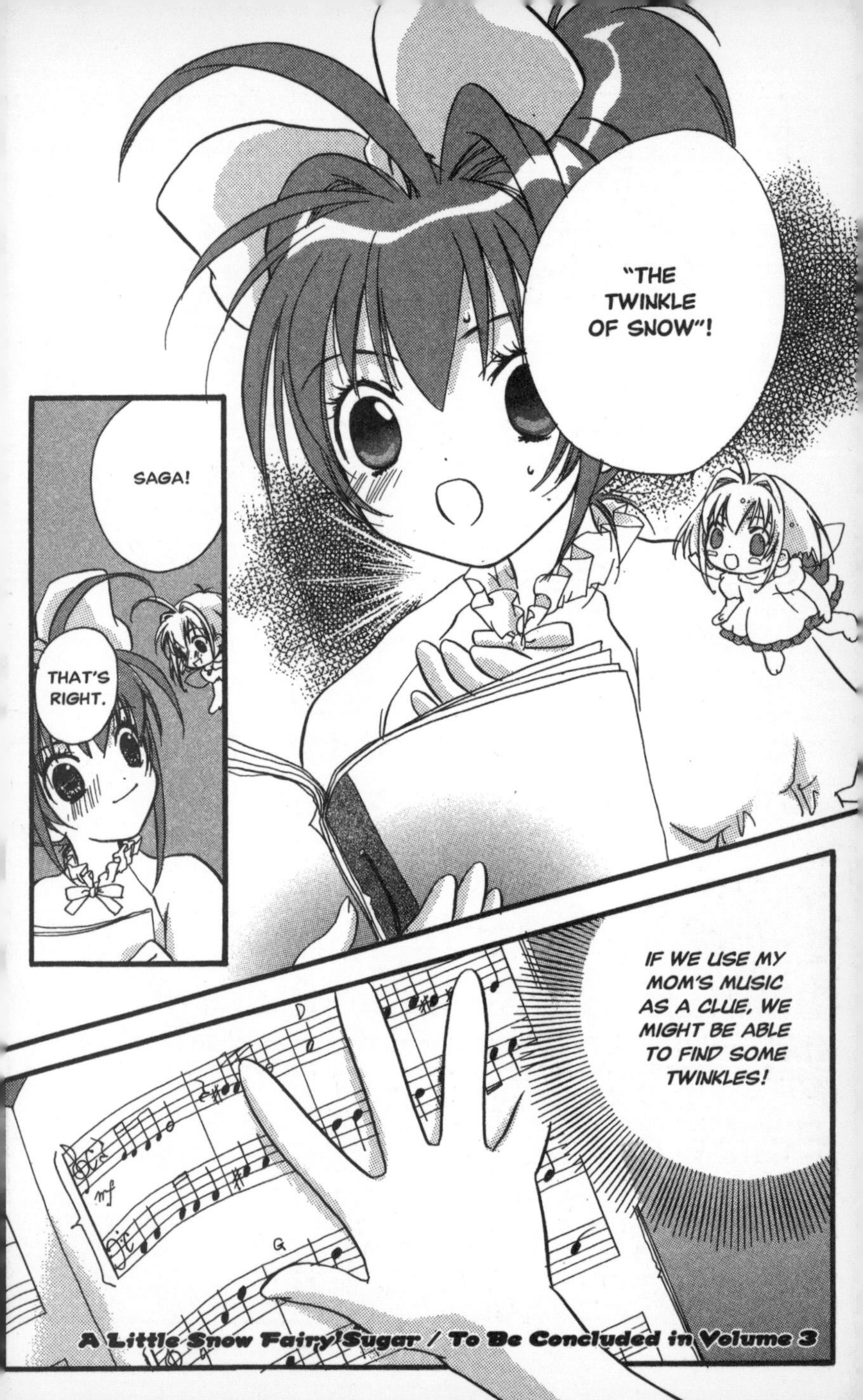
"THE TWINKLE OF SNOW"!
SAGA!
THAT'S RIGHT.
IF WE USE MY MOM'S MUSIC AS A CLUE, WE MIGHT BE ABLE TO FIND SOME TWINKLES!
D
G

A Little Snow Fairy Sugar / To Be Concluded in Volume 3

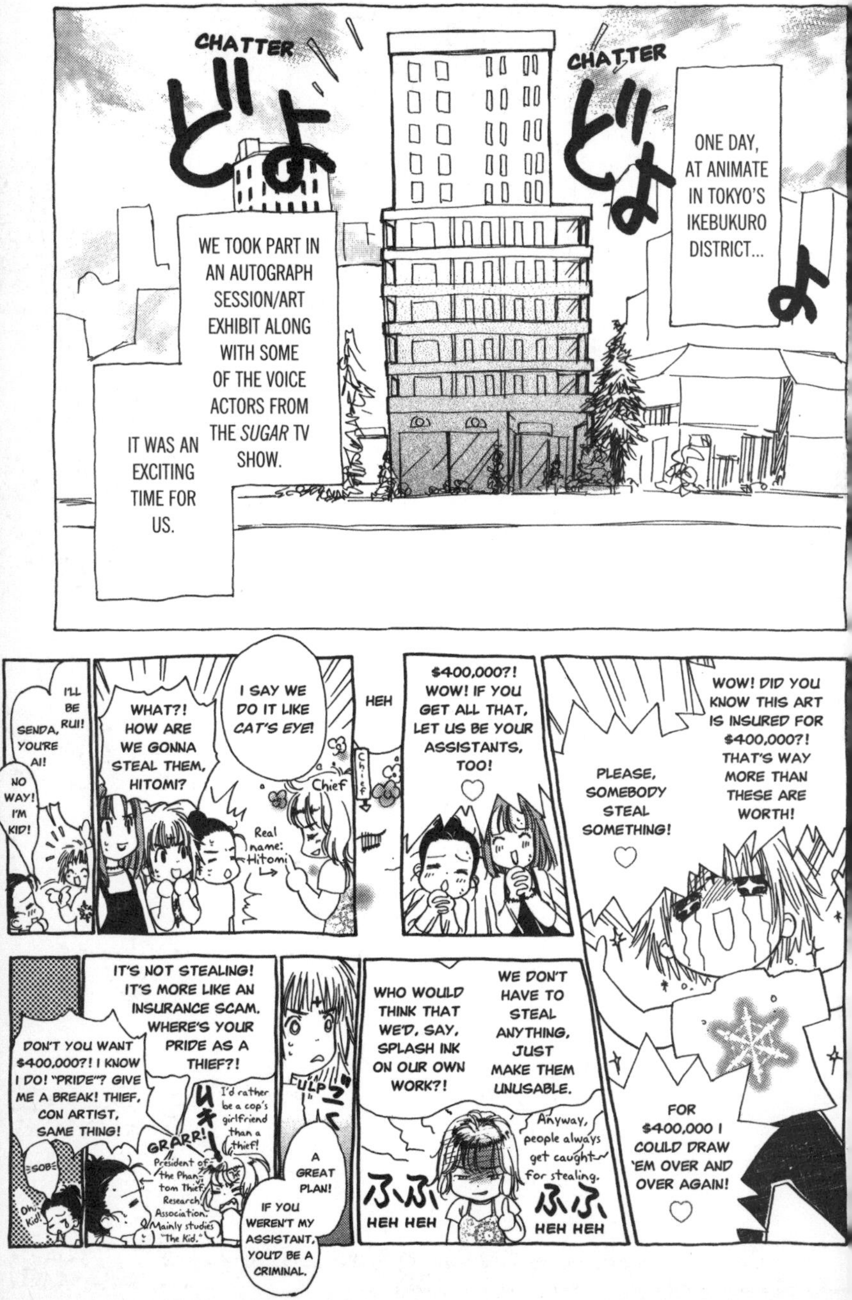

ONE DAY, AT ANIMATE IN TOKYO'S IKEBUKURO DISTRICT...
どよ
CHATTER
どよ
CHATTER
よ
WE TOOK PART IN AN AUTOGRAPH SESSION/ART EXHIBIT ALONG WITH SOME OF THE VOICE ACTORS FROM THE SUGAR TV SHOW.
IT WAS AN EXCITING TIME FOR US.
WOW! DID YOU KNOW THIS ART IS INSURED FOR $400,000?! THAT'S WAY MORE THAN THESE ARE WORTH!
PLEASE, SOMEBODY STEAL SOMETHING!
FOR $400,000 I COULD DRAW 'EM OVER AND OVER AGAIN!
$400,000?! WOW! IF YOU GET ALL THAT, LET US BE YOUR ASSISTANTS, TOO!
HEH
I SAY WE DO IT LIKE CAT'S EYE!
Chief
Real name: Hitomi
WHAT?! HOW ARE WE GONNA STEAL THEM, HITOMI?
I'LL BE RUI!
SENDA, YOU'RE AI!
NO WAY! I'M KID!
WE DON'T HAVE TO STEAL ANYTHING, JUST MAKE THEM UNUSABLE.
WHO WOULD THINK THAT WE'D, SAY, SPLASH INK ON OUR OWN WORK?!
Anyway, people always get caught for stealing.
ふふ
HEH HEH
ふふ
HEH HEH
GULP
A GREAT PLAN!
IF YOU WEREN'T MY ASSISTANT, YOU'D BE A CRIMINAL.
IT'S NOT STEALING! IT'S MORE LIKE AN INSURANCE SCAM. WHERE'S YOUR PRIDE AS A THIEF?!
I'd rather be a cop's girlfriend than a thief!
GRARR!
President of the Phantom Thief Research Association. Mainly studies "The Kid."
DON'T YOU WANT $400,000?! I KNOW I DO! "PRIDE"? GIVE ME A BREAK! THIEF, CON ARTIST, SAME THING!
SOB
Oh, Kid!

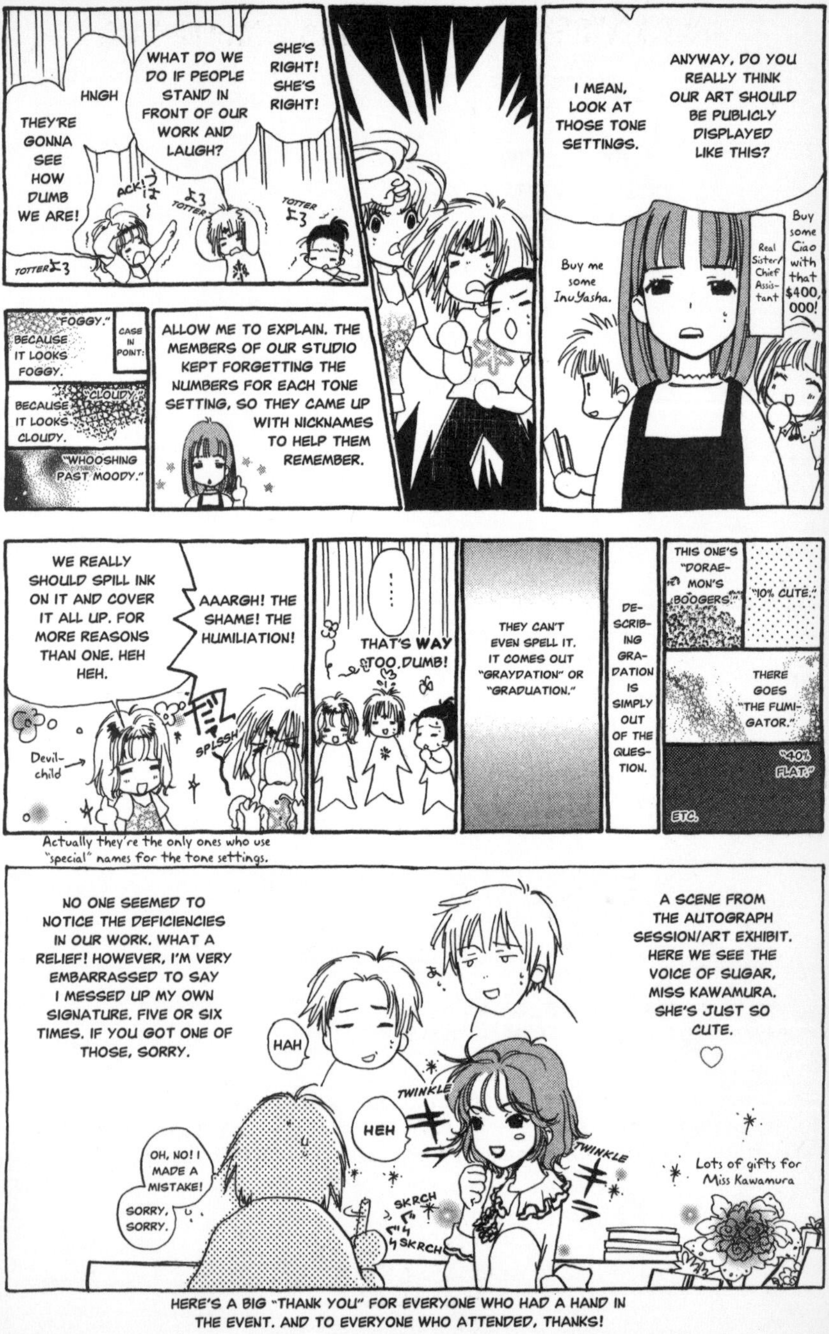
ANYWAY, DO YOU REALLY THINK OUR ART SHOULD BE PUBLICLY DISPLAYED LIKE THIS?
I MEAN, LOOK AT THOSE TONE SETTINGS.
Buy some Ciao with that $400,000!
Real Sister/Chief Assistant
Buy me some InuYasha.
SHE'S RIGHT! SHE'S RIGHT!
WHAT DO WE DO IF PEOPLE STAND IN FRONT OF OUR WORK AND LAUGH?
HNGH
THEY'RE GONNA SEE HOW DUMB WE ARE!
ACK!
TOTTER
TOTTER
TOTTER
ALLOW ME TO EXPLAIN. THE MEMBERS OF OUR STUDIO KEPT FORGETTING THE NUMBERS FOR EACH TONE SETTING, SO THEY CAME UP WITH NICKNAMES TO HELP THEM REMEMBER.
CASE IN POINT:
"FOGGY." BECAUSE IT LOOKS FOGGY.
"CLOUDY." BECAUSE IT LOOKS CLOUDY.
"WHOOSHING PAST MOODY."
THIS ONE'S "DORAEMON'S BOOGERS."
"10% CUTE."
THERE GOES "THE FUMIGATOR."
"40% FLAT."
ETC.
DESCRIBING GRADATION IS SIMPLY OUT OF THE QUESTION.
THEY CAN'T EVEN SPELL IT. IT COMES OUT "GRAYDATION" OR "GRADUATION."
.....
THAT'S WAY TOO DUMB!
AAARGH! THE SHAME! THE HUMILIATION!
WE REALLY SHOULD SPILL INK ON IT AND COVER IT ALL UP. FOR MORE REASONS THAN ONE. HEH HEH.
SPLSSH
Devil-child
Actually they're the only ones who use "special" names for the tone settings.
A SCENE FROM THE AUTOGRAPH SESSION/ART EXHIBIT. HERE WE SEE THE VOICE OF SUGAR, MISS KAWAMURA. SHE'S JUST SO CUTE.
NO ONE SEEMED TO NOTICE THE DEFICIENCIES IN OUR WORK. WHAT A RELIEF! HOWEVER, I'M VERY EMBARRASSED TO SAY I MESSED UP MY OWN SIGNATURE. FIVE OR SIX TIMES. IF YOU GOT ONE OF THOSE, SORRY.
HAH
HEH
TWINKLE
TWINKLE
OH, NO!! I MADE A MISTAKE!
SORRY, SORRY.
SKRCH
SKRCH
Lots of gifts for Miss Kawamura

HERE'S A BIG "THANK YOU" FOR EVERYONE WHO HAD A HAND IN THE EVENT. AND TO EVERYONE WHO ATTENDED, THANKS!

A LITTLE SNOW FAIRY SUGAR VOLUME TWO

© 2002 HARUKA AOI/TBS
© 2002 BH SNOW + CLINIC
Originally published in Japan in 2002 by
KADOKAWA SHOTEN PUBLISHING CO., LTD., Tokyo.
English translation rights arranged with
KADOKAWA SHOTEN PUBLISHING CO., LTD., Tokyo.

Editor **JAVIER LOPEZ**
Graphic Artist **SCOTT HOWARD**
Translator **KAORU BERTRAND**

Editorial Director **GARY STEINMAN**
Print Production Manager **BRIDGETT JANOTA**
Production Coordinator **MARISA KREITZ**

International Coordinators **TORU IWAKAMI & MIYUKI KAMIYA**

President, CEO & Publisher **JOHN LEDFORD**

Email: editor@adv-manga.com
www.adv-manga.com

www.advfilms.com

For sales and distribution inquiries please call 1.800.282.7202

 is a division of A.D. Vision, Inc.
5750 Bintliff Drive, Suite 210, Houston, Texas 77036

English text © 2006 published by A.D. Vision, Inc. under exclusive license.
ADV MANGA is a trademark of A.D. Vision, Inc.

ISBN: 1-4139-0351-7
First printing, November 2006
10 9 8 7 6 5 4 3 2 1
Printed in Canada

TRANSLATOR'S NOTES

A Little Snow Fairy Sugar 2

P. 8 | ***Speisekarte***
German for "menu."

P. 159 | **1) *Cat's Eye***
Here, the staff of *Sugar* are referencing the early-'80s anime/manga by Tsukasa Hojo. *Cat's Eye* tells the story of three sisters named Ai, Rui and Hitomi who by day run a café, but by night steal works of art.

2) Kid
"Kid" is a reference to kaitou kid, the so-called phantom thief appearing in the works of Gosho Aoyama (*Meitantei Conan*, aka "Case Closed").

P. 160 | **1) *Ciao* and *InuYasha***
Ciao is a comic anthology published by Shogagukan, while *InuYasha* is a long-running series by creator Rumiko Takahashi (*Ranma 1/2*).

2) Tone
In the Japanese manga biz, "tone" refers to sticky sheets of pre-drawn patterns used in shading and backgrounds.

3) Doraemon
"Doraemon" is the name of a robotic cat from the future, the brainchild of comic artist Fujiko F. Fujio. Why exactly the tone appearing on this page is thought to resemble Doraemon's boogers is something of a mystery.

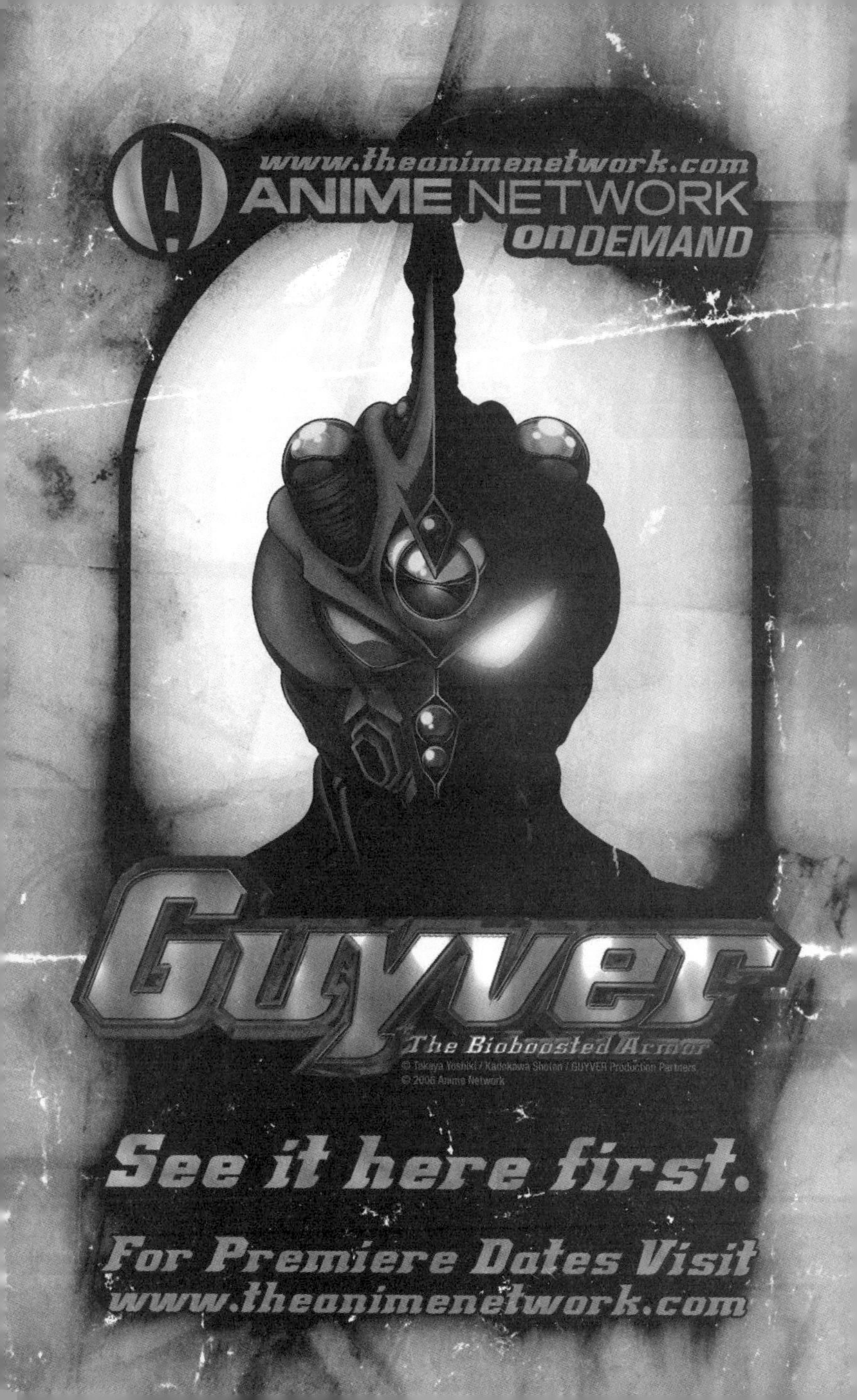
www.theanimenetwork.com
ANIME NETWORK
onDEMAND
Guyver
The Bioboosted Armor
© Takaya Yoshiki / Kadokawa Shoten / GUYVER Production Partners
© 2006 Anime Network
See it here first.
For Premiere Dates Visit
www.theanimenetwork.com

YOU'LL LAUGH.
YOU'LL CRY.
YOU'LL LEARN THE
BASICS OF SORCERY.

IN STORES NOW!

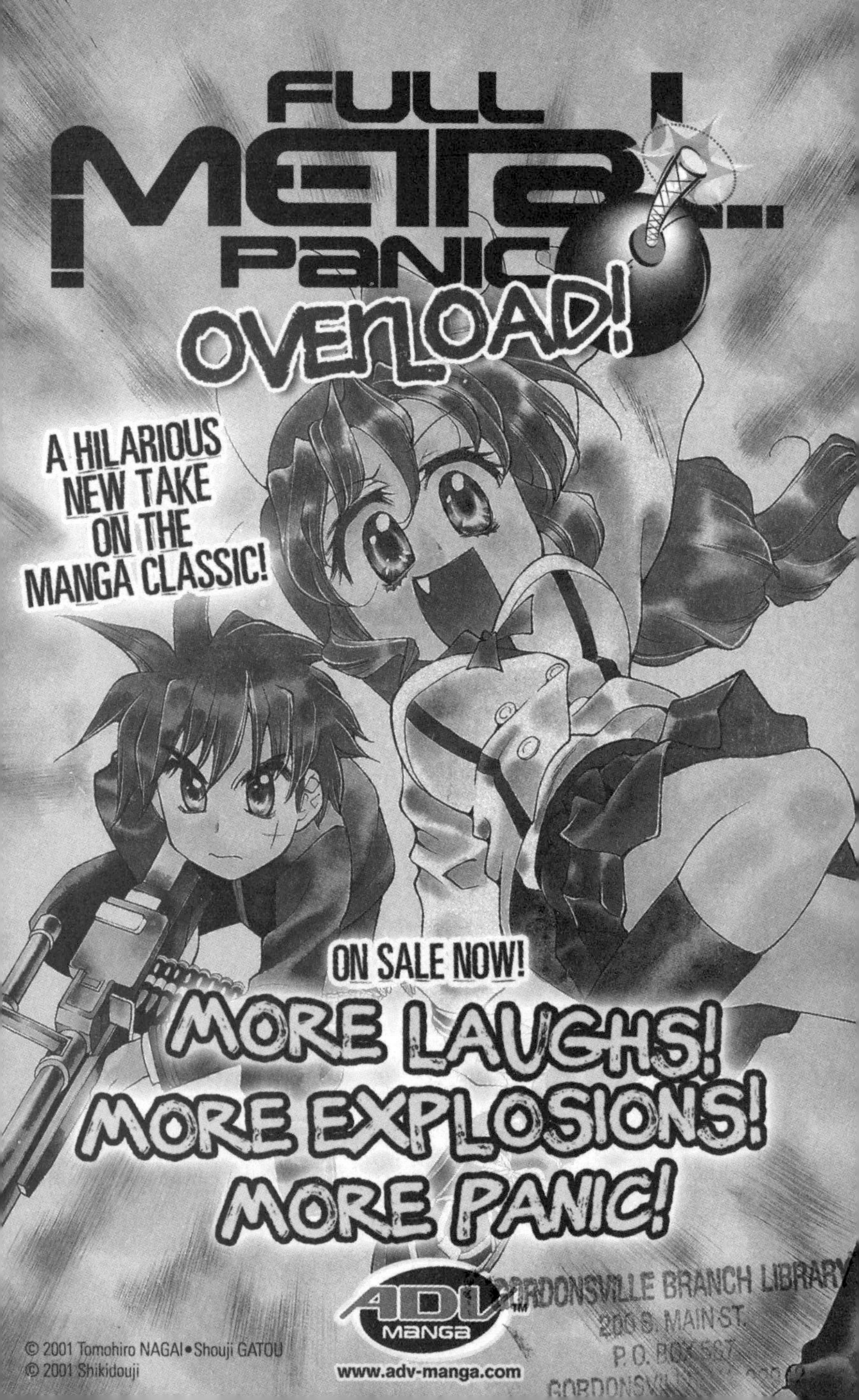
FULL METAL PANIC
OVERLOAD!
A HILARIOUS NEW TAKE ON THE MANGA CLASSIC!
ON SALE NOW!
MORE LAUGHS!
MORE EXPLOSIONS!
MORE PANIC!
ADV Manga
© 2001 Tomohiro NAGAI • Shouji GATOU
© 2001 Shikidouji
www.adv-manga.com

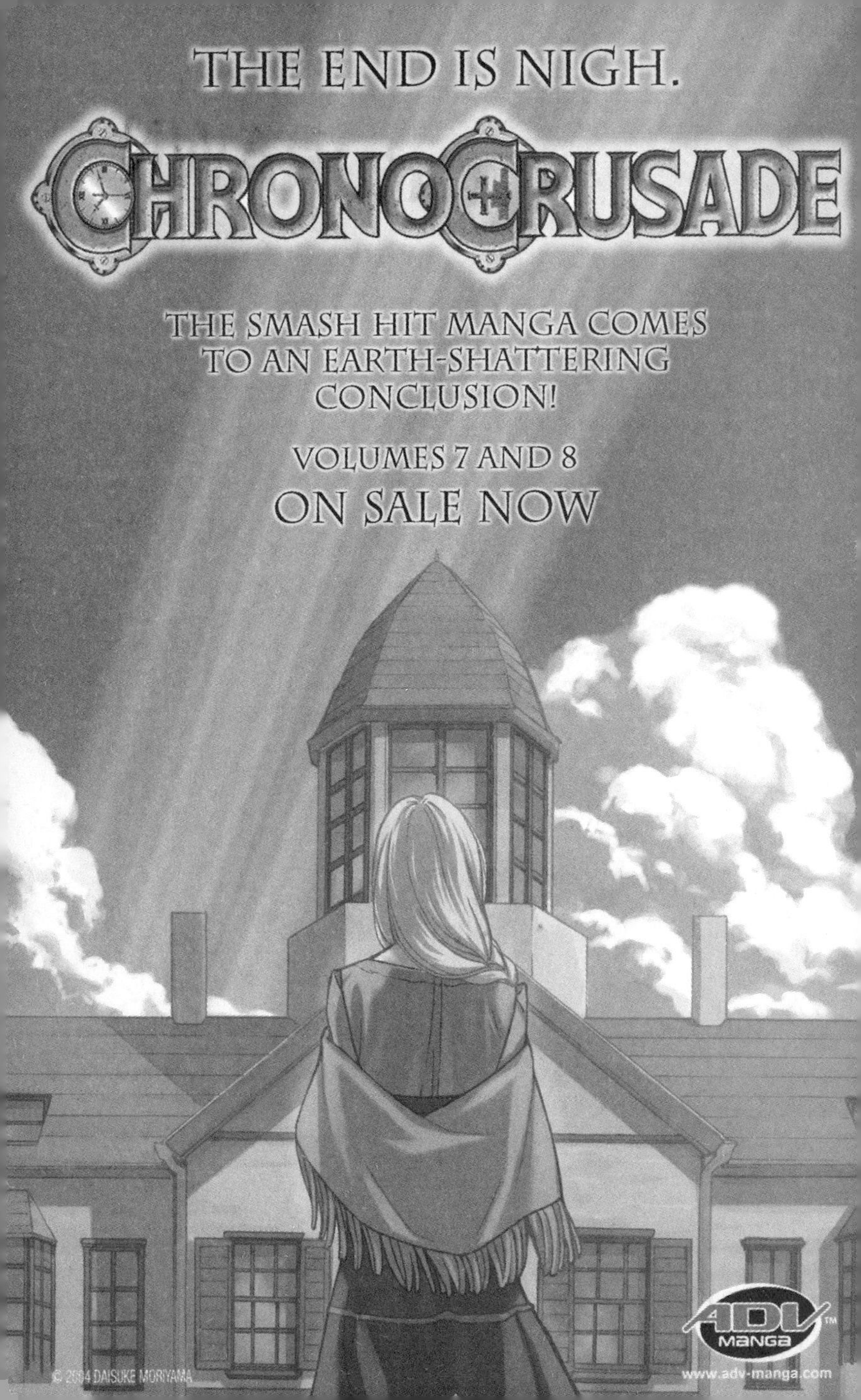

THE END IS NIGH.
CHRONO CRUSADE
THE SMASH HIT MANGA COMES TO AN EARTH-SHATTERING CONCLUSION!
VOLUMES 7 AND 8
ON SALE NOW
ADV MANGA
© 2004 DAISUKE MORIYAMA
www.adv-manga.com